First Edition

The Long Way Around

How 34 Women Found The Lives They Love

Edited by Emily A. Colin

Carolina Women's Press

The Long Way Around   How 34 Women Found The Lives They Love

Edited by Emily A. Colin

Carolina
Women's Press

An Imprint of:
Coastal Carolina Press
4709 College Acres Drive, Suite 1
Wilmington, NC 28403 U.S.A.
www.coastalcarolinapress.org

First Edition 2000

Book design by Maximum Design & Advertising, Inc.
Cover artwork by Alisha Kerlin

Printed in the United States of America
Applied for Library of Congress Cataloging - in - Publication Data

ISBN 1-928556-19-1

For my mother, who instilled in me a powerful love of literature, a passion for storytelling, and the confidence to pursue whatever dreams I conjured.

Table of Contents

Acknowledgements

The Secret to Their Success: How 33 Women Made Their Dreams Come True and *The Long Way Around: How 34 Women Found the Lives They Love* are sister volumes. When I began the project of telling North Carolina women's stories, I didn't anticipate the compilation of two separate books; but to my surprise and delight—and, initially, to my bewilderment—the response to my inquiries proved overwhelmingly positive. So many women were interested in participating that I had to restructure my ideas about what, precisely, this venture would entail. I must say that I am very happy with the result; I have learned a great deal from the women featured in these pages, and I hope that readers will, as well.

Needless to say, it would have been impossible for me to organize and compile these fine volumes without the help of a number of talented individuals. I owe substantial debts of gratitude to Heather Folan and Nikki Smith, for countless hours spent transcribing, entering edits, scanning photos, offering suggestions, and otherwise being of invaluable assistance; to Doris Elliott, for easing the transcription load; to Susan Comer, for lending her fantastic journalistic skills to this project, and for being so reliable; to Amy, Kelly, and Alex at Maximum Design & Advertising for another job well done—and for letting Stanley and me languish on their floor; to Alisha Kerlin, for painting an amazing cover, and being the most talented eighteen-year-old I know; to Emily Herring Wilson and Doris Betts, for their valuable advice and for writing fantastic introductions; to Dan Levy at the Mia Hamm Foundation, for taking time out of his busy schedule to speak with me; to Ms. Berry at Dr. Maya Angelou's office, for her patience and persistence; to Ellyn Bache and Julie Tetel Andresen, both contributors, for encouraging and supporting me in so many ways; to Georgeann Eubanks, Jean O'Barr, and Lynn Salsi, for their positive attitude and enthusiasm regarding this project; to the North Carolina Writers' Network, for providing much-needed information at a crucial juncture; to Celia Rivenbark, for her prestidigitation regarding our title search; to Bryan, for his constant words of encouragement, and my parents, for their continued support of this and other endeavors; to Ellen Rickert, for the conversation that birthed this project; to Dorothy Gallagher, Gil Brady, and Chris Compton for playing the name-this-book game (and further thanks to Dorothy for her patience with the graphically impaired); to Tony Norris, for listening to me talk about both books (and little else) for five months straight, and for aiding and abetting throughout their evolution; to Andy Scott, for taking a chance on me; to Zoë, Quinn, Niko, Sox, and Gray Cat for providing me with companionship, entertainment, and much-needed distractions; and, of course, to all of the women who so graciously and freely contributed to both of these fantastic volumes. I couldn't have done it without you!

Preface

The stories in this volume speak for themselves. They are mute only on one issue: their geographic relationship. The women featured here are from all over this country, and some are from another nation entirely. All have one thing in common: they have chosen North Carolina as the arena where they live, work, or play. Some, of course, were born here; but I did not make that the criteria for participation. I wanted, instead, to discover the twenty-first-century North Carolina woman.

This is what she looks like: dark-skinned, short, full-figured. This is what she looks like: pale, blonde, tall. This is what she looks like: voluptuous, rail-thin, stocky, muscular, blue-eyed, brown-haired, freckled, full-lipped. English may be her second language. She has started her own business, raised five children, written books, taught classes, counseled people in need, taken award-winning photographs, sold real estate, painted incredible pictures. She is Asian-American, Latina, African-American; she is Jewish, Buddhist, Christian, Muslim. She is gay and she is straight. She is from everywhere, and her story is every woman's story.

Emily A. Oz

Introduction   Emily Herring Wilson

"For all serious daring starts from within." Eudora Welty, *One Writer's Beginnings*

In the old days, little girls when asked what they wanted to be when they grew up were said to have answered "teacher" or "nurse" (it was understood that they wanted to be mothers). At least, so those stories go. In fact, as I remember the exercise, we knew the expected answers, but they had little to do with our lives. (Of course I said I wanted to grow up to be a teacher, and, in a word, I did, but that hardly describes—to my satisfaction—who I am today.) Me and my friends (memory trumps grammar) wore boots and spurs and climbed trees, with no more thought of what that or anything else might lead to than if the elders had asked us how a silly boy grew up to become president of the United States of America. Gender consciousness played an active role in our subliminal imaginations, but we had not yet encountered theory. We walked the walk, and in that respect knew that one step followed another and that a misstep meant you had to go to the back of the line, unless someone put you up or you could break in; otherwise, a sequence of events was not foretold. In 1954 when girls were said to be starching their crinolines (sure, I wore them), I beat the shame-faced boys in a foot race up a steep hill at the 8th grade class picnic and never thought a thing about it, except that obviously I was the best. That no one signed my prom card left me with a tinge of sadness, which of course I turned into living well.

The stories of 34 women living well in North Carolina at the time of the telling (one has since left Durham for Uzbekistan, and I imagine the other 33 aren't stuck in traffic trying to fight their way into The Mall), don't give us any easy answers as to what little girls grow up to be, no guaranteed role models for today's youth, and no high intellectualizing. (In current magazines, a debate over how little girls and little boys differ is quite the rage and sells quite a few books.) As the happy reader of these stories, I'm not going to dumb them down by summarizing their "themes." But I do want to whet readers' appetites for what's to come by introducing you to some of them. They come in different shapes and sizes—not the women (though that, too), but the stories— some are well-crafted essays, some are statements of purpose, some are long interviews, some are short interviews, and most left me asking for more.

The collection begins with "Homesick," by Eirene Chen, the most artfully written of the essays as she ranges over her life's territory like some free-range bird of paradise: though it begins in a car pulled into a gas station with our narrator searching her purse for a safety pin, we're not a mile down the road before we realize that we are sailing on the wings of metaphor ("safety pin"?): getting lost, leaving behind something of value, looping back to find it, and "flying the coop for alien terrain" (from the Citgo Family MiniMart off a NC road to a place only identified in the short bio after her story—find it on your own). Only a few times does she nod, and phrases like "caring community" and "working towards self-awareness" slip in—though one is never sure but that Eirene is mocking the talk. First and last, she is what her Asian-American immigrant father said she was, "a migrant soul." I can't tell you what she does for a living. She lives.

Fitzi Huber, interviewed by the book's editor, Emily Colin, comes from a circus family (her mother was born in New York and raised in Germany; her father is from Basel, Switzerland. Diversity is not a recent invention). Fritzi and her brother (a grip in the Wilmington film industry) have already made sense for themselves of what influences followed them into the present, and Fritzi explains being a seamstress, teaching sailing, papermaking, and, most recently, making books as the inevitable results of having begun as an aerialist. What's most important was that "working in air" gave her "a sense of wonder"—"what keeps people young."

Mirinda Kossoff begins her story at the bedside of her dying mother and looks back over her own life along a "twisted path, doubling back upon itself." Growing up in a household where her father's Jewish roots were entangled in a southern Baptist culture gave her a lifelong sense of being an outsider, an "alien." She found her way as a young girl ("a kid who just wanted to fit in") after attending a writer's camp—"a profoundly liberating experience"— launching her career as a writer. Nothing helps explain why her marriage didn't work out or offers a formula for bringing up children as a single mom: "kids are also resilient, and we muddled through somehow."

This willingness both to find meaning as they read their lives backward and to pick up the pieces of failed choices keeps these narratives moving. Even when the situations are familiar, readers are not likely to say, "been there, done that." Something about the particularity of story makes every one different. And there are differences. Consider where the women come from: a small town near Detroit; Chattanooga, Long Island, New Orleans; Lima, Peru; "I grew up everywhere"; Lillington, North Carolina.

Now they live in Charlotte, Mebane, Asheville, Durham, Wilmington. They teach; bake bread; kayak; run their own businesses; direct non-profits; protect sea turtles; practice law; ride horses; and write (often "in the wee hours of the morning")—whether in private journals or published novels and scholarly histories.

Consider this one story that encompasses so much: Cathy Holt grew up in south Florida, was educated in the Pacific northwest, wanted to be a missionary to India, decided she'd become an oceanographer, switched to journalism, studied psychology, made furniture and pots, bought a farmhouse and 36 acres in Georgia, and borrowed $2000 from her father to launch a new career. Today she's a professional goldsmith and a certified hatha yoga teacher living in Pittsboro. Go figure.

Along the crooked paths and highways that turn back upon themselves, these journeys have not been direct or easy or ever ended. The deaths of loved ones, divorce, disease, drugs, depression, poverty, and injustice litter a landscape that is always changing, always constant. According to these stories, women zig-zag a lot, and when they go down the wrong roads and lose their way, they weep or laugh, but mostly, they keep going. Advice, mostly indirect, turns up in many of the stories: never stop trying; work hard; take risks; don't settle—go for "the first choices in life"; devote yourself wholeheartedly to a venture; locate yourself in a beautiful setting; practice yoga; garden; and take advantage of whatever unexpected opportunity appears on your map. You'll grow up.

North Carolina is lucky that these 34 women and their husbands, friends, and lovers are here—by birth or happenstance or choice. (In every woman's story, there are other women, men, children, and pets.) Whatever it was that brought them here—an arts

school in Penland, a tech job in the Research Triangle, a small farm near a university town, an activist community working for good causes—North Carolina is, at least in these examples, a place to come home to. If I were going to be the next governor, I'd figure out ways to make North Carolina more receptive to these good lives. These women would be members of my kitchen cabinet. We'd eat well, laugh a lot, take care of families, and share the work. What better credo for statehood could there be?

Meanwhile, night after night, I have been dreaming of meeting these storytellers at some gas station off some highway in some heat of the night as they are on their way to yet another unknown destination. Always, I shout as they fly by, "You go, girls!" They laugh back, and keep going.

Homesick   Eirene Chen

On any given Friday night in any North Carolinian town, someone is at a gas station getting more lost than they were before they pulled up.

Those of you familiar with the North Carolina interstate system know what I'm talking about. Why are our gas stations, those beacons of coffee and guileless directions twinkling just beyond the frontier of the highway, such black holes par excellence? For the traveller adrift in a long night of weaving mile markers and books-on-tape, nothing seems more inviting than a canverserai fully stocked with soft drinks, $3.99 Waylon Jennings cassettes, and those treacherous cans of tinned pork. There's the Citgo I-40 Family MiniMart, so close to my house that I forget how deceptively exotic it must seem from the overpass. The Swan Quarter Texaco, Home-of-the-Slo-pitch-Bulldogs. Sam's Ataboy Best Hoarhound in the Mountains, Get Your Fireworks Here. A place to stretch and catch one's breath and bearings, and to thank the good Lord for indoor plumbing.

But this privilege must be reserved for only those who know where they are going. For the tourist lost in her own skin, there is only diluted powdered tea and exits that loop wickedly upon themselves, and the nagging thought that one has left something of increasingly looming value behind in the restroom.

Tonight the chosen object is my safety pin. Didn't I put one in my purse before I left the house?—but then isn't this also the purse with the hole at the bottom left corner, never mind its discount tag from Walmart Heirloom Collections? Maybe it's still perched above the washbasin at the Amoco from forty minutes ago. Maybe I don't remember because I actually set it down on Fred's kitchen counter while he was explaining his latest recipe for consubstantiation, which is begging for trouble because Fred is the only man of the cloth I know who has touched God—is, in fact, the only Freewill Southern Baptist Catholic I know who touches God regularly from the bottom of a jar of corn whiskey. Maybe I haven't partaken enough of the Spirit. 'My safety pin, Fred,' I holler half-heartedly from the backseat of Fred's girlfriend's jeep. 'Any y'all seen it?'

Of course no one has seen it because everyone is too busy trying to recover something of their own. Do you believe in life after love? Cher is squealing against a syncopated breakbeat while Fred's girlfriend scrambles frantically for the telephone number which promises directions to the party of our dreams. She turns around, waving a tube of coral lipstick in time to the chassis-rattling bass. 'Eirene you remember how to get to Wallis Street from here?' Before I have a chance to answer, Hetty is knocking on the window, her free hand primping a cascade of freshly bronzed curls—'Eirene? Where'd my woman go?' Hetty you trifling no-count, I want to shout, unpeel your eyeballs from that blonde by the Lowrider and start paying attention to your *gazelle du jour* before she disappears with the toaster oven! But Hetty, two hours out of a visit with her father in Hospice, is already walking towards the truck. 'Eirene, I bet that's Serena—I know I knew her from somewhere!' Now Fred is opening the door and rummaging under the seat. 'Eirene you seen my Cevin Fisher maxi-single—'

No, no, I haven't seen nothing yet. I figure it will all return soon enough when I find that pin. I'm finally wearing that red dress that I haven't been able to fit into for the past three years and sure as sherlock I am not going to bobble into the *fête d'été* clutching my hems, but I know that whatever zip and swish I'm feeling now will join Fred and the directions in the ethers as soon as I get out of the car...is this dress too tight? is my hair too short? what's my name again?

A cigarette—now that's what I need!

'Eirene I thought you quit smoking,' exclaims my best friend as she reaches over, drops something sharp into my lap, and helps herself to my new pack.

Well yes, I had tried. The gum, the patch, meditation at the Awareness Institute twice a week after work with housepainters and doctoral candidates. It was to be the year of the fresh start, of plans made and followed-through-upon, of aerobics and therapy  and Chinese lessons and letters to graduate schools.

Now, after several months of listless vigilance, I am ready to admit that I just can't make it without a narcotic.

'Oh come on, everybody needs a vice,' I say, and reach for my lighter. Gone.

⚯

How could I have known that the disappearance of one safety pin that thick summer evening would take me farther from home than any car, or boat, or plane? That its recovery would arrest my flight from myself long enough to open me to the enormity of a universe I had previously thought could only be found in tacks on a map and ornate phrases from literature anthologies? And that this universe would undo me so completely that, for a moment, I would no longer have any words left to describe who I was, much less where I was going?

When I was younger, my father liked to berate me. 'Eirene, you so busy running off somewhere in your head, you can't even see what's in front of you! Where I'm from we'd call you a migrant soul...'

'Well, I can't help it,' I never failed to retort. 'It's your fault! You shoulda stayed in China.'

Shoulda stayed in Tai-wan, shouldnta gone to Wisconsin, shouldnta gone to the roller rink in the mountains where that  quiet Chinese girl with the wild hair was drinking her Co-Cola. You shouldnta met her parents, you shouldnta pulled over at the Exxon in some foggy piedmont country when her water broke. Shouldnta exiled yourself from the known world and thought you could make a decent go of it elsewhere unless you were only look-ing for more heartache.

I don't like to admit it, but, over the years, migration of every imaginable sort has become so deeply ingrained in my family my-thology that I, too, have found it difficult to know myself apart from a series of dislocated constructions—name, birthplace, eth-nic background, schools attended. Not that we moved around much—I was born in central North Carolina and have lived here all my life. My father teaches economics at a historically African-American college and my mother conducts Sunday School les-sons at the primarily Caucasian Southern Baptist church where they have been members since my birth. I have a younger brother who currently attends college in the area, and who, with his long hair and twangy speech, is periodically almost unrecognizable to our parents.

But, like many Americans, especially those who were raised in immigrant or polycultural families in areas where the majority of the population claims a different body of ancestral values, I have found that a certain degree of tension between one's perception of herself and the perception reflected back to her from her environ-ment is inevitable.

Sometimes the tension is clear and palpable—accusations on the playground of being a Communist, wolf-whistles and imi-tations of karate-chop noises trailing behind the hapless first-gen-eration Asian-American as she carries her awkward adolescent bulk through the mall.

Sometimes the tension is less apparent and swirls uneasily beneath layers of well meaning and Southern hospitality—compliments from supermarket clerks for one's English being so remarkably accent-less, inquiries of whether one knows so-and-so who works in China as a missionary, of whether or not one is going to attend college on a scholarship, because isn't it true that Asian Americans excel at maths? At playing the violin? At depriving honest, hard-working 'real Americans' from jobs long shut off from their rightful claimants due to privations suffered at the hands of slaveowners, Yankees, Japanese auto manufacturers?

And sometimes the tension is downright absurd: 'Eirene, you will not be wearing lipstick/going on dates while you're living in this house because we cannot trust American boys—and we cannot trust you around them!'

Family members, usually a dependable source of cultural and intergenerational misunderstanding, are not the only people who can make life complex for a Daughter of the American Revolution. A high school principal once assumed I was the daughter of a local restaurant owner (due to shared surname) and continued to address me as such until very pointedly informed otherwise by my doppelganger. I was far too polite—in a peculiarly Southern way, I thought at the time—to correct him myself. Another school administrator suggested that I stay after school for some "extra tutoring," since he had "always wanted to spend some time with an fiesty Oriental tigress." Ahem. That, to me, sounded more like the name of a restaurant. With a massage parlor in the back!

Sometimes the tension is so muddied that it is almost impossible to discern whether the pressures they exert originate from social or familial expectations—and if this is the first filter through which one begins to examine her own internal expectations, it is not surprising, then, that a life on the lam from oneself seems infinitely preferable to a continual series of almost-successful re-adjustments to that first day in a new school cafeteria, whether at a Girl Scout meeting or Vacation Bible Camp or the Collegiate Asian Students Association, with a trayful of not-quite-foreign food and nowhere to sit.

Given the confusion from all these conflicting expectations, I found in language and music a convenient and enthralling escape hatch. As a little girl, I had always enjoyed talking, and when there was no one to talk to—or at—I often talked to myself, or to my invisible friend Ramona. As I got older I realized that I was not the only one who was schizophrenic. Everyone from Joan of Arc to Dante to Shirley MacLaine claimed to hear voices that no one else could recognize. I began to read voraciously.

My mother vehemently asserted that although there was good [Christian] literature—CS Lewis—and bad literature—pulp romance, Nietzsche—all literature was essentially glorified lying. At the time, I couldn't argue with her. But storymaking, for all its intangibility, has granted me the ability to remake myself at will, to suspend my shell of a body that was beaten for low test scores and scorned for its girth, and to disappear. While music transports directly, storymaking requires the mastery of codes and counter-codes through which one may gradually submerge herself into a vague under-overworld, where literal truths can lurk comfortably beneath layers of ironies for as long as one wants. And to this day, a trip to a certain used bookstore once again finds me hiding under the covers with my flashlight, sucking on beef bouillion cubes while riding with Robin Hood through Sherwood Forest, bottoming out with Anna Karenina at the train station, praying for redemption with any number of Flannery O'Connor grandmothers who have had the ill fortune to locate that elusive and terribly good man.

Perhaps there is no better roadmap for a journey towards safety than a lie told well.

Storytelling, my first love, gradually became the primary way through which I knew love. I have been fortunate to have had the support of many wonderful teachers in the North Carolina Public School System who encouraged me to continue exploring the world, and my place in it, through language. I am thinking of three in particular—one who introduced me to the writing of Elie Wiesel, one who breathed life into Sartre and the theater of the absurd, and one other, whose presence and guidance have been so inspirational to me that, for the first time, I began to wonder if teaching could not also become a way for me to share with others the clarity and hope that language and stories can bring in times of confusion, loss, and despair.

From 'Luna,' 1996

Despite mounting familial resistance to what was perceived as a pitch into unfamiliar and dangerously un-Godlike territory, I persisted in choosing for myself a path that would take me far from the comforting verities of the natural sciences, and into that tricky bog known as literature, where Coyote, the Monkey King, Plato and pious Augustinian televangelists converge in soap operatic glee...So that when I received a full scholarship to attend university, I descended into the bog whole-hog. Within one semester I had dropped all my math courses, dyed my hair green, and sworn off the family passport in favor of post-structuralist cultural theory, dinner parties with film students, and a form of chemical aviation better known as getting high.

Within two semesters, my family had thrown me out of the house!

⌐══

Sometimes a girl travelling alone on the interstate breaks out into a rare but potentially life-threatening panic. This tends to happen when she has drunk too much powdered tea, hasn't slept for ten hours, just smoked her last cigarette, and is running out of gas miles from a rest stop—all at the same time. One of the tell-tale symptoms of this panic is a moment of intense vertigo, during which her entire history of questionable choices flashes before her eyes and she begins trying to mentally unmake decisions that got her into this jam in the first place.

Had I known that a single safety pin would change the course of my life, I would not have left it at the Amoco off Highway 70. I would not have gone over to Fred's house for a drink. I would not have even met Fred at that party where I had too many PJs and woke up with my face in a strange corduroy lap, would not have been plucked off that lap by the woman who is now my best friend, would not have even known what a PJ was if I had not gone to the

blue two-story bungalow to rescue a forgotten philosophy text-book from an cocktail-loving astrologer who liked to go trainspotting with me, would not have stumbled upon the train tracks if I had not gotten lost en route to one of those film student dinner parties. And I couldn't have found the film students unless I had to chosen to elect a film course, which would have meant sacrificing an organic chemistry class, which would have meant preparing to dispose of an academic and career path that has been drilled into my head ever since I knew how to talk. And that would have meant talking back, which is the ultimate no-no to family, clan, tribe, community, the government, and even God Themselves. That would have meant having my tongue cut out. Death.

Which is exactly what I chose!

Over and over again, I slid my quarters into the slot machines and waited for the hangmans to pop up, three in a row. I learned the alphabet, I crawled under the covers with a flashlight and a Monkey King and an Emily Dickinson, and I held my breath. Held my breath during Sunday School verse recitation. During the school trip to the zoo where I made a boy bleed from his eye for calling me a Dirty Ching Wong Fong. Through-out ten years of music competitions when I was pouring my turbulent adolescence into sounds escaping from the end of a thin silver tube. In the middle of my interrogation at the police station when the officer pulled a pair of canvas sneakers from a plastic bag and asked why I did not pay for them, and I opened my mouth and could not speak.

I held my breath during my first rock concert at the university coffeehouse, where a man howled into an electric guitar, opened up a column in my spine and sent me spinning on my head. When, during a lecture, an Egyptian feminist rose and began to speak, her eyes ablaze with liberty, equality, a radiant city upon the ashes of an old order. When an eighty-four-year-old woman whom I assisted as a caregiver fired me for attempting to bathe her and then re-hired me after I served her breakfast.   When a fifty-five-year-old woman whom I had been teaching the English alphabet for over a year read me her name, written forwards, backwards, and later, her first letter—a prayer for her dying mother. When a car struck a friend and myself while we were helping an elderly gentleman cross the street, leaving him with multiple broken ribs, and us unharmed.

When, in a dream, I turned on a computer and had a conversation over the Internet with an unnamed phantom whose words touched my heart in a way I could not explain, and then spent the next two years wondering whether or not I had fallen in love with a ghost. When, in a dream, a poet showed me a book of three-dimensional woodcarvings and I fell, into layers of cool dark woods...into a snowy German morning on the eve of the Second World War, into a deep black lagoon where I could breathe underwater, into a galaxy awash with Jungian correspondences, hermes trismegistus, charlatans, miracles.

When, as if in a dream, I walked back into my ancestral home to find my mother painstakingly picking out Go Tell Aunt Rhody on the piano, tears streaming down her face for the life she could not give herself. When my brother took off his shirt and showed me the bruise from a trash can thrown by an angry classmate. When my father opened an atlas shortly after his prodigal daughter had graduated from college, and placed his finger here, here, these are all the places I want us to live, if only there was enough time...

When my physician placed her hand on my abdomen and said gently, Eirene, I know you're not insured, but there may be a tumor growing here.

When, as if in a dream, I stepped out of Fred's car on a gauzy summer night, pinned my hems together, and wobbled slowly up to a house veiled in thick swathes of gardenia and Christmas tree lights. When I opened the gate and almost collided with a girl whose entrancing gaze had haunted me for years. When, for want of a button, she asked me if I had a safety pin. When I unhinged the clasp, laid the pin in her hand, and let my dress fall.

⊷

My name is Eirene. As of this writing, I am twenty-five years old and I have a college degree in comparative literature. I was born to an East Asian immigrant family of modest means in a textile town and now live in a racially and religiously diverse part of the state known for its tobacco plants, its research hospitals and pharmaceutical firms, its artistic eclecticism and its history of grassroots social activism. While my new hometown is a mecca for all manner of creatively minded folks, it is still fairly difficult in this area for a young woman with an English degree and a propensity for daydreaming-on-the-job to find reasonably-waged employment as a full-time writer, so I have taken the route of many contemporaries and patched together a career out of serially polygamous temp-work.

At first my inability to find a job which combined flexible hours, health benefits and creative writing endeavors—as if!—was extremely frustrating. Upon graduation, I immediately began trying to hatch a plan to Get Out of Here. My first scheme was to learn how to become a proficient techno DJ, establish a place for myself in the electronic music entertainment industry, and travel around the world as an amateur ethnomusicologist, collecting and composing sounds for popular enjoyment.

Then it occurred to me that I was not even earning enough money to purchase a set of spare turntables, so I proceeded to my second and more abiding plan, whereby I would earn a certificate as English as a Foreign Language instructor and then move to

From 'Luna,' 1996

Cyprus, where I would bask in the hot Mediterranean sun, surrounded by lemon groves, trashy Europop bars, and dangling participles in three languages. From there I would take the Orient Express train overland to China, engage in some serious roots-searching, and then return to a North American doctoral program in the humanities. I would eventually earn tenure as a literature professor, move to a metropolis on the Eastern seaboard, and hopefully, along the way, meet up with a suitable Life Partner and Life Pet. I would invest in mutual funds, refine a regular pork-rich diet, and finally acquire those precious turntables of my youth. Delicious!

However, after three years of various stints as waitress, property auditor, data technician, personal assistant, bookstore clerk, secretary, and English instructor, I have learned that a job, a hobby, and a calling are very rarely the same things, though they need not—and should not—be mutually exclusive. Even a "permanent" job is ultimately a temporary economic arrangement whereby one trades some of her talents, though perhaps not the ones she enjoys the most, in the service of her community, in return for material comforts and opportunities. A hobby is closer to a calling, but requires more devotion and the acceptance that not all emotional priorities are going to be (a) economically feasible (b) socially acceptable at the time of introduction, and (c) congruous with other dreams of improving the welfare of one's fellows. And a calling— that commitment of all commitments, whether to a person or to a cause—is usually a much more rewarding outpouring of one's heart, but also one whose form often requires a lot of risky fumbling around to be recognized—and even that tends to change several times during the course of one's life!

There are probably many readers of this anthology who have found a very satisfying place for themselves in the workforce and enjoy mutually supportive relationships with neighbors, colleagues, friends, and family. There are also probably not a few readers who have presently found themselves in a stolen car with no roadmap, next to no sleep and even less gas in the tank. Right now, my story belongs with the second group.

I am relatively young and have yet to find a name for my calling, but I do know that I enjoy sharing stories, making music, travelling into unfamiliar territory, and learning from people of all ages and walks of life. I can finally name these passions after two years of intense depression, during which I was clearly suppressing my need for creative latitude and positive company by choosing a series of jobs and intimates that reinforced a lingering feeling of low-self-worth.

It was during this time of the obliterating skulk that three events converged upon my life in such a way to enable me to begin fundamentally rearranging the way I approached my life. It was a particularly unbearable summer when the air conditioning in my 1920's house petered out for good, I had just been asked to resign from my soul-depleting job as a property auditor, and I went down for the count with an excruciating case of poison ivy. Things couldn't have gotten much worse: my parents were not talking to me, nobody seemed to want to hire me, and I was violently single. To top it all off, I looked like the Bride of Frankenstein with a midsection the size of a flotation device and my skin unpeeling, layer by layer, as the weeks dragged on. This is a physiological condition otherwise known as necrolysis, a reaction to high-powered steroids, and it felt like one terrible, itchy molt. I was about as far from my dream of a glamorous metropolitan clubkid life as I could get.

There is a song by a singer/songwriter from Atlanta named Michelle Malone about times like these, times when "I've been in the weeds for so long now, it's starting to look like up to me...."

Nevertheless, change was inevitable. And how I dread change! But, finally, my body was granting my spirit permission to give up and take a chance on something, anything, that I truly hungered for.

For although I have been blessed with caring community of colleagues and friends, this was long before I consciously sought the company of people who were also working towards self-awareness. This was long before I decided to begin teaching math and English in earnest—first as a volunteer with the local literacy council, to adult non-native speakers, and later as a poetry instructor in a nearby public high school. This was definitely long before I respected myself worth a damn. My gratitude for the people I served as a teacher and fellow learner—and as a student, colleague, friend, lover, sister, daughter—was a long way from appearing in my consciousness. It seemed that in order to get any further, I would have to return to the beginning.

When a Southern girl runs out of gas on the highway, she does not think it silly to pull over and have a light nap first.

⇥⊨

Three months from today I will no longer be in North Carolina. Like a good migrant soul, I am flying the coop for alien terrain. Where I am going, there are no Citgo Family MiniMarts, no Swan Quarter Texacos, no Sam Ataboy Hoarhound and Fireworks Depots. There are very few forests, no tobacco fields, and no beaches. There I will find neither Down East pulled pork nor the Sichuan pork dumpling, for the prevailing religious proscriptions of the land forbid the consumption of hog. The people do not speak my language, nor do I speak theirs. Their water may react unpleasantly to my stomach. Where I am going, a woman driving alone at night means she is asking to be raped.

But, like a good migrant soul, I know that they are yet a people not so different from our own. They wake in the morning from a fitful sleep and groan about having to go to work. They prepare lunches for their children to take to school, haggle over the price of cucumbers in the market, pull at the elastic in their waistband and wonder how their dresses got so wide so fast while their purses only got thinner. They distill their own alchohol. They quarrel with each other and make up. They oil their hair and dream about falling in love. And when they can, they might go to the movies and watch a picture of a place such as ours, a place like North Carolina, and marvel at how a people could be so gracious and heroic, and yet so reckless and consumed with large houses, fast cars in a land already overflowing with abundance.

And when I walk into the secondary school classroom in this strange land where I am to spend my next two years, armed with only dictionary, a handful of stories and those trusty dangling participles, I am sure they will want to know where I am from, and what it is like to live here. And what will I tell them?

Will I describe to them the sound of old straw-hatted men fanning themselves slowly on porches overlooking winding tracks of Appalachian gold, red, indigo? The smell of salt spray and circling terns and a thousand hot, oily bodies surging towards the surf at the opening of the public beaches? Of glittering office towers, boxed suburban tracts, windowless ghettoes, peeling tobacco sheds? How will I knit for them the rich, twangy accent, the mournful banjos, the jump shot, the taste of sweet tea on a blistering July afternoon? How will I find words for the sight of a lone man swinging from a tree because his skin is too dark for his neighbors, or of a house of prayer lifting off the ground in a whirlwind of ecstasy, or of a freight train disappearing into the treeline, from whose railings my old perch would last as long as a blink, a green patch surfacing and dying amid the strange, wet eaves?

I will tell them a story:

North America is a vast continent, so vast and many-splendored that even its inhabitants are not familiar with its multitude of hidden corners, though they very much enjoy trying to seek them out. In North America, many people embark on long road trips when they have a chance, and girls of a certain age and older are allowed to make such trips unaccompanied.

Sometimes a girl travelling alone on the interstate breaks out into a rare but potentially life-threatening panic. This tends to happen when she has drunk too much powdered tea, hasn't slept for ten hours, just smoked her last cigarette, and is running out of gas miles from a rest stop—all at the same time. One of the tell-tale symptoms of this panic is a moment of intense vertigo, during which her entire history of questionable choices flashes before her eyes and she begins trying to mentally unmake decisions that got her into this jam in the first place. She can pull over now, or she can keep on driving until she plows into a WalMart rig.

And if she were raised in the American South, she is fully aware that there is not much else she can do besides sweat like a dog in August and pray, pray, pray. But her fatalism should not be mistaken for surrender. A Southern woman might temporarily abdicate responsibility, but she never abandons ship. She merely switches lanes and prays harder——sweet Jesus, Allah, Krishna, the Goddess, Ramona, I give up, help a sister out please!

For bargaining with God and smiling nicely for Highway Patrol are second nature to her. This is, after all, a woman who might take even her collards breaded, hold the Dukes please, and her bourbon double-strength—a woman who can bend like a wisteria vine if obliged to, but who has the spine of a steel car antenna. And perhaps if she endures long enough, she will tumble past all the thickets of disappointed prayers and unsung want that she knows as herself, and into a quiet and grassy slope, from where the road she has been searching for curls out before her in one unbroken shimmering stream, like a ribbon of light in the palm of her hand. She knows that yea, though she walks through the valley of the shadow of death, she is going to make it. That in the end, she is going to be just fine.

"…Change was inevitable. And how I dread change! But, finally, my body was granting my spirit permission to give up and take a chance on something, anything, that I truly hungered for."

Eirene Chen

Eirene *Chen*

Eirene Chen was born in 1975 in Greensboro, North Carolina. She received a BA in comparative literature from Duke University in 1997, Duke TEFL Certification in 1999, and has lived and worked in Durham since then. She has also served as an Adult Basic Education and English as a Second Language instructor with the Durham County Literacy Council. More recently she initiated and conducted a poetry workshop for ESL students at a public high school in Durham.

In addition to the interests discussed in her contribution, Eirene enjoys drawing graphic novellas, for which she was awarded a Benenson Arts Grant in 1995, and which may also be found in her colleagues' superb Durham-based international comix zine, *Zoom-*

cranks. Other pastimes include learning languages, playing the flute, spinning records, studying astrological depth psychology, baking pies, kite-flying, and making long road trips.

From 2000 to 2002, Eirene will be teaching English at a secondary school and working as a U.S. Peace Corps community development aide in the Republic of Uzbekistan. She would love to hear from you, and will return all correspondence! Interested parties may contact her via the following:

email: mooktone@yahoo.com

snail mail home: c/o Maria Horvath
1335 Cole Mill Road
Durham, NC 27705

snail mail away: US Peace Corps, Attn: Eirene Chen
c/o Halquaro Poctamt
4 Turkestanskaya Street, 700015 Tashkent 15
Republic of Uzbekistan

Fritzi Huber   an interview

Tell me how you grew up.

OK. I was born in a circus family. My mother's side of the family has gone back hundreds of years. My father was first-generation. He was Swiss, from Basel, Switzerland. My mom was born in New York but raised in Germany in the Convent system. That was considered a good education for women at the time but she very early on came to this country. And her story is incredible and long.

I have one brother. He was also born in the circus. Our parents decided that we should be permitted a childhood, so we didn't have to go to work in the act like most kids did right away. We went to correspondence school, mainly. Went to public schools on and off. My dad died in '61 when I was eleven and we went to public school after that. I went to work for a costume-maker in Houston where we were living. Decided after I left home and moved to California that the only way I was going to see my family—being my mother and my brother—was if I went back to the circus and worked with the circus. So about three months out of the year I would go back, and I worked with them on these Texas dates and some other dates until I was twenty-eight. And then I

decided that I would have to decide what I wanted to do.

I was going to college, I was being a seamstress, teaching sailing... Always doing something in the arts because I grew up with that. That was always a continuum and I did other things to earn money. But at a certain point there's just too much on your plate and you have to say, 'Something has to stop.' So, I stopped circus and focused completely on my art, as well as teaching sailing, because I had to make a living.

I still know people in circus. I still go to the circus. My mom is still very much involved with folks there. We still have friends who are like relatives to us.

I did trapeze. Aerial ballet. It's not flying trapeze, it's more like gymnastics in one place. You use riggings. I still have a trapeze in my studio. I still have rings in my studio. It's a great way to unwind and to relax in the middle of the day of hunching over a piece of paper. It's still a part of me, but I've chosen not to have that as my life.

What was it like for you growing up in the circus?

Well, you know, it's hard to be objective when you're in it. I remember kids used to ask me that all the time when I would come out and go into public school. 'Wow! What's it like?' It's like saying 'What's it like living in your home?' I remember the first time my mom let me have a friend outside of the business—to actually go to their home. She met their parents and my mom and dad agreed I could go away for the day and visit this little girl. It was up in Canada. So, I went to her home and I came back that evening. My mom said, 'Did you have a good time?' I said, 'Yeah, I did. But it's really strange.' I still remember the Pepto-Bismol pink of this girl's room. She said, 'Why was it so strange?' I said, 'She's been in this room for *eight* years.' It just floored me that someone could stay in the same place, in the same room for eight years. My mother said, 'I'm going to have a talk with you. This is how most people live. You are the unusual one.'

What did you think at that point?

Oh, I...it just took me aback. It had never dawned on me that this was a possibility. That someone would stay in a room, in the same house for the majority of their life. It struck me as sort of a place of fantasy. You know, like some kids dream of running away with the circus? We'd drive through foreign towns at night and you'd see people at dusk in their pajamas already and running around the front yard or whatever and lights on in the house...I'd think, 'Wow, what's that life like?' So, to say, 'What was it like?'...it's hard to be objective about what it was like. It was a lot of travelling. It's easier to answer specific questions than a vague 'What was it like?' because it encompasses the whole...realm of being. Spending lots of times in dressing rooms. Knowing that you could

be friends with people for very short, intense times and then you might not see them for a very long time. But when you saw each other again it would be as if no time had passed. So, carrying these friendships on for a whole lifetime where maybe you only see people for very short, intense stints of time...

Were you happy?

Yeah. Yeah, I was.

Was your brother happy, too?

Yeah, we both were. We enjoyed it tremendously as kids. It was great. Because we got to travel. We got to learn different languages. You know, if you were working with someone on the show who was from China, or from India, or wherever they were from somewhere in the world...you just go next door to that trailer and you were in that country, because they would carry their culture with them. You would eat that food, practice those cultural habits and...it was wonderful.

How did you know that what you wanted to do was trapeze? How did you choose?

My parents were aerialists. My mother was actually an acrobat and my father was a high-wire walker, and she worked in the air with him once they were married. My grandfather also worked in the air. It just was a natural thing for me. My mother, being an acrobat, was incredibly comfortable on the ground. I wasn't comfortable on the ground. I'm a lousy acrobat. It doesn't work for me. But as soon as I was in the air and was suspended in the air and working off of my arms, something came over me that changed me completely. My whole sense of being, my whole physical sensibility...It was transforming, I guess would be how it would best be said. A transformation occurred as soon as I left the ground. I felt confident and competent and secure in the air. It was a natural place for me to be. Not the ground. If I were to try to do a somersault, which I can't even do...I'm OK with a cartwheel. If I tried to do that I would be fixed with an obsession of falling on my head, of throwing myself wrong, of injuring myself. That makes you hesitate and then you do get hurt. In the air, none of that happened. In the air I could visualize myself moving through a maneuver, moving through a trick, moving through a regimen of activities without a trace of fear. So, that was a natural place for me to be.

Was there a typical working day in the circus for you?

Certainly. After you would get to your location and get set up, you'd go in and do your first rehearsal so you knew where everybody's rigging was, where your place was in the show, what the music was going to be like, how you were working with the music, what the costumes were if they were different from the last place—you get all of that out of the way. Then an average working day would be getting up late in the morning, because you wouldn't eat until after the last show at night. You'd get up late in the morning and do whatever activities you needed to do, like laundry or cooking and mending your costumes, making a new costume—whatever. Then I would go out and check the rigging, make sure the rigging was fine. Eventually you would get ready for the first show. You never ate before the show. On weekends you'd do two to three shows a day. Weekdays it would be one or two shows a day. Days off were only travel days or layoffs between dates. After the last show you would clean up, eat something and then you wouldn't want to go to bed on a full stomach so you'd stay up late and you'd visit with other performers or maybe go out somewhere, or do whatever it was you needed to do that you didn't finish during the day. Again, lots of times that was costumes.

As a child, somewhere in the middle of the day we would do our correspondence lessons and basically be self-entertainers. My parents wanted to give us more time in one place rather than travelling everyday, which is really hard on a family, so they broke into parks. It used to be Palisades Park in New Jersey, Kenwood Park in Canada, and you'd stay anywhere from two weeks to the whole summer. During that time maybe you wouldn't encounter any children other than children who lived in the town, which we stayed rather separate from. So, we became self-entertaining and my brother and I were best friends because of that. You know, you make your deals about who gets to play dolls today and who gets to play cars. Half the time the dolls became performers and we'd build riggings and they'd go on the roof. A reflection of life. Kind of like, I guess, kids would normally do with Barbie dolls, they get in the car and they drive to work. Well, it's the same thing. You build your rigging and you get in the vehicle and you go to work. So that was a normal day as a kid. As an adult, you just do whatever else you need to do. I used to love to see what museums were in town, see what music was going on, what kind of gardens—that sort of thing. You'd find somebody else on the show with you who would go and visit.

How do you think being in the circus and travelling like that has specifically shaped your attitude in your adult life?

I've been talking to my brother about this a lot. I said something to him the other day about, you know, we'd both chosen not to be in the business. I said, 'But look what we've done here.' He's a key grip in the film industry. I said, 'You load up the trailer, go to location, offload, do your gig, load up again and take off. I'm getting ready to go to ECU to do a several-day workshop. I have to do all this prep, load up my car, get there, unload the whole

thing...you do the act or the job, load it all back up again and disappear. We're doing the same thing.'

It's like there's nothing there...you unload this big show, you do the whole thing, you pack it all up and you're gone. And all that's left is some residue or a memory of this performance. I said, 'We think we've gotten away from it and we haven't. We are as addicted as we ever were and have fooled ourselves all our lives that we're not doing this.'

I think there's an element of surprise that's important to both of us, not just me. You want to hang on to a sense of wonder and encourage a sense of wonder and feel it yourself—not just that it's something you're imposing on the world, but something that you want to feel on your own. Because I think ultimately, that's what keeps people young, is a sense of wonder. If that slips away you've lost a real sense of youth. It just goes away for you and you wonder what *can* make your life interesting today and what can you *do* to make your life interesting rather than life *being* interesting. I think that's the main thing.

What were your greatest challenges growing up, do you think?

Adapting to not being in the circus was a huge challenge. That was really tough. There are other young people that I knew that left the business and it was tough for them, too. That's one thing we have in common when we speak to each other, because one of the things that's not common for all of us but for a good number of us is that we usually don't tell people that we're performers—or had been performers—right away. Until we get to know them a bit.

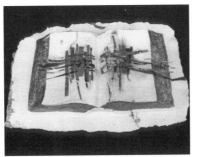

"The Woven Word #1"

People tend to see you as that and not as who you are. They're colored by what that profession is.

There's a whole mystique about circus. Not that many people know so much about it. So, learning that it's OK to be vulnerable, to be open, to let that be known and not use it as a gimmick or not use it as anything like that. But just to say, 'OK, this is who I am. This is who I was.' And not be afraid of what kind of questioning that it will bring in and what people will make of it. Or...the possibility that you can't be invisible in a crowd.

What skills do you think you took away from your time in the circus that have helped you survive in your life?

The obsession with mechanical skills. When I started teaching sailing, that was so easy for me because it was a transferral of all that knowledge about riggings. And of course, what I taught was surf launching on catamarans in California. So you come with this little package and you put up the whole rigging and the sails and the whole thing and you go out and you do the surf launching. Then tear it all down and it's back in its little package and you leave again. I'm still doing the tent.

You have not escaped.

I did not escape then either. I just thought I did. That type of sailing is incredibly physical and so that was transferable. From as early as I can remember I've made costumes, which makes you very textile aware—fabric aware. Lots of times you're making costumes out of remnants of things. This has carried over so strongly for me because what I do when I make paper is I recycle fabrics. If I want blue, I use blue jeans. If I want white, I use white shirts. If I want purple, I'll maybe use a plaid shirt that's blue and red and it breaks down. So, an awareness of fabric, an awareness of doing a lot of things in a small space—those have carried over.

I have an obsession with recycling and an obsession with water. One of the things that happens when you get to a location and you're just setting up with your trailer is that you look for water. How far is it? How much can you get? Can you hook up to it? Do you have to haul it? When do you have to cut off from it? All of this stuff with water. If you didn't get there first and you're way down the line, how much water pressure are you going to have? I've always felt that water is an incredible wealth. So, as long as I'm close to water I feel like I have a great richness in my life, no matter what the other circumstances are. Papermaking is water-intensive. You're up to your elbows in water. You're sloshing around in the stuff. There's water everywhere. I'm working with fabric and breaking down fabric and creating other things with the fabric that are very much like costumes.

I had one performer friend who was helping one time when I had a lot on my plate. I was doing a lot of commissions and I needed an assistant badly. She was an ex-circus performer and she came in to help me and she was watching me go through the steps and she said, 'You're just making costumes.' I said, 'Yeah, I am.' It was the same approach.

I tend to have a sensibility towards a decorative quality—in terms of what I'm putting in the paper as well as what I'm applying to the surface. Lots of times what I apply to the surface has microparticles in it. Sometimes it's even what they call an interference color, which will give you a duotone. I'll put ground-up sequins from costumes—I'll put all kinds of stuff in the pulp so I come up with this relatively decorative surface to begin with. That's less intimidating than stark white anyway. You've got a collaborator. You're working *with* the thing rather than *on* it or doing something to it. I like that sense of collaboration—even if it's not another person. It comes with its own history. The Japanese have a sense of history about some of the paper they use when they put inclusions in it like ground-up newspapers. If you can read a word or a bit of a word, the paper itself is telling you a piece of its own history and what it's come to you with.

So, how did you find your way to papermaking?

I was doing a lot of printmaking in California and I was wanting to do blind embossing in the surface. So, I'm doing a blind embossing and it was getting deeper and deeper and deeper into the surface and I couldn't find a commercially-made paper that I wasn't breaking surface with. Every time I tried to do something that was an inch or two inches deep it was just ridiculous to do that with an industrially-made paper. Even a fine-quality printmaking paper wasn't going to do it. Then there's problems with the presses when it gets that deep.

I was coming in in the middle of the night to do my printing because I was doing some color things and didn't want any dust in the environment. A friend of mine was coming in in the middle of the night to do some projects she was working on. She saw that I was having this problem and she said, 'Why don't you just let me teach you how to make paper?' This was 1976. I said, 'Oh yeah, right.' She said, 'No, I'm not kidding. I'll show you.' So, she showed me and I learned an Oriental technique first which is the more difficult. When I learned Western technique I thought, 'This is great. I can do this.' For two years I juggled back and forth whether I really wanted to do paper or not. Not even asking the question, just consistently being drawn back to it and finding reasons to do it because I liked it so much. Eventually I just said, 'This is really what I want to do, so I'm going to be a papermaker.'

One of the things I'm doing more of now is, I'm doing a lot of handmade books. I've always done books and part of that goes way back to the circus again, too. Some of my books are cast three to four inches deep. You can't page them. They're solid.

I'm computer ignorant. I was over at my friend Sara's house, wanting her to look up something on the Internet for me. I'm over there and her little boy comes running into the room and he's got a red skirt on around his neck. He drops to the floor and the skirt puffs up around him like a big mushroom and he says, 'Look! I'm a rock!' And I said, 'Oh, Ayers Rock!' because he's in the middle of the floor and he's on this flat plain and here's this big red puff of a thing. He says, 'What's that?' and I say 'It's this thing in Australia. A wonder of the world.' I go to their two sets of encyclopedias and they go to the Internet. They're rummaging around to find Ayers Rock on the Internet. I've got the two books open in my hands saying, 'Look, here it is. Here's Ayers Rock,' and they're all looking on the Internet and asking 'Are you sure that's the way you spell it?' I say, 'Yeah, look. It's right here. It's right here.' And all three of them were looking at the screen—Sara and her son and daughter. So I said, 'Well, look up Australia.' So they get Australia up there and there's Ayers Rock. And there was just this incred-

ible, magical moment where a breeze passed through and turned the page of one of these books and I thought, 'I'm holding relics. I'm holding relics.' I wanted to make icons to these relics and I started doing the cast books.

As I'm doing the cast books I'm remembering things about bookmaking. This is one of the reasons I'm doing more of it now with the painting, and doing the larger, flat pieces.

As a child, I couldn't have a library card while I was on the road. My father, before he had gotten into the circus, was a bookbinder's apprentice in Basel in Switzerland, so he had a great love of books and he exposed me to it. I so wanted a library that I made my own books. Before I could write I sewed little handmade books that I still have. I have maybe three of them. They're one inch by two inches and they're crudely sewn, but I was binding these little books with images and finally words and that sort of thing. When I was able to have a library card I would check out as many books as I could possibly get my hands on and take them all home. I would open them all up, I would smell them, I would sleep with them. I would go to libraries and I would choose books by walking down the aisles and smelling. The areas that smelled the best, I would get those books. Lots of times they were older papers.

So, there was this whole sensual thing that occurred with a book for me. Learning papermaking and having my hands in the paper and doing this thing from scratch just fulfilled that desire so well and made me so close to that love that I've always had for the book. Not just the written word, but the book as physical object.

So you started college but then you left to do papermaking?

Yeah. I consider myself a late bloomer because I didn't even get to college until I was twenty-two. I was going back and forth and doing other things. I had become friends with some of my professors and said, 'Look, I don't really want to teach, and I feel like I'm really late getting started in this. All I really want to do is get in the studio and work and figure out what I'm doing.' What was suggested to me, since paper was what I had chosen to do, was, 'Why don't you just choose some people to study with?' I thought, 'OK, that's good.' So, I did. I chose three people to study with. I chose a paper chemist and artist. Then I chose a paper toolmaker who I'm still very good friends with from up in Boston. I'm so lucky—he trades me equipment for artwork. So I get equipment through him. I studied with these three people and just started working.

So, no, I never finished that sort of an education...but then, the kind of education that I grew up understanding was, 'It's out there in the world. If you want the information, you can get it.' If you get a piece of paper for it, you have to have a specific reason for that piece of paper. I mean, is it just so you have a piece of

paper? Or is it because it's essential to taking you someplace that you want to or you need to go? For me, since I didn't want to be in the university system teaching and I didn't know what else I would use it for at the time, I just thought, 'OK, well, I'll get out and I'll work and I'll learn.' So, that's it.

How did you come to North Carolina?

My brother came down here when Dino DeLaurentis opened the studios, and started on the first films with him, and helped set up some of the studios in terms of rigging. In fact, that's how he was spotted. He was called out for *Firestarter* and they needed a full moon shot at night and there was no full moon. He quickly, with a friend of his, threw together a rigging and rigged up a lighting system that looked like a full moon. They said, 'Who is that guy?' Here we go again. The rigging thing. Both of us...any opportunity, 'Oh, I can do that.' Down, boy. Down, girl.

So, he moved out here and he decided he was going to move my mother out here. Well, that meant the two people in my family whom I would normally leave several months out of the year to go be with on the road, weren't going to be on the road anymore. She was going to be here, he was going to be here. I had been in Southern California for seventeen years at that point. We're all from Texas originally. Not my mom. My brother and me. We had a home there as well. He said he wanted me to move out.

'Come look at it. See what you think.' I came out here and I thought, 'You know, this looks a lot like Southern California did, but more lush. More green.' When I had moved there in 1970 I thought, 'Well, hopefully they'll be more ecologically conscientious and growth-conscious and pay attention to the environment more.' They were *here*, and I thought, 'Well, I'll come out.'

So, was your mom leaving the circus at that point?

Yeah, she's relatively older. Mom's eighty-three now and she had gone back into wardrobe every now and then. But the neighborhood she was in in Houston was becoming not such a good neighborhood anymore. We were worried about her health and we were worried about her living alone and being isolated there with him on this coast and me on that coast. It was just a better thing to move her out here. She loves being here now. She works as an extra in the film industry all the time. It's hard to find an eighty-three-year-old woman who's enthusiastic about doing twelve hours.

I was going to say...it must have been interesting for her to not have that schedule anymore.

Oh, she didn't like it at first at all. People would ask, 'How do you like it here?' and she'd say, 'I hate it.' For her, there was no life here. Now she has a life here.

Was it a challenge for you to meet people and trust friends in the outside world when you left the circus?

Making friends was not a problem. Allowing people to be very close was a problem. Then, you know, maybe a lot of people are like this, maybe not. I have no idea. It's like a complete pendulum swing for me. I go through my extremes before I find my middle ground. Lots of times when I'm working through a body of work, I end up having to do maybe twenty or thirty pieces. Not all of them end up going out into the world...What? It's all good? No. But I have to go to one end before I know where that zone is that I was trying to get to in the first place. So, I think, in regard to the friendship thing, I'd be either wide open and let everybody close, or closed down and not let anybody in.

As we're talking I keep thinking of Wallace Stegner. I loved his writing. He's only been dead a few years now. He wrote a fabulous book called *Angle Of Repose...*

Oh, that's my favorite book of his.

Oh, thank you! I love this book!

It's a great book.

I love this book. I kind of feel like where I've come to now, at this point in my life—you know, we don't know what's going to happen beyond—is I've kind of reached an angle of repose. All those rocks have stopped to roll. It means that I know that the one extreme doesn't work for me and neither does the other but there is a moderate ground. It's probably—even though I'm in the midst of some personal insanity—a least insane time, because I feel like I have a solid ground of perspective. More so than I have in the past. It doesn't mean I know everything, but it's more solid than it was in terms of relating to people and who I let in and who I don't.

Was it hard in terms of having romantic relationships or starting to date, when you were never in the same place for very long? Did you come late to dating?

Yeah. I mean, this gets into kind of a strange area. I don't know. I've been married a few times. Right now I'm going through a divorce and it's not pleasant. But that's also having reached an angle of repose again. So accustomed to intense relationships that my marriages lasted for short periods of time. Also, my mother had been married three times. My father had been married before. It's a terrible, sarcastic sort of thing to say but it's almost like that pair of shoes didn't fit and I didn't know it until I bought them. I don't mean to be flippant but...that's one way of putting it in terms of, 'How did you deal with long-term relationships?'

The funny thing is, my parents had the most incredible relationship with each other. They thrived on over-exposure. If they had an argument, one would leave until they cooled down. Not leave, period, but leave the trailer or go out and work for awhile and mom would go work on costumes. They'd come back, they'd talk about it, they'd work it out and that was it. So, I always had this ideal of what a relationship should have been. What a good relationship was like. It didn't have anything to do with the reality of most relationships.

How did you begin to recognize that in yourself?

I thought that this wasn't a problem. I thought I was fully capable and fully committed. I didn't go into anything thinking this is short-lived. I thought 'I found my lifelong love.'

What accomplishment do you think you're the proudest of?

That's a tough one. Come into my angle of repose. It's all about...where is your place in the world? Are you doing anybody any good? Are you doing yourself any good? Is there anything that you have to share? As long as that pendulum swing is so broad, you just every now and then touch on something valuable. Something valuable doesn't happen consistently. It only happens when you hit that middle there when you're at your sane point and not at the insane extremes. Also, though, the insane extremes bring you to those moments of sanity—if you want to call it that; I don't know that we're ever completely sane. So, I think the closer that we can get to...a sense of being in balance, being more valuable to ourselves and to others that our lives touch. That doesn't really sound like a tangible accomplishment, but it's about as tangible as I think you can possibly get, in reality, to being in relation to the rest of the world and with people in the world. If you can come to some point of balance, then you are more valuable to yourself and to others.

Do you have any dreams that you still want to fulfill or goals that you want to work towards?

Oh, God! Always. Death is the end of growth. I'm not the only one to say it, I know. The only thing that's constant is change. So, I hope to change into a better, more valuable person. That's vague and broad, you know, but that's about it. To be able to see and express more clearly. If I have a piece that someone responds to—because when they want to do commissions, what do they do? They look at slides of work that I've already done, and I'm off somewhere else by now. What I do when I'm doing the work is I listen to music—music without lyrics, because lyrics form images and I don't necessarily want the image. It's just going to take me wherever it's going to take me. So, if someone has responded to a piece, I keep a little diary of what music I was listening to. I go to that music and I'll play it again. I'll play it maybe four to six times or whatever...until the same emotional state is invoked. It's not

like I'm trying to answer anything mysterious, you know. It's just that it evokes a certain emotional state or psychological state. Then I'll just begin to paint.

Now, the painting is simply the vehicle for tapping into that emotional or psychological state, as far as I'm concerned. The closer that I can get to people feeling that and saying, 'That's it,' the closer I am to having accomplished touching another life. Communicating with another person. I don't know why you would make art if you don't want to communicate something in the first place.

What would you tell either a young woman who's just starting out on her path or an older woman trying to find her career, her goal in life?

I don't mean this in a harsh way, but it's really important. Don't worry about taking no for an answer. No is much more prevalent than yes, and before you ask for something you have a no already. So what do you have to lose if someone tells you no? Take a chance and do it.

I'm going to bounce back to Wallace Stegner again because it's funny, he's just been coming up a lot lately. When he died this magazine did a little article on him and he was talking about the differences of your concept of beauty, living in the West and living in the East. How in the East your concept of beauty has to do with gardens and green and lushness. How in the West it has to do with space—because that's what you have there. You don't have lush and green so everything changes, everything shifts. One of the differences is that that kind of space puts you in a land of desire. This kind of lushness puts you in a land of fulfillment. So, on the one hand, you are in the lush land of fulfillment, which is the bed of feathers. And then you have the land of desire, which can actually be the bed of nails. You can't always have the two together. I don't know if it's even *possible* that you can have the two together. So there's always that struggle down the middle...Are you comfortable? Do you have enough? Do you want enough? If the balance is off, don't let that scare you. It's just a path to some- where. Never expect to have the whole thing, because only very few and very fortunate ever have the whole thing. If you ever get it, that's great, but it's worth the search and the struggle. The struggle can be wonderful.

Interviewed by Emily A. Colin.

"The Woven Word #3"

"The only thing that's constant is change. So I hope to change into a better, more valuable person."

Fritzi Huber

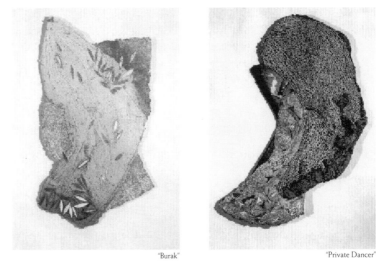

"Burak"

"Private Dancer"

Fritzi *Huber*

Fritzi Huber has been a hand papermaker and painter for over twenty years, but has been an artist for all of her life. As a child her involvement in circus work—and costuming connected directly to it—inspired her to develop a life-long romance with fiber that is evident in her work.

Huber is in corporate and private collections throughout the United States, including the permanent collection of Duke Medical Center. Her work is in museum collections in Finland and Hungary and she was invited to create an ornament for the White House Christmas tree to celebrate "The Year of American Craft" in 1996. She has shared her expertise from locations such as the Mingei Museum in San Diego, California, the Savannah College of Art and Design and Pyramid Atlantic in Washington, D.C. Recently she has taught at the San Antonio Center for Art and Craft in Texas and at Eastern Carolina University in Greenville, North Carolina.

Publisher, Help Thyself   Julie Tetel Andresen

It all started about five years ago when I bought *The Artist's Way* by Julie Cameron, a twelve-step recovery program for artists. I loved the book so much, I did the entire twelve-week program twice in one year. After that, I started reading other self-help books about creativity (creative journaling, creative visualization) which, in turn, inspired a look at self-help books involving other kinds of recoveries (dreams, past lives). These led straight to the long shelves of self-help books about financial recovery.

I did whatever these books instructed. I wrote out exercises, made time lines, kept notes, recorded observations, used different colored markers. After I cleaned up my financial mess (okay, I'm still working on that one a bit), I turned my attention to the house, and this produced an extended and satisfying period of practicing feng shui. My bed is now positioned for optimal sleep. My desk is facing in absolutely my best direction (southeast). The Japanese garden in the back yard completes the missing Wealth and Fame sectors of the house ba-gua. The flow of ch'i couldn't be better, especially since one of my books revealed to me the true secret of harmony with the universe, which is:

Decluttering.

Unused and unwanted junk in cabinets, drawers and storage spaces, unused and unwanted furniture—all gone, gone, gone with the help of self-help books, along with about thirty years' worth of books. The removal of my unused and unwanted clothing opened up my closet and the way to reading books on personal style. The decluttering also gave rise to a spiritual dimension in my life, and so I moved happily into *Anatomy of the Spirit* by Caroline Myss. There I hit bottom. Myss noted a condition which I will call self-help book addiction. This evidently can happen when a person gets stuck in fourth chakra issues. I couldn't miss seeing myself in her passage. I was aghast. *Did she really expect me to give up my self-help books?*

I sucked it up and quit cold turkey about a year ago. I had a little relapse this past weekend when I ran across an intuition workout book that had not made it out the door during the decluttering. This time, however, I didn't really do any of the exercises—and there were some really neat ones involving bubbles—I only imagined doing them. Sort of like an ex-smoker catching a whiff of second-hand smoke, I suppose. It gave me a buzz for sure, but I didn't inhale completely.

The problem is, I have a long history of self-help activity, mostly without the books. I suspect that I have a 'self-help personality.' My mother tells me that from my earliest childhood, whenever I was learning something new, I would tell her to go away and insist "I can do it myself!" In high school, my friend Josie and I wrote out and revised extensive Self Improvement Plans, mostly during French class. Our S.I.P.s revolved around losing weight (which required a strict diet and exercise regimen), improving our complexions (which involved a liberal application of Noxema boosted by a judicious use of sun lamps), and getting more popular (here the plans became somewhat vague). In college, I took a course in logic. I remember that, on the night before the final, I realized there was no hope for me in the class unless I could devise a complete new system on my own. My semester grade was a D. I was happy I didn't flunk. The further good news was that college was a lot more fun than high school because the very categories of my high school S.I.P. were no longer relevant. Self improvement had occurred, after all.

⇥⊙

Clearly, not all my do-it-myself results are perfect, but that's quite all right. In fact, getting something perfect would be awful. It would mean The End. Nothing left to do. I'm not saying that I like to fail, but I am saying that I don't really mind it so much. I see it as part of a larger process, along the lines of Irving Berlin's motto: "I write six songs a day just to get rid of the bad ones."

A few years ago, after publishing fifteen mass-market romances with major commercial publishers and getting tired of the insecurity and low pay, I started my own publishing studio. I didn't even notice my life pattern at first, until a writer friend of mine remarked with some surprise that I seemed to be enjoying myself. I laughed and replied without thinking, "You can't believe how typical this is of me!" Suddenly I heard the echo of a little girl's voice piping up to say, "I can do it myself!" Did I need somebody else to publish my novels? Heck no. Why send my already-digitized stories to some bloated commercial publisher and let them have all the fun designing, marketing and distributing them? I'm not sure whether many of those New York guys and gals are having so much fun in commercial publishing anymore–but that is another story entirely.

Now in my third year of operation, I am starting to get the hang of studio publishing. What I have learned overall is: *I cannot do it all myself.* This is the wisdom of my middle years. There are simply too many jobs: writer, editor, copyeditor, designer/artist, typesetter, printer, accountant, marketer, shipper, legal consultant, business manager. I joyfully do the jobs I love, and I find talented professionals who know how to do the jobs I would only botch. I am learning to work with assistants and independent contractors and other writers whose work I am acquiring and publishing. I have long known that writing a book is a solitary endeavor. I am now learning that producing and promoting a book is a wonderfully collaborative experience.

⇥

I had no idea that I was a born entrepreneur until I became one. Before launching my publishing studio, a significant part of my adult professional life had been spent in an academic career, the kind that involves the truly wretched process of tenure. Fortunately for me, I had been selling romance novels to mass-market publishers while I was an untenured assistant professor. I say 'fortunately' because many of my colleagues were convinced that this activity would sink me in the academy. What they didn't know—and what I couldn't fully articulate to myself at the time either—was just how corporate the academic world really is. That is not a criticism, since there is nothing wrong with corporations. All I knew was that selling myself to the tenure committee was a test of my commercial writer's mettle. Since the tenure committee bought my case, I have no idea how I would have dealt with a

failure on that score. I am sure I would have felt badly, but I would also like to think that I would have interpreted the experience as one of the "bad songs" that I had gotten rid of. One thing is certain: the founding of my publishing studio was inevitable. I was bound to discover, sooner or later, that starting my own business was the way to maximize the glorious and thrilling process of learning from mistakes. No, wait. That's life.

I am not trying to run my publishing studio perfectly—that would be no fun—but I am trying to run it profitably which, I hear, *is* fun (I'll let you know). Starting up a business is a great game of: solving problems creatively, getting financial records in order, avoiding clutter, finding and projecting a studio image and style, and operating within a strong spiritual framework. How about that? All my self-help reading prepared me well. Now, if only there were a self-help book to help with self-help book withdrawal...

⇥

As a commercial writer and an academic, I learned about writing for an audience. As a studio publisher, I am learning what it is to write and produce books with a soul. These two learning experiences are by no means necessarily mutually exclusive, and in any case publishers have to produce books that people want to read in order to make the profit that keeps them in the game. However, taking the publishing reins in my own hands has given me to know through experience that profit is a by-product, the epiphenominal effect of offering the right book to the right audience. For me, "rightness" is evidenced when a soulful connection is made between author and audience.

I caught my first glimpse of this a few months ago when I attended a booksigning at a local bookstore featuring Robin Greene. She was reading selections from *Real Birth: Women Share Their Stories,* the launch title for my non-fiction imprint, Generation Books. During the reading I felt Robin capture the attention of her audience. I could see the connection in the expressions on her listeners' faces. I understood what it meant to be a part of something larger than myself. After the reading, I overheard a woman say, "I just came for the reading not expecting to buy any books. Now, I am going to buy two, and I am going to send them to my daughters, because they've got to read this." It's nice to sell books, but it's even better to produce books that make such an impact on a community of readers. For me, this experience at the bookstore was more satisfying—as corny as this sounds—than any of the awards or fan mail I have received for my own novels. Believe me, I enjoy ego gratification as much as the next person, and I have long dreamed of writing a self-help book and becoming the next Julia Cameron or Caroline Myss. But here's the thing:

I don't think I have a self-help book in me. I wouldn't even know where to begin. Now, I do know a good one when I see one, and suddenly my busy brain is saturated with an idea, surely one of my "good songs" for today. I have just realized that my path as a publisher may well be to bring a fabulous self-help book to life, and it occurs to me that publishing a really terrific self-help book for the greater good of the community has got to be a fifth chakra issue, at least.

Think about it. Now I can justify my addiction, feed it and claim spiritual progress all at once. Oh, yeah. There really is something to this soulful publishing thing. Very nice.

⊷⊐◉

So, if you or anyone you know has a good self-help manuscript, send it on in to Generation Books. Make sure to include plenty of exercises. I'm already reaching for my colored markers.

Bruce R. Feeley

Julie Tetel Andresen

"I had no idea that I was a born entrepreneur until I became one."

Julie Tetel Andersen

Julie Tetel Andresen grew up in a suburb of Chicago and has lived in Durham, North Carolina since 1976 with her husband, Marcel Tetel, and two sons, Francis and Gerard. She has taught at Duke University since 1986.

In 1997 she founded her publishing studio, which has two imprints: Madeira Books (fiction) and Generation Books (non-fiction).

You can visit her at *www.madeirabooks.com* and *www.generationbooks.com.*

Of Psychics, Singing, and Soul-Searching Diane Brandon

Life sometimes takes us down roads we don't anticipate. This is definitely true of me: I never foresaw myself working as a professional intuitive, or "psychic," as people often refer to the profession. However, that is precisely the work that I have found myself doing in the past seven and a half years. So how did I come to be doing this work that is so atypical for the type of person I saw myself as? Please allow me to share my story with you.

I was born and raised in New Orleans in a middle-class family and did all the "normal" things a child did growing up in the '50s: I went to church and sang in the church choir; I was in the Brownies and Girl Scouts; I went to summer camp and went on trips with my family. I was always an extremely avid reader and loved to read just about anything, including Nancy Drew mysteries. One year I read a lot about Greek and Roman mythology. The next year I was interested in astronomy.

I was always quite innately fascinated by psychic phenomena and felt that there was a connection between spirituality and ESP, but could not have verbalized what that was. Although I had a strong interest in metaphysics and was quite spiritual from an early age, I saw no implications for what I wanted to do "when I grew up." In fact, I had always wanted to be an actor and a singer, and indeed I knew from my earliest memories that that was what I was to do in my life.

I started singing solos in talent shows in second or third grade and availed myself of what few resources there were back then for the budding performer. I started taking voice lessons in junior high and also went to a summer drama program for teens in junior high.

In spite of my strong interest in performing, however, I had other interests as well. And academic pursuits were one of those. I gradually found that my "group" in junior high tended to be the "brains" (albeit the more creative rather than the dry ones: we collaborated a couple of times to put together skits for talent shows), and I attended a college preparatory high school for academically gifted. What I have come to realize about myself in the (many, many) intervening years is that I have eclectic tastes and am not easily pigeon-holed. I have also come to realize that this eclecticism has strong implications for the type of person I am and for what can satisfy me in terms of a career. Self-knowledge, or self-awareness, is one of the greatest gifts or tools we can acquire,

I have come, perhaps belatedly, to realize. But I'm getting ahead of myself.

As one might not have expected with my strong interest in acting and singing, I pursued a straight academic curriculum in college. I majored in French at Duke University. In fact, although I took voice lessons at Duke and sang in both the Chapel Choir and Glee Club, it wasn't until my senior year that I was in a play. When I graduated from college, I moved back to New Orleans and worked for a couple of years, first as an accounts payable clerk and second as a bilingual executive secretary. (At that time, there was very little open to women other than clerical work, irrespective of what one's academic background might have been.) I did do some theatre while in New Orleans and continued to study voice.

I then decided after this two-year stint to go to graduate school in media. Although I applied to and was accepted by different schools, I consciously felt myself pulled back to North Carolina for some unknown reason and decided to go to University of North Carolina at Chapel Hill for radio, television, and motion pictures. This turned out to be a very significant period in my life for personal change. Both the academic program and the social influences in Chapel Hill had a profound effect on me. I started to see things in life quite differently as my perspective and total outlook shifted. I started to see myself as the artist I had always been with its attendant implications, but had never defined myself as. I also started to perform on a much more regular basis in local theatre productions. There was such a personal and artistic flowering for me in this period of my life that one would have expected that it would lead directly to a professional flowering. In fact, I did move to Los Angeles to pursue acting, but found myself feeling disenchanted by what I saw in the industry there and left to return to North Carolina after a couple of months.

The next ten years or so found me working in regular jobs (from secretary to research assistant to corporate manager, the latter as the first female manager in the department I was in) while pursuing acting and singing on the side. From my present vantage point on the far side of fifty, I now look at those years as the "lost years." Far from the promise of my early years in theatre, I was really floundering. "What went wrong?" I asked myself over the intervening years.

Before I fast-forward to the present time, allow me to answer this query quite simply: I later learned that I was the one holding myself back. My personal self-doubts, coupled with my passivity and inability to be more proactive, held me back.

So what happened to make me realize this? Actually it was a confluence of factors.

First of all, I left the corporate world in the early '80s and opened a performing arts store. This served to set me on the path to working for myself and gaining more autonomy. This more autonomous mode of working gradually led me to realize that I was a more independent person than I had previously seen myself as.

The second factor had to do with my entering a major period of personal growth in which I worked on some of my personal self-defeating issues—and evolved. The growth was so significant that I came to view it as exponential. I now feel light-years away from the person I was before, although my essence—my core on the inside—remains the same. There were many catalysts for this personal growth, including a women's support group and a difficult personal relationship (as I've come to see through my intuitive work, relationships are often the stimulus for growth, if we're willing to learn!).

And the third factor for my change had to do with an intense period of spiritual growth. I have always been strongly spiritual, as I mentioned earlier. It was not my spiritual *orientation* that increased; that was always there. Instead, it was my awareness and understanding that grew. The initial impetus for this growth was a spiritual group that I participated in that was facilitated by an intuitive for whom I had a strong respect. This group also marked the first time that I was in a group of people interested in metaphysics. Prior to my involvement in this group in the late '80s, I had rarely been in a room of people who shared those interests.

Of course, the time period itself was a facilitative factor. In the late 1980s, more people in our society were opening to metaphysics and becoming more interested in personal and spiritual growth.

These were the major factors, among other, lesser ones, that brought about significant changes in me. I gained more self-esteem, came to understand, know, and accept myself more, and lost my former people-pleasing ways.

In 1987 I closed Theatrics, my store. My plan was to teach voice privately and get an agent for acting, so as to get on-camera acting work that paid, rather than continuing to focus on local theatre that either didn't or paid a miniscule amount. For the first several years, I got an increasing number of on-camera and voice-over jobs. However, the work, and hence the income, were unpredictable. In early 1992, I started working part-time as a church secretary for extra income. Going back to clerical work after my years of being self-employed was both a shock to my system and a wounding to my pride. I had finally, if belatedly, come to realize how very independent I am and how working in a support position went very much against my grain.

It was at this point, and somewhat in desperation, that I started to work as a "psychic." Had the mitigating factors been otherwise at the time; had I been getting more income from teaching and performing; and had I not been miserable working once again in a clerical position, I would likely never have come to be doing the work that I'm presently doing. I would say that it was serendipity, were I not a believer in the workings of the universe often steering and guiding our actions. In other words, I feel that I was *led* to this work. It was certainly not anything I would have consciously and deliberately chosen!

In essence, I started working part-time as a psychic for a 900 line. Talk about a far cry from an undergraduate degree at a fairly prestigious university! Needless to say, I did not exactly leap at the opportunity to do this work. This venture came about in a quite off-handed manner. A friend suggested this to me because he knew another person working for this line. My initial reaction was negative. "I can't do that," I thought. However, after my initial rejection, I gave the idea more consideration. I had learned through working on self-esteem to catch myself in those initial knee-jerk reactions of "I can't." I remembered that I had been encouraged by my revered metaphysical teacher to do spiritual counseling. The only problem was that I had never considered myself to have any psychic or intuitive ability. Other people did that type of work, not me, was my thinking. I had bought both tarot cards and an I Ching book in grad school, and played around with doing readings for myself and my roommate, but had never gained any sort of proficiency. In this manner, I found myself seesawing back and forth in my mind about the possibility of doing this type of work.

I finally decided to give it a try. I practiced doing a few readings on some friends and then applied to the line. I was required to give three sample readings as a test of my "abilities" and subsequently was approved for hiring, much to my surprise.

I won't belabor the progression of events in the seven and a half years since I started working for the 900 line. I initially approached the work with a great deal of trepidation, feeling that I really didn't know what I was doing. This was compounded by the fact that I kept trying to do what I thought a "psychic" was supposed to do, which mainly consisted of fortune-telling. However, I kept getting positive feedback on my readings. So I was getting continual encouragement that, somehow, I did indeed have some sort of intuitive ability. After about eight months, I got up enough confidence to have business cards printed so as to start doing private readings. I really felt my way along initially. However, as I continued to do the work I gained more insight into it and, moreover, into what I was doing. My concept of what a "psychic" was—or could be—evolved greatly. If I had been less open about letting this work evolve, or had I more rigidly clung to my concept of what I thought a "psychic" should do, I would never be doing the type of work that I now do.

In spite of the fact that I continued to feel conflicted about being seen as a "psychic," I personally gained more insight over time into what my work was evolving towards. I came to realize more and more that my work is more that of an intuitive or spiritual counselor, or personal facilitator. I am really just using my intuitive abilities to provide insight and be a guide to others. I cannot do a session and just provide superficial information to a client: who, what, when, where, how—or whether one will win a lottery. It is the underlying meaning of events that captures my attention. What is really happening to us through the external events in our lives and how does that speak to us of change, especially of our own inner and personal change? I have come to realize that my greatest gifts may come in reading people, both my clients and others in their lives. Not who they are in a superficial sense, but who they are on the inside, their essence, the energetic template for their being, if you will.

This work and its very nature have taught me a great deal. Through this work and my struggle to understand my role with it, I have come to tease at the inner workings of things. No great leap for me, as I've always been somewhat of an armchair philosopher. However, it's not just the inner workings that I've found myself teasing; I've also striven to understand what intuition itself is as a phenomenon. I must admit, though, that it still rankles quite a bit to hear someone refer to me as a "psychic!" The word belies the great strengths that this work can have in facilitating others.

This work has indeed grown tremendously for me. After my initial tentative printing of business cards, I started going to a few metaphysical stores to do sessions. I was gradually asked to participate in expos and psychic fairs and started doing some traveling within the state. I was also asked to write metaphysical articles. I've done some radio and T.V. appearances. I started incorporating other modalities into my work, in addition to just doing readings: I do individualized guided meditation; dream interpretation; regression; and some healing work. I also started teaching some workshops on topics such as developing intuition, working with dreams, and personal empowerment and wholeness (that I designed a system to work with). I've done presentations on some of these metaphysical topics as well. I've even worked at some parties as a fortune-teller. (Ah, well, it draws upon my performing background!) And I now have a web site that explains my work and contains the articles I've had published. After about four years, I was doing well enough from my private sessions and my work in stores, the expos, and psychic fairs that I was able to quit working the 900 line and just focus on the private work. I also stopped teaching voice for the most part.

I have gained a great deal from this work. It has certainly increased my self-confidence. Because of this work, I have started writing and have found my own voice. I have also learned a great deal, both about people and about metaphysics. (At present, I'm working on a book explaining some of what I've learned through this work.) And through this work I have tapped more and more into my own knowing. Being in touch with one's knowing is extremely powerful—so powerful, in fact, that I strive to facilitate others' tapping into their knowing as well. In addition, I've had some wonderful feedback from clients. For example, I've had several clients tell me that I had helped them to transform their lives. I was quite taken aback the first time a client told me that. "What a high compliment!" I thought. I am humbled at the thought that the little I thought I was doing could be that helpful. I do know that some clients regard me as a guide or mentor, and I do know that I have felt more self-actualized myself through this work. And I also know that had I not already started to realize my own independence or adhere to my awareness that one has to follow one's own path, rather than living the norm or the expectations of others, I could never have done this work. So there have been many benefits accrued from doing this work, as well as personal satisfaction.

That is not to say, however, that I find this work the end all and be all, or that it isn't fraught with a downside. Working for oneself is indeed a mixed blessing. It's wonderful to be autonomous and make one's own decisions. On the other hand, there are no corporate benefits (retirement, pension, health insurance)—and there's no guaranteed weekly or monthly check or paid vacation. The income can be highly variable, and one is subject to the whims of societal trends. There is also the social connotation as-

signed to this type of work to contend with among those who are not aware of what the work can be.

Finding the fulcrum, or balance, between the work and my own privacy can be difficult. As anyone knows who works in a helping profession, the needs of others and what they may be going through emotionally can not only tug at our hearts, but also often drain our own energy and psychic reserves. I've had to learn how to erect emotional boundaries. This issue is complicated by the fact that I often work out of my home and have needed to find a way to ensure privacy—and reduce phone calls coming in in the middle of the night or very early hours of the morning.

At the present writing, I find myself experiencing some of the troughs in this form of self-employment. The fluctuations in income seem to be heightened, due to the vicissitudes of the market of late. There are fewer fairs and expos. And perhaps there are more people doing this type of work. Although a few years back, I had felt that the universe was moving me out of performing into more and more of my spiritual work, I now find myself wanting to do more performing again. Singing pulls on me more and more all the time.

Am I saying that I might give up my metaphysical work to go back to performing? No, I'm not. One of the things I've come to learn is that, just as life is a process, so too is career—rather than either a linear progression (up the corporate ladder, for example) or a sole focus on one career activity. I find myself ebbing and flowing more in my career—and accepting that ebb and flow. And I've also come to realize that a career may be composed of more than one activity. Thus, even though I never stopped performing completely (I've continued to do intermittent on-camera, voice-over, and singing work), the mixture may become more fifty-fifty, rather than ninety-ten. Career may be not just a matter of what can garner us income and financial security, but what can also bring us personal satisfaction and quality of life. As I've learned through my intuitive work, the greatest career (or fulfillment of our purpose) may have more to do with expressing our essence and interests through our work than fitting ourselves into some preconceived slot in the economy. And for creative people, like myself, carving out our own niche and allowing ourselves to walk our own path may not only be what we *should* do; it may also be the only thing we *can* do in order to feel whole and fulfilled. It's simply a matter of one's personal comfort level and choice.

If I were to offer any words of advice to others based upon my experiences and regrets over any "should haves," it would be to ferret out, work on, and exorcise any self-defeating behavior that can hold you back—and then to know yourself, accept yourself, build on your strengths, know what brings you joy, and allow yourself to express your true self insofar as possible. Sing your own song.

"Self-knowledge, or self-awareness, is one of the greatest gifts or tools we can acquire."

Diane Brandon

Diane *Brandon*

Diane Brandon is an Intuitive Consultant, Spiritual Counselor, Personal Facilitator, workshop leader, writer, and speaker, residing in Durham, North Carolina. She conducts individual sessions that include intuitive consultations, regression sessions, guided meditation, dream interpretation, and Natural Process healing. She is also a professional actor, singer, and voice-over artist, and has taught voice privately.

Diane has designed a system for working on personal empowerment and wholeness entitled "The 15-Fold Path to Personal Empowerment and Wholeness" and conducts workshops on this topic. She also conducts workshops on developing intuition, interpreting and working with dreams, and Natural Process healing and has spoken to groups on dreams, intuition, heart-centeredness, and personal empowerment.

Born and raised in New Orleans, Diane has had a lifelong interest in metaphysics and been an avid student of it for over thirty years. She is a member of the Institute of Noetic Sciences, *Intelligentsia Metaphysica*, and IANDS: The International Association for Near-Death Studies. She attended a high school for academically gifted in New Orleans, graduated from Duke University with an A.B. in French, did graduate work at the University of North Carolina at Chapel Hill in radio, television, and motion pictures, and attended TUTOR, a language institute in Geneva, Switzerland for French studies. In addition, she pursued group metaphysical studies with Tomiko Smith.

Diane has appeared as a guest on several radio shows in North Carolina, Maryland, Massachusetts, Texas, and Wisconsin and has made TV appearances as well in North Carolina. She has contributed articles to *Connexions*, *Innerchange*, and *The Journal of Tar Heel Tellers* and is currently working on a book entitled *Invisible Blueprints — Insights of an Energy Reader*. She has also produced "Yes, You <u>Can</u> Sing!" a self-instructional audio tape.

Diane newly resides in Durham after twenty-six years in Chapel Hill and was included in the 1997-98 edition of *Who's Who in the South and Southwest*.

Mara Bishop an interview

What career dreams did you have as a child, and how did those dreams evolve as you grew into adulthood?

I was kind of all over the place. I went from psychiatrist to archeologist. Certainly artist was always an important dream of mine—always loved art. Those were probably the big ones. I've had my own graphic design business, so I've gone from painting and fine art to more commercial art. That was more as an adult though.

Art was the closest thing to being a consistent thread from childhood to adulthood, and I still do artwork now. I don't think I realized it at the time, but now, in looking back and answering a question like that, I feel that creativity and spirituality are very closely linked. And I think that, as a child and as a person in college, doing artwork was the closest place for me to feeling a spiritual connection. And I was only able to get so far. I always had this kind of edge of frustration with art. It was like I felt this potential for getting to this place, but I couldn't quite get there. What I believe is it was more of a spiritual place that I was looking for. And that work has evolved into more of the type of practice that I do now, using my intuition, tapping into higher sources of

spirituality and creativity that I was doing when I was doing art. I had kind of a taste of it, but it's actually evolved into the more spiritual and healing practices that I do now.

When you say you had an edge of frustration with your art, do you feel that you were unhappy with the quality of what you were putting out or was it simply that you didn't feel a connection to it?

I wouldn't exactly say I was unhappy, no. I like some of the stuff that I did. It wasn't that I gave up on art because I didn't enjoy it or I didn't feel like I was good enough. It just kind of evolved into something else. My attention shifted. And I find some of the most satisfying moments that I have—although they're few and far between now because I'm so busy—is when I'm painting or sculpting or doing some form of art where I really just feel 'in that creative flow.' And as I said, it's a very similar feeling to being in that spiritual place for me, feeling spiritually connected.

Where did you grow up and go to school?

I grew up and went to school in Danbury, Connecticut, until college and then I went to Clark University which is in Massachusetts. I also spent a semester in Provence, France, studying art. And I'm currently enrolled at Greenwich University in a master's program for energy medicine. It's a distance learning program in Australia.

Recount for me the path you took to get from where you started out, majoring in art—and, I suppose, originally intending to do only that—and where you are today. How has your life's work evolved?

Long and convoluted path there. After college, I was the assistant director of an art gallery so I got a little taste of the other side—of not actually creating the art, but showing it and placing it in corporations. I liked that.

I've always had an interest in—I guess metaphysics would be the closest word that I can come up with. Interested in intuition, interested in spiritual things. Maybe since I was a kid, but it became quite strong when I was in college and in years thereafter. And that interest just really started growing. I started reading and practicing, and I studied with a woman for a number of years to learn how to hone my intuition and use it practically.

I also did artwork for the State of Massachusetts for some educational, environmental programs. And I was always doing some fine art on my own. Along the way, I also had some of my more long-term full-time jobs, more in technology, at the college level. I worked in an international programs office and I did all of their technical support and designed databases and designed web sites and things like that. So I have kind of the left brain/right brain thing going on, I think.

But anyway, my interest in developing intuition in shamanism became greater and I sought out places to learn. A good friend of

mine introduced me—and actually my mother and my grandmother at the same time—to shamanic journeying. And that felt like a very important moment for me after I took that first shamanic journey because it felt very familiar, and I realized that I had had some spontaneous journeys on my own that came about through meditation. It felt very comfortable. From that point on, I really sought out more ways to learn about shamanic journeying—and shamanic healing in particular. So I embarked on that path and started seeing clients. I've been doing intuitive readings for longer than the shamanic work. And I guess that's where I am now—is having a practice and doing intuitive consulting and shamanic healing.

And you also still design web sites?

Yes, I work at Duke, actually, at the business school. We do executive education programs for corporations and we customize them for their specific needs. And, for many of the programs, there's this distance learning component where they are using the Internet to continue their learning through web sites and bulletin boards and chat sessions.

Do you have a particular childhood event or recollection that foreshadowed that you would become a shamanic practitioner or intuitive consultant?

I had precognitive dreams. And they weren't momentous, huge events—sometimes even just mundane things, but that were unusual enough that, when they happened a day or two later, it really started me thinking about the nature of reality. 'How does this work? How is it possible that I saw this exact scene happening in my dream two nights ago, and then here we are in the drugstore or walking in the woods with my dad and he says that exact thing or he slips?' I remember one where my dad was slipping in the mud. And then a couple of days later, there he is—we're walking in the woods and he slips in the mud in exactly that same way. So a series of precognitive dreams was kind of an indication that something was going on. And I think everybody—or at least a lot of people—have those. It's not necessarily some kind of great omen that I was going to be doing it professionally, but it got me thinking. I did have-maybe in high school—an incident in which I really sensed someone's pain.

Did you know whose pain it was?

Yes. I didn't know the person, but I looked over and saw him.

Did you actually feel the pain? I mean, did it hurt you, too?

Oh, yeah. It wasn't physical pain. It was emotional pain. And that was confusing and kind of difficult to process because I just got this hit off this man that he was just in such pain.

What exactly happened?

I was at church with my parents and I just, at one point in the mass, looked over and there was a man sitting there. There was nothing particularly unusual about him that jumped out at me, but I just got this feeling in my chest that he was in a great deal of pain. My sense was that it had something to do with his daughter, but I didn't get a lot of intellectual information about what was going on. It was just kind of this emotional hit.

Was his daughter there, too?

I honestly don't remember. The focus was so much just on this man. And my initial reaction was—I wanted to comfort him somehow or just pat him on the shoulder and let him know that someone was thinking about him or caring about him. I didn't really know what to do—was the confusing part. Obviously, it would've been inappropriate for me to rush over to this man and say, 'I'm feeling your pain,' you know? But it was so tangible in my body that it was very disconcerting. And that is what it's like when you're actually doing a reading for someone if they're in that kind of pain. If I'm doing an intuitive reading, I'm kind of opening up my energy to their energy and, frequently, that involves feeling some things that they feel. And things like that started happening spontaneously—walking into a room and just picking up somebody else's emotions. You know, you're feeling perfectly happy and you sit down with a friend and, after five minutes, you just are miserable? Kind of being a sponge for other people's energy?

And what I learned from my teacher was how to separate my energy from someone else's. To be able to—at will—sit down with somebody, open myself up, and sense things from them in order to give them, hopefully, valuable—or, at least, useful—information, but then to go back and be centered in myself and not carry around their energy—being able to distinguish someone else's emotions from my emotions.

So this is something you can't really turn off until you will yourself to?

Well, it actually is kind of the flipside of that. I turn it on. I mean, I get gut feelings if I meet somebody for the first time, like a lot of people do. I have intuitive feelings about people, but I don't walk around kind of doing a reading on people and having to turn it off. It's off until somebody gives me permission and asks me to tune in to them, and then I can turn it on.

As a child, did your precognitive dreams frighten you at all?

No, they didn't frighten me. The precognitive dreams, I remember more as a teenager or a bit later on. No, because I didn't have anything sinister happen. It wasn't like I dreamt something horrible happened and then it did and I felt like it was my fault or something.

I do remember one time—and this was when I was a little child. My mom and I—and I don't recommend that anybody do this, and I wouldn't do it again—we had some people over for dinner and we were using a Ouija board and it started moving. It spelled out something like 'Tell her that I'm fine. Love, Richard,' or something along those lines—I don't remember the exact words at the moment. And it didn't mean anything to us, but we looked over and one of the dinner guests was crying. Her brother Richard had died very recently or something like that. And that was pretty dramatic at the time. But then I don't remember doing anything with it after that when I was a young child—my mom and I, we just went about our business.

What did you make of your abilities back then?

I don't really think I thought about having abilities particularly until I was older and thought about developing them so that they were practically useful.

What have been the greatest challenges throughout your path? I tend to be—oh, what's my word for this?—not quite 'overachiever' but it's a little bit 'perfectionist,' so I can be really hard on myself and set goals that are maybe unrealistic and then beat myself up over not reaching them. So being a little bit too hard on myself is a challenge. It makes me stressed out.

Practical challenges? The things that I am the most interested in are pretty alternative—the practice that I have or even just wanting to be an artist. And, I think, in and of itself, that's kind of a challenge. You know, if your life's ambition was to be a doctor, nobody really questions that or thinks 'Wow, what do you want to do that for?' or thinks that what you're doing is completely unreasonable. You never feel like you have to be explaining yourself. So being in a field that is alternative and unusual, it's a bit of a challenge in just communicating that to other people. Being very careful about how you present yourself. You know, I'm not a flaky person, but I'm in a field that some people would just completely write off as being, if not outright fake, at least flaky. So I make sure to fight against that image.

Is it ever difficult for you at times when, say, you're at a gathering and somebody asks, 'What do you do for a living?'

Much less than it was before. I think when I first started out, I was very judicious about who I told what I did and I was very careful about the way I talked about it. I tend not to talk about it very much. And I still do use my judgment about who I open up to.

But now I'm really out there. You know, if that article's in the front page of the 'Body and Mind' section of the Herald-Sun, you can't really hide. I've been doing this work for awhile and, you know, part of having a practice is you do want people to come to you. (*Laughs.*) So it's kind of a catch-22. You want to be out there,

but you want to be out there to people who are receptive. So I don't consider that a problem anymore, but I think that was a challenge for me in starting to get into this field. I wasn't feeling comfortable in sharing that part of myself.

What are your sources of inspiration or renewal in times of disappointment or strife?

Well, the first thing that pops into my head is my mom. (*Laughs.*) I go to my mom first for support. And my husband, too. But as far as kind of a deeper inspiration, it's my spiritual practice. I look to the spiritual support that I feel that I have to get me through things at that level. And then on a practical level, it's my family and my friends.

What aspect of being a practitioner brings you the most gratification and joy?

When people say to me, 'That session that we had really made a huge difference in my life.'

What are the goals of a session?

Well, it varies, since I do two things—I do intuitive consulting and I do shamanic healing work, and they're related, but they're really separate. When I do an intuitive reading for someone, my only goal is to try and give them information that's going to be for their highest good. That's one of the intentions that I set before doing a session. I want to get information for them, but I also want to get information that's going to be helpful. Other than that, people come to me and they ask me questions, so I don't really have an agenda. I follow what types of information they're interested in hearing about. My goal is to be as sensitive and operating from as loving a place as I can. And, by that, I mean—if I'm sitting with someone, sometimes I'll get information about them that if I just blurted it out, really could cause them more harm than good. So I work very hard to be not only tactful and sensitive, but also really judicious about how I present information and what information I present to people.

And the shamanic healing work, there is certainly an element of getting information and answering questions and giving people insight into a situation. But there's also more of a direct healing component, and that could be emotional healing, physical healing, spiritual healing. From the shamanic perspective, all illness, psychological or physical, has a spiritual origin. You're dealing with the spiritual component of illness that can then manifest in physical or psychological healing, but you work from the spiritual side down, as opposed to the physical side up.

Do you run into the same syndrome that medical doctors run into, where you're out someplace and someone asks for an impromptu reading or healing session?

With the intuitive stuff, on occasion. Not that often. But sometimes people call up and say, 'Can you just answer one question over the phone?' Not so much that it's a problem.

Tell me about your family.

Well, I have a wonderful husband and an adorable little baby girl, Violet Miranda, who is four weeks old today, who has been taking up all of our time and energy, as you might imagine, for the last—feels like more than a month. There was a lot to do to get ready for her to be here. So we've been pretty involved in being parents and preparing to be parents for awhile.

I'm an only child, and my parents still live in Connecticut and I'm very close with my family. Both my mom and my dad were here since the baby's been born, and my mom stayed for five or six weeks and helped us out. I have one grandmother left, my mom's mom, and we do a lot of the shamanic work together.

Do you anticipate any difficulties in balancing family and career?

Yeah! (*Laughs.*) I was having difficulties balancing *career* and career—*and* school before she came. Working on my master's and having my practice and then working at Duke and trying to have a life with my husband and trying to fit in friends. I was feeling like that was on the verge of being way too much. And now with

Violet here, obviously some things have got to go or change. So I'm not really sure exactly how that's going to play out as far as where my time goes, but I know my number-one priority is to be with her. So however it shakes out, that's my goal—to spend as much time with her as possible.

What are some ways you relax?

I love to be in nature. I don't get a chance to be out there as much as I like, but I like to take walks. Duke has a lot of acres of forest and there's some lovely gardens to walk in. I like to read. I love to nap. I have not had much chance to relax, it seems, that much lately. Basically, hanging around with my husband.

Do you have any special personal interests or goals that you're pursuing or would like to pursue in the near future?

I would love to landscape my yard and have a beautiful garden with flowers and a pond and really make our outdoor environment nice. I also would like to be more involved, if I could, with some animal preservation organizations. And this is definitely a pipe dream right now with my time constraints, but one thing pops into my head. There's a wonderful organization out in Pittsboro called the Carnivore Preservation Trust, and they rescue large cats, particularly, and they do projects with their breeding animals— carnivores—to be reintroduced into the rainforest. And they have this whole compound out there. They've got ocelots and leopards and a lot of tigers. I would like to do more to help organizations like that.

What are some of your favorite things?

My favorite color is purple. My favorite scent is lavender. My favorite food is mango. My favorite season is spring. I enjoy collecting found natural objects like bones and feathers.

What personal qualities do you consider to be of the most value in life?

Integrity. Honesty. Operating out of love instead of any other motivation. That sounds kind of hokey, but I think a lot of times people operate out of fear as a motivation, and that manifests in a lot of different ways. Trying to have a loving and open heart.

What is the one way that you have evolved as a human being that makes you proudest?

I feel like I've gotten to be a strong person, a lot stronger than I used to be. I really feel like I could handle a lot of different things. And part of that comes from dealing with different situations, and part of it, I think, also comes from the spiritual work that I've done.

What qualities do you possess that make being a practitioner a natural vocational choice for you?

Empathy. And, I think, a natural intuitive ability. I think everybody has intuition and everybody can develop it. It's not just something that certain people have and certain people don't. But I think I'm inclined to operate from that sense, so it doesn't feel like it was that difficult for me to develop. I think that's kind of an innate quality. Patience. And, I think, a real desire to help people.

Conversely, what qualities of yours create conflict or struggle that you must constantly work to overcome as pertains to what you do in your practice?

I guess I would have a tendency to want people to understand what I'm saying to them. And I don't think that's a fault, but there are plenty of times when I'm saying something to someone and I can see that they're hearing me but they maybe aren't really getting it. So I think it's important to not become too attached to really making people see and believe what you're telling them. You can only do so much.

I don't feel I'm having a lot of challenge with personality issues of mine while I'm actually seeing clients. As far as, in general, in my life, not feeling like I have to be too in-control—and worrying. You know, I tend to be a worrier.

Of what professional accomplishment are you most proud?

Well, this one pops to mind—and I'm not sure if this is exactly

it. But Sandra Ingerman, the woman I studied with, who's kind of figuratively and literally 'written the book' on the technique of soul retrieval—it's a shamanic healing technique—has a referral list. When people call her, she has just certain people that she will not exactly recommend, but whose names she will give out. I have an incredible amount of respect for this person and, after submitting case studies to her, she's put me on that list. So that's just something that happened recently, and, anyway, it feels nice to be accepted by somebody whom you have that much respect for in your field.

And of what personal accomplishment are you most proud?

I gave birth to that baby! (*Laughs.*) And, man! You *know* you can't *know* what it's like until you get there. But you don't *know* what it's like until you get there! And it was hard—it was really hard. But nothing quite compares to that feeling of seeing your baby for the first time.

What dreams do you have that are yet to be realized, both personal and professional?

I'm a pretty lucky person. (*Long pause.*)

I was about to say, 'Total control over my day,' but that's one of my faults. I have to watch out for that. I guess I'd like to be able to do whatever I wanted to do each day, and that's kind of a pipe dream. You know, obviously I want to take care of my daughter and I want to spend time with my husband. But being able to go and spend six hours in the studio one day—and the next day, be able to do something entirely different. Having absolute freedom with my time is probably the thing I would crave the most.

What advice would you give young women just starting out in a career or older women considering a career change?

I guess the first thing is to figure out what you love to do and then try and work it from there. I know, for me, that's always been a challenge because the things that I love to do have not been particularly lucrative. So you can say, 'OK, I love to paint,' but you really have to be a committed person because the odds are against you that you're going to be able to make a good living being a painter.

But figure that out first. Figure out what your ideal is before telling yourself why you can't do it. I think we so often will get information about what we want, what our hopes are, what our dreams are. But before we actually can even get it straight what our dreams are, we're already saying that we can't do it. You know that old saying of 'Follow your bliss'—what's the thing you most want to do? And then at least try to have some kind of organized plan about achieving it. And ask people for help.

What, if anything, would you do differently if you could turn back the clock?

I don't know that I would do anything differently because of where I am now. I don't really want to change it. And I think that even individual decisions that I may have made that I might say, 'Oh, you know, what if I went to that other college that I was accepted at?' Or 'What if I moved to a different city?' Or 'What if I didn't hang out with that group of people?' or whatever. 'Didn't take that job' or 'Did take that job'—I don't think we ever really can know what those little decisions along the way mean to our life in the bigger picture. And I like where I am right now. I like my family, I like my friends, I like where I live, I like my professions, I love my husband. And if changing the color of shoes that I bought in 1983 somehow would alter where I am right now, I wouldn't want to take that risk.

Interviewed by Susan L. Comer.

Mara *Bishop*

Mara Bishop is an intuitive consultant and shamanic practitioner in Durham, North Carolina. She has studied intuition, shamanism, art and communications. Mara has a bachelor's degree in art and communications *summa cum laude* from Clark University and is a master's candidate at Greenwich University for a degree in energy medicine focusing on shamanism. During intuitive sessions, Mara accesses information for clients from non-physical, universal sources. Mara uses the following shamanic techniques with clients: soul retrieval, power animal retrieval, extractions, and healing and divination journeys. She also conducts lectures and workshops on shamanic journeying and intuitive develop-

ment. In addition, Mara is an artist who works primarily with paint and clay. Her artwork is frequently inspired by her spiritual work and journeying. For more information call 919-419-1074, send an e-mail to mara@wholespirit.com, or visit www.WholeSpirit.com.

Kathi Middendorf an interview

Why don't we start with where you grew up and went to school?

I was born in Akron, Ohio, and I went to public school until I was in third grade and hadn't learned how to read. I got shifted to a private all-girl Catholic school and wound up spending the next ten years of my life there, which was very interesting because I wasn't Catholic. So that was quite an experience. I got my bachelor's degree from the University of Akron in Akron, Ohio, and that was in speech therapy. I got my master's degree at Sacramento State College, California. And that was a master's in speech pathology. My doctorate is from North Carolina State University in social psychology. And I also attended the New Seminary and am ordained as an inter-faith minister of spiritual counseling. And, I did training for Coach University to become a personal and professional coach. I completed that last June.

Going back to your childhood, what was your difficulty in reading, do you think?

I was very good in art, and I happened to be in a situation where my first and second grade teacher were the same person. Instead of making me do the reading class, she would allow me to do artwork. I can't remember which method they were using to teach reading, but once I got to the Catholic school they were using a phonetic method, and I learned.

I had a wonderful former Mother Superior who was my tutor, and as I said, I wasn't Catholic and was attending the school. And when I first got there, I didn't know the difference between nuns and angels. I thought she was an angel. She was so sweet and so wonderful, and I learned how to read. I didn't learn how to spell well, but I learned how to read.

How did you find your career path?

When I was young, probably in grade school, I read a story which was about Tom Dooley, who was a psychiatrist, and I decided that I wanted to be a psychiatrist. I thought that would be the most wonderful thing in the world, to be able to help people. When I got to Akron U. I was in pre-med, I had come out of a school where I had six people in my physics class, and maybe eight or ten in my chemistry. And when I got to Akron U. I think three of my first five courses were televised, and that included algebra, trig, and chemistry, and the psychology, and maybe one or two others. And it was overwhelming. I mean I was in classes of 600 people, and if we had questions, we had to raise our hands and then the proctor would ask the question of the professor. It was a very inventive way of putting the best professors in front of the most students. So, in that way, it was groundbreaking. But for me it was overwhelming, and I wound up flunking chemistry. I went to talk to the professor after the fact and to tell him that I wanted to sign up again because I wanted to be a doctor, and he verbally patted me on the head and said, 'Well, dear, there are some things that women just aren't prepared to do.'

How did you react to that?

I backed off, because at that time, that's what we did. This was at Akron U. in the sixties. So then I didn't know what to do. I loved theater. I was very involved in the university theater. I had done acting in high school. But I was also still attracted to psychology. I was torn about whether I should go into theater, but I am six feet tall, and I thought well, what sort of a future would I have as a six-foot-tall actress?

One of my friends was in the speech therapy program, and he said, 'Why don't you come over and watch what we do and see if it is something that would interest you?' And I did, and it seemed to me to combine speech and psychology, which it does very heavily. Plus I had an aunt who was born with a cleft palate, so I had seen the effect on someone's life of not being able to communicate effectively. So, I made the decision to go into speech therapy at that point.

Then how did you get from speech therapy into this whole spiritual side of yourself?

That happened many years later. I was working on my doctorate, and I spontaneously ruptured three discs in my lower back. I had completed all my coursework and had just collected all the data for my dissertation, and had an initial meeting with my advisor and my results, walked into my bathroom and spontaneously ruptured the discs. That put me on the floor literally for three months. I could not walk. I couldn't lie in a bed, because the give in the mattress was so painful. I believe, and a lot of spiritual teachers will tell you, that if you are marching along in the wrong direction, God will give you a chance to review your life. I think that's what happened; that I was put flat on the floor and, you know, there is little you can do when you are flat on your back but think. And I did a lot of thinking and reassessing of my life. Not that I was doing bad things or wrong things. But I wasn't doing my thing.

Anyway, a friend told me about Reiki, which is hands-on healing, about three years later. I had a spinal fusion. I was in a body cast, and I went to a Reiki session. And I was amazed, because I could feel the energy, and this was just so far beyond what I had conceptualized as being a part of our material reality. Then I heard about a summer conference that is held every year. And I attended that. That is a conference that focuses on things metaphysical, spiritual, psychic, etc., and during the last day of classes, something major shifted within my consciousness, and I had an opening or awakening. I don't even know what words still to put around it, you know. I know how it felt, and I know it changed my entire life, because I had come there with all of my attitudes and classifications, etc. When I had the experience at the conference, it caused me to open my eyes to a new level of reality. And, then at that point, I became just ravenous for information, because it was like this whole new area that I just didn't know anything about, and I started reading. And I read at the rate of about two books a week for seven years straight.

What kind of books were you reading?

Anything about, well, all the religions of the world; metaphysics, consciousness, psychic phenomena, life after death, near-death experience, UFO energy. Anything beyond what we consider normal.

I know you went to a Catholic school, but you mentioned you weren't catholic. Were you religious growing up?

I was. I was a confirmed Episcopalian and attended the Episcopal Church until I graduated from high school. No even after that, I think. Yes. So I was religious, but what I have come to understand is that spirituality and religion are not the same thing.

The way I look at it spirituality is the highest level of reality. The fastest vibration is at the spiritual level, and then it is mental, emotional, physical. You know, there are variations within that, but reality begins at a spiritual level. What we look at as religion are ways of approaching spirituality that were based on the spiritual awakenings or awareness of individual leaders. And those people did not found the religion. I mean, if you look at Buddhism or Christianity, Islam, you find that these were people who were engaged in living out their own awareness of what it meant to be spiritual and live a good life. And it was their followers that codified rules to become like them.

How did your realizations change your life in an active way?

What I found was that some of my longtime friends, I didn't enjoy being with them and doing the things that they did as I had before. I think it was Eleanor Roosevelt that gave a quote about 'small people talk about other people.' That bigger people talk about events, and the most outstanding people talk about ideas. So it was as though I let go of close relationships with people who were focused on talking about people, and moved up to associate with people who were focused on ideas and concepts of what life is really about: how do we improve the world by expanding the consciousness of individuals? How do we bring people to an awareness that there is more in life than making a lot of money and having the biggest house and driving the fastest car?

And how did your day-to-day life change as a result of this?

I began living with a sense of constant presence of something beyond the mundane. You know, it is hard to put into words a quote when you refer to the Godhead. It is, 'He about whom naught could be said.' Because anything you say diminishes the hugeness of what it is, but our reality is just a small speck in what the hugeness of life is all about. So, I walked in constant gratitude and awareness and openness to things. I look for guidance in my everyday life. I might be reading a book and a sentence would jump out. And it would be an answer to a question I had, or a thought that I had. It was like there was a constant interchange between me and a greater reality that was there all the time, but was not available to my awareness until I was open to it. So it was like, instead of just, you get up and get dressed and you go to work and do your job and you come home and you watch television and go to bed—it was like walking in awareness all day long.

And then, from there how long was it before you became ordained?

Let's see. That was probably five or six years later. And the reason that I attended the New Seminary—I attended as a correspondent student because it is based in New York City—I felt like I didn't have the structure that I needed for all this information

that I was accumulating, and I knew that the New Seminary was founded by people who were a step beyond what we would just call an insular religion. The New Seminary was founded by a rabbi, a swami, a Catholic priest, an Episcopalian minister, and some other people. And their idea was to pull the sum total of knowledge that we have together about religion, about psychology, and about spiritual healing, and put it into a package together. So that was a two-year study to become ordained for the New Seminary, and that was the focus of the study. And once I had completed that I realized that it was not that I wanted to be a minister, but that I want my life to be a ministry.

So, from there, how did you start The Spirit Coach, how did that come to you?

Well, that was still a long way off. I think I got ordained around 1993, and at that point I was working at IBM.

Were you at this point making any use of your work in speech pathology?

No. My last position as a speech pathologist was teaching at North Carolina Central University. I was teaching in their master's degree program, and enjoyed that a great deal. But I did not have a terminal degree, so I couldn't get an ongoing contract, and I was raising my daughter alone. I realized that I had to put myself in a position that I could get a job where I could depend on being employed, semester-to-semester, beyond a semester. So, I applied at Duke, UNC, and State to get a doctorate in speech pathology, and I didn't want to take my daughter out of the state. I wanted her to have close access to her father. So I decided to stay and pursue a further degree in psychology, and was admitted to State's program. They don't have clinical, but they have social psychology. And it sort of fulfilled an earlier question. The job before I went to North Carolina Central was at C. A. Dillon School in Butner, North Carolina. I worked there for three years. This is a high-security reform school in the state, and it is the only one that has fences and barbed wire and everything. And it's for people who fail reform school. These are kids from twelve to eighteen. And I had never in my prior jobs been in association with kids who were so damaged. One of my questions to myself as I was working there was, 'What are the forces that bring a child to this kind of institution?'

I knew that I didn't want to study sociology, because that is very broad and high level. I didn't really want to do social work, but when I found social psychology, it was a combination of psychology and looking at the larger patterns and sociology. But it looks at effects on the individuals or small groups. When I got to State and they had the program in social psychology, I said, 'Ah, this sort of taps into my background at C. A. Dillon and will give me some answers I was looking for at that point.' So I launched into my degree in social psychology.

I was collecting the data for the dissertation when my disc ruptured, and about six months after that happened, my advisor told me that there was an opening at IBM where I could continue to be a student, but I could also work and make some income. And at that point in my life I needed some income. I started working there as a Human Factors Engineer, which dealt with improving the usability of software, and we would do things like write test cases and bring lots of people in and let them go through the test paces and find out what the problems were with the software and report that back to the development team, so that hopefully they could fix the problem before the product was shipped. And I became aware through those years that we were too late in the development cycle to really effect change. So my last period of time with IBM, I had teams that I formed, called Customer Information Research Teams, and we would bring groups of customers in and run electronic focus groups so that we could get their requirements for future products. We also did surveys and things like that. We were very focused on being at the beginning of the development cycle and wanting to create products that people really wanted and that would fill their needs.

Some friends of mine were going on a trip to India, Nepal, and Tibet and I decided to go, because I had never been out of the country. And it was a spiritual pilgrimage. I went; experienced that; came back and got laid off. I mean it didn't have anything to do with the trip, and yet, at a higher level of reality, I believe it did. Because during that trip, I committed myself to be of service in any way that God wanted me to be. I also knew that layoffs were coming at IBM, and that the type of work, and my position, since I didn't write code, was more vulnerable to being laid off. So, coincidentally, I make my big spiritual pilgrimage; I come back; and I have no job.

So what did you decide to do?

I wanted to find a job that would combine spirituality and helping, and I didn't have a definition for what that was. I tried two or three different positions, because they looked like they would be what I wanted. But for whatever reason, the first several ones I tried were not the answer.

I had read a newspaper interview with a woman who was doing coaching. As soon as I read it, I said, 'Oh, this is what I want to do!' But, in fact, I didn't even approach the coaching training for another two years. I was still looking to see if there was something I could step into, because, my goodness, I have enough training for anybody in the world, you know. So the thought of starting all over again and getting another training in something was not something I embraced right away.

How old was your daughter when you got laid off from IBM?

She was not living with me anymore. She was in college. I think she was married at that point. So, she was not my dependent anymore. I was the only one that I was supporting, although I had bought a big house that I hoped would eventually serve as a center, you know, where we could do workshops, etc. At that point, I was program chairperson for Spiritual Frontiers Fellowship, which is an organization that was formed about forty years ago, and it was formed as a way of looking at the very questions that I had been looking at on my own. We hosted speakers and workshops. But I was living on very little income. I had to decide if I wanted to go back into business, or if I wanted to actually step into what I thought would be my life-work. And my decision was to sell my house and take the equity and support myself long enough to return to Coach University, which is taught by e-mail, phone, and faxes. So, I did that.

It was a hard decision, but it was really interesting, you know. You think about, do you know when you are doing the right thing? because that is a question that I asked. 'Am I moving on the path the way my higher self intends me to?' rather than the ego-level decision. I decided to sell the house. It was a wonderful house. Cleared and cleaned and sorted and put the house on the market myself; sold it within six days. I had two full-price cash offers. Now, to me that is a confirmation that I did the right thing at the right time. It was so easy.

People talk about being in the flow. You know, when you are in the flow; when you are moving down the path that's appropriate for you, doors open, things happen. It's almost magical. So I sold the house, got rid of about two-thirds of my belongings and moved into an apartment under 1,000 square feet. I had an office, a bedroom, and living room, and a kitchen/dining room. I spent eighteen months studying through Coach University.

And then from that point, how did you decide that you were ready to start your own business?

Well, it wasn't that I decided that I was ready to, but that was my step in preparation to do it. In Coach University, they encourage you to start coaching immediately, whether you think you know how to coach or not. So there were a number of people that I was doing pro bono coaching with, so that I would develop my coaching skills as I was studying the material. Some of the pro bonos turned into paying clients. Paying clients started coming in other ways.

The majority of coaches that I know, although they probably have a spiritual aspect to their coaching, they don't talk about being spiritually based. And I felt like that was the niche that I wanted to reach out to—people that had actually stepped onto their own spiritual path and didn't have the guidance that they needed. In ancient traditions, you would have a guru, or a teacher, or a mentor who would help you move along your own path to spiritual realization. So I wanted to combine the coaching with working with people. Not that I exclusively would coach people who were working on their spiritual growth, but most of the people who are drawn to me are at some level.

How would you describe what you do for them or with them?

One of the things I do with Spiritual Frontiers is that I write a Dear Spirit Coach column, and my most recent column sort of answers that question. Could I read it to you? It's real short.

Sure.

This is part of the answer. It is not all of the answer, but it may can give you a sense of what my role is. The question is: 'Dear Spirit Coach: please clarify what we are doing in spiritual coaching and what your role is.' 'Dear Sharon: In response to your question, I see you as someone who has stepped actively on her own spiritual path to her unique expression of her core essence. One of the challenges with spiritual development is that there are no maps to tell you exactly how to get where you are going, since you are the pathfinder. Each individual journey will be a bit different, although there will be similarities. One of the first things we did with you was to find those things in your life that you truly love to do, not that you were doing to please others, but because you can do them. You committed to certain actions and were pleased with the joy that came from them. You also took steps that brought up your shadow in full force. While I didn't fix any of the stuff coming up with the shadow, I supported your willingness to embrace it and forgive whatever might show itself in the process.

You ask me what my role is. As a coach, it is to move you toward expressing your gifts into the world, creating a happy, fulfilling life and holding you to your intention. As a spiritual teacher, it is to be your witness, your guide, and your mirror, so that you can see where you are and how you are progressing. In closing, here is an excerpt from a note from one of my students. I appreciate you and the part you have played and are continuing to play in my becoming one with God. Thank you for your patience, tolerance, steadiness, structure, ever-developing ability to connect with me and my unorthodox process; and last, but not least, for giving me a figure of authority to push against in order to grow. What I am experiencing is so much like childbirth (you are the stirrups). I am birthing my new self.' So that was the extent of that spirit coach question.

What I do with clients is, I don't have an agenda with them. Most everybody in your life has an agenda in relationship to you, whether it is a spouse or a parent or something. They know what they think is good for you. And as a coach, when I am working with someone, I support them in doing what they want to do. I work on the phone three or four times a month; we exchange e-mails. I have something I use called a Call Prep Form. At the end of each coaching session I send a Call Prep Form to the client, and it lists the actions they have committed to take during the following weeks. And then prior to our next coaching call, they fill out the form and they say what they have accomplished. What were their wins? What were their challenges? What do they want to focus on and what are they grateful for during the week? So, this is a way for both of us to track their progress as they are moving towards their goal or their intention. Those are kind of tricky, because a lot of us have been taught to create goals, and then we blindly march toward them. And sometimes the goals we create are not going to get us where we want to go.

So when I am working with a client, it's not so much that I hold them to goals, as I hold them accountable to doing their best. If their best means changing a goal, then that's okay. A coach is not somebody that stands over you and smacks your knuckles with a ruler if you haven't done what you said you were going to do, because sometimes you step into something and you go, 'Whoa! This is not going to take me where I want to be!'

Did you find that having these revelations about how to live your life affected your relationship with your daughter? Did it change your parenting style, for example?

She is one of the most focused people that I know. I don't know that it changed my style with her, because I think my style was always very supportive. I think that we have a strong feeling of support for each other, although her path is not my path. She is taking a very traditional religious path, and, standing from that point of view, looks at mine and questions it.

When did you decide to get married? Was it when you were still in school?

Oh, yes. It was when I was in college. I mean everybody did that. That was the thing to do.

Did you meet your husband in college?

Yes. On the stage. We were in Molière's *School for Husbands*, and we were playing opposite each other. We just had so many similarities in things that we liked and were interested in, and it seemed like my way of stepping out of the family structure. I lived at home when I went to college, so I didn't have that experience of being somewhat independent at that point.

After you got married, did he come to North Carolina with you while you were in school? Were you still married, then?

I came to North Carolina with him. He was with IBM, and he first went to Poughkeepsie, New York, for several months' training, and then came to North Carolina. So he came in before Research Triangle Park was built. That's how I got here.

Was your daughter alive at that point?

No. She was born here. She's a North Carolinian.

And did you find that your spiritual revelations served to adversely affect your relationship with your husband? Did he have problems dealing with them?

No. We were divorced at that point. We are friends now, and he supports me in what I am doing.

Was it a challenge for you to balance your career and raise you daughter, when she was younger?

It did present difficulties. Yes. Partly when I was teaching at North Carolina Central. I was in a different city, and she would go to school and then go to after-school care. I would pick her up. Just the mechanics of doing that on your own is challenging. How do you do your work, have a social life, be primary caretaker for a child, and have the energy to get everything done well?

What do you think enabled you to do that?

I think I didn't have any choice. I just had to do it. I was thinking about when I decided to go back and get a doctorate. I made the decision at that point that I would stop dating, because I knew that was going to be so consuming of time and energy. You know, taking care of a house and taking care of a child, and trying to do a doctorate. So I let go my associations. I had done a lot of work with Raleigh Little Theater. I let that go. I let go of other social activities, and just knew that I had to take the amount of energy I had and use it in what I thought was the best way possible at that point.

So, now that you are a spirit coach, have you picked up other things to relax? What do you do in your free time?

I still like to read. I belong to a lot of groups and different associations. It's mostly spending time with people that I enjoy.

Do you have a goal that you are moving towards, something beyond what you are doing now?

That's a good question. I don't see what that would be at this point. I love the coaching. I think that, for me, it is a wonderful profession that I could do for years and years. I don't know that I want to step into something more formalized, like creating a foundation or something. Although I did incorporate and I am the president of my business, and at some point I might want to start hiring coaches to work for me and mentoring them. But I don't

see that as an immediate step. I would love to do some more traveling.

What personal accomplishment do you think you are the most proud of?

This is not a personal accomplishment. But I had something happen that was phenomenal. My daughter had a gerbil, and she was taking care of a friend's gerbil. And the friend's gerbil died, or it appeared to be dead anyway. I had just learned Reiki, which is hands-on healing, and I asked her to give me the gerbil. I just sat and held it with the intention of healing it, and it came back to life.

Oh, wow! What did your daughter and her friend do?

Well, she was going to pick her friend up at the airport, but my daughter said, 'Don't put her down!' I don't know that that is a personal accomplishment, except that I sat with the willingness to be the avenue of healing energy to come through. I mean, I have had things like that happen with people, not with bringing somebody back to life—but if somebody has a headache and I am able to touch them or talk with them...I had a woman that I counseled for one session—this was back before I became a coach. I was calling myself a spiritual counselor—and she had had migraine headaches for forty years, and she had gone to every sort of doctor that she could think of and had every test and medication. We sat and talked, and just through listening with an open heart, I heard the root cause of the headaches and was able to mirror that back to her, to put it in words so that she could see what the pattern was. She was from out of state, but she wrote me letters and said that the headaches were gone. When I talk about working from a spiritual level, that's what I am talking about. There was a pattern with her, such grief over a decision she had to make about a handicapped child.

I've talked about the shadow, the place where we push those parts of ourselves that we can't look at because they are too scary or too dark or too negative or too frightening to face. So we shove them back inside of ourselves. And then what happens often, is that it comes out physically or it comes out emotionally. The things that are in the shadow drive our behaviors without our conscious awareness. So, when I am coaching somebody, or in the case with that woman, just hearing, being present to what is being said at multiple levels of reality—once I ask them the question, they can see the pattern themselves, and they have the *Aha* experience that empowers them to make the changes, or to release the guilt, or whatever it is that needs to be done for them.

Is that what you find the most satisfying about being a spiritual coach, or is there something else?

My philosophy is, we each have something that we can do very, very well, and when we tap into that and express that to the world, then the whole world is benefited. It's like there is extra light in the world, when we are doing what we are meant to do. When I say, 'What we were meant to do,' it is not necessarily saying predestination, but with the sum total of all of our training, skills, awareness, background, experiences, we are unique in the world. To be able to work with someone and help them step into their own point of personal power—and that's what I think it is, it's when you have touched into your core essence—you are standing in your power and you are radiating that into the world.

What advice do you think you would give a young woman who was just starting out and had doubts, or an older woman considering a career change?

What I say often to people is, 'Think back over your life and think about the things that you love to do, because we naturally gravitate to those things where we are being our best selves and expressing our best selves. What are the things that you do when you lose time?' It makes me sad for people to go to a job and hate what they are doing.

And for someone who is perhaps in the middle of their life and never really found what they wanted to do, what advice might you give them?

Immediately what I wanted to say is, 'Call me.' What you are talking about, I call divine discontent. At a very powerful level, some people know that there is something for them, but they don't know what. It's the healing crisis that people go through. I don't know if you have heard that term or know what it means, but it is like, 'things are darkest before the dawn.' In the healing crisis, you have got to the point where you go, 'I know this is not the way my life was supposed to be. I know there is something for me to do.' You just have this feeling inside that is so powerful, but it is so frustrating because you don't find the answers. So what I ask people to do is look back and say, 'What did you love before? What have you done where you have been joyful? If you had one week to live, what would you choose to do? If you were guaranteed success, no matter what you did, what would you choose to do?'

Why do you think so many people seem to get stuck at the point where they are just going to their job every day? They have a dream, but there is some crucial break, it seems to me, between having that dream and feeling that they can realize it. Why do you think that is?

I think a lot of it is because of programming we got as we were growing up. Our country is based on a Protestant ethic, you know, that you work hard, you don't complain, and there is not anything wrong with that, unless you are working hard and not complaining and you are doing something that you hate. And there are people who are doing things that they hate. I don't

know if you have a sense of energy, but you walk into a room where somebody has had a fight and you can almost feel it in the atmosphere. In a church, you can feel a different type of presence. When people go to work with an energy of resentment and hatred, they carry that energy into their working place. It is physically bad for them, and I think it is physically bad for anyone that they interact with at a physical, emotional, mental, and spiritual level.

What do you think causes so many people to get stymied at that point and not be able to effect change?

Fear. Isn't this why abused women stay with their husbands? Because it's known. You know what is going to happen. If you are going to a job that you hate, at least you know what is going to happen. And you know if you hang in there long enough—or at least you used to—you retire and then people would live their lives. But by the time they got to retirement, so many of them were burned out and sickened by working at the wrong job, that they never had the joy that they want. A lot of companies talk about 'golden handcuffs.' I don't know if you have heard that term.

No, I haven't.

It's that there is so much invested in the years that you have put into the job, that, you know, 'How can I leave at twenty years? Because then I lose all of these benefits.' And they can list off the benefits that they are going to lose. I think a lot of us make our choices out of fear rather than making them out of love or joy.

So, what would you do for someone who is poised at that moment, full of fear, yet wanting to change? What do you think you could do to help them?

That would be a very individual thing. I would ask them to start adding into their lives things that they really love. To focus on things they really love, so at least they could get a sense of what it feels like to do things you love rather than doing things you hate. I have had several clients who have come to me because of wanting to change jobs. The first thing I ask them to do, and we work to do, is to improve their performance in the job they are working. One of the people that I worked with last year, within three months of doing that, she had gotten a $15,000 raise. That was not the intention for doing it, but that was one of the outcomes.

All right, so the first thing is to improve the way you are doing your job. No matter how bad your job is, there are some aspects that only you have control over, and if you can look at those and you can make them better, you are going to do a couple of things. Your life is going to feel better, and the job is going to go better, and people are going to regard you in a better light. So

improve your own job performance. Change your attitude.

We have something like 48,000 thoughts a day. Seven thousand are self-referent. Can you imagine the power of someone saying something to you 7,000 times a day? And yet, that is what is going on in our minds. So if the messages we are giving ourselves are, 'I hate this job,' or 'I am miserable,' or 'Why do I have to do...' I mean, if it is that kind of self-talk, it is going to make everything seem bleaker and darker, just because of the way we are thinking about it. So one of the initial things I do with people, also, is to get them to start monitoring their own thoughts. When they are aware that they have had a negative thought, to stop and change that around and make a positive statement.

OK. So, you can improve your job performance, you can change your attitude, and then you can leave your job. But it is not good to leave a job when you are dissatisfied, because you carry that with you.

How do you think that, in your own life, you had the courage or conviction to go down the path you felt was right for you?

I don't know. Often, it has just been an awareness like, 'OK, it's time. It's time to make this change.' You know, it was like getting the house ready to sell. I had done everything that I could do to make it ready. And then it was time. I put it on the market, and it sold. So I get myself ready, most of the time not knowing what the job will be, but knowing it was something that I felt compelled from inside to do, to make myself ready for whatever was going to come next. It's like seeing life as an adventure rather than a burden.

Interviewed by Emily A. Colin.

"I think a lot of us make our choices out of fear rather than making them out of love or joy."

Kathi Middendorf

Kathi *Middendorf*

Kathi Middendorf came to coaching as a natural evolution in her career. Her master's studies in speech pathology were grounded in the physical. Her doctoral studies in social psychology expanded into the psychological. Her explorations into metaphysics and spirituality and her studies for ordination as an Interfaith Minister of Spiritual Counseling have focused in the mental and spiritual realms. Her training through Coach University has given her the skills and tools to incorporate her training and experience in a way that fulfills her desire to aid in expanding spiritual consciousness and awareness.

Kathi has formerly held memberships in: The American Speech, Hearing and Language Association; the North Carolina Speech and Hearing Association; Mensa; the American Psychological Association; the Rosicrucian Order; Niscience; A.R.E.; the Self-Realization Fellowship; the Coptic Fellowship; the Mayan Order; and Science of Mind.

She presently holds memberships in: the Association of Interfaith Ministers; the International Coaching Federation; Spiritual Frontiers Fellowship International; Sanctuary of the Beloved; the Theosophical Society; and the Institute of Noetic Sciences. She is chairperson of the Raleigh Chapter of Spiritual Frontiers Fellowship International.

The Chance to Hit One More Ball Donna Noland

Hello, my name is Donna Noland and I am an elementary school counselor. I say that with the same pride and feeling of accomplishment that might be felt by a successful surgeon or a professional tennis player who is competing at Wimbledon.

Many people ask me, "What does an elementary school counselor do anyway?" Most people have never heard of having a counselor at an elementary school. These same people would never believe how challenging a job I face each and every day, working with the wounded spirits of the kids who enter my office door. But I believe I was led into this profession by some divine intervention. You see, many years ago, I was one of those students whose spirit was wounded.

I never felt I was gifted academically, as I had ADHD (Attention Deficit Hyperactivity Disorder). Of course, it was not recognized as such in the 1960s. Today, thankfully, we can recognize learning-disabled students and obtain resources to help them level the playing field and find success in place of failure.

If it hadn't been for the threatening posture of the Catholic nuns who carried a big stick to keep us in our seats, I would never have made it further than the eighth grade. Now I realize it is really wonderful to have all of that incredible energy—when you know how to channel it. Creativity is a positive side effect of ADHD. The impulsiveness gives you the courage to try new things, to take risks, and to challenge yourself beyond your expected ability. I look upon my ADHD now as a gift; for I am able to utilize the positive aspects of this disorder to help the young students I see every day.

What could be positive about having ADHD? Well, I am not afraid to try new things, which might explain the fact that I have had three careers in my lifetime, often applying for my initial position without the proper qualifications. For instance, in 1968 I applied for a position as a flight attendant for Eastern Airlines. I had never been out of my little rural town, nor had I ever been on an airplane. The day I went for my interview, I got desperately lost and had trouble finding the airport. However, I got the job!

I went to live in Boston as a flight attendant. On my virgin flight (that's what they called it), I met and fell immediately in love with my future husband, Jim, who was the pilot. Does this really happen? In my case, it certainly did.

It thrilled my parents, poor immigrants from Eastern Europe, whose mantra while I was growing up was to "marry a good provider." Little did I know that I would end up being "the good provider" for my family.

We married shortly after and immediately had two children, bought a 100-acre broken-down farm in New Hampshire and started on "happily ever after." That is, until 1976, when Jim was diagnosed with multiple myeloma—cancer of the bone marrow. His pilot days were over and he never flew again. This was so sad, as it was his passion. He would have flown for free, and often said, "Can you believe they actually pay me to do this?"

⟜⟜

He was unable to work—at any job—as his chemotherapy was debilitating. Every time he was hospitalized, we never knew if he would come home again. This continued for the next nine years. During those years of treatment, he lost three inches of his 6'3" frame from the effects of five collapsed vertebrae. In spite of the severity of his illness, his spirit was unshaken. He was truly the greatest influence in my life. He had more faith in me than I had in myself.

When he was initially diagnosed he said to me, "Well, the first thing we need to do is get you an education." I didn't think I could get into college, having barely made it through high school; but I took the SATs and the CLEP exam and did well enough to be accepted as a full-time student at the University of New Hampshire. This was a totally unexpected joy, and I framed the acceptance letter.

During my years of college, we lived on my husband's disability of $18,000 annually. If Jim wasn't in the hospital or on chemotherapy, he was pushing me every inch of the way. He tutored me in math and statistics, drilled me on Spanish vocabulary, and was the original Mr. Mom, taking care of the children whenever he was able.

I graduated with honors, with a bachelor's degree in business and a minor in psychology. I really enjoyed the study of human behavior, but was advised that those in 'helping professions' just don't make any money. I needed to get busy finding full-time employment, so I could fulfill my role as provider.

Shortly after graduation, my husband was reading the Sunday *Boston Globe* and passed me the employment section. He had circled a job for a pharmaceutical representative for Smith, Kline and French in Philadelphia.

I said, "I can't do this. They're looking for a pharmacist or an R.N. with five years experience." He said, "Try it anyway. It sounds perfect for you." Well, you can imagine my astonishment when I was offered the job from a pool of three hundred applicants.

The woman who interviewed me was the first woman to hold the title of district manager for a major pharmaceutical firm in the very large, competitive market of Boston's teaching hospitals. (In 1982, this was a male-dominated industry.) She later commented about the situation I was dealing with at home; she felt that anyone who could manage stress like I was, while working part-time doing family mediation, obtaining a college education, and raising two children while caring for a sick husband, would be most able to meet her expectations. She hired me.

It was one of the most thrilling moments of my life. I came home and jumped up and down on my husband's bed. The salary far exceeded my expectations, especially for rural New Hampshire. I had the Boston territory and I worked my heart out for this woman, she had such faith in me. I ended up becoming the number two representative in the New England District.

With no medical background, I had to learn all of the new material very quickly. I walked around constantly wearing a headset, listening to tapes on antibiotics, the circulatory system, the G.I. tract, IV infusion, bolus injections and adverse reactions. It was all foreign to me. But I was so eager to learn and so grateful for the job.

I had been working for Smith, Kline and French for five years when I took a three-month leave of absence to be with my husband as we attempted a last-ditch effort for a bone marrow trans-plant. The only place that would take a high-risk patient like him was University Hospital in Seattle, Washington, which was 3,000 miles away. We flew out with Jim on a stretcher, taking up seven first-class seats. My teenagers were at home, with my seventy-year-old parents. I was not surprised, after three weeks, to receive a call from my mom, telling me that the children were becoming difficult. That was an understatement. Jim insisted I go home, as they were still unable to get him 'up' (healthy enough) for a trans-plant. I left the following morning.

As soon as I arrived back in New Hampshire and walked through the door, the telephone started ringing. It was the Exeter Police Department. My daughter, Carry—who is now my best friend, and who, incidentally, will be receiving her Ph.D. this Saturday—had just had a car accident. The laminate on her driver's license had not yet even dried.

Carry was not injured, but when we got back home, a message was waiting from Jim's doctor. She told me to return to Seattle immediately, as he was in a coma, and was not expected to live.

I got the next flight back out to Seattle at six a.m. It was the longest flight of my life. What if I missed being with him when he died? It was like being in a nightmare when you can't run.

I arrived that evening in time for the staff to give me a pair of pajamas and tell me what would happen when Jim died. One by one, the oncology nurses and doctors (he had many) came to say goodbye. They genuinely cared a lot. I was so touched. It was an incredible experience. Jim always said that he was lucky to be surrounded by so many who cared for him and tried to make him comfortable. He compared it to the soldiers on the march to Bataan—alone, real sick, dropping in the mud so far from home. He felt fortunate.

I got into bed with him, just as I had for the past sixteen years. I held him. Even though he was in a coma, I told him how well the children were doing. I told him that we would be fine and that he could go now, if he needed to. When he took his last breath, I got up and stood beside the bed. I could actually feel his spirit lift from the body that I knew so well. I didn't see anything. I just felt it. There are no words to describe the experience.

His death was a turning point in my life. When you no longer fear death, it is a tremendous freedom. Experiencing a death gives an insightful meaning to life. You realize how important it is to enjoy each and every day. I stop myself when I wish even one day away due to a stressful week or a heavy workload. My only regret is that the children were not with us, as they had a very difficult time dealing with their father's death. Closure took a very long time.

Adolescence is a very difficult time to lose a parent. My daughter was sixteen and my son was thirteen. His death was an immeasurable loss to all of us. He had spent so much time with them while they were growing up. I always told them they had more of their father than a lot of other kids do. It made it harder, not easier.

A week after my husband's death, I was back at work. My children both began to "act out." Remember those old washing machine wringers that you put the clothes through? Well, that is what my kids put *me* through. I was traveling out of town one night a week, working seventeen-hour days, and dealing with my own grief and loss as well.

The final breaking point came when my daughter was admitted into the Emergency Room with anaphylactic shock from medication given to her while she was having her wisdom teeth extracted. This was only nine months after Jim's death, and now I had almost lost my daughter. I was overwhelmed and eight weeks later I quit my job. It was one of the most difficult decisions I had to make.

I cashed in my 401K, my company stocks, my savings plan, gave up the company car and took the summer off to be with my children. We hiked through Yosemite Park in California, played a lot of tennis and began the healing process.

I didn't have any benefits from the now-defunct Eastern Airlines and I lost Jim's meager life insurance benefits through a bad investment—another story for sure. The children were receiving social security, but I still had a mortgage to pay, no health insurance, and college tuition to begin planning for. I needed to go back to work. I began my job search, but nothing compared to what I had just given up.

When in doubt…go to graduate school.

In 1981, as an undergraduate, I had done an independent study for a new model program in family mediation. I really enjoyed the concept, and my research had yielded results indicating that mediation was a viable alternative to the court system. At this time, I considered becoming more involved in this field; but I would need a graduate degree in counseling in order to open a private practice. Fortunately, I had enough financial assets to keep us afloat until I finished graduate school in 1989.

The week I graduated, the local school counselor died suddenly of a heart attack. I had not thought about being a school counselor, preferring to go into private practice, but here was another opportunity presenting itself. I went for the interview. I got the job!

I have been in school counseling ever since, starting in high school, then middle school, then, for the past eight years, at Topsail Elementary. I've enjoyed this age the most, I guess because I'm just an old "kid" myself. It has been a humbling experience at

times, and a privilege at others, to be able to sit with these children and really listen: listen to their play, listen to their stories, listen to their pain, their confusion.

You see, as a school counselor you don't just see the children six times and send them on their way, as you would as a private counselor. You see them every day in their classrooms, in plays, on the playground year after year. You cheer their accomplishments and feel their embarrassment when they forget their lines. You're excited when the scores come back for End of Grade and the student you've been tutoring passed to the next grade. You really do get attached.

I truly have learned so much more from them than they from me. Their honesty and directness is refreshing. Their emotions are on their sleeves. What continues to amaze me is how resilient children can be, especially if there is just one other human being there for them. So often it's a teacher or a coach, a friend's parent or a foster parent. It keeps them going in the worst of times.

W orking with students in a divorce group prompted me to open a private Divorce/Custody Mediation practice here in Wilmington, as I saw children caught in the middle of bitter custody battles. If parents really understand what their children are experiencing, it doesn't have to be like that. The parents I saw in my practice were usually so hurt and disillusioned—their dream of happily-ever-after turning into a nightmare—scared, financially stressed, et cetera. It is difficult to tend to children's needs when your own are so great.

I always asked the couple to bring a picture of their child or children to the session . I would set it in the middle of the table so we could always come back to the children when tempers would flare. It usually worked, as most parents love their children very much and want what's best for them.

I closed my practice after a year, as I was working my day job and mediating Wednesday evenings and Saturdays, writing contracts in every spare evening. But I really believe in the concept of mediation and might try to do something again, as I experienced some good results. We do student-led conflict resolution at school, and I am amazed by the talent and mediating skills of some of my fifth-grade students. I think this is one of the best skills we can teach our students. It should be part of the curriculum. I tell them, not only will it make them better friends but also better employees, employers, and of course husbands, wives, and parents. They giggle.

-→=◎

You can't really do this kind of work with people unless you have some sort of outlet, stress reliever. Tennis is my absolute salvation and passion, and has always gotten me through any-

thing. I just pray for continued health to be able to hit just one more ball. Even when I'm down 1-5, love-40 in the third set, I still get excited about the chance to hit one more ball and stay out on the court just a little longer. I never get tired out there. I never want to quit. Tennis got me through my husband's illness for ten years, occasional bouts with loneliness (I've been single sixteen years) and any other "not in my control anyway" situations.

I am ever so grateful for tennis. And, I might add, tennis people are wonderful. For years, I used to hit balls with the pro at Empie Park for an hour every Sunday, used to tell him it was my therapy and he was my therapist.

I never played a team sport in high school. They simply didn't have women's sports when I went to school, so, at fifty-two, being able to go to a state competition with my team was one of my most memorable moments.

-→=◎

I had one student in grief group in first grade for the loss of her father to lung cancer, again in fourth grade for the loss of her mother to ovarian cancer, and just recently for the loss of her grandmother and guardian, whom she was living with, to stomach and liver cancer. I was the first person she called when her mom died at four-thirty in the morning. She said, "Mrs. Noland, Mommy just died." I'll never forget it. I said, "I'll be right there," hung up, sat on the floor, and wailed.

Diana continues to be in my life and I will always be in hers, as long as there is breath in me. She has just been adopted by the most wonderful, loving couple in Winston-Salem, a family that God Himself has dropped out of heaven. Diana is an inspiration to me, as she has lost so much in her thirteen years and still truly longs to be happy and to accept the love that is out there.

Just as Diana's life will begin again, I too, will start on a new adventure. My life has taken another turn in the past month, allowing me an opportunity I must take. My adventurous, creative, risk-taking attitude compels me to to see what else is out there.

I have just been notified that my husband's death was service-related due to exposure to Agent Orange. I will receive widow's benefits (small, but I am grateful) and full educational benefits. I've never had the luxury to "just go to school." I have so much more to learn, skills needing sharpening. This computer to master. It can do so much, and I know so little. TIME to LEARN. I love it. I will be taking an educational leave of absence from Pender County Schools and would love to return writing my own job description.

Since this all happened so recently, I don't know what I'll be doing; but then again, I never really have anyway, and my journey has been rich. All I know is that, at fifty-two, I am so very grateful to be able to have the chance to hit one more ball!

Donna *Noland*

Donna Noland, M.A., N.C.C., N.C.R.C.P., is a National Certified Counselor and trained mediator. She has over thirteen years of human service experience in mental health, school, and career counseling, as well as interpersonal skills training and business management. She is currently on an educational leave of absence from the Pender County School District and lives in Wilmington, North Carolina.

"Experiencing a death gives an insightful meaning to life. You realize how important it is to enjoy each and every day."

Donna Noland

Courage to Change Ann Newton Spooner

I have been fortunate in life and have had many excellent opportunities. Unlike most young people, I didn't rebel as a teen and was the model child. I suffered rebellion and mid-life crisis simultaneously at the age of thirty-six. During that time, I made a conscious decision to change a very unhealthy lifestyle and begin family healing. I didn't want to live the rest of my life as it was. Thus began my mission to create the life I wanted, not what my parents planned or was expected by others. I am now fulfilled and content with life and am honored to have the opportunity to share my experiences. I sincerely hope to encourage those living in unhealthy, abusive situations to take charge of their lives and begin a new, more enriching lifestyle.

I was fortunate to have inherited both musical and artistic talents. I had a wonderful musical mentor as a young girl in the church and our youth group was close and active. No one considered alcohol or negative behavior; our focus was on music, the church summer camp, and our youth group activities.

At age eighteen, encouraged by my parents, youth minister, and music director, I auditioned for the Continental Singers of Los Angeles, California and was accepted. Two singing tours took us across the United States, to the Caribbean Islands, and Alaska. That wonderful experience taught me to be comfortable with meeting new people and rid me of the fear of new experiences for as an only child, I was very much the shy introvert.

When I was twenty-one, the director of the Continentals offered me a full-time job in Los Angeles but because my dad had recently died of a heart attack, I was a loyal, caring daughter to my mother and refused the opportunity. I was also dating a young man who seemed to be "Mr. Perfect," and was very much "in love," or so I thought. I acquired a job in the medical field and was ready to settle down to start a responsible adult life. "Mr. Perfect" and I married shortly thereafter. I soon acquired a very good job working for the director of Pediatric Medical Education a tour local teaching hospital.

Our first year of marriage was one of adjustment. I was not particularly happy but thought I was having difficulty settling down. My husband began a long series of health complaints and depression. Thus, he began years of trips to the psychiatrist and physicians with a steadily growing dependency on prescription drugs.

After three years of marriage, I decided that a baby was the answer to happiness and our first daughter, Carin, was born. She was a very good baby but I was still unhappy. I resented seeing other happy couples and their "perfect" children. My husband's medical complaints, depression, and need for medication continued to get worse, so I dedicated myself to my new position at the hospital working with the director of the Internal Medicine Residency Training Program. I received positive strokes for a job well done and regular pay raises. My job was the one area of my life that I had under control, but my home life was quite the opposite and the resentments grew. Even though I tried to be a good mother, I now realize that my daughter suffered terribly. My mother was a great support during those early years and the three of us grew close.

When Carin was six, my mother died suddenly. I was devastated by her death for she was my mother, my sister and emotional support. I decided another child was necessary, not only to carry on her namesake, but also to give my only daughter a sister to share life and family memories with after our death. Sara Michele was born in 1980 and to my surprise, she was not as quiet or easy to care for as Carin. Therefore, life at home became even more difficult. I was the mother of two daughters, but I had difficulty accepting the fact that I was no longer someone's little girl myself. I was also the caretaker of a prescription drug-addicted husband who worked a 4-12 shift and contributed little to our home life. I was angry, resentful, lonely and unhappy with an abnormal need to control everything and everyone.

Carin remained a well-behaved child and caused few problems, but Sara developed emotional problems almost from the start. She showed all signs and symptoms of living in a sick household. Her behavior was a constant cry for help. I denied the severity of her problems and certainly denied that our family needed help. Even though I tried to be a good mother to my children, I was constantly angry and resentful. We all developed unhealthy behaviors and the vicious cycle in our family grew worse. My husband's addiction worsened to the point that he was taking eighteen to twenty Darvon a day when some occurrence scared him into admitting he had a problem with drugs. I don't know what happened to scare him; he simply announced one evening that he had a problem with the pills. The next day he voluntarily went to an outpatient treatment facility. After only two or three sessions, the severity of his addiction became apparent. He was quickly referred to inpatient care and entered an eight-week drug treatment program. That made me even more resentful and angry. I was left with the sole responsibility of two children and regular visits to a drug treatment program that forced me to learn about the family problem I denied. At the end of his treatment, a family session was offered and I became aware of my involvement in the struggle. To my surprise, I realized that in many ways, I was sicker than he. I began to attend Al Anon and began a slow learning process about the disease of alcoholism and its effect on the family.

My husband remained clean for about nine months while I continued to attend Al Anon, though not regularly. I still denied the severity of our problems even though he was clean. Ignoring it made it go away. Our family relationships did improve slightly but I had not seriously taken control of changing my attitudes and feelings. Slowly the dependency and family illness began all over again, this time with both prescription drugs and alcohol.

The medical education department of our hospital offered regular nursing education courses. One day I happened to overhear a discussion between two nurses about a seminar they were attending on the effects of alcohol on the family. One was telling the other about a family with whom she was working. Her description was identical to my own situation. She made the statement that the mother was really the major problem in that family because of her anger and resentments. I now know that God placed both of us there that day. I actually heard and understood how emotionally disturbed I was. I made the decision then to seriously break the vicious cycle that existed in our family and began seeing a professional counselor.

On the very first visit after hearing the description of our family life, she made the simple statement that my husband WAS an alcoholic. I was ready to hear the truth about our problems and months of serious counseling began. It had taken years for me to admit the need for help and admit the reality of our predicament. When I did, our situation began to change. I then realized I was gambling with my future and my daughters' futures by staying married. My counselor told me that if my husband was involved in a drunk driving accident, he might kill someone and our lives would be devastated. That reality gave me the courage to make a firm decision to leave. As I prepared to move and my decision to leave became reality, my husband used his refined manipulative skills to block my exit. In an effort to scare me, he predicted I would fail, that I would be in the street. He vowed then to take care of his children, not me.

The doubts and fears I felt about raising two girls alone were tremendous. They didn't understand and were angry with me for creating an unsteady situation in our family. Sara's emotional problems worsened from the change of lifestyle I was creating. I didn't know how I could afford to leave but knew I couldn't afford to stay. In one session, my counselor asked what I wanted most in life. I quickly answered that I wanted both girls to be emotionally stable and well, and that I wanted to be a designer or be in a creative field. At the time, I felt both were a dream.

The girls' anger with me for disrupting the life they were

used to grew, although they had been miserable. They grew even angrier when their dad's condition worsened drastically after our move. Our family went through severe emotional struggles over the craziness that this disease brought. I could tell many stories of those incidents and our reactions to the craziness during those early months.

It was difficult telling my Christian friends of my decision to separate but to my surprise, their reactions to my announcement were not judgmental or condemning but supportive and positive. All were much in favor of my decision and, to my surprise, one friend even said he would pray that God would send a contractor to work with me on creative projects.

The girls and I moved into a tiny duplex apartment that was too small for the three of us but I quickly realized that even though we still suffered emotional problems, I was much happier. I felt relieved and released. I wanted the girls to remain in their schools and near their father, so our apartment was only three blocks from the home they knew. I did my best to make that difficult change easier for them.

Shortly after our move, I began dating a man that was introduced to me by a close friend. Our dating relationship began as a simple friendship and dinner out together. Ed and I didn't even hold hands for the first four months of dating. He was amazingly patient and calm with my daughters' outbursts and stepped in at

times to mediate our differences. I was amazed that he was not scared off by the illness of our family, but he too had experienced an unhappy family history and was taking the proper steps to change an unhealthy lifestyle. I so appreciated that he drank nothing but water! Ed began classes within that first year with a goal of obtaining his contractor's license. When he told me of his goal, he knew nothing of my friend's prayer that God would send a contractor. Certainly marriage was not in either of our plans at the time.

Sara was hospitalized for severe emotional and depressive problems. I was convinced I was doing the best thing for all of us and was never tempted to move back. I was told that my husband had to reach his bottom. It was no longer my responsibility to take care of him.

Carin was angry also, but was more affected by a severe lack of self-esteem. She felt the need to take care of her father, which she did as long as it was her decision to do so. When she thought her father expected it of her, she rebelled. Both girls spent a great deal of time running back and forth between their father and myself and became expert at playing one against the other. They defended his behavior but knew deep down that he was a very sick person. Carin was most unhappy both sharing a room with her troubled sister and spending time with her dad.

My ex-husband's illness grew worse as did the craziness of

the alcoholic lifestyle. I remained in counseling and was gaining emotional and mental health as the broken family situation worsened. God gave me strength to continue my own personal struggle and I held on to the hope that life would get better. I am now convinced that God removed my ex-husband from our lives.

The house that I left had been on the market for some time but my ex-husband's poor housekeeping, lack of care, and unpredictable behavior turned prospective buyers away. Miraculously, though, immediately after one particularly bad alcoholic incident, we received an offer and sold the house. He moved some distance away from us.

Carin decided to move with him. I worried terribly but felt she needed to come to her own conclusions about her dad's illness. Within a few months of the move, she announced that she was moving in with her boyfriend. He confided that she was scared of her dad and he was scared for her. I was not pleased with her decision but told her that if living with Sara and I was not an option, I would rather she live with her boyfriend than her dad. Needless to say, she was surprised at my reaction, or lack of it. That was the first sign that change was occurring. My caring response rather than over-reaction and control began the healing process between my older daughter and me. Meanwhile, my younger daughter grew worse and was hospitalized a second time for depression and severe behavioral problems. She left the hos-

pital in worse condition than she went in, and was so overmedicated that she would fall walking from the living room to her bedroom. I was terribly concerned that she too would develop a problem with prescription drugs but could hardly stand the pressures of living with her without medications.

I next faced the battle of fighting for child support from the man who swore he would take care of his children. I fought long and hard for each child support payment, wrote letters to Social Services Departments, governors, and anyone that I thought might help. Finally, I hired an attorney who in the end did help to win my case, but the three-year battle with the legal and child support system left me wondering why the system is so protective of the "bad guy" and has so little regard for the welfare of the children. Toward the end of my battles for child support, the laws began to change in favor of needy children.

Ed and I dated over two and a half years, during which a very ugly divorce was finalized and my younger daughter's problems grew even more severe. I continued the healing process for myself and felt secure in the relationship between Ed and I. We announced our engagement on July 4th and were married on October 3rd of 1992. Ed's contractor's license arrived in the mail on our wedding day. Both of my daughters and my husband's daughter were bridesmaids in our wedding. It was a happy day. By this time, though, Sara was extremely violent and was headed for total destruction. We feared for our own safety as well as hers. Ed was resented by Sara but stepped in as the rock-solid strength and father figure of the family. He was clear about the severity of her problems and helped me to take the necessary steps for help.

A sympathetic nurse whom we had known from Sara's two hospitalizations recommended a psychiatric treatment facility for young people in Knoxville, Tennessee. My prayers were answered when she was admitted to that facility. The experience gave her a new life and my husband and I an opportunity to develop and grow our relationship during our first year of marriage.

Ed encouraged me to leave my job of twenty-five plus years. I had become quite bored with the same job for that length of time and, after gaining mental and emotional health, no longer needed my job as an escape. My change in attitude and behavior created difficulties for those with whom I had worked for so long and the change affected job relationships as well. I no longer needed to control everything and everyone, and the change of attitude was interpreted negatively by those with whom I worked. My creative needs were not being met either and Ed knew of my heart's desire to do design work. He encouraged me to begin my interior design studies. I had the new goal of making my dream a reality.

Sara remained in full-time psychiatric treatment in Tennes-see for slightly over a year. She was discharged a changed young lady and displayed a totally different personality. She developed maturity and the ability to make healthier decisions for herself. She actually grew into a cute young girl with a teasing personality and became a pleasure to be around.

My two-year design education took three and a half years to complete, but I graduated and began my professional interior design practice. My dream finally became reality!

Carin remained with her boyfriend and made the decision to marry him. To this day, I do not feel that she loved him; he was a means for escape. At the very beginning of their relationship, I disliked him but appreciated his insight and patience with our family problems. Even though I felt she could have chosen better, I learned to like him. After their marriage, they struggled endlessly over finances. He never seemed to mature and spent more time with his friends playing the guitar and smoking pot than he did with Carin. Her car was repossessed. She began working for a maid service that provided her with a car, but her self-esteem went to an all-time low. My husband encouraged me not to get involved or step in to help, that she would come to her own conclusions about making changes much more quickly if I didn't interfere. I listened to him, though it was hard to watch her struggle. Our mother-daughter relationship improved and she finally admitted to me that she knew I was right in leaving her dad.

Finally, after four years of unsuccessful marriage, she showed up on my doorstep one evening having made the decision that she didn't want to live that way any longer. She revealed her dream to join the Navy, get a college education, travel and make something of herself.

Today, I own a successful interior design practice in Charlotte, North Carolina. I am president of the local chapter of the Interior Design Society, and an Allied Member of ASID. I have won a number of designer showcase awards. I am active in showcase events to benefit several worthy fundraising organizations including The Relatives, the Leukemia Society, and the March of Dimes. The Relatives is dear to my heart, for its purpose is to assist troubled teens and their families in improving relationships.

Carin is now stationed in San Diego, California in the Navy and is currently enrolled in three college courses. Sara turns twenty this year, lives on her own, is growing into a responsible young lady and is now also considering the military in her future.

The girl's father has disappeared from their lives. We do not know if he is living or dead but the relationship between mother, daughters, and their step-dad is strong and healthy.

Ed and I are happily married, are working together to build my business, and are working slowly on renovating an older home. God brought us through some difficult times and has given us life, health, and the pursuit of happiness while on this earth.

I speak from experience when encouraging women needing the courage to improve their lives to seek counseling. Having grown up in a very strict religious atmosphere, I was convinced that I had chosen my original path and it could not change. Counseling helped to change that thinking and afforded me the ability to give God the opportunity to heal our family. He gave me the strength, courage and ability to make those decisions and act on them. He has truly blessed us. Again, I am now fulfilled and content with my life, but I still have goals. I am honored to have the opportunity to share my experiences in order to encourage other women to take charge of their lives, create their own opportunities and achieve personal success.

Ann *Newton Spooner*

Ann Newton Spooner is a Charlotte, North Carolina native, a successful businesswoman, an award-winning designer, and an educator. She has a degree in interior design from Central Piedmont Community College and is a graduate of the Charlotte Small Business Owners Program. She opened her design practice in Charlotte in 1994. Her business was placed in the January 2000 Book of Lists by *The Business Journal* of Charlotte/Mecklenburg County.

She has been president of the Greater Charlotte Chapter of the Interior Design Society for over two years, and is an Allied Member of ASID. She is also the showhouse chairperson for the year 2000 March of Dimes/ IDS Designer Showhouse in Charlotte. Her rooms have been featured in numerous publications, most recently in the spring issues of *Today's Charlotte Woman* and on the cover of *The Business Journal.*

A Writer's Journey Deborah Ellis Daniel

Never give up on a dream. In the middle years of my life I've discovered that a dream, once thought to be lost or unreachable, sometimes merely incubates until you're ready to reach out and grab it.

I've always admired those who let nothing stop them from their goals, their talents, their path in life. Yes, and envied them too. Stumbling blocks, detours and life's unpredictability always seemed to push my ambition to become a writer further from my grasp. Defeated, I nearly gave up hope. Than I turned forty and had a revelation! Perceptions and priorities shifted and my life came into focus with a clarity I found startling. Before I could come into my own as a writer, I'd needed to take a journey. A journey that only decades of living could give me, and all that I've experienced—the triumphant, the ordinary and the tragic—enriches me as a writer.

This journey began at the tender age of eight. I was a passionate reader, so it seemed a natural progression to move from reading others' words on the page to writing my own. Lying on my stomach on our living room floor, I began by creating my own fairy tales. Those first literary efforts were neatly printed on lined notebook paper and lovingly illustrated with whatever colored pencils I could find. I remember being prolific as a young writer, fascinated by my own words. The act of writing itself "spoke" to me and, with a child's innocence, I accepted that this was who I was...a writer. Never realizing that I'd have to fight hard as an adult to reclaim that unquestioning faith in myself.

Fairy tales gave way to short stories, poetry and playwriting in my adolescence and teen years. Every form of writing appealed to me and I tried it all. In school, I relished writing assignments and discovered a love of research. Often the process of unearthing the information held my interest far more than the facts themselves. Although still in junior high school, I became one of the youngest reporters for the high school newspaper and found my niche. My first "professional" interview was with the adult star of a visiting theatrical group to the school. Little did I know that it foreshadowed my work in movies three decades later. My course was set for a career in journalism. Or so I thought.

During this period of discovery, my home life was falling apart. We lived in a rural community in south central Pennsylvania called St. Thomas during those early school years. My father was the town's only physician, a country doctor who still made housecalls at all hours of the day and night. My mother, who'd left nursing school to elope with my father, helped out at his office on occasion but I remember her being unhappy with the life of a country housewife. Dad was frequently away from home on medical emergencies, leaving her with an active family of four children in an aging house with no heat. Their escalating arguments could be heard late into the night. A few months after my fourteenth birthday, my mother committed suicide and life as I knew it ceased.

The rest of my teen years are painful to remember. As the oldest child, I felt a great responsibility for my brother Tom and my sisters, Susan and Barbara. My father, already a heavy social drinker before my mother's death, slid into alcoholism, neglect and verbal abuse. We were fortunate that our Aunt Arlene, my mother's sister, and our maternal grandmother stepped in to help. Ultimately, in a showdown with Mother's family and a series of child custody hearings, my siblings and I were torn apart. It was the mid-'60s and my pleas to keep us together and away from our abusive father fell on deaf judicial ears. Susan and I went to live with our aunt while Tom and Barbara remained with our father. I spent the rest of my teen years mourning the loss of my immediate family. How had things gone so tragically wrong? To my great joy, although living hundreds of miles apart now, my siblings and I maintain a strong, loving bond that I cherish.

In my senior year of high school, I received yet another blow. Journalism school wouldn't be possible. I qualified for a student loan but only as a commuting day student to a state teacher's college in the next town. My guidance counselor further argued that journalism was a "risky" career choice and that I should major in something more "practical." She convinced me that I had no other options. The following year I entered Shippensburg State College as a library science major, minoring in English. After two years of feeling that I was wasting my time, I dropped out and took a job in a convalescent home as a nursing aide—a fateful decision, as it turned out.

Although a doctor's daughter, I never aspired to a career in medicine but I discovered that I had a talent for nursing. After observing my work for several months, the director of the nursing home took me on as her personal project and pushed me to apply to the local vocational-technical school's nursing program. To the delight of my grandmother who believed that nurses would always have a job, I was accepted and did well in both the scholastic and clinical aspects of the profession. The work was challenging and gratifying even though my heart wasn't in it. The writer in me lay dormant, pushed aside for the business of learning a new vocation and making a living.

Two days after my graduation from nursing school in 1973, I packed all of my belongings into a used Rambler sedan and moved to Hickory, North Carolina. I had a job in the intensive/coronary care unit of Catawba Memorial Hospital, a room at a local women's boarding house and my own car. A brand new life had begun and it didn't take long to fall in love with North Carolina. I felt a sense of "coming home" here and that's stayed with me to this day.

Time flew by in my twenties and thirties. I was caught up in the hectic pace of life, and my dream of writing became a dim memory. In those years, I married twice, struggled with infertility and moved several times—from Hickory to Salisbury, North Carolina, then back to Hickory, to Virginia Beach, Virginia and Louisville, Kentucky—often as a result of job transfers for my husband. Each new city meant starting over and I took jobs in doctor's offices when possible to get better hours, holidays off and benefits. I also worked as a restaurant hostess and supervisor, taught adult education classes in needlework techniques at a community college, opened a small needlework shop with a partner and worked as an assistant manager for Petite Sophisticate in Louisville when nursing jobs weren't available. My resumé resembled a patchwork quilt of skills.

My husband Pete and I returned to North Carolina from Kentucky on April Fool's Day, 1985. Once settled in Wilmington, I looked for work once again and took a job with a local optometrist. Pete's new position required him to travel four or five days

a week and I found myself alone much of the time. My job kept me busy but I began to feel the old stirrings of that life-long dream. But how could I reclaim it after neglecting it for so long? I feared the prolific writer of my youth no longer existed. Despite my fears, I took any adult education writing classes that UNC-Wilmington offered. In 1989, an unexpected twist of fate pushed me onto another path. A path that ultimately led to the dream I thought I'd lost.

An old injury to my back resurfaced with a vengeance and I lay helpless and in pain for weeks before and after two surgeries. The lengthy recovery period forced me to resign from my job, giving me plenty of time to think. I was approaching forty and my life so far had been shaped by family situations and husbands' jobs. What did I want? What defined me? What gave my life meaning?

I found some of those answers in an unexpected place. In January 1990, I became a volunteer tutor for the Cape Fear Literacy Council in Wilmington. During the eight years that followed, I also became a tutor trainer, a supervising trainer, a creative writing teacher for New Readers and a member of the North Carolina state training team for volunteer literacy. Working with illiterate adults in their struggle to learn a skill I'd taken for granted, I learned gratitude for the blessings of education. I'd never realized how fortunate I was to be raised by parents and family who valued reading and teachers who encouraged me to reach for excellence. Our students taught me that I should never stop learning and I decided that, if they can reach their goals and change their lives, so could I. Now, at last, the time was right to reach for my most prized ambition. It was time to start writing.

Although not writing professionally over the years, I'd taken writing courses, attended seminars, read how-to books and articles, joined a writers' group and talked to published authors. I learned that the best way to become a freelance writer was to act like one. That meant putting myself in front of the computer and seeking out ways to build a portfolio. Whether it was a small article in an organization's newsletter or a paid assignment with a local publication, I needed experience. I started out by co-writing a tutor handbook for the literacy council, writing a monthly column for my writers' group newsletter and contributing to a local corporate newsletter.

My first paid assignment as a freelance writer combined three loves—writing, Southern history and the movies. In April 1995, a small regional magazine bought my article (plus photos) about the extensive use of Orton Plantation in Brunswick County as a filmmaking location. That article led me to a job with *Reel Carolina: Journal of Film and Video*, a monthly film industry magazine covering North and South Carolina. In four years, I've progressed from film history columnist to contributing writer to

Wilmington editor. Suddenly I was working in a profession I loved, interviewing celebrities and filmmakers, visiting movie sets and learning the behind-the-scene world of filmmaking. Contacts I made with the magazine led to other assignments and I started my own freelance writing business in 1997, naming it Synchronicity Freelance Writing Service. The term "synchronicity" seemed to fit the unexpected ways in which my writing career fell into place.

At times I marvel at how humbly this second career began with that fortieth birthday resolution and how far I've come. I was prepared to fall flat on my face if necessary and as often as I had to in pursuit of that eight-year-old's dream. I've had help, of course, and owe a debt of thanks to my husband, family, friends and colleagues who believed in me and cheered me on when my confidence reached a low point. I'm thankful too that the inspired child who started out with illustrated fairy tales stayed with me throughout a long and arduous journey. To honor that spirit in me and the unflinching faith she possessed, my signature includes the surname she used as author.

"In the middle years of my life I've discovered that a dream, once thought to be lost or unreachable, sometimes merely incubates until you're ready to reach out and grab it."

Deborah Ellis Daniel

Deborah Ellis Daniel

Deborah Ellis Daniel, a freelance writer in Wilmington, N.C., is the author of numerous articles for regional publications and *The Insiders' Guide to N.C.'s Southern Coast and Wilmington*, 6th and 7th editions. Deb is currently at work on *Binding Threads: Coastal North Carolina Quilters* for Coastal Carolina Press.

I'll Be Seeing You Mirinda J. Kossoff

Just nine days past my birthday, in the year 2000, I became a middle-aged orphan. For the two weeks leading up to my mother's death on February 13th, I stumbled through my days at work and at home with a feeling of dread lodged in the pit of my stomach. I had no way of knowing that in the wee hours of February 10th my mother would enter the hospital for the last time. But I had a visceral sense that it was coming. In some inexplicable way, I felt a physical connection with my mother, an extension perhaps of that time when I was part of her body, when her blood flowed through my veins. Though by no means the favored child or the one closest to my mother over the years, I was the first-born and the first to be expelled, bawling, from the safe haven of her womb. Now I am finally and irrevocably separated from her physical presence.

When she was lying, semi-conscious, in her hospital bed, a morphine drip entering a port inserted in the back of one withered hand, I experienced an almost-desperate desire to crawl into the bed beside her and cradle her in my arms, much as she must have done for me when I was a baby. A sense of hospital propriety and the presence of my siblings stopped me. I also knew that my mother, had she been of sound mind and body, never would have welcomed such a gesture. She wasn't given to overt displays of affection or sentimentality.

Her first two days in the hospital were marked by brief periods of consciousness when, as if surfacing from the bottom of a well, she recognized her children and grandchildren. Then she smiled, and in slurred but still-understandable words she said: "My beautiful family."

My twenty-year-old twin sons moved to either side of her bed, each taking one of her blue-veined hands in their big, healthy ones. She squeezed their hands and shrugged her shoulders in delight. She looked like a young girl at her first prom.

"Mom," I said. "You seem happy."

"I am happy," she replied, with more clarity than before.

Then she crooned, "I love you, I love you, I love you."

"We love you, too, Grandma," the boys replied.

"She's talking to relatives on the other side," my sister said.

My maternal grandmother, Elsie Mirinda, had died some thirty-some years earlier at the same age.

I moved to the head of the bed and stroked Mom's hair. As she looked up at me with eyes that seemed to gaze past me to another plane of existence, she called out, "Mama."

More than anyone else, it was her mother she wanted in her time of need. And when she called for her mother, I answered.

"Mama loves you," I said, over and over again. I said it as an affirmation of her mother's love for her and as an affirmation to myself of my mother's love for me. In the years before her illness, ours had been a difficult and bumpy relationship, but I knew the love was there. And in her hospital room, its presence was palpable.

On the afternoon of the third day, my youngest sister and I took a break from our bedside vigil and walked a few blocks around the hospital as my brother kept watch in my mother's room.

"I know this sounds weird," I said to my sister. "But suddenly, I feel the urge to buy something."

"Oh, you wouldn't believe all the money I've spent in the past month," she replied.

We are sisters, after all—even if ten years and tastes and preferences separate us.

⊷

On the fourth day, we all knew the end was near. Mom was in a state of deep unconsciousness. Her shoulders heaved with the effort of taking each breath. At times the period between breaths lasted so long we thought the previous breath must surely have been her last.

We had wanted to be with her when the end came. But it was just like her to wait until we left the hospital for the evening to take her final breath. She was with one of the caretakers we'd hired to look after her over the last few months. Her breathing slowed, the caretaker said, until it finally stopped. No struggle. No sign of fear or pain. We needed to hear that.

⊷

My parents met and courted in Greensboro, North Carolina when Dad was assigned to the Overseas Replacement Depot in 1943. Mom was working as a nurse's aide at Sternberger's Children's Hospital, on the three to eleven p.m. shift, and living with my grandmother in an apartment on 5th Avenue. That fact that Dad was only nineteen at the time and my mother twenty-six didn't seem to deter either of them. Mom claimed he lied about his age so she'd go out with him. He didn't mention being Jewish, either, and for a long time, Mom didn't know that he was. Given his last name and his looks, my mother might have had some questions, but the young woman who grew up in Wilkes County probably had never known a Jew before, so she had no reference point.

She wouldn't go out with Dad on Sunday nights, because she sang in the choir at Magnolia Street Baptist Church. So one night, Dad showed up in the sanctuary for the Sunday evening service and slipped into the back pew. It was an answer to Mom's prayers. He'd been in a church before, a Methodist church somewhere during his military training, and she'd been hoping he'd find a need to return to church.

Dad was known to fabricate passes so he could get off base to see Mom. He'd meet her at the gate at Sternberger's at eleven p.m. and walk her home. Often, he'd stay out past curfew and slip back into his barracks unnoticed. His ingenuity in getting around the rules never failed him.

It wasn't long before he was a regular at my mother and grandmother's dinner table. He took to the Southern fried chicken and greens my grandmother cooked up for him, and he definitely took to her habit of putting the man first. Catering to the men of the clan was a long tradition in my mother's family. Her grandmother, Granny Holler, often remarked that "men are superior."

I think Dad must have been attracted to the warmth and ready acceptance he experienced at the little apartment on 5th Avenue, something he seemed to have lacked as the only child of critical and distant parents.

My father was born in Manhattan to Sadye Herman and Herman David Kossoff. I have his Hebrew prayer book, with his name embossed on the front and spelled with only one "f." Hugo Kossof. They named their first and only child Hugo, after Victor Hugo, since Grandpa was a well-read man and something of a Francophile. Grandpa, a talented pianist and Russian immigrant, had hopes that some day Hugo would be a great musician. Instead, Hugo changed his name to Hugh and refused to have anything to do with the piano. When he was as young as ten or eleven, young Hugo would take the subway from Mt. Vernon into Manhattan and spend the day by himself, wandering the city.

My father, an only child, questioned whether he was planned or wanted. Herman and Sadye stopped sleeping together after Dad was born. They had separate rooms with chaste twin beds in each. That would explain some of Grandpa's well-known extra-curricular activities. He taught piano and played concerts nine months of the year and spent his summers in Europe, most often without Dad and my grandmother.

Though Mom couldn't say what it was about Dad that had attracted her, I think it was his brash, can-do attitude and his exotic good looks. He was different from the southern men Mom had dated. He steamrolled into her life. Over six feet tall, slender with a thick crop of dark hair, Dad had heavy eyebrows that grew to a point in the center over hazel eyes. His nose was strong and straight, and he had a fleshy lower lip that gave him the look of a matinee idol.

My mother, Nancy Ozelle Whitfield (her twin was named Martha Mozelle) had wavy auburn hair swept above a broad, unlined forehead, blue eyes and a translucent complexion. She must have seemed like an angel of mercy in her white nurse's uniform. Before he shipped out to England, Dad asked Mom to marry him— several times. But she refused, saying she didn't know him well enough and didn't want to end up a war widow. During the two years he was flying bombing raids over Germany, he never wrote, and she didn't know if he was dead or alive.

In 1945, she got a phone call from New York.

"Are you married," my father asked.

"No."

"Are you engaged?"

"No."

"Are you seeing anyone?"

"No."

"Do you want to pick up where we left off?"

"Yes."

"You've told every g-damned cat and dog in the street before mentioning it to me," was Grandpa Herman's response to the news that Dad planned to marry Nancy Whitfield. My grandparents did their best to prevent the marriage. On a pre-nuptial visit to New York, my parents spent a few days with Grandma and Grandpa Kossoff. The first day, Grandpa sent Dad out on a trumped-up trip to the bakery to buy bread. While he was gone, Grandpa and Grandma unleashed their scheme to sabotage what they considered an inappropriate relationship.

Their first line of attack was Grandpa telling Grandma to "go get those letters." So Grandma produced a stack of love letters written to Dad by other women, which she proceeded to read to my mother.

"He's not ready to settle down, my grandfather argued. "He doesn't know what he wants or needs yet. He should marry some-one of his own kind."

My mother left the living room and went to sit at the dining room table, weeping silently. When Dad returned to the apartment, he found Mom still crying at the dining room table. Upon learning what my grandparents had been up to, Dad called his father a g-damned SOB and abruptly left with my mother in tow.

My parents were married in Greensboro on December 23, 1945 in the living room of Mrs. Grubbs' house. My mother and grandmother had been living in Mrs. Grubbs' upstairs apartment. It was a modest wedding, because neither of my parents had much money.

In their wedding photograph, my parents are standing arm in arm in front of a mirror over the fireplace. White poinsettias and candles decorate the mantel. My mother is wearing a light grey suit, hat with veil and long white gloves that flare at the top. My father wears a slightly darker double-breasted suit. While my mother has one gloved hand around his elbow, neither are looking at each other; only my mother looks as if she's staring into the camera, with a faint smile on her lips. She's wearing no makeup, her hair piled high above a broad, smooth brow. Dad is looking away from the camera, his face a blank.

I was the first product of this unusual union. Born in a hospital that no longer exists in Greensboro, I was a toddler when we moved to an apartment in Chapel Hill's Victory Village while Dad earned his degree at the University of North Carolina. This was followed by a D.D.S. from the University of Maryland. During Dad's dental school days, we lived in a working-class Baltimore neighborhood called Middle River, next door to a Catholic family. When one of the daughters was confirmed, I was entranced by her confirmation dress, which looked to me like the most beautiful wedding gown I had ever seen. I wanted to be confirmed, too, and was disillusioned when I learned that the Baptist church offered nothing so captivating to mark its children growing into the faith. All I had to look forward to was getting dunked in a baptismal pool in a plain white shift.

My sister Martha Ellen was born in Baltimore, followed eighteen months later by Robert Hugh, whom we called Bobby. When my brother was born, Dad said, "I want to name this one." Bobby was the boy Dad had longed for, and he named him after himself and a cherished boyhood friend.

Martha was called by both her given names, Martha Ellen, so that the two were run together and came out "Marthellen." But I was always Jean, not Mirinda Jean, just plain Jean. This was fine with me. I didn't like my first name; it was too exotic for a kid who just wanted to fit in.

After graduation, Dad was eager to get back to North Carolina—my mother's home turf and his adopted geography. But North Carolina rejected him. He wanted to practice in Winston-Salem, near my mother's twin sister, and we moved there briefly while Dad took the North Carolina dental boards. He was told he flunked. When he learned the news, he wept, knowing he had done well on the exams.

Mom queried her dentist, Dr. Poindexter, who told her he was the only one among the dental examiners to vote for Dad. He said the board didn't want another dentist in town. Translation: they didn't want another Jew, this despite the fact that Dad had converted before marrying Mom. Even in Danville, Virginia, where Dad ultimately established a practice, he was often referred to as "that Jew doctor."

The tension between my Jewish and Southern Baptist halves would become an ongoing struggle for me, the search for identity a twisted path, doubling back on itself. It was, and still is, a non-issue for my siblings, who've always considered themselves Protestants.

When I wrestle with my dual identity, I think of the writer

Adrienne Rich's essay, "Split at the Root," about a similar dualism in her Jewish/Protestant family. Maybe it's the lot of the first-born to be more sensitive to the legacy of the past. Whatever the reason, I always felt I was toeing a tightrope between two, sometimes warring, cultures. If I teetered too far in the direction of my Jewish relatives—who were, in fact, more interesting, cultured and intellectual than my mother's family—then I would be disloyal to my mother, who felt rejected by Dad's Jewish relatives.

To my Jewish grandparents, I was "little Jeannie," a marvel at the piano and a budding multi-linguist. And so I wanted to please them, too. I wanted their love and attention for the needs and accomplishments my parents were too busy with my younger siblings to notice. When, at age forty-two, my mother gave birth to my youngest sister, Bonnie, I felt irrevocably relegated to the ashheap of benign neglect, except, of course, when it came to discipline. Neglect didn't extend to my being able to stay out late or have friends stay overnight.

For his part, Dad did his best to pass as a good ole boy, hanging out at Curtis Hanks' country store on the weekends where he'd rock back on two legs of an old wooden chair, a plug of tobacco tucked inside one cheek, and trade hunting and fishing stories with the locals who accepted him for who he was and simply called him "doc."

Dad's plunge into what I then considered redneck culture embarrassed me. I had cousins on my mother's side who collected Civil War and Nazi memorabilia and serenaded me with a smutty rendition of reveille: "There's a soldier in the grass with a bullet up his ass, get it out, boy scout, get it out, get it out." They were hugely obese, drank sugary iced tea from mason jars and embarrassed me even more.

The same feeling washed over me when we'd meet people for the first time and they'd say, "Kossoff—that's an unusual name. Where y'all from?" Or "Kossoff—you're not from around here. What kind of name is that?"

"Well," I felt like saying, "you found us out; we're aliens."

I don't think the questions about our name were meant to be unkind. Southerners have a need to place you in context. But the constant curiosity about our name and background made me feel like an outsider, a feeling that I would carry with me all my life.

Dad was so determined not to be Jewish that he had plastic surgery to "correct" his Jewish nose. My mother would tell me long after Dad's death: "He didn't want to look Jewish; that's why he did it."

I was about twelve at the time, and Dad's transformation was sprung on us when he stepped off the plane after a trip to New York where we were told that he was having surgery to help him stop snoring. I hardly recognized the man who crossed the tarmac to greet us. His nose was shorter and broader, making him look less refined and definitely less handsome in my eyes. I felt hurt, betrayed and bewildered.

As determined as Dad was to reject his Jewish past and embrace Southern culture, I was just as determined, when I left home for college, not to be Southern. My first month at William & Mary, I dropped my thick accent—as easily as shedding a coat in summer. I didn't want anyone to confuse me with my ignorant Southern relatives.

⊶

When I was a toddler, my mother would sing to me: "Bye baby bunting, daddy's gone a-hunting, to find a little rabbit skin, to wrap the baby bunting in." My response was to wail inconsolably. I was afraid my mother was singing that Daddy had gone away and would never return.

Years later, when I was a grown woman with babies of my own, that's exactly what he did.

It was September 30, 1980, a sunny fall day. I had come home from work and was unloading groceries from the back of our new Subaru station wagon. I kicked open the screen door to the kitchen with my foot, my arms filled with grocery bags. As I struggled into the house with my load, my husband, George, walked in, without his usual smile and greeting. He didn't come forward to help me with the grocery bags.

"I've got some bad news," he said.

"What?" I asked, dumping the bags on the counter, my mind a blank. Then a jolt.

"Are the kids okay?" My heart was beginning to slam against my rib cage. Our twin sons were just eighteen months old.

"It's your father," he said. "He's killed himself."

I felt my whole body sag, as if a weight had been dropped into my empty arms. Then the numbness set in, my emotional anaesthesia.

"But how? He was being watched. How could it have happened?"

"I don't know the details. Your mother was pretty upset. She said to call Martha."

I walked into the bedroom on wobbly legs, sat down on the bed and dialed my sister in Washington. I was dry-eyed, purposeful. Only my shaky hands gave away my emotional state.

How many times had I imagined the unimaginable. Like thinking a lingering sore throat must be throat cancer. I imagined the worst to keep the worst at bay, to demystify it, to feel in control. Now that the worst had happened, I couldn't believe it.

There were times in the past when I thought: "He might as well go ahead and do away with himself; he's threatened it often enough, held us all trapped in the barbed wire of his misery." But there was no sense of relief or closure in the brutal fulfillment of what I had let myself wish for.

When Martha answered, I blurted, "What happened to Dad? Is he really gone?"

I could tell she'd been crying. "He hanged himself."

"But how? How did he do it?"

"With the belt from his bathrobe."

"But I don't see how he could have done it." A robe belt seemed so insubstantial, so incapable of inflicting death. "How could he have hanged himself with only a cotton belt?"

"All I know is that he looped it over the hook on the bathroom door, tied the other end around his neck and leaned against it."

A picture of my father, ashen faced, slumped against a grey institutional door rose in my mind. He must have wanted to die so badly that he transcended the impulse to save himself at the last minute. He didn't step off a chair and dangle helpless in mid-air; he simply put all his weight against that belt while his body was on the floor. At any moment he could have stood up and released the pressure on his neck. Instead, he must have leaned against the belt with a superhuman determination that I could never begin to understand. It was like choking yourself to death with your own bare hands.

What must have gone through his mind in those last moments. Did he think of us? Did he think of me?

I didn't say any of this to my sister. Instead, I said, "He was supposed to be on twenty-four-hour suicide watch at the hospital."

"I know," my sister sighed. "But they couldn't watch him every second. He evidently figured out when they'd check on him, and he timed it to happen in between room checks."

⊷

Dad's suicide was a pivotal event in my life, triggering a major depression and compelling me, for the first time in my life, to seek psychotherapy. I would learn that the history of mental illness in Dad's family was a legacy I would have to confront again and again in my life.

Those summers when Grandpa Herman went off to Europe would sometimes precipitate a catatonic depression in Grandma Sadye. She'd go into a room in her mind where none could follow. She'd become completely mute, and only a course of electroshock therapy would bring her around. Dad must have felt abandoned by both parents during those times. My mother was also abandoned as a child; she lost her father when she was only two, to the influenza epidemic of 1918. Abandonment surely was an unconscious thread that bound them together when they met.

When we children left home for college and lives of our own, Dad must have re-experienced that abandonment. Those feelings, combined with his identity issues as a Jew who had rejected his heritage, and a struggle with chronic back pain, were more than he could live with.

For my own peace of mind, I needed to understand Dad's mental state during his last hospitalization on the psychiatric ward of University of Virginia Hospital. I had to go behind my mother's back to get access to his medical records. To her, such things were private and none of my business, so she refused to give me permission to see the records. But I found a way to get to them; I had to find some connection with the father who had been so emotionally remote when he was alive.

Hand-scrawled notes from residents, nurses and physical therapists detailed the course of Dad's final days.

The psychiatric resident says, "A difficult patient, obsessed with control and unable to gain insight about his condition."

A nurse's entry marked August 25, 1980 observes: "The patient was crying. He seems to have regular crying spells, but when I asked him about it, he replied, "A man doesn't cry; I've never cried.""

Someone else writes that in a rare, unguarded moment, my father admitted to sabotaging his therapy and suggested that maybe he really didn't want to get well.

The resident reappears, quoting my father in a fit of pique at being pressed to talk: "If I have to talk about feelings again, I'll vomit. Feelings are the wind, the woods, the water, times when I'm out of doors. They don't have anything to do with people." As I read that entry, I felt numb. My emotional anaesthesia had kicked in, a learned response when things get too hard to bear.

There's a note about the last visit my mother and I made before Dad's death. The chart says he called for help because of severe chest pains. He's convinced he's dying of a heart attack. The resident orders an EKG and bloodwork. Nothing. His note concludes: "The patient's symptoms were most likely an anxiety attack about the upcoming family visit and whatever issues and feelings the visit might stir up." I know about those anxiety attacks, too. I've had several over the years.

The concluding chart note details in a dry, clinical tone: "On the morning of September 30, 1980, the patient was found hanged by his robe belt on the inside bathroom door hinge."

Reading those chart notes confirmed my sense that my father had been psychologically damaged from an early age, that his suicide was not my fault, that no matter how pretty or how smart or how good a daughter I had tried to be, I never could have won the relationship with him I had craved. His demons were bigger than I could wrestle. I could let him go. I could try to move on.

It's ironic, but not surprising, that in my choice of a mate, I married a man whose sister had committed suicide—at age eighteen—just a few weeks before we met, though I didn't find out about it until we had been dating for some time. The man I married would prove to have his own abandonment issues, which we couldn't resolve. The years after my father's suicide and before our divorce were difficult ones, with each of us depressed at different times and dealing with the depression in drastically different ways.

I realize now that I must have been depressed most of my life. The signs and symptoms were there from high school on—a feeling of grayness, that the world and my life lacked color. I was withdrawn and sometimes weepy. This created its own vicious cycle; the more withdrawn I became, the more isolated and lonely I was. I didn't know how to reach out to others or make things happen for myself. But it wasn't until a couple of years after my divorce at thirty-six that I experienced a second major depression—when a man I thought I was in love with abandoned me in a cold and dismissive way. I couldn't sleep and then couldn't get out of the bed in the morning. It was as though I was attached to the sheets with velcro. The every day tasks I had routinely managed seemed insurmountable; I was wracked with anxiety and fear. That was when I began analysis with a psychiatrist and a course of anti-depressants.

I often wonder if Dad would still be alive today if he'd had access to the new generation of anti-depressants, the SSRIs like Prozac, Paxil and Zoloft. Paxil saved my life. I doubt therapy alone would have done the trick.

Writing and my sons have given my life the meaning it seemed to lack when I was depressed. When I began writing, I reclaimed my first name, Mirinda—the creative, imaginative child who had been shut down by dutiful, first-born, good-girl Jean. I enrolled at a week-long writer's camp in the mountains of North Carolina and decided I would introduce myself as Mirinda. I was new to the camp, and no one had known me before as Jean. It was a profoundly liberating experience, and that's when I started writing regularly. Shortly after I returned to Durham from camp, I began writing commentary for public radio.

My greatest regret about bringing up my sons as a single parent, with shared custody, is that I didn't get on anti-depressants sooner. I was short-tempered and sometimes overwhelmed by the demands of parenting without the support of a spouse. My sons suffered from the divorce. They were only six when my ex and I split up. Instead of finding comfort in each other, they competed for my attention. It was as if they believed love was finite, and there wasn't enough to go around. They kept strict accounts of who got what and one always thought the other was getting the better deal. But kids are also resilient, and we muddled though somehow. Much of that period of my life is a blur of work, parenting, exhaustion and getting from one paycheck to the next. The times I remember are the times I carved out one-on-one trips or special activities with each of my sons alone. Then they could relax with me without the "twin monster" taking over. When they were old enough to understand, I told them the truth about their grandfather and the aunt on their father's side whom they will never meet. I told them about my depression and how much I regretted that it got in the way of my being a more patient, available parent.

I've taught them to be alert to signs of depression in themselves. They understand they're at risk, from both sides of the family. But I hope they've also gotten the message that depression is manageable, if not conquerable.

I've seen my sons grow into bright, capable and independent young men who, unlike me at their age, have made good things happen for themselves. They've backpacked through Europe, planning the trip and earning the money themselves; they've grown into their talents as musicians and into their own as college students. They've become fine young men who are both sons and friends.

They were an emotional anchor when my mother was dying. Though they didn't get the attention from her I would have wished for, they intuitively understood the impact of her loss on my life. My mother's death put an end once and for all to my childhood.

Every one of her generation who would have remembered me is gone. In their absence, and especially in her absence, I've lost a part of myself and my past. I mourn that just as I mourn the passing of the mother who gave me life.

About a month after Mom's death, I dreamt about her and Dad. They were sitting side by side on a park bench. Dad leaned over to kiss Mom on the cheek. At first she seemed hesitant and withdrawn, unsure that she was ready for reconciliation or for Dad's affection. He had abandoned her long before he killed himself. But in the dream, she turned to him, and he kissed her tenderly.

From the World War II era song: "I'll be seeing you in all the old familiar places, that this heart of mine embraces all day through..."

Duke University Photography, Photo by Les Todd

Mirinda Kossoff

Mirinda Kossoff has worked for *The News & Observer* and in communications and public relations for Duke University and the Hunt administration, where she won an award for speechwriting. Currently, she is communications director for Duke Law School. She is a regular columnist for the *Spectator,* a Triangle-area arts and entertainment weekly, and has been an on-air commentator for WUNC-FM and an occasional commentator for public television. She has published articles in *Self, Psychology Today, The News & Observer,* the *Louisville Courier-Journal,* the *North Carolina Independent, The*

Herald-Sun, MetroMagazine and several university alumni publications.

Mirinda has taught writing, specifically the art of the personal essay, to classes through Duke Continuing Education and the North Carolina Writers' Network and has served as a judge for several creative non-fiction competitions in North Carolina. Recently, she also co-hosted a radio show, "Avenues," that was distributed in North Carolina through the North Carolina News Network. The show is in currently in hiatus but expects to make a comeback soon.

Her twin sons, Matthew and Andy Danser, are her proudest accomplishment. Like the children of Lake Woebegon, they are smart, talented, good-looking and way above average. In the spring of 1998, the three had an adventure in Eastern Europe. They share a love of travel.

It's Not Over 'Til It's Over   Brooks Newton Preik

"It's definitely cancer... I strongly recommend a mastectomy."

I was in the recovery room of the hospital. The anesthesia was slowly wearing off. Through the crushing pounding in my head, the surgeon's words echoed. I wanted to scream, but I lay paralyzed as if imprisoned in a nightmare, trying to cry out for help, but unable to make a sound. Any minute I expected I would wake up and be able to say, "Thank God, it was only a dream." The moment came. I could finally open my eyes, and then I knew the nightmare was real. My husband sat beside me, squeezing my hand, visibly stunned and very frightened.

During the week before the surgery, I had prayed for a miracle. I prayed as I had when I was a little girl, begging God to make everything all right, trying to strike a childish bargain. "Dear God, if you'll just let it be benign, I'll..." and all sorts of promises followed. I thought of myself as a good person. I attended church on Sunday. I had sung in the choir for more than forty years. There had been ups and downs in my life, but my faith was strong, and things had always seemed to work out for the best. Surely my prayers would be answered. It took months for me to understand that they had been—but in a way far different from what I had imagined.

I grew up believing in fairy tales. Nothing in my early life prepared me for two divorces, the awesome responsibility of being a single parent to my young son and daughter, or the almost-five years of caring for my mother who suffered from increasing senility and the ravages of a stroke. At fifty-six I had dealt with my share of adversity, but my life had still been full and exciting and each time of sadness had brought with it an equal measure of joy.

For thirteen years I had been married to a wonderful man who made up for the two who were not. My children were grown and had turned out just fine—in spite of me. I had long since given up a career in teaching for the more flexible schedule of a real estate broker. Though I missed teaching, I loved what I was doing. Life was good!

Even through the pain of a mastectomy, the frustration of getting used to the aftermath, and the threat of recurring breast cancer, life remained good. In fact, it became better and better. Forced to re-examine my priorities, I soon learned the only control I had over the disease was my attitude. It was not easy, but I refused to give in to a crippling fear. Fortunately I had the support of a large and loving family and the genuine concern of many special friends. With the illness came a new awareness of the preciousness of life. I could not bear the thought of wasting a single moment.

All my life I had longed to be a writer, but I always had an excuse for not getting started. I had even taken a short writing course several years earlier and joined a writers' group, but I never seemed to be able to do anything more than critique someone else's work. As I recovered from my surgery I began to write. At first it was just a short essay about going crabbing with my dad and my brothers when I was a child. Reliving some of those fun-filled, long-ago days took my mind off myself. I soon had a piece that I thought was worthwhile. I phoned a small bimonthly publication in Southport, my hometown, and asked if they might be interested in it. They were enthusiastic but said they only paid $25 an article. Even that sounded great. Later that same day I got a call from a friend in my writers' group. A professional writer, she had just had a call from a regional magazine wanting a short article with a coastal flavor. She was not interested in the project herself, but she had given them my name as a possibility. "Don't tell them you're not a writer if they call you," she said. "Just say yes, and I'll help you with it."

They did call, and I sent them my crabbing story. They paid me $50 instead of the $25 the other magazine had offered, and they even asked me to send some vintage snapshots to use with it. The result was a beautifully designed two-page article entitled, *A Childhood Memory*. From the minute I saw my article in print, I was hooked.

My writers' group was thrilled for me, and I felt brave enough to try a few more things to show them. They cheered me on. Writing became my tonic. I didn't have time to think about myself or to worry about my illness.

A very welcome pathology report showed that my cancer had been detected in an early stage. There was no lymph node involvement. I met with my oncologist and chose not to have chemotherapy. I did agree to take tamoxifen, a much-publicized cancer drug, which had shown some very positive results in early testing. Things were definitely looking up.

My real estate work kept me busier and busier, but somehow I managed to find the time I needed to write.

The *Wilmington Magazine*, a new publication in the area, wanted a real estate article. I was contacted. The subject was an easy one for me, and they liked what I wrote. Since that time I have written thirty-five more articles for the *Wilmington Magazine* and other regional publications.

A short time later, I had the opportunity to write a ghost story for a magazine series called "Coastal Ghosts." My assignment was to write about the ghosts of Thalian Hall, a 150-year-old theatre in Wilmington, long thought to be haunted by famous actors who had appeared there. I didn't know the legends about Thalian Hall, but ghost stories had always held a fascination for me. My mother was a wonderful storyteller, and I was raised on her chilling first-hand accounts of the supernatural. I remembered, too, how much my students had enjoyed listening to spooky tales in the years when I taught elementary school. I couldn't wait to get started.

Soon I became a regular "Miss Marple," hot on the trail of anyone who had had a ghostly encounter with the thespian specters. The story was written and published and it became the catalyst for a collection of such stories that I was soon to write.

A publishing company in the area asked me to put together a book of local ghost stories. I was both flattered and apprehensive. With constant encouragement, I was able to finish the book in less than six months. *Haunted Wilmington and the Cape Fear Coast* arrived from the printer just in time for Halloween. My first book signing at Books-A-Million was a huge success; I sold over a hundred books. I couldn't have been more thrilled. I felt like a celebrity for sure.

For many months after my operation, I continued to feel better, but one problem persisted. Unable to take estrogen, which I had taken for the preceding five years, I had trouble sleeping at night. Working on the book was my salvation. During the day when I could slip away from my real job I did my research, poring over hundreds of old documents and newspaper articles in the local history room of the library. I talked with dozens of area residents, many of whom were anxious to tell of their own personal encounters with the spirit world. Others gave me helpful information and furnished clues to the elusive details of the stories. At night I would sit at my computer and write, sometimes until two or three o'clock in the morning. One night I was working on a story from the early 1800s about a man who was buried alive in St. James Churchyard. I tried to picture the story in my mind as I wrote. The process worked amazingly well and the scenes became so vivid I was scared to move—even to go downstairs to bed!

My research for the book led me in another direction as well. In gathering details for a story set in Southport, I came across some information about a great aunt of mine, Kate Stuart, who had lived there during the Civil War period. I vaguely remembered what my Aunt Josie had told me about her when I was young. It was rumored, my aunt said, that Kate and a young navy signalman, the poet Sidney Lanier, met and fell in love when he was stationed in Southport in the early 1860s. I decided to try my hand at a short story, and blending fact with fiction, I wrote about Kate and Sidney Lanier. I entered the story in a contest sponsored each year by the Lower Cape Fear Historical Society. My story won first place.

I was absolutely beside myself. It seemed as if an unseen hand might be guiding me, placing opportunities one after another in my path. I cannot decide to this day whether the opportunities had always been there and I had been too preoccupied to see them, or if an almost unbelievable sequence of events had come my way at a time when I was in great need of them. Though I had prayed for one thing, I had been given instead something that changed my life in a most remarkable way. How often that has been the case for me.

It has been almost six years since a diagnosis of cancer sent me down the path to a new career and gave an added depth and meaning to my life. My collection of ghost stories is now in its fourth printing and is still selling well. I have told those ghost stories to more than three thousand school children of all ages who love them and clamor to tell me their stories. I have spoken to civic groups, newcomer clubs, book clubs, writers' groups and many more, and my passion for writing has grown greater by the day. I've shared my personal story with countless women who have had their own experiences with breast cancer, giving them hope, and receiving inspiration from them in return.

My son and my daughter, my husband, and all of my family seem so proud of my achievements that I am truly touched. I feel that I have accomplished something in my life that will survive me and bring pleasure to others long after I am gone and that is important to me. There have been other physical problems, including an operation two years ago to remove my ovaries and a pre-cancerous ovarian cyst. But nothing keeps me from my writing for very long. I was delighted to learn that even my doctor is a ghost story fan. He was surprised and very pleased when I gave him with a copy of *Haunted Wilmington*.

For as long as I can remember, my favorite ending for a story has been "…and they lived happily ever after." Though I've faced lots of convincing difficulties to the contrary, I have somehow managed to hold onto my "fairy-tale mentality." I still wake up each morning with an almost childlike sense of wonder, waiting eagerly for the next adventure. At age sixty-two, I've come to accept that I'm never going to sing on the stage of the Metropolitan Opera as I once dreamed of doing. I also know my chances of writing a number one bestseller are pretty slim, although I'm not ruling out the possibility, nor have I given up yet on pursuing an acting career. After all that, too, is something I've always wanted to do!

Brooks Newton *Preik*

A native North Carolinian, Brooks Newton Preik was born in Southport and grew up there. She graduated from St. Mary's Junior College in Raleigh in 1958 and from the University of North Carolina at Chapel Hill in 1960 with a degree in elementary education. She taught in the public schools of Virginia, Massachusetts, and North Carolina for ten years. In 1975, she received her N.C. Real Estate Broker's License and is currently a broker and relocation director with Intracoastal Realty Corporation.

In 1995, Brooks won first prize in the Lower Cape Fear Historical Society's Short Fiction Contest for her short story "Kate." In the fall of 1995, her book *Haunted Wilmington and the Cape Fear Coast* was published by Banks Channel Books and is currently in its fourth printing. The book, a collection of "true" ghost stories, has become a regional bestseller.

Brooks has published articles in *Carolina Style, Wilmington Coast Magazine, Encore,* and *Coastwatch.* She is a feature writer for the *Wilmington Magazine.*

Maudy Benz an interview

Generally where we start is just at the beginning, where you grew up and where you went to school.

Well, I grew up in a town called Adrian, Michigan, which is kind of a triangle between Toledo, Ohio, and Ann Arbor, Michigan—a couple hours from Detroit. A town with about 20,000 people, with a couple of small colleges, one called Adrian College. The schools were good. But it was definitely a peripheral manufacturing town for the auto industry. And then there were the executives and the doctors—but it was, in a way, a poor and a wealthy town with more poor people. Very industrially influenced.

And when you were a child, what were your career dreams? What did you think you might do?

Well, I was always going to get out of Adrian. (*Laughs.*) And I think I first wanted to be a neurosurgeon. I came from a medical family and so I felt like I had to be in a medical field. It was one of my first dreams. But I always wrote; and there was a lot of appreciation for art and literature, because my father grew up in Ann Arbor. We spent, probably, three days a week there. And I went to all the serious plays, including Arthur Miller reading from his own work on 'Adam and Eve.'

I saw such incredibly new work, cutting-edge work. Gosh, the great poets. I think Auden was there, and Brodsky...Donald Hall was teaching there. I really was steeped in the culture of literature and theater, so I often wanted to be an actress. I wrote all the time, too, but I didn't really give that validity. 'Cause I thought that was something that wasn't a profession, that I couldn't do. But I did it secretly. I sort of hid my work.

And then as you grew into adulthood, how did your dreams change? Did you keep writing, or did you put it aside?

Well, I did keep writing. I always wrote poetry. Poetry was, for me, almost a religious form that I went to for spiritual comfort. So, I read many of the major poets, more women than men. Not the intellectual poets; more emotive poets. I always continued to write poetry throughout my life. And my dreams...actually, I started out studying English. English literature, my first year. I didn't like the college I went to. It's called Depauw and it's in Southern Indiana. It was really frat/sorority-oriented and there really wasn't any culture there.

That sounds debasing...I was just used to being in a college town where there was a lot happening culturally. There wasn't anything going on there. The Indy 500 was the biggest thing and it was like an hour away. I wanted to transfer, so I went back to

Michigan. And they couldn't read my handwriting on my application, so it got shuttled aside and I didn't get in until very late. At that time, I entered the nursing school, because I could get in that late. Then I was going to transfer out, back into literature. But once I got into nursing...you know, I have a real need to communicate; that's why I like teaching and helping people. I really became quite seduced by the field of nursing, in particular the hard sciences. I was taking anatomy and physiology, which were really kind of like art, when you get to the higher levels of it.

So, I stayed in nursing, which was probably a mistake. But I still wrote. In fact, I skipped nursing school for two months, I didn't go to a single class in my second year, and I attended Donald Hall's poetry class. And I wrote an essay. This is really kind of sad, but a good story in the end. I wrote an essay on a James Wright poem, 'Lying In Hammock on William Duffy's Farm in something Minnesota.' I can't remember the town. It's a beautiful poem.

The T.A. called me and said, 'You know, you really have a gift for writing and writing about literature.' And I went home to my room and cried for several hours, and never returned to the class. I see it now, after years of therapy, as the inability to succeed in what I really loved and perhaps to be vulnerable, I think, to exploring emotions? And all that was sort of brought up. So I left the class, and twenty years later, when I went to Bennington, there was Donald Hall teaching.

And there I was writing with Donald Hall again. And there he was telling me I had a gift and then I got my M.F.A. in writing, which was a triumph. But, you know, it took me all those years to accept that this is what I loved. And it was OK to be good at it. And, you know, I could pursue it and I did.

So, can you recount for me the path of those twenty years, in brief—what you did and what directions your life took?

Well, I always wrote poetry. I worked in nursing for a couple of years around Michigan. And then I decided to go to North Carolina, mostly because I really wanted to. I fell in love with Chapel Hill while I was looking at colleges. And they didn't take women at the time. You had to go to Greensboro.

So in my mind, I kept thinking, 'OK, I want to go to graduate school in Chapel Hill.' And I decided to study developmental disabilities in kids and stay in the medical field. I came down here and got a master's in pediatric nursing, in developmental disabilities, and then I started working with families who had babies that were born with problems. And, you know, I think it was a really worthwhile and rewarding occupation for a single person as I was then.

But I still wrote poetry. And at that time, in the late seventies, I was beginning to publish poetry and do readings. I was in a poetry group at the art school, first formed in Carrboro. Once I moved down to Chapel Hill, got some separation from that medical model of my family, I began to pursue my work more seriously.

And then I decided I was leaving nursing. That was a really big moment. I started working at a restaurant because I could write during the day and work at night. So, I did that for several years and then I got married and started having children and I decided I would do a business. Umm...and that's why I developed my floral/catering business. I was a painter at that time, as well as a poet.

Had you always painted, or did that come later?

Well, it came really as a result of taking art classes and design classes, because I was really trying to discover what form of creation I would be best fitted for. I was always trying to go into something practical like interior design, still holding to this idea that one had to be practical. (*Laughs.*) Then I took some art classes. And once I took the art classes, I married an artist. I would do automatic drawings on cocktail napkins when I was bored at parties. And then these paintings came out of drawings that were really from the unconscious. So then the floral business came out of liking to compose; you know, compositions and arranging flowers are really sort of like painting. And it gave me something to

do that was mostly on the weekends; I could write during the week and take care of my children.

So I did that for eleven or twelve years, here in Chapel Hill. And then in the early '80s, I just one day wrote a story instead of a poem. I think it had to do with having children, in that their lives were always full of something happening that was like a narrative rather than poetry, with more spirituality. That was the beginning of writing stories. And then I won a little prize for that story, and I thought, 'Oh my gosh, wow!'

That's pretty amazing. So did that scare you off in any way?

No, it didn't—I guess because I had gone to a shrink for a long time (*laughs*) to help me accept success. No, it didn't scare me. I kept writing and then I studied with Lee Smith. I heard her on the radio and she sounded so...I just loved her voice. It was calling me to come to her class, so I called her and she said 'Come on in!' So I did. Then I began more seriously writing the short story. And I still was doing the floral thing. And then I decided to write a novel.

I told Lee what I wanted to do, and she said, 'Well, all I can say is that you've got the skills, so just go and do it!' (*Laughs.*) So I did, but it was just really hard. And it took me many years.

What was your feeling when you finished it?

You know, maybe I did seven drafts. And after the first draft, I felt that I had crossed a great body of water, in a boat without oars...or a sail...or anything. (*Laughs.*) I wasn't in a writers' group or anything. For some reason I had this notion that I had to write this book completely on my own. I didn't want people to know, I was very secretive about it. So, I think it took longer. I don't know that I would do that now. It was always hard to finish each draft, kind of sad, you know? It felt like you were leaving that world. It was like closure.

Then I went to Bennington, because I felt there was still something about the book...it was getting interests from agents and such, but not really settling into a place. I just felt it needed to be worked on in an environment where there were mentors. So that was my decision, to go to Bennington, along with the idea and commitment that I would make writing my life instead of the extra thing I did.

When the book was published, did that make a significant change in your mindset or in your life?

It had a great amount of confidence-building. The most elemental thing is that the story was important to me to tell. And I had communicated it and it had gone out into that river of literature beyond me, which is what you hope for your children and you hope for anything that you love and have influence upon—

that it will go out and become part of something that lives without you. And just to go out with it and meet some of the people who were influenced—women would write and tell me that it had helped them deal with sexual abuse. I think that to communicate is the end product, the last state where you want your piece to be—to be a communicator. If it's not published, it's very hard to accept that you haven't been able to say what you set out to. So, that was the best part.

The accomplishment, the book world, all that is very confusing because the book world has become very commercial and that's why presses like yours are very important now. The book world wants to develop careers, personalities, and there is a lot of hype and glossy material. The industry has really...contracted...to maybe having five or six companies in New York that will look at your work now. All the imprints are owned by one bigger company. So, the downside of this was facing the capitalism of publishing. And you know, coming to terms with that, after publishing with both the small press and then the big presses and seeing the differences...it has changed my life in many ways. In other words, I'm going into writing a new book and I really go into it with all the innocence taken away from my view of the publishing world. And I'll write a book just because, once again, I love it and I want to write it and it's the story I want to tell. Not because I'm trying to have a second book for the publishers to turn out.

There was a little period where I had to deal with that mentality and sort of shake it off. And a little bit of an adjustment to what I see is a brutal capitalistic situation in publishing that I don't like. But, it's there. Although I do think that university presses and small presses are taking the place of what the literary editors did at the bigger presses.

What do you think have been your greatest challenges along the path of your life thus far?

Well, I think it has partially has been that vulnerability or lack of confidence, the fear of success that drove me out of Donald's class. And even now it's hard writing a second novel, having had some success, in terms of getting to be a noteworthy paperback in *The New York Times*. It's a little hard for me to internalize what I've accomplished and build on it; that's probably been one of the hardest things. That and this need to equate—I think this comes from living in a capitalistic country—accomplishment with making money. And when you write literary novels, unless Oprah finds you, you generally do not make a lot of money from the books. You can do all right teaching, which I love, but you know, that has been a struggle for me.

Has it been a challenge for you to balance your family and career throughout all the different careers that you have had?

Well, more now because I think my children have needed me in the last year in really very poignant ways. But, generally, I've been able to do that and I think it's been very good for the kids. They went on my book tour with me. And, you know, my son would get up and tell stories about me in the question period time (*laughs*) and my daughter would be like, 'I don't want anything to do with her. This book is too upsetting for me to read...' But they each had their role in that. When I was doing flowers, they were walking around, pulling the flowers out of the containers. I did things in my house so I could be around them, and so that's how I balanced it. It's always hard, timewise.

Was it difficult given that your husband, at the time, was an artist too—were there jealousies that arose from that in trying to balance both of your creative work?

Yeah, there were. It was hard when I started writing because it wasn't his medium and he tried to critique things, which he shouldn't have done. And it would be very difficult. When I had successes he seemed to be happy, and I was happy for his successes. I think what happened more was that the difficulty of succeeding in artistic endeavors can be daunting. And if we both got into that feeling of it being so hard, it wasn't good (*laughs*). But I actually think that we helped each other, and it was actually common ground for us—that we both loved art.

What personal qualities do you consider to be of the most value in life?

I think an inner vision that is solidly one's own, that is not dependent on the opinions of others to sustain it. Not to say that one doesn't need other people for love and everything. We are interdependent, but the vision—if you're an artist, writer—really is one's own. And to able to adhere to it and stay with it, without needing others to say 'Yes, it's right' or 'Yeah, I get it'—because there are so many opinions that could change what you do.

I have a writer's group and I take them things I can't work out, which for me is a new thing—to go to a group and show my work when I'm working on it. And I listen, but the vision itself needs to be one's own and one should have confidence in it.

Is there one way that you have evolved as a human being over the course of your life that makes you the proudest?

I think I have followed my dreams, which have been difficult for me to achieve. I didn't just go to school at Hollins and start writing, which a lot of people have done. But I got there, finally, in my own way. So, that makes me proud. The other thing I'm really happy about is that I promote the arts by writing reviews. I wrote a review for the *Washington Post*, a dance review just recently, and I've reviewed a dance festival here. And I'm writing a cultural arts column for *Metro* magazine, where I try to promote the arts that I think are really important and need support. That's kind of a mission I have, aside from my own work.

How did that evolve? Did that come before writing your own work, or was it something that came afterwards, as people recognized your name and asked you to write?

It really came before I had the success of my novel. I simply decided. I was studying non-fiction at Bennington, because I'm interested in non-fiction as well as fiction. So, I did book reviews and I decided that since I was doing book reviews I would actually do them for newspapers, as practice, because that's taking it to another level. And so I started doing reviews, and then the N&O hired me as a literary correspondent and I did some interviews. I did Joyce Carol Oates. It just came out of my pursuing something I was doing in school.

What advice would you have about breaking into doing literary reviews, in terms of the process?

How did I make that happen? I think it's good to start with a paper that is local and easier to access, and that's what I did. Once you get a review or two, then you can go out to other papers and use those reviews as examples of your work. And I think you just have to call the editor; I think they are always looking for people to do freelance journalism. It's not something that is that hard to break into. But it's like a catch-22. You've got to get your first review so you can show it to them. Take a class on book review writing. Just get the form down. And then you just have to get on the phone. (*Laughs.*)

What qualities do you feel you possess that make your career a natural choice for you?

That's a very hard question, because I think a literary career really requires a person to have two areas in which you're strong, that are very different. One is to be a very interior person who develops stories, impressions, idiosyncratic impressions of events, stored memory in a sort of narrative way—a somewhat dreamy, poetic person who is reflective. That's very important, and there is the will to create the work and the drive, the continuing momentum. The ability to say, 'This is going to be good, even though it's taking so long to create it.' To keep moving through something, to stay with it. That's the more introverted side, the person who will stay inside and work for seven hours writing, and then look at what they've written for days at a time. And then there is the other side of being a person who is more extroverted, who can go out and communicate the work, meet people, be an ambassador for the message or the book itself. That takes a totally different kind of person. It's great if you can have both of them. It's a funny combination—I think I have it. I have to keep it in balance, though. Sometimes one gets...I think the promotional

part of me got overdeveloped when the book came out. You know, I'm into hibernating again.

Are there qualities of yours that you need to work against in order to sit down and write and then showcase your work?

I think I have to let go of promoting my baby, when the book finally runs its course. Just recently, when I went to Santa Fe, I could have gone to bookstores and signed books. And I just let it go, because I just feel like I have to move on to the developmental stages of my story collection, which I think is going to come out in the coming year or year and a half. I have some work to do on that, and this new novel that I'm working on which I'm halfway through. I have to let go of trying to make things work all the time, for the work that's out there. Because I'll spend a lot of time on that.

Of what professional and personal accomplishments do you think you're the most proud?

Well, I think, personally, it's definitely raising the children. And, being a good friend. Developing long-term relationships. I feel I am responsive to my friends, and sensitive. And I think as a writer, sometimes you're working, and you know, it's just as easy not to return a phone call (*laughs*), but it's important to do that. And professionally? I guess the publication of my novel has been a great validation for me. And teaching. I absolutely love teaching. I find my students actually often give me the courage to do more work. Because they're so honest, and forthright, and vulnerable. I teach memoir, so they're not hiding behind the fictional world, like I do some of the time. But I do write some memoir, too.

In terms of disappointment or strife, what sources of inspiration and renewal do you turn to?

I think...the lives of other writers and artists who held to their visions. And, I have to say, who also held to lives that, I feel, are lives well lived. Lives in which they cared for their children, their family. And I admire people who have taken a position, politically or otherwise, to help the world.

Is there anything that you would do differently if you could turn back the clock?

You know, that's such a hard question. I have to think of the clock now. And of these two works that await my attention. There are writers who live extremely solitary lives. Philip Roth is now holed up alone writing seven days a week, and I don't want to aspire to that. 'Cause I want to be with my family and children, I have to be. So, the clock, I think, has already run this far and I don't like to think about—you know, had I stayed in Donald Hall's class, I might have been a professor of literature and not written a novel. I don't like to ask myself that question too much 'cause I'll beat myself up. (*Laughs.*)

What advice do you think you might give either young women just starting out in a career, or older women considering a career change?

I think, do something you love. Something you have a real passion for. It's the same thing when you marry; you should marry someone you really love. You want to get into a career that you really love, and have a passion for, and then get some education and support, get connected. Let some people help you and don't try to go at it alone; I think that's very difficult. But loving something and having people whose opinion is critical tell you, 'You're doing a good job and this is something you can do.' That's certainly edifying.

What dreams do you have that are yet to be realized, both personal and professional?

Well, I'm remodeling a house. So, my dream is to finish the remodeling, which has been hard to balance with writing. It really has. But once I get in there, I intend to really get to work on the new novel and, in the interim, work on the stories. The dream, I think, is to finish the next novel. And personally, to have a relationship, with the man I'm with, and with my children, and my friends, my community, and to support causes I believe in, and to continue to support the arts. And my writing.

Well, wonderful. Thank you.

Interviewed by Emily A. Colin.

"Do something you love. Something you have a real passion for."
Maudy Benz

"Poetry was, for me, almost a religious form that I went to for spiritual comfort."
Maudy Benz

Maudy *Benz*

Kirkus Reviews called Maudy Benz's novel *Oh, Jackie* "a stylish first novel" and "a frank and convincing portrait of a young woman's painful coming of age." In *The New York Times Book Review* Sally Eckhoff wrote, "Benz tells North's story with tenderness and impressive control." *Oh, Jackie* has been on Ingram's "distinctive title" list, was featured in Borders stores nationally and was a finalist for The Discover Great New Writers Series. The paperback edition in Berkeley's Signature Series was named noteworthy paperback by *The New York Times Book Review*. Ms. Benz's lead story from her collection *Dear Princess Di* appeared in the Winter issue 2000 of *The Virginia Quarterly Review*. The collection is a continuation of

Benz's exploration of female icons and how they affect the women who admire them. Other stories have been recently published in *Ontario Review, Farmers Market* and the *Madison Review*. Earlier stories won citations from the Nelson Algren Award, the *Mademoiselle* fiction contest, and *Sing Heavenly Muse's* fiction contest. Maudy Benz has written on literary culture for *The News & Observer* and has written memoir for *The Oxford American Magazine*. She has covered the American Dance Festival for several years for *Spectator & The Independent*. She has reviewed dance for *The Washington Post*.

Benz performs text and image shows from her fiction. *"My Novel, My Life"* was performed at the Duke University Museum of Art in 1998. She was a fellow in fiction at the Wesleyan Writers Conference; taught at Writing Women's Lives, Santa Fe; and will teach at the Iowa Summer Writing Festival as well as at Duke University.

Elizabeth Cox an interview

Why don't we start with where you grew up and went to school?

I grew up in Chattanooga, Tennessee, and lived for the first twenty-one years of my life in a boys' private school—Baylor School, where my father was headmaster. I went to a public school, city high school there. Then I went to the University of Tennessee. I ended up graduating from Ole Miss. I went there the same year James Meredith went, which had an effect on me. It felt as though I was in a war, seeing the anger and the turmoil of that semester.

What career dreams did you have as a child, and how did those change?

Well, I was raised in the forties and fifties, so I really wasn't expected to be anything except a wife and mother. Wasn't encouraged to be anything except that. I married young—when I was twenty-one—I met my husband when I was sixteen. I had children in my twenties. In my early thirties I began to write poetry. Both of my brothers had published books of poems and I thought, 'I can do that.' I had written poetry as a child—I had a little book of poems—but nothing much was said about it. You know, I really wasn't encouraged in that way.

I had a few poems published and I went back to get my master's at University of North Carolina in Greensboro working with Fred Chappell and Robert Watson. I got my M.F.A., I did my thesis in poetry, though during that time I began to be interested in writing fiction, and I wanted to write a story. When I did, it felt as though I already understood more about telling a story than I did about writing a poem. I began writing stories and then I went to a writer's conference in Saranac Lake, New York. I met a man named Charles Simmons and another man named E. L. Doctorow. They praised a story I'd written—it was my first story—and they suggested that I write a novel. So, that...began. I had that story published and so I began from there...writing fiction.

What do you think had been your greatest challenges along your path to that point?

To that point? Trying to believe that I could do something other than being a wife and mother. As I began to get published my marriage ended and I was raising children by myself for about twelve years. Then I remarried a man who lives in Boston and is Editor of the *Atlantic Monthly*. My greatest challenge was having the confidence to continue to write, when, growing up, I really wasn't encouraged to do anything.

In those times when your marriage was ending, what were your sources of inspiration or renewal?

Just my own imagination. I love waking up in the morning and I've always loved that, even in tough times. Nothing ruins waking up in the morning. Probably that sense allowed me to stay in touch with the imaginative process. I had ideas for stories, I had ideas for novels, and I wanted to try and make them work. I did have encouragement from people in the business at writer's conferences I would go to—agents, editors. An editor from *The New Yorker* named Chip McGrath—Charles McGrath—encouraged me. So, that was very helpful and I'm grateful for that.

How did you come to teach?

I adored teaching. When my first novel was published, someone at Duke—Victor Strandberg—suggested that I teach a course there. I don't have a Ph.D., but I guess my novel—or my novels—are my Ph.D. I began teaching there about sixteen years ago. I was Adjunct for several years and then they brought me on to the faculty. I continue to teach there even though I live in Boston. They have graciously allowed me to teach one semester a year, so that I get to still be part of the Duke community—and I love that community.

But I also taught when my first husband was in medical school. I taught in Memphis and Kentucky, and wherever we lived, in special education. I taught kids who were retarded or brain dam-

aged or hydrocephalic. I had a class of about fifteen students of very different kinds of problems and capabilities—a cerebral palsied boy was in that class. It was interesting because each child in that class...the age range was wide and the abilities were varied, and I had to reach into each child's capability and help them to be whatever they could.

It's very similar in creative writing. It helps me to teach in that way. To not have a blanket way of doing something, but to listen to each student and see the kind of voice or the kind of writing or the kind of imaginative process that is their own.

What do you think are some of your greatest joys about teaching?

Watching the students awaken to their imaginations. Seeing this kind of light come into their face as they become aware of the possibilities of that imaginative process.

Was it hard—a challenge for you—to balance your family and your writing in a time when you were raising your children on your own?

My son was sixteen, so he was going off to college and my daughter was twelve. My husband provided alimony so that no, it wasn't hard because I had the time to do both teaching and writing because of the money that he provided. He was very generous. I had helped him through medical school for about twelve, fifteen years and he helped me through the years until I got on my feet with my writing.

And when you're not writing and you're not teaching, how do you relax?
I read, I travel, I take long walks.

Do you have personal interests or goals that you're currently pursuing?
I just finished a book of short stories. I am working on a novel that I want to finish. It has to do with violence children do to other children...and the world it's created...the world we create that allows that to happen. I have a book of essays I'm working on that have to do with teaching and writing and place. I'm still working on a manuscript of poems that was started many years ago that I'm trying to publish. I have started another book that's sort of a journal. I'm not thinking too much about publishing it but as I'm writing it I'm thinking, 'Well, this might be publishable.' But I'm just trying to stay true to each day and see what patterns develop. I have ideas for more stories which would go into another book of stories. And I'm still teaching, so...

What do you think is the one way that you've evolved as a human being that makes you the proudest?
Well, I don't think I've gotten there yet...but I think to be more awake and more present in every moment of the day. I think I've progressed along that line. I think I still have a long

way to go.

What personal qualities do you consider to be of the most value in life?
Love and honesty.

Are there concrete ways that you've tried to pass that on to your children?
Oh, yes. Reminding them of ways to be loving. Being aware of the ways I'm not loving and admitting it. Accepting that part of myself so that I accept that part of them. Believing in them...believing in them completely. And encouraging honest conversation.

Of what professional accomplishment do you think you're the proudest?
Professional? I was going to say my children...Professionally I think my novels and my teaching.

Did you find that motherhood came naturally to you, or was it something that you had to work at?
Came naturally.

Why do you think that was?
Well, because of my own mother, I think it came naturally. I had parents who were very loving—as well as demanding, but very loving. I found that with very young babies, it was more

difficult than when they got old enough to relate to and where they had a stronger sense of themselves. That complete dependence, when they were real babies, was not my favorite time.

What, if anything, do you think you might do differently if you could turn back the clock?

Well, you know, I really don't have any regrets. I do feel that the failure of my first marriage was a huge failure. But somehow some very good things came out of that, and I am so completely happy in my marriage to Michael Curtis that I can't imagine feeling any regrets.

Who were your heroes, both growing up and now, too?

Anyone who risks something for the sake of others. Anyone who does that. Mother Teresa *(laughs)*. You know, Gandhi...Martin Luther King. People who, no matter if they have other things about them that may not be wonderful, they have done something with their life that has affected others. Maybe...maybe if I think of regret at the end of my life...if I have not done that, then I will regret it.

What advice do you think you would give a young woman who was just starting out in a career, or an older woman considering a career change?

To do it. Do it. To not let a lack of confidence stop you,

because nobody is confident from what I can see. *(Laughs.)* Everybody is sort of faking it. I know that with students—especially those who are middle-aged—I teach in the Bennington Writing Seminars, a graduate program; and the students will talk about confidence and not having it. They're kind of waiting for it. I tell them not to wait for it because as far as I can see, I'm not sure that it comes except in spurts. Just to love the work, whatever work you choose, and to be faithful to that and not to think about whether you're getting attention or praise or the amount of...publishing or...not to wait for someone else to tell you you're good.

What dreams do you have that are yet to be realized, either personal or professional?

Well, I want to write more novels and stories and essays and journals...but I want to do something. You know, I told you of the people I admired...I haven't done something that has made a difference in other people's lives yet, and I don't know if I ever will. Teaching does. My writing doesn't yet; it would be nice if it would. I don't know yet what I will do—that I *hope* I will do—that will be the thing that finishes my life.

Interviewed by Emily A. Colin.

Elizabeth Cox

Elizabeth Cox earned her undergraduate degree from the University of Mississippi, and a master's of fine arts in creative writing from UNC-Greensboro. She has published three novels: *Familiar Ground* (Atheneum, 1984; paperback Avon, 1986), *The Ragged Way People Fall Out of Love* (North Point Press, 1991; paperback HarperCollins, 1992), and *Night Talk* (Graywolf Press, 1997, paperback, St. Martin's Press). The latter won the 1998 Lillian Smith Book Award, given to books that raise the social consciousness and promote harmony between the races. She has also written essays for *Ms. Magazine*, *North Carolina Magazine*, and *The Oxford American*.

Random House has recently offered Ms. Cox a two-book contract for her collection of short stories, *Bargains in the Real World*, to be published in spring 2001, and for her next novel, *The Children's Hour*, to be published in spring 2002.

She teaches writing the spring semester each year at Duke University, and has taught in the graduate writing programs at the University of Michigan, Tufts University, Boston University, and in the undergraduate programs at the University of North Carolina-Chapel Hill and Bennington College. She has taught for five years in the Low Residency Graduate Writers Program at Bennington College.

Ms. Cox, who has two grown children, lives in Littleton, Massachusetts, with her husband, C. Michael Curtis.

Jaki Shelton Green an interview

Where did you grow up and where did you go to school?

I grew up in Efland, North Carolina, which is in Orange County, during the advent of desegregation in North Carolina. I actually was one of about nine African-American students who were a part of the 'Freedom of Choice.' There was this 'Freedom of Choice' kind of experimental plan where you could just send your kid—you signed up. And my family signed 'yes,' so I was one of about nine kids to integrate this junior high school, and life was not fun! And then, of course, after that, they consolidated. They closed the one black high school, which was Central High School, and all of the African-American students went to Orange High School.

I got kicked out of Orange High School in the tenth grade for helping to organize—and participating in—a walkout in a list of demands about the inclusion of African-American students on student government bodies, the inclusion of African-American literature in courses to select from. I think one grievance was, you know, 'hire more African-American teachers,' etc., etc., etc. And we all were kicked out. I think it was about eighty-some of us.

And the criteria for which people were allowed to come back to school was if your family would sign a paper stating that their child or student would never participate in any other civil disobedience act—would not demonstrate or participate in any marches or walkouts or whatever. About five students held out—those five transferred to other schools—and my family said, 'No, we're not transferring her out of Orange County schools. This is where we pay taxes,' and 'No, we're not signing away her civil liberties and agreeing with you to violate her right to protest, because this is what we've taught her—to question wrong—and she's coming back to school.' My family threatened a lawsuit and I was allowed to come back to school. I was branded once I came back. I was back in, but there were some pretty racist older teachers in that school system and people were terrified of me. You know, 'this little troublemaker' was back in school. So my grades plummeted. I was a really good 'A-B' student and it was like—if I sneezed, I was in trouble.

So, to make a long story short, I applied for and scored very, very high on SSAT examinations to go to secondary private schools—and pretty much had my choice of where I wanted to go to school. I selected and was accepted to go to the George School. And this was through the 'ABC' Program which stands for 'A Better Chance.' It is out of Boston, and it still continues to recruit and place gifted African-American students in secondary private schools who, historically, would not have the opportunity to go there, pretty much based on economics which was my case—my parents could not have afforded to send me away to a private school. So that was really, I would say, the beginning of a different kind of education for me. You know, I was in Pennsylvania, I was in a Quaker school. The codes were different, the norms were different, the nuances—it was just totally different.

What career dreams did you have as you were growing up?

That's really interesting because my biggest dream was to become an oceanographer. And my daddy pretty much—early on, my family showed me there was no ocean in the backyard, I had never been to the ocean, I didn't even know where the ocean *lived*, and they didn't think this was very practical.

I come from a family of teachers. Everybody in my family is a teacher, has a degree in education. My mom's sisters, one of their husbands is a professor, their children *(laughs)*—and I really didn't want to do that, but I ended up getting a bachelor's in early childhood education which I have used very little.

Umm, *never* wanted to be a writer, never said in life I wanted to be a writer, did not see writing as a vocation, growing up. Did not know any writers growing up, didn't really have my arms around it. My grandmother continually would tell me a story about her grandmother who had been punished for the knowledge of knowing how to read and write. And so my grandmother

always had this very, almost—how can I say this?—sort of romantic, sort of mystical place in her being about reading and writing and education. I mean, for her, it was just the epitome, as it should be, for people who want to empower and be achievers. So her thing was, 'This is what you will do. You will be a writer. You will read. You will write.'

So I started writing when I was very, very young. And my favorite place to write as a child was—I would sit in church and I would write stories, predominantly about the women's hats, and make up stories about their hats and would just sit there and be fascinated by the theater of church and all that went on. And funerals and rituals. Really, community ritual has been one of the things that's really informed my writing and is sort of, contextually, how I create characters and place and stage ambience for situations in my poetry as well as in the novel I'm working on.

Do you have a career in addition to poet/playwright?

Yes. For the past ten or twelve years, I've been a paralegal for Legal Services of North Carolina, and I work out of North State Legal Services which is an office in Hillsborough. And I have a master's in community economic development.

How do you balance the two?

Well, since I started writing as a child, writing was this outlet for me. It was this place to go. It was this escape. And growing up in Efland is a whole 'nother story we can have because it's a very rural community where I learned to be present but also kind of have this other life going on in my head through my writing, because I was bored all the time. So that sort of duality of existence, I carried on into my adult life.

I married pretty young—had children pretty young. So I had to balance being a mom, being a full-time caretaker. Fortunately, my husband was a professor, we had a pretty affluent life then, and I could stay home. I was a homemaker and mom. And my day—my days, my weeks—were centered around being a nurturer, and I was like sort of the epitome of 'Mother Jones' for my children. It was the seventies. (*Laughs.*) We were vegetarians and baking bread and—nothing commercial going into my children's little bodies—you know, puréeing fruits and doing all this stuff.

And then I would write. I would write in the wee hours of the morning, I would write during their naps. I managed to learn how to capture that time for myself, and perhaps that's something I learned from my mother who had to work really hard to raise us, but she always made sure she had time for herself. She had her rituals. And I grew up creating those rituals for myself, making sure that I had my own sacred space where I needed to go. For me, it was writing. Now, I embrace writing a little differently because I will not allow writing to be my life. It's one of the

things I do in my life, one of the things I enjoy doing, but I don't want to be a slave to it anymore than I want to be a slave to my nine-to-five job. So, you know, I would create those times to write. And I had a partner who was willing to, when he came home from teaching, make it possible for me to just sort of go to what I needed to go to—the library or a long walk or to the bedroom, to seclusion, to just write in my journal or to work on some poems I was revising.

So I continued that balance. I've always been a working-class writer—never had the resources to just go off and say, 'I'm going to the beach for the summer to work on this novel' or 'I'm going to my little chalet to work.' I have been blessed that I've gotten fellowships and grants over the years where I did go away to the Virgin Islands. I was doing some research, but also it was a very restive time alone to get some serious writing done. And *Conjure Blues* sort of was a product of my having that downtime to just write. But I don't flourish on needing retreat space. I have to create it because, again, for me to write a poem—even to *read* a poem—to me, to take on all that language gives me a lot of energy. And that energy kind of comes out as an activist, even activist for the work I do with low-income people as a paralegal, or a creative-artist activist. So I kinda like being present, you know what I mean? I need to know how to make art—how to do this the same way my ancestors did this. They didn't name themselves artists, but the incredible pottery and the quilts and all of the art forms I've managed to keep, to preserve, kind of 'memorabilia' of my family—I know those objects were not made in studios. That art was a part of their living, was a part of the life, it was utilitarian, it was functional. So that's what drives that balance.

How did it feel to have your very first work published?

Oh, it was terrifying, just absolutely terrifying. Because then you're out there, you know. I was very excited, but then it dawned on me—people are going to see it. They're going to have things to say. I won't always agree with the things they want to say. So it was learning that, when you do this, you don't own it anymore. People say, 'Well, how do you deal with rejections and negative reviews?' I say, 'Well, you know, it's like once you put it out there, it's not yours anymore.' I mean, you have no control over the response to it. I made it, but when people buy my books, I don't know if they take 'em home and read them or if they use them for door-stops or they're holding up the commode—I have no idea. So I just have to celebrate the fact that I wrote these words, people come to listen to them, people enjoy them, sometimes people are challenged by them. I name it my art and I don't create it to shove down anybody's throats. I think the politicization of it for me is to be a woman and then to be a woman of color who has the audacity to have voice in this culture.

So it's always exciting, you know, and as I grow older and see new works come out, it's very, very exciting and it's humbling. And there's something very mysterious just about—you know *where* you wrote these words and *when* you wrote them and then you see them gathered all together in this professional book and you look at certain poems and go, 'Hmm, I wrote you on the back of the light bill.' Or this poem was written on the back of the bag from Sears in the car on the way home. Or this was written on the back of the bar napkin. Or this was written on a sticky pad in this boring board of directors meeting. It's fun to see these little ramblings show up in book form.

Do you save the Sears bags and sticky notes and bar napkins?

I have. I used to. I used to have just bags and bags and boxes and boxes, you know, where I was calling 'the archival material.' (*Laughs.*) I have some of it, and of course, over the years, I've trashed some of it as well.

Some things can be tough to let go.

Yeah, yeah. (*Laughs.*) But you can't keep it all!

In times of disappointment or strife, what are your sources of inspiration or renewal?

Writing. If I can *write* it out, the healing starts. I can feel the healing at the base of my fingertips, you know, *if* I can write, if I can just get rage to page. That has been very cathartic for me.

The other thing is housecleaning. (*Laughs.*) When I'm troubled, I clean. And people who really know me know that, when my house is messy, I'm kind of just in a state of bliss and just walking through my days and kind of insular and not paying attention to the external. But when there's a fly in my eye, I clean. I have created this wonderful sacred space in terms of my home that I really love and enjoy. And so that's another source of inspiration.

The other source is to bring forth—to hear the lessons that I've been taught by my grandmother, my mother, my aunts, wise women in my life, women that helped, when I say 'raise me,' I mean just *that*. When I think of my childhood, I think of the way we raise barns or raise houses, you know, or raise buildings in the architectural world. That raising is built on the lessons I've learned sitting at the feet of women and being a witness. You know, working with legal services, you're very humbled by people's problems. And just knowing that I've somehow survived the crises in my life, somehow I know that I'm blessed. I've survived a lot of real crazy stuff in my life—two crazy divorces, a child who became ill just slam out of nowhere, and continuing to be a caretaker for that child who's an adult now. And divorce left me penniless for awhile, and having to overcome that. But fortunately

and prayerfully, I had these incredible models around me—of women who had made worlds out of nothing. And that's the fabric that I'm woven from. That's who I am. And I can celebrate it with a lot of pride and a lot of confidence.

And then another thing is prayer—just knowing how to be prayerful and respecting the gifts of nature and the gifts from lifesprings and life sources and knowing how to go there and get it when I need it. And then reading I should not discount. I have just an incredible appetite for reading. Reading has sustained me. When I can't write, I read. When I can't do either, I dance.

Tell me about your family.

I have three children—Imani's twenty-nine and a psychologist and a wonderful woman. My son Segun is twenty-seven and just a real beautiful young man, very gentle and sweet and warm. And he's a licensed barber by trade, but has not been able to have his profession due to an illness for the past four or five years. And there's Eva, my baby, who's named for my grandmother. And she will be twenty this year and she is a sophomore in college, Spanish major. They've grounded me—and the writing too—and made me realize, just by their existence, that writing is what I do—it's not who I am. And making very sure not to neglect them because, you know, art is a very jealous mistress. She *wants* you when she *wants* you when she *wants* you. And I've had to be careful in wanting to give so much energy to my writing. As a divorced single mom, that balance was fragile for me. It had to be in check at all times.

What are some personal interests or goals that you're currently pursuing?

I really want to be able to throw myself full-throttle into this novel that I've been working on for about three years. And this is where I really would like a big fellowship. (*Laughs.*) To just have a year—I just want a year—to write. I've never had that because, as the only source of income for my family, I've had to work. But now as my children get older and now that I'm thinking of remarrying after seventeen years, I feel like I can give myself permission to look at that differently, to let go a little bit of needing to be totally in control of my life and maybe being a little reckless by trying to negotiate with myself—and my job—how I could do this.

Gardening. I really want to become a good gardener because, for me, the connection of earth to life—to *my* life—is so important. And, you know, my grandmother was a woman who would dig in the earth every day of her life. I don't care how cold, how hot, she was out digging, hands in the ground. And as a child and even as a young adult, I remember she was always talking while she was working, while she was digging. And when she was troubled, that's what she did—she went to the earth, she went and planted something or *replanted* something or weeded something or plucked something. And I have that same need right now. You know, writing the novel—continuing to be able to write and produce, to print word—I guess I'm more inside of myself right now in terms of what I want. I feel if I can continue to evolve as a human being, then that evolution is going to show up in my work. And, hopefully, in very good ways.

What are some of your favorite things?

Shoes, hats, asparagus, ummm, veggie-burgers. (*Laughs.*) Sunsets, sunrises, praying with my soon-to-be husband, receiving letters. Being able to re-experience memories through photographs. Visiting my ancestral graves. Umm, let's see. I'm not a big T.V. person, but there's some movies that ring out in my mind—'Sankofa,' 'Daughters of the Dust,' 'Black Orpheus.' Ummm. Kisses, beaches, feathers. Oh God, candles. And baths!—I could say 'baths' about ten times—wonderful baths. Flowers—flowers are a necessity to my life. I have to have fresh flowers all over the house. It's the one indulgence I allow myself on a weekly basis. Uh, grandchildren that I don't have, so babies. Brazil nuts, mango juice, brown rice. Let's see. Soccer, basketball. Umm—books, books, books, books, books. African art, which I have a tremendous collection of. I like to feast my eyes on just wonderful art.

What personal qualities do you consider to be of most value in life?

Patience, forgiveness, *self*-forgiveness, to learn grace, laughter, good sense of humor, humility, discipline, self-discipline, respect for other people and self-respect, discovering your truth. Umm, let's see. Faithfulness, trustworthiness. Those are the things that just automatically roll for me. Knowing how to laugh at oneself and with oneself.

What are some ways that you have evolved as a human being that make you proudest?

Embracing disappointments. I've learned to really embrace them as what they are and not let them just totally destroy me or bury me—and accepting disappointment, accepting rejection. Understanding how vulnerable and insignificant we all are in the scheme of life in terms of just the natural order of being—being present to it. Learning how to celebrate myself—self-love and self-celebration. And right now, embracing transition and not mourning the loss of—you know, I'm going through menopause and looking at my oldest daughter really flower into a woman. And I've learned how to embrace that as newness instead of a loss of something. And, most importantly, being able to forgive myself when I feel that I've allowed myself to be hurt—or hurt myself by being present to unhealthy stuff.

Of what professional accomplishment are you most proud?

The publication of my books. Being able to be a real advocate for marginalized, non-traditional, outside-of-the-academy writers. And perhaps for me, that's academic. I mean, to have the perseverance to continue to make art and to create it and to go with it. Because publishing has been very difficult—just showing up in the publishing world is difficult. Being published is a major accomplishment.

And pursuing and achieving this master's in community economic development while, at the same time, raising children who were still in school, and traveling out of state to do it and maintaining a full-time job at the same time.

And of what personal accomplishment are you most proud?

Raising my children as a single mom with very, very little help from their fathers.

What, if anything, would you do differently if you could turn back the clock?

Marry when I'm forty-five.

What advice would you give young women just starting out on their path or older women considering a change in path?

To make sure it's *your* path and to make sure that you're self-directed on that path and to be able to ask the real *hard* questions of 'why I'm on this path' and 'what do I want to do?' But then to give oneself permission to not have to know. To sometimes just trust what you're feeling and not need to have all the answers and have the map totally drawn out. To just trust putting your feet out there in some rough terrain and trusting and, if you fall, you might even get bumped and bruised, but you're *not going to die*. That it will be OK, that it's part of the walk, it's part of the journey.

For older women like me, I think—in terms of age, in terms of background, in terms of race and ethnicity—to celebrate who we are, to really be able to celebrate the life we've created. And lately I've been thinking about healthy wealth and wealthy health. It's kind of being healthy on that path, and only the individual knows what that means, you know, where the bad health in them is and what they need to do to be about getting healthy.

For me, it's about *owning* that—owning that piece of that path, I mean owning the decision to go. And, especially if it's writing. I still say writing—and any other art—is such a jealous mistress, and you have to be real clear that you want to dance with her because she'll keep you up and out all night. And I think you have to know that you want the energy to do it and where's it gonna come from and how are you gonna have a life in addition to it. I've never wanted to be a writer who writes in a vacuum. As a child, I used to believe—and as a teenager and a young writer—I

thought writers had to be very mysterious and total weirdos and house themselves up at the end of the street, you know, with the fence around it. And now I'm saying 'No! Writers go to Wal-Marts and we show up at softball games and we go to the church picnic.' You show up in your life, you know. But if your life is the secluded house, that's OK, too.

But I think we have to find where we need to be on the path and not kind of look at somebody else's life and decide 'I'm gonna be that' and then realize that you can't be—you know, you have this difficult time *becoming* that, because it's not yours.

What have been the greatest challenges along your own path?

Money. Money. Gosh, money. Because I made a decision— I'm kind of a rebel, just by nature. I think I get it from my mom. You know, everybody was saying, 'You have to get an M.F.A. You have to get an M.F.A. If you're gonna do anything with this writing thing, you have to get an M.F.A. and you have to go teach.' So my early writing career, those were the only options people were suggesting to me or mentoring to me. And I was like, 'No, I don't. I don't want to get an M.F.A.'

Now, personally, I'd *like* to get an M.F.A., but not for the reasons that everybody thinks I should have an M.F.A. And part of that is, you know, writing for me—and poetry, the poetry I've done because that's where my publications are—it's an oral tradition and, for me, it comes from the people that inform my writing. When I'm writing a poem, there are certain faces that just come and look right at me and I'm sitting there laughing. And, for me, it's that way of giving that word back that I've usurped that energy from. It's giving it back to that force.

So I've not had the money that perhaps I would have had over the years if I had chosen to go teach poetry. I do a lot of teaching by invitation, in terms of residencies and writers' conferences or writers' camps. I've done the Young Duke Writers' Camp and I do Hot Ink—I'm doing Hot Ink again this summer which is UNC's Young Writers' Camp—as faculty, and then faculty for North Carolina Writers' Network. And I've done residencies at different universities and have done all of these scholarly presentations on my work. And I love doing that, but I don't want to go do it seven days a week and be in a classroom.

Like the other day, I took the day off and I spent half of the day with a literacy class of adults at one of the literacy centers here in Durham. And it was so rewarding to be with these nearly literate writers. But I'm not making money doing that. I believe that everyday language and experience are very valuable and are at the core of what poetry's all about—or what *making that writing* is all about. But in making this decision to deal with these marginalized writers and disenfranchised writers, I'm not inside of that canon and don't have a lot of the big-buck invitations ex-

tended to me. You know, every once in awhile. But it's a conscious decision I've made that this is the work I want to do. I don't want to get an M.F.A. just to go teach at a university. I have enough friends who are in those positions who bring me to their campuses—and pay me as well. So, in making that decision, the challenge has been having a full-time job to support myself and my family and getting the writing done. And as I get older, it's becoming more and more exhausting—just physically exhausting—to do this. And I don't want you to think I'm saying that I think people who do that have sold out, but it's not where I've wanted to be everyday.

What qualities do you possess that make being a writer a natural choice of vocation for you?

I have the ability to live in both worlds, in the eye and the ear. And because I do as much stage reading, it's the page that's most important for me because when it's going to an editor or to a publisher, it's gotta be a good read—it's gotta be good writing on the page. But I think one of the things that has been a strong point for me is that, for me, poetry is alive and it's oral and I come from a very traditional oral tradition. It's to be able to hear it. When I'm writing a poem, I'm hearing it. I hear the cadence, the rhythms, the form. And in my early writing career, I was also a dancer. I mean, I danced a lot and taught dance and studied dance.

And if I could dance it, it worked. So, for me again, I think I have a good sense of seeing how a poem is going to function. And seeing how it's going to work in terms of imagery, in terms of colloquial words, or if I choose to read a poem in a particular narrative voice.

The other strong point is—I'll take risks. I will step out of the box and not care about who attacks it or that it may not be regarded as traditional 'poetry.' And also to be able to see the science, the social services, the chemistry, the mathematics, to see all of the other humanities—to see other things in my writings. That's been a strong point.

What does writing do for you on the most basic inner level?

The sense of power, a tremendous sense of ownership that those are my words, those are my thoughts. You know, even if they're not unique *(laughs)*—it's kinda like my mother was always saying, 'Well, you know, everything's been said. It ain't too much anybody else can say. It's all been said and done.' But, you know, the power, the ability, that dance to rearrange and to arrange, to play with language, to play with dialogue. When I can conjure up characters and just bring them and sit them right down at the bed beside me, sort of like a painter with a model, and write that character and make that character, give it voice, give it body.

And the other—probably the best feeling I get is from an audience. A good audience really, really feeds me. So knowing that I'm making myself accessible, that when I'm reading, especially to people who wouldn't traditionally show up—you know what I mean?—at a writing, at a reading. Being able to take poetry down from the tower. There used to be a time when people believed that the poet was placed on a pedestal—had no obligation to his or her audience other than to show up and read a poem. Well, I just have a different take on that. I think that we empower audiences by taking it down from the tower and making it available to the so-called masses. And also poetry that answers their questions and helps them seek opportunities and understand that their voices are important, that *my* voice is *their* voice. So that's kinda where I am. You know, Walt Whitman once said, 'To have great poets, there must be great audiences.' And I believe that. I get a lot of just real wonderful inspiration from sitting in front of an audience that hears you—that *allows* itself to hear you—I mean, *really* hears you and examines the words and rolls them over in the back of their memory or their ears, just rolls 'em over and over and over the way we savor good food. That's what really feeds me.

And then to have people actually write to me or call me up to talk about how moved they were by a poem I read. Or what's always funny is when people buy the book and they read a poem—then they hear *me* read that poem and go 'Oh, wow, I'm so glad I heard you read this poem.' Those things mean a lot. I mean, we all love those strokes and those slaps on the back and those nice letters and those great evaluation forms. We live for it. So that's the joy of it and, for me, that's the recycling of it also, because those accolades actually get recycled into the next piece of work. To know that it's meaningful to someone even if it got four reject slips or if it got a bad press review by some guy who has no clue what I'm writing about. The fact that the guy at the service station says 'I heard you on NPR this morning. I really like your poem.' Well, that means more to me—you know what I'm saying?—than NPR running it. The fact that this guy got it!

When *Pete and Shirley: The Great Tar Heel Novel* came out—I don't know if you know about this book—it was a collaborative work in progress. Well, I'm Chapter Sixteen. So I was actually on my way to some press conference or something to do with the book and I was speeding out on Forty and I got stopped. And this officer came to the car and took my driver's license and said, 'Ms. Green, you know what you were doing?' I was like, 'Noooo, but I think you're gonna tell me.' And he kept looking at me and saying 'I know you, *I know you*.' And I said, 'Well, I haven't been locked up lately!' So then he started asking all these questions, 'Where do you go to church? Where'd you go to school?' And finally, he said, 'I got it! I got it! I remember! I know you! You're Chapter Sixteen!' Because *The News & Observer* published a chapter a week

and they put the writer's picture beside their chapter. He said, 'I can't *wait* for the book to come out.' And I just looked at him and this stupid comment came out of my mouth. I said, 'Highway patrolmen *read*?' And this poor man, he looked at me like he wanted to shoot me and he said, 'Yeah, *some* of us actually *can* read.' And I said, 'Oh, please, I didn't mean it that way. I didn't mean to insult you. I'm just blown away that you *know*!' I said, 'The book is out. And if you wouldn't consider it a bribe, I have a copy that's signed by all nineteen of us, and you're welcome to it, even if you do give me a ticket.' So I gave him the book. This guy was jumping up and down like a little kid. He was like 'Wow! Autographed by *all* of you!' (*Laughs.*) So then he said, 'You get back in that car and you get yourself to Raleigh and I better not ever hear of you speeding again. Do you hear me, young lady?' And I said 'Yes, sir!' And I told that story when I got there, of course. That meant a lot to me.

You know, I feel great when Reynolds Price or Fred Chappell or some of these people whom I really admire—Lee Smith—call me up and say, 'I saw that piece you had in USAir last month. It was great.' Or 'I really like such-and-such a poem you read.' That's meaningful, too. But it's the ordinary people—the guy at the service station, the woman at Biscuitville—those people that recognize the work. *And tell me they're reading it!* That's what's really empowering to me since I have chosen to be this struggling working-class writer—that the class that I come from *embraces* the work. And that helps me not be disenfranchised from this whole process and *not* feel that I'm in my own little literary circle of one.

Interviewed by Susan L. Comer.

"Art is a very jealous mistress. She wants you when she wants you when she wants you."
Jaki Shelton Green

"When I can't write, I read. When I can't do either, I dance."
Jaki Shelton Green

Jaki Shelton Green

Jaki Shelton Green holds an undergraduate degree in education and a master's degree in community economic development. Her published works include: *Dead on Arrival* (Editions I and II), *Masks*, and *Conjure Blues: Poems*. She has been awarded two emerging artists grants from the Durham Arts Council. National Public Radio featured "Eva I," a poem written for her grandmother, in a radio documentary about African-American women and hats. She is a community arts and literacy activist and consultant, teaching workshops directed towards—among others—the newly literate, the elderly, disadvantaged children, and abuse survivors.

Ms. Green lives and plays in Mebane, North Carolina, where she is working on her first novel, *Dandelion*, and on an ongoing Juke Joint Project which is partially funded by grants from the N.C. Arts Council and the Durham Arts Council.

Ruth Ann Binder   an interview

What career dreams did you have as a child?

I didn't necessarily have that one dream that was going to carry me through my life. I think I went through a lot of different periods. One of them was wanting to be an interior designer, which makes me laugh now. One of them was wanting to work in theater in some capacity. And I think also teaching at some point, too.

And how did those dreams evolve as you grew into adulthood?

Well, I think that other dreams took their place—and more of a sense of how I wanted to live my life than career goals that took me from one place to another. For example, Judaism's a pretty important part of my life, and in high school, I was involved with a number of Jewish activities. And having that be a part of my life and be a part of my community was a stronger pull than, say, wanting to be a director and then trying to get my life to that point where I could be a director. So I'd say it's more the way that I want to live my life and how I want to spend my days and my time, both professionally and personally, that was a stronger guide than anything.

Where did you grow up and where did you go to school?

I grew up in Northridge, California, home of the big earthquake. And I spent kindergarten through ninth grade at a private Jewish dayschool, so that had incredible influence on my life. We were taught that every child is special, and the teachers had incredible interest in each of the students. And I went to a public high school that I think, honestly, to this day, was a waste of my time unfortunately, because of the [particular] high school. And that was also in Los Angeles.

I went to undergrad at University of California-San Diego and graduated there in '93 in anthropology and women's studies. And, since then, I've done a lot of things. Well, mostly what I've done is try to explore a lot of different things and make sure that I always have time to play. After I graduated, I traveled through the national parks for a few months, teaching—working with a group of students. And then I gave myself an opportunity in that following year to explore different things—lots of different classes in the community. I was living up in Santa Cruz, California, at that time. Then I went traveling overseas to the South Pacific for three months, and it was a wonderful experience. It was the first time I traveled by myself, and I think that it still infuses what I do today because, in a month, I'm leaving to travel by myself again for four weeks. I remember that sense of adventure and independence, and I want to have that again.

After I traveled, I dabbled in a couple different things, and one of them was experiential education, working with junior high and high school students and teaching them about the environment—the wetlands and different ecosystems—leading them through conflict resolution, exercises in team-building. That was in New Hampshire—when I first came to the East Coast five years ago. And it was there that I met my partner—I met the man I'm now going to marry. And that was definitely the best thing I got out of those six months teaching. Decided after the six months, I didn't want to work with students—that being a teacher, although it seemed like a really noble profession, was just not the best match for me.

After that, I moved to New York City. In New York, I worked as the director of a women's center for a couple of years for the National Council of Jewish Women. And that was really where I think I started to get a lot into nonprofit work and understanding how the nonprofit works—and what I want to do and what I don't want to do. And I was able to really explore my interest in women's studies, but I also found it really difficult to work with an organization that was not very interested in change.

Three years ago, I moved to North Carolina. And my life now is very exciting. Actually, this year, it's full of incredible change for me. I will be going to graduate school at Carolina in the fall for a master's in city and regional planning. I want to focus either in community or economic development. I've wanted to go back to school for years to really figure out how I can help poor communities help themselves. And over the last several years, I've tried to figure out different ways where I can make an impact, a contribution. I've explored being a teacher and I've explored working directly with women's issues and, along the way, have felt good about what I've done, but I've also realized that, at some point, I need a master's. So I've taken this path, and although I could've ended up in public health or even in business school, I'm choosing planning because I really want to focus on community and economic development.

What brought you to North Carolina?

It was a lot of things. I was looking to move out of New York and my partner was looking to go to law school. We had both applied to grad schools, but in different places. I decided not to go to grad school at that time. I was going to go get a Ph.D. in anthropology, and after I got accepted, I decided not to go. And we thought, 'Hey, what are our best choices?' and Duke was one of them. I had checked out the nonprofit community here and heard it was really great, so I wanted to come here. Now Matt is at Duke, studying law. And it's been an incredible place for us.

What have been the greatest challenges on your life's path so far?

I think it was probably, over the last several years, not *having* a path. When I was in college, it was very clear what I was supposed to be doing and even, to some extent, who my friends would be, and there was this set community. And I think, along the way, one of the challenges has always been—being in a place where I have a community. Other places, I haven't been able to establish that. And I've been able to establish that here. That's why it's been so great to be here, to have that sense of community—the Jewish community, a women's community, a community of activists. And also, within that, knowing what I wanted to do to give back, to contribute. Here, I've been a volunteer with the Rape Crisis Center. I was finally able to make the time and the space in my life to do that, and I've really enjoyed it. I also volunteer with the Dispute Settlement Center of Durham, doing conflict mediation and resolution. But there's been other places where I couldn't quite find my place, and that, I think, has been really difficult along the way—figuring out what I should be doing and how I'd go about doing that. Now I'm getting married in the fall and I'm going back to school and I'm traveling this summer, so there's a lot of exciting things happening.

What aspect of the life you've created brings you the most joy?

Well, I would say it's a couple things. It's the relationship I'm in that is full of love and respect. It's a relationship that is some-thing I never thought I would have and something I almost thought I never even wanted. And the community that I have here is wonderful. A couple friends and I have formed this group of Jewish women. We call ourselves 'The Cool Jewish Chicks'—someone named us that. I get together with these women—we talk about all sorts of things and it's a lot of fun. And I live in a beautiful place—I'm sitting in my house looking out at gorgeous trees. So it's the home I've created here, too. It brings me a lot of joy—and pride in being able to create this.

In times of disappointment or strife, what are your sources of inspiration or renewal?

I think when things are personally feeling difficult, I do a couple of different things. Sometimes I write in a journal when I just need to get stuff out of my head and onto paper. I'll do some physical activity sometimes—some yoga or work out at the gym or go running. There's certain people I can turn to to talk through things with—Matt or close friends. I'll tell you though—I've been very lucky in my life. I haven't had incredible tragedy. I've had to make things happen for myself, but I've also been really blessed. I've had a lot of great things in my life.

What personal qualities of yours create conflict or struggle in your daily life?

Well, I try and get rid of a lot of conflict. There's everyday challenges, but I would say there's nothing that I struggle with on a daily basis, and if something comes up, I really need to focus on that for awhile, which is what I do. But I don't think living my life should be a daily struggle and, if it is, I need to look at what's going on there. I think it should be much more about joy and enjoying everything that's around us.

Are you at all a worrier?

(*Laughs.*) There's a friend or two who might say I am. I would say, 'Somewhat,' and there are things that come up that concern me. For example, there's a man who sells newspapers and he's not very well-off—he mostly just has the clothes on his back and the paycheck he gets from selling newspapers. And he's someone who I have been worrying about lately and I've started to talk to, and I've brought him some clothes and I've wondered about ways I could take care of him. So there's things like that that concern me on a daily basis. And then I feel like I'm juggling 10,000 things, and that, I would say, worries or concerns me, too—and that ebbs and flows, and right now, there's a lot going on.

What are the ways you relax?

I write. I spend time talking with friends, and walking with friends. I read—it's a great way for me to unwind. Occasionally in the winter, I'll take a long bath to take care of myself.

What are some of your favorite things?

Gardening, being outside, hiking, looking at the stars, celebrating moon rituals, walking in the forest after it rains, and laughing—anything that makes me laugh. I don't have a T.V., and whenever I watch, I have to watch something that's funny and makes me laugh. Hmmm, that's pretty wide open! Activism—protests and marches are actually a lot of fun. Reading a variety of books, spending a weekend at a yoga retreat, traveling, being in the Outer Banks in October, celebrating different life cycles with friends, activities with different life-cycle rituals. Just really laughing aloud, spending time with the people I love, my family.

What are your pet interests or goals, from a personal standpoint?

Well, I think I try to lead more of a Jewish life. And I'm doing that by going to Israel this summer for a month and bringing more Jewish ritual into my house and having more friends who are Jewish. In trying to learn to take better care of myself, I'd like to create some kind of daily ritual—or, if not daily, a few times a week—a ritual which will help me relax and focus, whether it's more journaling or more yoga or whatever it might be. Indulging a little, taking more risks, having more adventure. Funny, some people look at my life and think that I have a lot of adventure, but

I still strive for more—and things that are riskier. Having a very full life—I think I have that now, and I'd like to continue to have that. And in time, that'll involve probably having children and welcoming them into the world.

Given the importance of Judaism in your life, how do you handle the fact that you are Jewish and your fiancé is not?

That has been an incredible process. We have struggled with that. And he does not practice any other religion, so it makes it easier and, over the last five years, he's really come to embrace Judaism. He doesn't talk about converting at this time, but we celebrate Shabbat and we celebrate some of the Jewish holidays together. His aunt died a week ago and he is finding comfort in the Jewish Mourner's Prayer, and that's pretty incredible. We're going to have a Jewish wedding, we're going to bring up Jewish kids, and Matt will have to decide for himself how and when—if—he wants to make religion more a part of his life, Jewish religion. But we've reached a pretty great place in that right now, although it was a huge issue for my family. It was also an issue for me. I didn't know if I wanted a partner who didn't practice this. It wasn't just a matter of his being Jewish—it was a matter of his living a Jewish life in some way. But between finding this group of 'Cool Jewish Chicks' and having more Jewish friends now and me belonging to a synagogue, we're more a part of the Jewish community.

Who you fall in love with is who you fall in love with.

Yes, I think so. It's not the easiest path, that's for sure. And it was a huge struggle with my family basically until the week we got engaged. Since that time, my family has really come around and they've really accepted him and embraced him. It wasn't that I didn't see their point of view. I understood where they were coming from and I felt some of it the same way. But I also knew I am with this incredible man, so I wanted to try and see what I could do with that.

What personal qualities do you consider to be of the most value in life?

I would have to say integrity and living and speaking one's truth. And living life in a way that honors that.

What is the one way that you have evolved as a human being that makes you proudest?

I think the depth and the emotion of my relationships—that love that's there in my friendships and in my relationship with Matt.

Of what accomplishment are you most proud?

I would say building a community, having a really full life

that includes fun and seriousness and adventure and lots of different kinds of people.

Can you think of any particular childhood event or recollection that foreshadowed that the career plans you now have would one day emerge?

There's not an event. Something I actually recognize about my life is that when I think back, I remember a very rich, a very fun childhood, but there's not these specific events that have changed my life or turned my life. I think it's about process for me. It was about the exploration of things in college, when I just got to be this person who could explore whatever I wanted to—and then post-college and allowing myself to explore things. It was that process rather than one event specifically. And now I know I want to help poor communities—I want to do economic development, but I still don't know what that means in some ways. I don't know exactly what I'll be doing or how I'll be doing that. And then, I think, in another five or ten years, that will shift and become something else—to give back in another way. Perhaps it will be teaching in universities about this, or it'll be living abroad and doing this. I don't know exactly what it will be.

What advice would you give women just starting out on their paths?

Listen to your heart and take risks. This is it. We can't follow what other people are telling us to do or what we think we *should* be doing—that's where I've seen people really struggle, is doing what they think they're supposed to be doing. But I would say— just doing what's right for them and always giving something back in some context to the world around them. Find something you're passionate about and *live* it, enjoy it, whatever it might be, have it be a part of your life.

And I recently heard Sister Helen Prejean speak—she's the nun who worked with death-row inmates and wrote the book *Dead Man Walking*—and she said to always have a room in your house for poor people, for people less fortunate. She said this to law students about their legal careers, but I think it's true for everyone. I thought that was really wise advice.

What are your greatest dreams that are yet to be realized?

I have huge world dreams like people not being homeless and really being able to help each other and strong communities and women being able to really be who they are and fulfill their own dreams—for every woman and for every person. And for myself, I'm really kinda curious how things are going to unfold for me. I'm looking forward to getting this degree and seeing what will come up and what I'll do with it. I know broadly what I want to do. I've always known broadly that I want to make change and I want to give back. I still don't know how specifically, other than— now—economic development or community development.

What, if anything, would you do differently if you could turn back the clock?

There are some things I definitely would change, although at one point, I swore I would never regret anything and now I think it's OK to do that. Certainly, there are job situations that I've been in that were not supportive of who I am or how I like to live my life, and I would've gotten out of them earlier, because they took a toll on me. And I also think I would've, at some point—and it's easy to say now—but taken a few more risks in my younger years and done a few more crazy and adventurous things. But I'm only twenty-nine, so I can still do those.

Interviewed by Susan L. Comer.

"Listen to your heart and take risks."

Ruth Ann Binder

Ruth Ann *Binder*

Ruth Ann Binder was born in 1970 in Northridge, California. Her parents, Farla and Hershey Binder, had three red-headed children; she is the middle one. After growing up in suburban Los Angeles, Ruth Ann attended University of California-San Diego, where she earned a bachelor's degree in anthropology and women's studies.

After college, Ruth Ann worked on the Blackfoot Reservation in Montana, taught outdoor education in New Hampshire, and ran a women's center in New York City, before moving to Durham, North Carolina in 1997. In Durham, Ruth Ann has assisted low-wealth and minority entrepreneurs start and expand small businesses and raised money for a non-profit that helps older adults

manage and afford their medications. She has also volunteered at a rape crisis center and is a trained mediator.

In the fall of 2000, Ruth Ann will be pursuing her master's degree in city and regional planning at UNC-Chapel Hill. She will soon marry the love of her life, Matt Rossiter, to whom she proposed a year ago.

Learning Keeps Me Green   Billie Granger

What would I do with the rest of my life? This was the question I was asking myself on June 25, 1985 as I walked out of the textile plant that had been my workplace for the past twenty-five years. The plant had closed its doors and there was no more work. There I was, a forty-nine-year-old woman with only a high school education. I had spent most of my adult life working as a weaver, working shift work that rotated all three shifts, every two weeks. It was hard work, but the pay was steady and substantial and it was necessary. There was nowhere in the area to get another job as a weaver. The only thing that I was trained to do was out of the question. What was I going to do?

The only things I had going for me were my health and my faith in God. I had been taught to believe that God does not close one door without opening another. I was just going to have to look for that door. One thing was for sure, I would need to be trained for some other type of work, which would probably mean that I would need to go back to school or find a job that offered job training. But who would want to hire a forty-nine-year-old woman with no experience? The other question I was asking myself was: what kind of work would I like to do?

The company I had worked for had arranged with the local employment office to offer all employees job counseling and help with preparing a resumé. We were also eligible to draw six months' unemployment benefits. There were no retirement benefits. I knew I would need to find work of some kind, but where? And what? Financially, we would be able to get by for about a year. Then I would need a job with a steady income. Some decision must be made.

Three days after my last day at the plant, I went to the employment office to meet with the job counselor and to sign up for unemployment benefits. The counselor talked with me about my job history, the kinds of work I had done and my experience. It wasn't a long list. I had been a waitress in a family-owned restaurant. I had worked as a cashier in a neighborhood grocery store and I had worked at the plant. Not too much for a resumé. The one impressive thing was my longevity at the plant.

I was given a twelve-page questionnaire to take home and fill out for another session the following week. I could not believe all the questions. I was to start with my childhood days and list responsibilities and achievements in my life, including family, community and employment activities. I really didn't understand how all this was supposed to prepare me for the future, but it would be interesting to see what the counselor would come up with.

As a child, I learned what work and responsibility were. I was the oldest of six children—four girls and two boys. My father was a small tobacco farmer. In those days, farming was a family business and every member of the family was expected to do their share of work. My grandparents lived on the same farm, but Grandpa had given up farming and ran a small fish and vegetable market in town. Grandmother helped out with farm work and was always there to give us advice and support, helping when the new babies were born or when there was sickness in the family.

My dad was a hardworking man and believed that everyone should do their share. I can remember him saying that he had no use for a lazy person. He would tell us that, even though we were poor, if we would work hard and be honest we would never go hungry. He made sure that everyone in his family understood this. Although tobacco was the main thing we raised on the farm, it was not the only thing. We planted potatoes and vegetables to sell at the farmers market to help supplement income. We also raised our own food, such as pork, beef, and chickens. We had our own cows that supplied us with milk and butter. Taking care of the animals was also a responsibility. During the winter months when there wasn't a lot of work he could do on the farm, my dad worked at a sweet potato warehouse as a night watchman, to earn extra money.

My mother worked equally as hard. Not only did she take care of the children and the house, she worked in the fields and at the tobacco barns. She did the laundry by hand and had to draw wash water from a well. Food had to be prepared from scratch—that included harvesting and preparing. Most of our meat was pork or chicken, which required butchering before you could prepare it.

These are just a few of the things that were our way of life. Children were expected to do their part as soon as they were old enough, and that was very young in my family.

The first responsibility my parents gave me was when I was five years old. It was summertime and time to harvest the tobacco. At tobacco harvest time, everyone had a job and we usually had neighbors that came together to get the tobacco in the barn for curing, which had to be done as the tobacco became ripe and ready to pick. In return, we would help the neighbors. This particular summer, my mother had given birth to my second brother in March. She was needed to work at the tobacco barn.

Taking young children in the fields and to the tobacco barn was a natural thing. There was a crib for the babies to stay in and other small children would play close by under the watchful eye of the women. My baby brother had been very sick the first two months of his life and really required a lot of care and attention from my mother. Since I had already been taught to rock the baby, my dad told me my job was to take care of the baby during tobacco harvest. No, they didn't leave a five year old at home to take care of a three-month-old baby. They took a rocking chair to the tobacco barn and I was to sit and rock him under my mother's watchful eye while she worked.

It seemed there were always chores to be done. Dad could always find something for everyone to do, even the children. Even when we went to school, we had our work to do when we got home. Sometimes we would help with fieldwork for one or two hours. Then, my job was to make sure that firewood was brought in to last through the night and to help the younger children bathe while Mother prepared dinner. By the time we had dinner and the dishes were washed, there wasn't much time for homework or reading, but somehow we managed to get it all done.

One thing I remember about my childhood was I was always afraid that my mother would die. It seemed she was sick a lot. As I look back now, I realize most of her sicknesses centered around difficult pregnancies. When she wasn't real sick she was always working.

When I was twelve years old, my mother was hospitalized for two months because of a difficult pregnancy. This was in January and February, so there wasn't a lot of farm work going on. My aunt took my twin sisters—age four—to her house. Since my brothers, aged seven and ten, and I were in school, we stayed at home with Dad. That is when I was given the responsibility of taking care of the house, preparing meals and doing the laundry. By the time Mother came home with my new baby sister, I had learned to do many things that would help her in what turned out to be a very difficult year for all of us, because she remained very sick. As I look back and remember that year in my life, I don't remember ever resenting having all those responsibilities. All I can remember is trying to do all I could to help Dad hold things together. He worked so hard, but he always took time to teach each of us how to tackle a new job and he always praised us for what we did.

My teenage years mainly consisted of school and working on the farm. There wasn't much time for dating and a social life. I married my first and only boyfriend, who just happened to be the boy who lived on the family farm next to ours. We had always known each other and had worked together on the farms as our family helped each other in tobacco harvesting time.

After marriage, my husband and I left the family farm in Columbus County and moved to Wilmington, where my husband went to work as a shipping clerk for a milk and ice cream company.

In the first eight years of our marriage, I gave birth to four children, all boys. I had gotten a job as a waitress in a family-owned restaurant. My next-door neighbor who had two little boys, took care of the children when my husband and I were at work. Most of the time, we worked opposite shifts so that one of us would be home with the boys. Later, I got a job at a neighborhood grocery store where I worked until I got the job at the plant. The next twenty-five years were pretty much routine. My husband and I continued to work opposite shifts. I was always involved in school, church, little league, Boy Scouts and all the other activities that are connected with raising children. My life was centered around church, family and work, each of which I gave 100%.

On the questionnaire the job counselor had given me was a place for me to score myself on the things I had done in my life that I enjoyed most and the things I really didn't like to do. After the counselor had reviewed the questions, he advised me that I needed to be in some type of human service work, because I was very much a people person and enjoyed helping others. He pointed out the leadership and organizing skills that I had developed over my lifetime. I had to agree with him, but where would I get a job doing this?

In the meantime, I had decided that while I was not working, I would like to do some volunteer work in the community. I had always wanted to do this, but had never had the time. I happened to make this statement at church one Sunday in the presence of Marsha Cook, the Christian Social Minister for the Baptist Association. The next week I was taking part in backyard Bible Clubs in different parts of the city. This went on for three weeks, five days a week. The day of the last Bible Club, Marsha asked me what my plans were now. I told her I was signed up to take the training to become a volunteer literacy tutor. She got real excited and encouraged me to follow through. Little did I know that her wheels had started to work. The day I completed the training, Marsha called me and invited me to lunch the next day.

At this lunch, I got my first lesson in volunteer recruitment. She began by talking with me about my reason for getting involved in the literacy program. I explained to her that I had worked with a man that could not read. He was the best machinist in the plant and I had always admired him for his achievement even though he did not have reading skills. I really felt God had directed me to help people like him. This was a skill I could pass on. I was very excited about the training and was ready to get busy. It was then that she shared with me that the Literacy Council was in the process of obtaining its nonprofit status and becoming a community program instead of a Baptist Mission Project. An advisory committee was already in place. This committee would later become the Board of Directors for the Council. Marsha was serving as the chairman. The Baptist Association would continue to give the council office space and the use of their training room. There was no money to pay staff, so volunteers were needed to help get the agency up and going. Since literacy was only one of her many community activities, she needed someone to help her with recruiting volunteer tutors and students. She asked if I would be willing to help. I agreed to help her all I could while I was not working, if she would just tell me what to do.

Within the next two weeks the nonprofit status had gone through and the Literacy Council was on its way as a new non-profit agency in our community. By this time I was really getting excited about all the people we would be able to help. I was already volunteering forty hours a week and could not do all the things that needed to be done. I was so busy in my volunteer job that I almost stopped looking for a paying job, but I knew that I would soon need to find work that would pay. I had about three more months that I could afford to be unemployed.

It was about this time that I learned that the Board of Directors had applied for a Vista Grant for two Vista workers. Marsha once again invited me to lunch and asked me if I would be interested in one of the Vista positions. I would be expected to work forty hours a week for a stipend of $68 a week, and I would be expected to make a one-year commitment. One other benefit of the Vista plan was that I could sign up for career development training. I would be assigned a supervisor who would train me in

volunteer administration management. Marsha would be my supervisor. My first reaction was: no way. I told her there was no way I could afford to work for $68 a week, but I wanted to keep on volunteering as much as I could. She told me to pray about it and we would talk again in a few weeks. We still had time before the grant started.

I did pray a lot about it in the next few weeks. The more I prayed, the more excited I became about the direction the Literacy Council was going in and about how much I wanted to be a part of it. I was witnessing people being helped and learning about the need for such a program. I knew that I wanted to take this position more than anything. One night as I was praying, I remembered that God had promised that when one door was closed another would be opened, but that I must be willing to walk through. That was when I realized that God was working in my life.

When I told my husband what I was thinking and how I felt, he told me that if I felt God was calling me to this work then we would somehow be able to get along financially and that I should accept the position.

For the next year and a half, I worked as a Vista volunteer. The pay was not much, but the training I was getting was unreal. Marsha was one of the most intelligent and hardworking people I have ever known. She had so much knowledge of the community and human service work and I was determined to learn everything I could from her. She very quickly became my mentor and friend as well as my supervisor.

In 1987 I became the first director of the newly formed Cape Fear Literacy Council and I have continued to serve in that capacity ever since. In 1985, the organization had a budget of $500 and worked out of donated office space. Today, we are housed in our own building with an annual budget of over $175,000. Seventy percent of our annual income comes from community donations. I feel this is a sign of the support and trust we have been able to establish in the community. Even more important is the impact on the lives of everyone involved in the program. Year after year, I have encouraged and inspired everyone—tutors and students alike—to achieve results and been inspired by them in turn. This mutual encouragement has translated into annual program statistics that are well above the national average for similar programs. The vast majority of our students make measurable progress toward their literacy goals.

I have asked God daily to give me the wisdom to steer the Literacy Council on a steady road of sustainable growth, strategically emphasizing the need to continuously improve the quality of our service. With the support of committed board members and the dedication of an outstanding volunteer training team, we have strengthened each of the major areas of the council by:

- Developing a robust and compelling vision for the organization
- Broadening the client and volunteer base
- Designing, delivering and evaluating effective literacy services, shaping the program according to the needs of the community
- Developing resources and training to meet current and future needs
- Growing the base of financial support, and
- Establishing collaborative relationships across the community.

The result is a thriving, independent non-profit agency that has received local, state and national recognition.

Establishing and managing a viable and effective non-profit organization takes hard work, enormous energy, enthusiasm and an unerring ability to take advantage of every opportunity. God gave me the ability to see people's needs and potential, and I work hard to provide people with the opportunities they need to learn and grow and give. For the clients we serve, I try to understand where they come from and encourage them to take advantage of the services we provide. Because of the obstacles I have overcome in my life, I can relate to them with honest and sincere encouragement.

Each time I interview a new client, I learn something new about the problems and burdens they have to overcome daily. In many cases, they have become my heroes. For instance, there was

Mrs. Louise, a seventy-two-year-old lady who had retired at age sixty-five from working as a housekeeper. She had managed to raise her two children and each of them had a college degree. It was her time now.

She had enrolled in the Adult Basic Education class at the local community college with one specific goal in mind—to get her GED. She attended class four mornings a week, and wanted a literacy tutor two afternoons a week, because she was still having a lot of trouble with reading. She explained to me that she was not afraid of hard work. She had waited all her life for this opportunity and she was determined she would make it. When I looked at her skills I was doubtful about whether she would be able to meet her goal, but I knew she had the ability to improve her skills. She would be getting one of my best tutors, someone who would work with her as long as she was able to work, even if it took the rest of her life.

After the interview and testing was over, I had one more question for her. I said, "Mrs. Louise, why are you doing this at your age? Why don't you just sit back and rest and enjoy life?" I will never forget her response and the impact it has had on my life. She closed her eyes and looked upwards and then looked straight at me. "Because I want to stay green," she said, "and the only way to stay green is to keep learning. When you are green, you are living, but when you stop learning, you begin to turn brown. You know what happens to the leaves on a tree when they start turning brown. Soon they die." I had to agree with her and at that moment, I don't think I have ever admired anyone more.

With volunteers, I look for their special skills and try to find work for them that is rewarding and meaningful. I believe people work best from their strengths. I am continuously amazed with the volunteers that work with me. Whenever and wherever there is a need for special skills and talents, God just sends someone along to fill that need—tutors who teach clients new skills, trainers who train the tutors, volunteers to work on special fundraising events, board members who set policies and raise funds to keep the program going and growing. I am very protective of the time and energy of my board, staff and volunteers so they can accomplish their work. All of them have been willing to go the extra mile to make a difference in the lives of others.

Although I have been successful in leading our organization to where we are, I am still not willing to sit back and enjoy our success. Each day brings new challenges and I am determined to stay on the cutting edge of any new or better technique that will help our clients meet their potential.

Recently, the organization has received two major statewide awards. In 1998, it was chosen as one of the Best Practice programs at the Governor's Summit. In 1999, it received the Nonprofit Sector Steward Award.

As I look back and remember the day in 1985 when I was forced to look for a new career, I think about how afraid and unprepared I thought I was. I did not have the formal education needed for the kind of work I really wanted to do and I thought I was too old to do anything about it. My only resource was to put my faith in God and be willing to follow his guidance when doors were opened. As God began to open these doors, I remembered what my father taught me about being honest and working hard. The time I worked as a Vista volunteer, I learned so much from Marsha Cook. I know there is no way I would have learned as much in an educational class. I guess this is why I am still so committed to one-on-one training. Not only did Marsha teach me new things, but also she made me aware of the skills and experiences I already had but did not realize were there. I remember telling her how much I admired her organizational skills and how I would like to be able to do as she did. She looked me straight in the eyes and said, "You have the skills and don't know it. Anyone who organized their life the way you have with work, family and church, has to be a good organizer. Life is much more difficult to organize than a job." It was then that I realized I could do this job with God's help and with hard work. I also made a commitment that this work would not be just for a job for me but would also be my ministry.

Managing the council and bringing it to where it is today has not been easy, but it has been challenging and rewarding. It has helped me overcome my own insecurities and skepticism about others. I have proved to myself and to others that a country-bred woman with limited formal education could effectively lead and manage an up-and-coming nonprofit organization, specializing in providing education services. This experience has deepened my commitment to helping others to meet their full potential, especially when they lack educational advantages. It has strengthened my faith in God and my fellow man and made me understand more fully how much we need the support and encouragement of others in our lives. If I can just continue to pass it on, I will feel that I have met my challenge and God's purpose in my life.

I also recognize that the love, support and encouragement of my family were the most important source of help I received. Even though I have put a lot of time in my career, I have always made my family a priority. I feel so blessed to have their support and love, especially my husband's (who is, by the way, still my first and only boyfriend). He has stood by me in the good and bad times, encouraging me to keep trying. He has also been willing to put up with my working so many hours over the years. I know he sometimes felt neglected. I also know that I would never have had the strength to tackle such a challenge if he had not told me that if I felt that God was leading me in that direction, I should go.

Billie *Granger*

"God gave me the ability to see people's needs and potential, and I work hard to provide people with the opportunities they need to learn and grow and give."

Billie Granger

Billie Granger was born on a family farm in Columbus County, North Carolina. After working twenty-five years as a master weaver in a factory, she launched a second career as the director of a non-profit organization, the Cape Fear Literacy Council. In the past fifteen years as director of the Council, she has touched the lives of over 7,000 people, working across the community to provide learning opportunities for adults who seek to improve their literacy skills. Next to being a grandmother, she says, nothing has been more rewarding than helping people learn. Recently honored as a YWCA Woman of Achievement, she has her priorities straight: God, family and work, in that order.

Connections   Ilana Dubester

DEDICATION:

I wish to dedicate this essay to my best friend and wonderful mother Anita Libel.

PHOTOGRAPH:

By my dear friend Paul Cuadros.

I moved to Chatham County from Chicago in the early nineties. I was attracted to this area because of its climate, rich farmlands, and rural nature. The original dream and goal was to become an organic vegetable farmer and live off of the land. Those were the early days; I had no idea of the turns my life would take. Much took place to lead me to Chatham County and to my current path as executive director of the Hispanic Liaison.

My earliest memory of community involvement in North Carolina took place during a regular shopping trip to a local pharmacy. I was in Siler City, a small town of then 5,000 people, looking through the aisles of a drugstore, when I noticed a Spanish-speaking woman struggling to understand what the pharmacist was explaining to her. I decided to listen in for a moment, and realized that the woman needed medicine for her baby who had a high fever. The communication between the woman and the pharmacist wasn't going well; they simply couldn't understand each other. Given that I knew Spanish and English, I interrupted to offer my assistance. I wanted to make sure that the woman understood the instructions given by the pharmacist, and I showed the Spanish-speaking mother how to read a thermometer in Fahrenheit (we use Celsius in Latin America). This and similar experiences at local stores, banks, and other businesses left me wondering why Latinos were moving here and how they were getting along. I continued living my own life, and a few years passed before I found out the answers to these questions.

Being a voice for someone else was not a strange concept to me. I was a precocious talker; according to my mother, I began speaking at nine months of age and was forming three-to four-word sentences by the time I was one year old. This ability became extremely useful to my painfully shy older sister who relied on my "interpreting services" as a child. I remember being four years old and accompanying my nine-year-old sister to the corner store to serve as her voice. She would whisper in my ear, "We need grape jam and two bags of milk." I would then tell the storeowner what we needed. This went on for many years as my sister struggled to overcome her shyness. The experience of being able to reach out and help someone just by being who I am has permeated my whole life and, unbeknownst to me at the time, shaped my future.

I had a rich childhood in Brazil, even though we didn't have a lot of money. My father left us when I was three years old, and my mother devoted herself to raising my sister and me. At first she supported us as a seamstress, making clothes and party dresses, as well as all our clothes. When she was thirty-three, she decided to finish her higher education. She graduated from the Federal University of Rio Grande do Sul with a degree in mathematics, and became a schoolteacher. Although we struggled financially, my mom always made sure that we had access to educational, cultural and social experiences, either at no-cost programs or by applying for scholarships on our behalf. She wanted us to have opportunities that were not available to her, and to have the freedom to grow and explore the world around us. Most of all, I was encouraged to make my own decisions, follow my heart, and do what makes me happy.

I have always been very independent and outgoing, qualities that were well-suited for an experience that is probably the cornerstone of my career today. When I was seven years old, I joined a youth group called Habonim-Dror that was run and led by members ages seven to twenty-two. The philosophy of the movement was equality among members and shared leadership. This is an old movement that has members and centers throughout the world. We met weekly and held camp twice per year in different parts of Brazil. We owned a building where we held most activities, and we were responsible for all aspects of management, maintenance, and program development. In this safe setting we were taught critical thinking and were encouraged to analyze and question everything. We discussed politics, history, racial issues, religions, arts, social structure, and became increasingly aware of the world around us. All this was happening in the midst of a military dictatorship in Brazil that lasted from the time I was born until 1985, which was the year that I decided to leave my home country for good. The movement honed my leadership skills, taught me to speak my mind, share my views, and rely on myself. It also offered me incredible opportunities to travel all over Brazil and meet people from all walks of life. My love of travel was born.

After high school, my youth group with members from all over Brazil joined a one-year program to travel in Israel and experience life in a Kibbutz (socialist collective farm). There are nearly 300 of these communities (plural: Kibbutzim) in Israel; they vary in size from thirty to 6,000 members. Most of the vegetables, farm produce, meat, milk, and eggs in Israel come from these collectives. Each Kibbutz also has its own history and culture. For example, some were formed in the turn of the century by Polish immigrants, while others were formed in the '70s by South African immigrants. There are Kibbutzim founded by Argentines, Brazilians, English, Americans, etc.

I spent most of my first year in Israel at Kibbutz Gezer located between Tel-Aviv and Jerusalem, which was founded in the early '80s by Americans. We had a 1000-acre farm with thousands of egg-laying chickens, a dairy, cotton and sunflower fields, wine grapes, and an adhesive factory. I worked full-time in the cow dairy; there were 250 milkers and altogether 500 head of cattle. I loved my work and the country life. It was in Gezer that I learned to speak English with the help of some good friends and lots of dedication. When I left Brazil I only spoke my native language of Portuguese, which is not a very commonly spoken language outside of Brazil. I surprised myself in Israel by learning English, Spanish, and Hebrew in a period of six years.

During that first year in Israel, we toured the whole country, camped, attended educational seminars, learned some Hebrew and worked hard. The program ended but I decided that I wasn't ready to go back home. I wanted to travel more and wanted to live in an Israeli city. Once again, my mother supported my decision and encouraged me to do what made me happy, so I extended my airline ticket for another year. I traveled through Egypt with two dear friends, lived in Tel-Aviv for a few months, and then moved to Jerusalem, which is a spectacularly beautiful city and one of my favorite places in Israel. My second year abroad came to an end. I returned to Brazil with a heavy heart, unwilling to leave that beautiful land.

Arriving in my hometown of Porto Alegre, it was clear to me that I would not stay long. Even though it is a big city of two million people in the south of Brazil, opportunities were scarce, unemployment was high, and wages were low. I felt lost in a familiar place. I began studying at the Federal University of Rio Grande do Sul with a major in veterinary science. I always thought that I would be a veterinarian specializing in wildlife or large animals; this has been my dream since I was five years old. I was dissatisfied with my studies and I simply didn't fit in Brazil anymore. I wanted to be out in the world. So I devoted my time and energy to saving money to move back to Israel and continue my studies.

I decided to go into business for myself, and borrowed an idea from a couple I met in Jerusalem who had a small Tofu business. I was a vegetarian and knew many people interested in whole foods and healthy living. My neighborhood in Porto Alegre had five health food stores and restaurants. I already knew how to make tofu; I just needed to do simple market research. I went to all the nearby health food stores and found out that there was no one in my whole city selling tofu to this market. My home-based business was born. At the peak of the business, I made twenty lbs. of tofu a day and distributed it by foot twice a week. In less then a year, I became a small celebrity, with a couple of T.V. appearances, newspaper articles, and, later, Tofu Workshops. The business was growing and doing well, but I couldn't get over the feeling that I didn't belong in Brazil anymore.

Once again, I packed my suitcases and left. This time I was headed for Hebrew University in Jerusalem, where I only completed a one-year course in social studies. I went to work at a Dead Sea Hostel to save money for a trip to Europe. At the end of that summer, my mother came to visit me and we had a wonderful time traveling in Israel and then in Europe. Our journey together ended and I stayed in Europe for another two months traveling around, visiting friends and absorbing the history. Back in Israel, I moved back to Kibbutz Gezer; it felt right to be among old friends and my job in the dairy. I had really missed the slow-paced lifestyle of the farm. It was in the dairy that I met my husband Drew, who is originally from Philadelphia. It was because of him that I came to the U.S.

A couple of years after we began dating, Drew wanted to try something new in his life; he had been living in Kibbutz Gezer for more than ten years. So we decided to come to the U.S. and look for a quiet place in the country where we could have a small organic farm. We left Israel with very little money, our cocker spaniel named Hoagie, old books, and clothes to start a new life in Chicago. We needed to be in a big city in order to save enough money for a down-payment on a piece of land. We worked really hard for nearly two years, most of the time working seven days a week and saving almost every penny. My first jobs in the U.S. were as a waitress, cocktail waitress, and pet shop clerk. Drew worked as a carpenter doing remodeling jobs. We saved enough for a decent down-payment, and set aside a few thousand dollars to travel this immense country.

We packed our Mitsubishi hatchback, our dog Hoagie and all the camping equipment we could fit, and spent the next six months traveling throughout the United States looking for a place to live. I had never been to the U.S., and this was the best introduction to the culture that any outsider could have. We traveled out of Chicago going west northwest to the Pacific coast, then down the Golden Coast into the desert states, across Texas, up through Arkansas and out to the east coast, ending up in upstate New York at the home of old friends. Most of the time we stayed in National Parks and Forests, seeing old friends and meeting new ones who would receive us with incredible warmth and open hearts. I was amazed and moved by the natural beauty of this vast country. After 22,000 miles, we needed to decide where we wanted to settle down. One of my main criteria was the weather; after enduring two winters in Chicago (remember that I'm a tropical girl), I could only live in a warm climate with preferably no snow. North Carolina won.

We packed our belongings and moved to central North Carolina, south of Chapel Hill. As soon as we found a place to live we began looking for land. We found a beautiful ten-acre homestead in the heart of Chatham County, between Siler City and Pittsboro. It was everything we had dreamed about. It had two ponds, a pier, gazebo, flowers everywhere, fruit trees, open spaces, a few acres of pines, a tree-lined driveway, and a modest mobile home. Even though we didn't have jobs yet, we decided to purchase this property; we were resourceful and believed we would succeed. We began a vegetable garden right away, and even produced enough to sell at a couple of local farmers markets and restaurants. We soon realized that if we ever wanted to move out of the mobile home and build a house, we needed to get real jobs to start saving money again. Slowly organic farming became organic gardening, which granted us bountiful harvest throughout the year. Many years went by before we were able to design and build our own home. I was back working in pet stores and restaurants, and Drew started a small construction and landscaping company with an Israeli man we had just met. His business was doing well, but after a year his partner decided to leave. Drew and I decided that I would start working with him, doing carpentry, laying bricks or stones, landscaping, remodeling, tiling, etc. I had always enjoyed physical labor and working outdoors, so this came naturally to

me. This intense interaction began putting a toll on our marriage. We worked together for two years, until I came across an offer that I couldn't refuse.

Back in Siler City, the Hispanic population had grown tremendously. It became clear that they had unique needs, such as services in Spanish. In 1995, I responded to a job announcement from the North Carolina Cooperative Extension Service; they were looking for a Spanish-speaking person to implement a Leadership Development Series for Latinos in Chatham. At first I was reluctant to apply because I hadn't spoken Spanish in many years, and I was worried that they would require a university degree. My fears were unfounded. I was hired for my first "real job" to implement a leadership program developed by A&T University called Community Voices. I began my outreach efforts in the community by going door to door in various Latino neighborhoods to promote the program. My Spanish came back easily. After a few months, other areas of need in the community became evident and I began developing and coordinating other educational activities for Latino families, such as life-skills workshops about nutrition, schools, banking, child development, and driver's license classes. Soon after I began working with the Cooperative Extension, another part-time position became available. The new position was funded by the United Way of Chatham County to provide direct services to Latinos. Graciela Robinson, who is from

Venezuela, and I were hired to start what is today the Hispanic Liaison of Chatham County. A year later, the Liaison incorporated and was on the way to becoming an independent non-profit organization. Gracie moved on, and I became the Liaison's first director.

Working with my fellow Latinos has added to my sense of belonging to this area. During the past five years as executive director, I have become stronger, learned a lot about my community and myself, and learned all aspects of managing a non-profit organization. It is strange to look back and realize how I was thrust into this situation with little experience or knowledge. Luckily, I was quickly surrounded by wonderful people who trusted me and offered their support, expertise, assistance, profound knowledge, as well as a listening ear. Without them and the trust and support of the Hispanic community, this agency would not exist today.

Community service takes a lot of commitment and dedication. My job also put a toll on my marriage. I spent too many hours working, going to evening meetings, and weekend trainings, and being on call 24/7 for Latino victims of crime (one of the services of the Liaison). My outgoing personality got all the attention it needed, while my introverted husband spent most of his time alone at the farm building us a beautiful home that we had worked so hard and so long for. One and a half years later our dream home was finished, and so was our relationship. We had been together for eleven years when we decided to break up; my only family in the U.S. was torn apart. We didn't have any children, mostly because I never felt ready. Year after year I would say to myself that I was too young. I'm still waiting to feel ready, although I realize that this feeling may never come. I stayed at the farm and Drew moved to Australia. Thankfully, over time we were able to work out our differences and rekindle our friendship.

Leaving my birthplace and being so far away from my loved ones isn't easy. My mother, half-siblings, and most of my family are still in Brazil; my only sister lives in Tel-Aviv with her husband and children. Throughout my life I always had a sense of not fully belonging anywhere. This feeling motivated me to travel and visit new places. When I decided to come to the U.S. with Drew, I had nothing to lose; I could always go back to Israel or Brazil if things didn't work out. Through the years I learned to rely on myself to improve my circumstances, and the U.S. felt right for me from the very beginning. Perhaps knowing English before coming helped, but beyond that, I felt a sense of connection to this country, its history, people, culture, and language. I'm a naturalized American because I'm a strong believer in civic participation and voting. In 1996, I voted for the first time in my entire life. I was so happy that I flaunted my "I voted" sticker for several days after the elections.

I never dreamed or planned to live in the U.S., and I also never imagined that I would pursue a career in community service. One of the things that I have learned in life is that there doesn't have to be a master plan in order for things to work out. I took advantage of different opportunities, allowing myself room for new experiences and for making mistakes. Over the years I've grown to trust myself and to know that wherever I am, I will at least make do. This trust and knowledge allowed me to move around so freely, leaving behind familiar environments, friends, and family. Most of all, I have my mother Anita to thank for the sacrifices she made to raise me with a good head on my shoulders, and for giving me a sense of respect and responsibility towards humanity and the world we live in. I know that she trusted me to do the right thing during my comings and goings. That trust and her personal example inspired me.

I feel a little more settled now. I have many wonderful friends in North Carolina that are my surrogate family. I have a fulfilling career that feels more like a gift. I have the unique opportunity of helping hundreds of new immigrants adapt to this country, as well as helping the community at large understand their new neighbors. Sometimes I get overwhelmed with the responsibilities of my job; it would be false to suggest that this has been an easy road. One thing that helps me with the stresses of my hectic schedule is to gaze up at the birds and trees in my little homestead.

"Throughout my life I always had a sense of not fully belonging anywhere."
Ilana Dubester

Ilana *Dubester*

Ilana Dubester is originally from Porto Alegre, Brazil and has lived in Chatham County, North Carolina since 1991. She began working with the Latino community of Chatham County in 1995, as the Latino program coordinator for the N.C. Cooperative Extension Service. She was responsible for developing and implementing educational programs for Latino families. Also in 1995, she co-founded and a year later became the executive director of the Hispanic Liaison of Chatham County. The Liaison is a nonprofit organization that serves the multiple needs of the Hispanic community through resource referral, education and training, advocacy, and language services.

In 1998, Ilana was appointed to the first N.C. Governor's Council on Hispanic/Latino Affairs, where she chairs the Crime Control and Public Safety Committee. She was also recently appointed to the N.C. Domestic Violence Commission. Ilana is active in many Advisory Boards and committees such as Chatham Hospital's Immigrant Health Initiative, the Foreign Language Interpreter Task Force of the Administrative Office of the Courts, the Coalition for Family Peace in Siler City, and Chatham County Crime Stoppers.

From Peru to North Carolina a biography of Violeta S. Moser

Manco Capac, Atahualpa, De Soto, Pizarro: These are names that I had to learn when I studied history back home. These are the names of the mighty Incas and Spanish conquistadors who ruled Peru, the country where I was born, for many centuries. It has been a long time since those days, but the rich history and the diversity of my culture are part of the person I am. My mixed ancestry, influenced by modern cultures, and exceptional opportunities have contributed to my understanding and admiration of the diverse society in which I now live.

I was born in Lima, the capital of Peru, in 1955. Lima is an old Spanish colonial city that, in the fifteenth century, was the capital of Spain in the Americas. It is now one of the largest cities in Latin America, with a population of six million people. My family and I lived in the historical district of Old Lima in a large colonial house with many dark rooms and sunny courtyards, and with many people around us. There were times when our temporary family and guests could be more than twenty people living in the old house at the same time. My family included *mamá*, *papá*, two brothers, grandmother, aunts, uncles, cousins, and all who had one drop of blood of our known ancestors. Even our closest friends were considered relatives.

The adults in the family played a crucial role in forming the *niños* (children) of the house. Our respect for adults, particularly for our elders, teachers and mentors, was part of our formation. I went to crowded, full-of-life schools from elementary to high school into college. My family insisted on our education and endorsed every opportunity to study anything to build our knowledge. I was the *niña*, and the pride of my family who was expected to be the best of her class, and the best at everything that was academic. The other activities—dance, music, ballet, drama, art, sports—were just for culture.

From early childhood, my daily life was amongst people of different social classes, ages, looks, sounds, and colors with only one common denominator: our Catholic religion. Catholicism was not only our religion; it was a way of life at home, at school, and sometimes in government. Our family festivities, a baptism of a baby, a confirmation, a first communion, a wedding, a death, a blessing of a new home, a town celebration, our holidays, and our birthdays always included a ritual by our priest.

During my childhood I was also exposed to the *"gringo"* culture through my father's relationship with *el Cuerpo de Paz* (Peace Corps) that visited Huaylas, a beautiful little valley in the Northern Andes where my parents were born. The Peace Corps engineers used to teach the farmers how to grow better yields of crops. Hearing conversations in English I could not understand challenged me to listen closer, opening my interest in languages. I loved foreign music and accents. I began to take English and French lessons when I was seven. My brother and I listened to the Beatles for hours.

I also grew up during times of transition—there is always a transition going on in Latin America. By the time I was a student in college, a military dictatorship was the form of government in Peru. Censorship was a way of life. No meetings of more than five people were allowed without permission, curfew hours in the city restricted where people could go, the radio and newspapers were controlled by the government, there were long lines to get food, and "black markets" to find meat and other goods needed at home. The government told people that the *"gringos"* were not good people. Graffiti on the street walls read "Yanquis go home." The universities played an active role in the political life of Peru. The university I attended, Federico Villarreal, located in downtown Lima, was shut down many times in fear of rebellious manifestations against the government. I vividly remember times of frustration and fear as students marched in protest down the streets.

It was the time of revolution; it was also the time for many young people to look for other options to continue our only passage to success, education. By then my English studies were almost completed and I started looking for work to practice my bilingual skills. It was then that one of my cousins was coming to the U.S. and invited me to join her. This was my opportunity!

The priorities in my life changed at the very moment I learned of the opportunity to come to the U.S. I was eighteen and my new challenges were: 1.Get permission from my parents; 2. Be granted the grand prize of an American visa; 3. Find the money for the airline ticket and my *"bolsa de mano"* (expenses for stay); 4. Fill out dozens of paperwork and fight the bureaucracies and red tape; and 5. Stand in long lines to get all of the above done in one month!

In Latin America, this is indeed a challenge. It was a bright Friday afternoon when I left the U.S. Embassy in downtown Lima with a visa on my passport to travel to New York. I was granted a scholarship to attend a small college in New Jersey. It was only for one semester...that's all my parents would allow, and all the money I had.

I arrived at New York's JFK airport on a hot summer day of the Northern Hemisphere on August 3, 1974 full of dreams and expectations and looking for just an opportunity...an education. I wanted to get a degree from an American college and return home to get the best job in Lima, and live and travel around the world with my family. I wanted to be a diplomat or an ambassador for my country.

While in pursuit of this dream, I met many more challenges as I learned how to live in a culture that speaks a different language, a nation that holds different values, people who live different traditions and eat different foods. This became my rite of passage into the American culture.

I learned how hard it is to work and go to school at the same time. I had to work. My father could not afford to support me in a foreign country where dollars are the currency. I had to learn how to cook, clean the house, and launder my clothes. Back at home none of these chores were mine, I was a Student with capital S. All I was expected to do was to go to school and study hard so that I could get ahead. In my country, with a good education I could get a good job or a good rich husband. I could hire people to do the domestic work. What a change in culture this was!

Since no one knew who I was or how my life was in my country, I did not mind it too much. I was learning the new ways of the American culture. Things were done differently here, but necessity became my best teacher. When, many times, I ran out of clean clothes to wear, I taught myself how to use the washing machine.

A job was also something that I never had—even more, manual work was not considered for a *niña* like me! I got a job cooking hamburgers at a local fast food restaurant, four hours a day, three days a week. Many times I cut and burned my fingers, but I survived. The challenge was my customers, who needed to speak slowly while I took their orders so that I could understand what they said. Many times I felt like a fool when a customer became frustrated as I asked him to repeat his order for the third time. Many times I got yelled at when the order was incorrect. I realized that my impeccable record of more than ten years of English at home was not good enough. There were many times that I cried and I wanted to go home. I missed my family. There were other days that I felt my English was very good because my teachers and friends said it and my grades were showing it.

I shrugged off and went on. As long as my family in Peru did not know of the kind of work I was doing and the "sacrifices," all was fine. I did share with them the many times the bus driver got mad because I never had the right amount of coins for the fare. I always handed him a dollar bill—I did not know what a dime, a nickel or a penny was. My English teachers never taught me this in school. I did tell them that I saw white stuff coming down from the sky that I mistook as confetti on New Year's Eve. I had never seen snow before. I did tell them how my Peruvian coat was not the right kind for the winter in this part of the world and that my brand new Peruvian shoes were not made for walking in the snow. I did tell them that many people I met did not know where Peru was and that they did not call me American, not even South American, but Hispanic or Latina. I did tell them that I was invited to celebrate Independence Day on the 4th of July and that none knew of July 28 (Peruvian Independence Day).

After almost two years of total immersion in the American culture and finishing school, I was making plans to return home when I met a young Penn Stater. He came to work at a pharmaceutical plant where I got my first office job. Once again, another major change in my life and culture took place. At the surprise of my family and friends, I married a non-Peruvian in August 1977 in Summit, New Jersey. A new journey began as two young people with different cultural backgrounds set out on a life together.

Bob and I moved around up and down the East Coast, developing our professional careers. I entered the banking industry in 1979 as a management trainee in a bank in Connecticut. My English was totally improved! I was happy to take this opportunity, as my new plans were to move into a position in international banking to use my bilingual skills. English became my primary language and the American culture part of my life. International banking, however, was not found in Greenville, N.C. where we moved in 1983, one year after my daughter, Stephanie Victoria, was born. Around this time my mother, as a good Latin mother,

came to help me with the new baby. My mother did not speak English, Bob did not speak Spanish and we all had to learn to communicate with sounds and signs. Stephanie, on the other hand, benefited from growing up in a bicultural and bilingual household.

We had many laughs and sad times. The first time I experienced real sadness was when my father died in 1988. This marked another change in my life, as I became responsible for my mother's well-being. Life went on and I continued to pursue my banking career in this little and charming Eastern city.

It was also in Pitt County that I started another facet of my life, community work. I discovered the existence of migrant workers, most of them farmers from Mexico. I was able to use my Spanish skills by helping them with translations and organizing programs to attend to their primary health and social needs. I also realized that many people called Hispanics arrive in this country in search of the same dream I had…an opportunity to get ahead. I learned that our experiences and backgrounds were quite different, and that I was one lucky person for having an education and the knowledge of the English language. I learned that I was called Hispanic, just like the people I was helping, because we spoke Spanish, our common denominator. I knew that it was now my time to contribute, to help others realize the dream that also brought me here.

In 1992, we moved to Charlotte, a larger city with a more diverse population. I immediately became active in this Hispanic community, joining civic organizations and helping in the development of programs to assist the need for human services programs. I also saw the need for understanding diversity in the area. I became involved in projects to promote the Hispanic/Latino cultures, to bring awareness and stress the importance of diversity.

Parallel to these activities, my banking career continued for a few more years while I gained valuable experience with my involvement in the community. In the last two years I took another opportunity, making a change in my career and becoming a consultant. My current work involves the development of marketing and training programs for international and domestic Hispanic/Latino markets. I use my native language and teach language and culture to bring sensitivity into the workplace and in the community. I have become a speaker and an expert in the Hispanic/Latino cultures. I also develop curricula to teach Spanish to bridge the cultural gap as we move into a global economy and community.

It has been a long journey, one filled with fun, excitement and challenges. It is a journey I would gladly walk again. There is no other way that I could have learned to appreciate the value of the cultures, the value of diversity, the value of languages, the respect for all people. I now understand better that it is the link to my ancestry and the confidence with my identity that gave me the solid base that supports the person that I am. That no matter how big the dream and how hard the challenges, they can be overcome as long as there is a line that anchors us to our roots.

Violeta S. Moser

Violeta Moser is a native of Lima, Peru. In the middle seventies, forced by political and economic instability in her country, she came to the United States to pursue her college education. She attended Montclair University in New Jersey. Her goal was to obtain a degree in business and return to her homeland. Her dream was to travel the world as an ambassador for Peru. Three years after her arrival to this country, and to the surprise of her conservative family—all of them still live in Peru—she married a North American. She and her husband Bob have a teenage daughter, Stephanie Victoria.

Violeta started her career in banking, focusing on bank and mortgage operations and administration. She has also taught Spanish and cross-cultural programs for schools and corporations on a part-time basis to keep connected to her native language and culture. Her personal background, along with her professional and community service experiences, provided her with expertise to become a consultant specializing in Latin American markets. Violeta's principal experience in the textile industry derives from her work with major textile companies operating in Mexico. Her domestic work with ReMark Inc. includes research, marketing, public relations, and training programs development for private and public institutions with interest in the Hispanic/Latino population.

Violeta is president of the Latin American Coalition. She serves on the Governor's Hispanic Economic Developments Committee, the Mayor's International Cabinet, and on the boards of CPCC Small Business Development and Children's Theaters.

May Craven   an interview

Where did you grow up?

I grew up as a sharecropper's daughter in the Sandhills of North Carolina—a little town called Ellerbe, ten miles from Rockingham. Very rural community. We farmed tobacco. Lived there until I married at seventeen.

Then what?

Went to the university. We moved to Columbia, South Carolina. Stayed there for four years, then moved to Wilmington.

And you've been in Wilmington ever since?

That's right.

What career dreams did you have as a child?

Because I am a former stutterer, I always wanted to be able to speak without stuttering. Therefore, I took every opportunity that I could to try to get up before an audience. I was the first female president of our student body association in my high school. This was 1963.

It would seem that a young person who stuttered would've avoided public speaking, not have sought it out.

I know. A couple of reasons for that, I think. One, that I had this intense desire to be something a whole lot more than how I had grown up—poor. I am the middle child—I have an older sister and a baby brother. Now, I am not the oldest, I'm not the youngest, I'm not the only girl. I think many times—most times—middle children strive to achieve. We either are shrinking violets or we will be overachievers, and I was an overachiever. I got my education by simply *wanting* it—wanting it badly enough to do those things that it took and working hard to get it. I stuttered so badly until I was in about the ninth or tenth grade, but in fact, I made very good grades. No matter what I did, I always wanted to top that and do something better, be something better. And I don't know why *(laughs)*—but I had no qualms about a woman achieving in a man's world.

Even at a time when that wasn't the norm.

That is correct. That is correct.

Were you aware that it wasn't the norm?

Absolutely. I surely was.

Did you know yet at that time what you wanted to achieve someday?

All I knew was that I wanted to do something where speaking was concerned—public speaking—and I wanted to do something where I could help other people, especially stutterers.

When did your own stuttering stop? Was there a point when you said 'I don't stutter anymore'?

It stopped gradually, just as all of my evolving has come about. It stopped gradually about the time I graduated from high school.

How did you overcome it?

By learning to speak so very slowly. And practicing, practicing, practicing. I would read. I would ask my teachers, my professors, to call on me to read in class. I was very, very fortunate that almost all of them agreed to that. And we'd never heard of voice or diction lessons. Therefore, I knew that it was something that I could do on my own. I never thought for one moment that I couldn't do it.

Do you now find it unusual that you didn't have any training on how to overcome stuttering and yet instinctively felt you could do it?

Mmm, mmm, I think so. There's no doubt in my mind that I can do anything I want to do with enough time and enough training. Shoot, I could be a brain surgeon if I wanted to. All I'd have to do is just go to medical school and learn how.

To what do you attribute such optimism?

Lots of struggles throughout life and just living life on life's terms. I'm fifty-five. My life is the most content it has ever been. I feel comfortable in my own skin. I feel comfortable about others. And happiness is an inside job. That is so good, to feel comfortable about myself. I haven't always felt that way. It's great, and this is what I want to pass on to younger women.

Recount for me, if you would, the path that brought you where you are today.

We moved to Wilmington, because of my husband's job. We were married about five years before we had our first child. Then, in a little over a year, we had the second child. So I did the usual things, PTA, volunteer work, worked here and there, you know, just to pick up a little pin money, enough to where I could have and say 'Hey, this is my very own.' It seemed as if in my twenties, though, I was always searching for something that I could call my own, especially as far as a career was concerned. Now, I had a wonderful husband—oh, my goodness, just a doll. That man was just as exciting to me at forty-three as he was at seventeen. And so I was very blessed there. We actually grew up together.

Then I started volunteering with entities such as the Greater Wilmington Chamber of Commerce, the United Way, and I joined the Wilmington Toastmasters Club about twenty-five years ago.

And that's a club that is dedicated to public speaking, self-improvement. I knew then that that was going to help me a lot.

Then I would get free speaking engagements—'May, would you consider speaking free for the Lion's Club, for the Kiwanis?'—giving speeches in my Toastmasters Club, going to statewide conventions, things such as that. Through doing those freebies, I learned, 'Hey, people are beginning to respond to what I have to say.' Little did I know that I had not lived so much of life at that time.

I definitely was not a 'know-it-all' because I had such an inferiority complex—my roots of being poor and always trying to achieve. I did not have the self-confidence, the high self-esteem that I always wanted. I didn't feel as good as some people, especially women. I thought that a lot of other women—not only older than I, but even my age—had a secret that they were not telling me, because they seemed so much more well-adjusted. But the more I made it on my own, then I realized that I beginning to come out of those feelings of 'less than,' feelings of not being 'as good as.' And, of course, from the outside I looked so good, you know. I remember I made seventy-five dollars the first speech I ever made—oh, I was probably in my early thirties—and I went to Belk's and bought a hundred-and-fifty-dollar suit. Took me six months to pay that off. But I knew that I needed to be dressed for success with the shoes and the handbag and the suit. So I started

writing and giving different programs, making a little bit of money.

Then, ten years ago, something happened that drastically changed my life. Ray Craven, my husband of twenty-six years, came home from his office, loosened his tie, we had dinner, we sat down on my son's bed, and he fell over in my lap and died. He had not been sick. He had a series of strokes in the back of his head. Now, here was a good-looking forty-three-year-old man who had been healthy as a horse, and he was barely breathing. I gave him CPR and he lived in a coma for eleven days before he died.

Now I knew that I really had to put the pinch on to make a living for myself. I was forty-three, I had never lived alone, I had gone straight from my mother and daddy—'Momma and Daddy,' I called 'em, *their* home—to being married. And it was time for both of our sons to leave home. So I went from a bustling family of four to just May. I had to learn to live with May. It took me three years—three years of fighting as hard as I could, three years of crying, praying, cussing, reading, seeking, not feeling as if I was finding.

Today, I know that real growth comes from a broken heart. My heart was broken. I had great successes with my late husband—and I had great regrets. Had I told him I loved him enough? Had I shown him I loved him? Could I have done anything? Should I have given him CPR? All of those things kept flooding back those three years. There were three years of sheer Hell.

Then finally, *finally*, I began to see the light. And the light was that there are others out there who have been through that. There are others who will help me. I can depend on friends. I can trust people. 'Give it a try, May.' Taking baby steps. Taking three steps forward, two backward. And I started writing new programs. I wrote a new program, which sold very well, on grief—the loss of a spouse, the loss of both parents. So here again, I regrouped, reinvented May Craven, went back to what I did to overcome the stuttering—keeping at it and keeping at it until I thought I was gonna die. But I didn't. So my real growth came from my heart being broken.

Where do you find inspiration and renewal today?

I find renewal from God. And I'm not one of these holy-rollers who's a Bible-thumper. I am an officer in my Presbyterian church. That's the highest honor I've ever won. I've won beauty contests; I have been voted into offices—by men and women—that women had never won before. But the highest honor is when the peers in my church voted me in as an officer. I'm very proud of that.

I'd always gone to church from the time I was married. I didn't grow up in church—my parents did not go. But when I was sixteen, I got down on my hands and knees in the tiny little Meth-odist church—about sixty members—that I had attended and first joined so I could chase boys. And I got down on my knees in that church right by myself and I said, 'God, if you're up there or if you're anywhere, I need some help. My stuttering is getting better, but I want to *be* somebody. I want to help other people, and, in turn, I want to help myself.' See, we get what we want when we help others get what *they* want.

Tell me about your career today.

I teach classes, but mostly I am a keynote address speaker. That's what I do. I give the keynote address at conferences, conventions, business meetings, association meetings. I do that more than anything else because I have a powerful story to tell and it's not just for women—it's for men, too. I tell them about growing up on a tobacco farm. And I'm a motivational humorist. I'm very proud of that. I help motivate people through my own life story as well as the life stories of others. And using a lot of humor. A sense of humor has helped see me through in my worst times when I have done stupid things—had a car wreck or my dress flew up over my head. See, I can laugh about 'em now. And then, I would cry and squall and take on. But I'd never forget my country roots. Something that I thought would be so bad—a terrific Southern accent, a very pronounced Southern accent—has turned into quite a jewel, north of the Mason-Dixon line.

So you travel all over the country?

I surely do. And I teach 'Stress, Coping and Energizing Skills'—that's my most popular. I also teach 'Dealing with Difficult People.' I teach 'Making A Positive First Impression.' Those are my three hottest sellers. I've written two new ones, for women only, 'Living, Loving and Life,' because women's roles both at work and at home have changed drastically since our mothers and grandmothers told us about living, loving and life—if they told us *at all*. And planting ideas, planting the seed—just a little mustard seed even—that can grow when women learn to live life on life's terms. And then I have just finished—and will give it for the first time next month at a college—for women over fifty, 'Feeling Fabulous after Fifty.' Now see, I'm *there!* That gives me credence. That gives me credibility.

How do potential clients hear about you?

Word of mouth. I've been doing this twenty-five years. If you're good, if you're funny, if you're sincere and have integrity, you'll get work.

What are some ways you relax these days?

Cooking. Gardening. I've learned to meditate—somewhat. I'm getting better at it. That's a goal of mine. I always have *something* in my life to look forward to, some little something to look forward to. It might be eating a lobster dinner Saturday night.

Now I remarried a year and a half ago—remarried a man I'd known thirty years. He's wonderful. Now he's undergoing chemotherapy. So this is a real strain on him and, of course, I'm the caregiver. He is a joy to be around though. (*Laughs.*) Oh, I can't tell you how blessed I've been with two good men.

It must be difficult to face the illness of a spouse after you've lost one husband.

Mmm, mmm, it is. I knew he had lymphoma going into the marriage. This is a choice I made and I'm very glad I made the choice.

Tell me about your sons.

Oh, they're wonderful. My sons are in their early thirties. I have one who is a sales manager for an automobile dealership. He and his wife have two little children. My younger son, who is seventeen months younger, works for a graphic design company. He and his wife have one daughter who's nine. And they live, oh, within thirty miles of me.

Do you see them often?

Well, keep in mind, honey, that I grew up in the country. Therefore, I'm a good country cook. Growing up in the country doesn't make you a good country cook, but cooking is one of my hobbies. When I fry chicken, have butterbeans, scalloped potatoes, lemon meringue pie—they come. (*Laughs.*)

They can probably smell it thirty miles away!
Oh, yes.

When your sons were young and you were getting started as a professional speaker, how did you balance home and career?

Well, I really was not doing it as much then to make money. I was just doing it just to get some experience. And a person has to have a support system. My friends have been my support system. My friends have been my family. Because, after seventeen, I've never lived close by to my family. And my husband was a very devoted family man and he had the kind of job where he could be a little bit late for work or he could come home a little bit early to keep the children if I had a speaking engagement, which really made it nice. One has to have a good support system, whether it's in the form of a babysitter, a neighbor, a mother, sister, whomever. You've got to work out that support system, whether it's little children, whether it's emotional support when you're crying and squalling and cussing over something. And I've done it all.

Do you have personal goals or interests besides meditation that you are

currently pursuing?

Yes. Constantly upgrading May Craven. Regrouping. Finding ways where I can help others. Now, remember, we get what we want when we help others get what they want. I think that is sooo important. Shoot, I didn't realize this until I was about forty-five.

My biggest concern is health. My health is good—I want to keep it that way. For the first time in my life, I'm exercising three times a week. Exercise has always been a four-letter word to me. But I know that if I expect to live well, live a full life, and live long, I must take care of my body, just as I take care of my car, my home, my husband. We women over forty-five face life just as frenzied, I think, as we did when our children were babies. Today, we juggle aging parents, a career—a career that may be coming to an end if we're facing retirement—spouse, teenage children or grown children. And something that I face, too—raging hormones. (*Laughs.*) And, of course, these result in mood swings, muscle fatigue, loss of memory, and intense food cravings. Now, there's something else that I have to watch and that's my weight. Oh lord, I would love to be able to eat a dozen doughnuts, two dozen chocolate chip cookies, all washed down with a real North Carolina Pepsi-Cola. I remember when I would eat three tomato sandwiches with mayonnaise on them and not worry about it. Now, if I continued to eat the same amount of calories as I did when I was twenty, just in those twenty-five years until I was forty-five, I would be forty-two pounds heavier and at risk for health problems.

And I want women who read this to know that, over forty-five, this is the second half of my life—I like to speak in the first person, and that way, I hope I can help others—and I alone have the power to make my future years as rich and rewarding as possible. Not my children, not my husband, not my career, just May. And those persons with whom I surround myself—are they healthy? Are they fun? Do I really enjoy being with 'em? Or do they drag me down emotionally?

And what do you do when someone drags you down emotionally?
I make as smooth an exit from them as possible.

What personal qualities do you consider to be of the most value in life?
Honesty, open-mindedness, and integrity—I think that is so important, someone who can be honest with me. Somebody who will lie to you will ultimately steal from you, and may not steal something that is tangible that you can touch, but they'll steal your time, your energy. I have a lot of places where I want to put my energy. And being with somebody who's not honest with me—or honest with themselves mostly—is not my idea of spending a good time. But thank God roles for women have changed.

There has never been a better time to be a woman than today, and I'm so proud of that. And I'd like to think that when I leave this earth, I would have had a part in helping that positive change. I mentor for young women—that has been one of the greatest joys of my life.

How did you reach the point of being so 'comfortable in your own skin,' as you put it earlier?
Lots of work. Lots of work and struggles. Example—when my husband died, when I wondered if I would have enough money to last me through the month, if I would have more month than I did money, when somebody had wronged me, hurt my feelings, my car broke down, I had a kitchen flooded from the dishwasher. Through those struggles and keeping at it—perseverance, perseverance, perseverance, I cannot stress that enough—then you know, 'Hey, I can do this. I am my own greatest resource, other than God. And there is a God who is looking after me. That God *made* me; now I've got to do some work, some footwork, to make good things happen for me.' I like to say that the good Lord gave me two ends—one to sit on and one to think with. Heads, we win—tails, we lose. Our success in life depends on which end we choose. Example—if I'm going to sit on my backside and just let life pass me by and say, 'Well, God's taking care of me. Honey, I'm not gon' worry about it,' I am going to be out of luck, out of

cash, out of a good time. But if I get up off my backside and use my head, even if I make mistakes, sooner or later, I'm gon' hit on somethin' *good*!

It seems as though perhaps you've had more tragedy than the average person.

I don't think so. I don't think so at all. Each person has her own Hell, whether that's lack of self-esteem, shyness, no confidence, no money, no man, no children. That's all right. The station of life we're in can be good, if we want it to be badly enough.

What advice do you give women for making their lives better at any stage?

Little things we women can do—just little things help so much. For instance, keeping our homes up-to-date. Have you ever been in an elderly woman's house? She'd lived alone for years, and she had a bunch of cats jumping up and down on the furniture, and her house smelled stale and musty? Sure. And the drapes had probably hung there for thirty-five years. And the same carpet, if there was carpet on the floor, had been there at least forty years. 'Update your surroundings' is something that I tell women. Have your house smelling clean and fresh. Have *yourself* clean and fresh. Doll up. After forty-five, I don't believe in the natural look. I love to paint up and powder up as much as I can—makes me feel *good*

about myself.

And other little things like—'Make sure that you're driving a clean car,' 'Hire somebody to come in and straighten up your house once a week,' 'Don't have pictures out of your brother and your daddy in World War I and the Korean conflict and W-W-Two.' 'Change your pictures at least once every six months.'

And if you're sixty years old, don't dress like you're sixteen, 'cause even if you still *are* small, you're not gonna have the figure that you had when you were sixteen, unless you've had a little cuttin' done. Of course, one thing that I do is not eat s'damn much. Now, I love to eat—Lord *knows* I love to eat—but I know, like I say, that I can't eat those three tomato sandwiches anymore. I'm gonna have to cut down on it and exercise. Now that doesn't mean that I wear a size ten. Shoot, I'm a size fourteen to a sixteen. But when I dress up, honey, I look *good*! And I do little things like always using a lighted, magnifying mirror when applying my makeup because you can see little flaws. Cover 'em up! Honey, if you got a roll around your belly, don't show it off. Cover it up!

Keep bestselling books out in your den, in your living room. You never know, you just might read 'em. Put a new comforter and sheets on your bed. Buy new lamp shades. Do some things for yourself to make you feel good because a man's home is not just his castle—a *woman's* home is her castle as well. Change to softer lighting, especially if you're over fifty-five. Zsa Zsa Gabor always had pink light bulbs. And keep fresh towels in the bathroom. Don't have those nasty-looking towels there. And buy a bright new tablecloth or something just to make *you* feel better. Always have something to look forward to. Don't have dusty old fake silk flowers all over the house. Get yourself outside and do a little bit of yardwork and grow your own and bring you a rose in and put it in a vase.

I have a best friend with whom I can confide *anything*, I mean, anything. And I probably have two friends that I can do that with. Men will come and go. Good women friends will certainly stick by you, but you've gotta pick and choose, and it takes you a while to learn if you can trust them. This friend I've had over thirty years. Her name's Miss Kitty, and she and I are the same age. And she says, 'Yes, aging sucks, but the smart woman plucks.' That's why we have a magnifying mirror—if you have any little distasteful hairs on your face, pluck them out so you can get yourself dolled up for your viewing public.

Little things like fresh air, you know, letting in the sunshine. Burn scented candles, bake cookies, bake apples, or put a little bit of vanilla on the lightbulbs. This fills a room with a most welcome smell and the olfactory sense—the sense of smell—well, I believe it is the one which can trigger memories more than anything else. I *know* it is for me. Sometimes I'll just take a walk in the woods. I've got a fifty-acre farm up in my hometown, and the scent of the pine trees, the oak trees, the freshly-mowed grass—that can bring back sweet memories of when I was a child and would take walks in the woods and talk to God, talk to myself.

And as I said earlier, there is no better time to be a woman than today. I had knee surgery. It was just right after my husband Ray died. And that was one of my greatest fears for several years, that I would fall again, 'cause that was some rough surgery. I mean, having children's nothing compared to that. But things like hips are being replaced routinely. (*Laughs.*) And wouldn't it be wonderful if we would be able to relocate part of our hips to a more alluring spot? And laser surgery—my daughter-in-law no longer has to wear contact lenses because she had eye laser surgery. I think that's great—no glasses, no contacts. And there are new drugs that can dissolve blood clots. Lasers are removing wrinkles, age spots, things such as that. And of course, there's Viagra. And there was a woman who gave birth last year—she lived in England, I think—and she was sixty-three. And there's wonderful new cancer research being done all the time. And—I love to read facts—researchers have found the gene that triggers hair loss, so gene therapy to prevent baldness may soon be on the horizon. And, of course, scientists know how to regenerate the cells of certain human organs now. So there is so much promise. I hate to hear people say, 'Well, things aren't the way they used to be.' Hellfire, thank God they're not! Shoot, I grew up without a bathroom in the house. Today, I've got three bathrooms in my house and I go to all three of them. Just happy to have 'em.

Keep an optimistic outlook. Feel good about any age, any stage, you're in. I know women who are ninety-one, ninety-two years old, eighty-seven years old—I can think of three right now—who are so *much fun* to be around.

And *always* have something in your refrigerator that you can serve someone when they come in, whether it's a piece of cake, cookies, a Pepsi-Cola, cup of coffee. Make people welcome when they come into your house, young or old. That makes me feel so good, when somebody says, 'May, would you like a glass of sweet tea?' And then, have some fresh flowers there on the table.

And listen. Just *listen*. I asked my minister, Dr. Curtis Christian—he's forty years old—I said 'Curtis, I want you to tell me how you minister so well to those people whose parents have just died, whose spouse has just died.' I said 'What do you say to them at first that's of such great comfort?' Because he is very well-known for doing that. And Dr. Christian looked at me and said, 'May, I don't say anything. I tell them I love them and then I shut up and just listen.' That is what *I* do. I shut up and just listen. That makes me a very engaging companion.

I want to be the kind of person that other folks love to be around. And that's with a positive attitude. I want to be lots of fun and very honest. It's great to be my age today. It's absolutely great.

What would be an example of advice you give to women in the business setting?

Southern women, especially, tend to put tag phrases at the end of sentences. 'Mr. Jones, I made your appointment for five o'clock, as you asked. I hope that's all right.' Leave out the 'I hope that's all right.' Or you're in a board meeting and you say, 'This might sound stupid, but...' Leave out the 'It may sound stupid,' because that plants something in the other board members' minds. Right then, it says 'Hey, what she's gon' say is stupid.' Leave off tag phrases. These things I teach in my classes that have just come from being there. Been there, done that, bought the T-shirt!

Is there anything that you would you do differently if you could turn back the clock?

Not one thing. Even the mistakes that I've made are only lessons and they got me to where I am today. Not one thing. I couldn't have said that fifteen years ago.

What dreams do you have that are yet to be realized?

Well, I hope to go back to school when I'm sixty-five and then, that way, I can go free to the university here. I want to learn to be a good landscaper. Now, I have just found out that I love working in the yard. And I love to see things grow. Those are two goals that I have for myself.

What are some of your favorite things?

Chocolate chip cookies, cheese straws—see, a lot of mine involve food. A little girl's giggle. Hearing someone say 'Thank you, May.' The sweet smell of newly-mowed grass, I love that. I rarely watch television. I have one show that I really like and that's 'NYPD Blue.' Also, I like Westerns. I'm not going to admit to you that I like oldies but goodies, because I think we all should have friends of different ages. If I go around with all old women with those kinky permanents in their hair, their hair tinted blue, then I'm going to sooner or later become one—see, I don't ever want to be an old woman. I may *be* elderly chronologically but, in my heart, I'll always be fifteen, looking forward to my sweet sixteen birthday party. I love to be around people who are fun. That's probably my favorite thing to do, and to laugh. To be around people who are fun and laugh. And I love a Cadillac car. I look *good* in a Cadillac—a red Cadillac trimmed in gold.

Of what accomplishment are you most proud?

That's a tough one. 'Course most people say 'Healthy children, wonderful husband, nice home,' things like that. My great-est accomplishment has been the fact that I have stayed connected spiritually with God all my life. And that doesn't mean that I don't cuss and rant and rave. And I get scared. I have fears just like everybody else. But I know that there's something greater than *I* am that is helping me every single day. I am not alone. I think basically we all just want to feel safe. Today, I feel safe.

Interviewed by Susan L. Comer.

Olan Mills

May Craven

"There has never been a better time to be a woman than today, and I'm so proud of that."

May Craven

A former stutterer who grew up on a tobacco farm in rural North Carolina, May Craven says she knows how to regroup, recoup, and overcome obstacles in life. A popular, award-winning Professional Speaker and Trainer for twenty-five years, she travels nationally, giving her Keynote Address at conferences, conventions, and business meetings. She tells her own powerful story of winners, losers, struggles, and victories…all laced with an abundance of humor and motivation. Owner and President of Craven Consulting in Wilmington, N.C., May is married to Frank Clark and is the mother of two grown sons.

A Historian's Odyssey* Anne Firor Scott

Reading one's own words, some of them written nearly sixty years ago, stirs up memories, reflections, anxieties, questions. How did I get here from there? How did I come to choose this difficult discipline in the first place—one which it has taken me thirty years to begin to understand? Why did I fix upon history rather than zoology or literature? Why, indeed, did I choose scholarship rather than business or politics? Was it chance, or some half-understood personal predilection, which guided my choices? Historians are taught to be wary of autobiography, for who, after all, can tell the truth about oneself? Yet no one else is likely to try, and no other method (except perhaps psychoanalysis) suggests itself as a means of answering these questions.

Fortunately I do not have to rely entirely upon treacherous memory. Since 1937 I have kept a journal, which now approaches twenty volumes. Some of it tells me more than I really want to know, but the existence of a record made on the spot inhibits the inevitable human tendency to rewrite the past and make it nicer. I have no recollection, for example, of what was apparently a moment of despair in 1954:

I have been on a long jag of reading and doing little or nothing on my thesis. It almost amounts to a complete failure of will—over and over I resolve to sit down and write that damn chapter—but nothing happens. Nursery school had a holiday, but that is really no excuse. Probably the fact of the thing is that I have no business trying to be a historian, and only an undue consideration for what people will say if I give up now keeps me even theoretically at it.

Was I really on the verge of giving up? Was it really "what people will say" that drove me on? I have no idea; but in due course the "damn chapter" and its successors were written, and a few pages later certain journal entries foreshadow ideas which would evolve into a project not then even envisioned. The mind, as well as the Lord, works in mysterious ways...

Perhaps one should begin at the beginning.

It makes a good bit of difference when you happen to be born. I arrived in the world nine months after the suffrage amendment was added to the Constitution, so I never have to count on my fingers to find out how long women have had the right to vote. It was the year the number of women in state universities first equaled the number of men. It was also the first time women in other occupations outnumbered domestic servants among female wage earners. It was a year of sudden depression: my parents lost their savings in a bank failure and had some difficulty paying the doctor who had delivered me, at home.

My father, who had married late because he was helping to support a widowed mother and a younger sister, took to child-raising with enthusiasm. My brothers and I have been told that he began reading to us when we were babies, not from children's books—which he found boring—but from his own favorites. He also told us long historical tales, dealing with the Indian tribes which, he said, had lived on the hill by the Oconee River in Athens where the Georgia State College of Agriculture stood.

A rough analysis of the biographies of women historians in *Notable American Women* shows that three-fourths were either eldest children, only children, or only girls. I was both the eldest child and the only girl with three brothers. As far as any of us can remember there weren't intellectual distinctions on the basis of sex in our upbringing, and if anything, more was expected of the firstborn. When I read now that "society" convinces all girls of their own inferiority, I am struck by the fact that parents who did not share the common view countered the supposedly overwhelming social messages so effectively that I was twenty-one before it crossed my mind (thanks to a rude comment from a favorite philosophy professor) that being female would in any way limit what I did in the world. (I should make it plain, of course, that the assumption that their male and female children were equally intelligent did not prevent my parents from bringing me up to be a proper Southern lady in behavior, speech, manner—but that is another story, perhaps not relevant here.)

As far as I can tell, I began to do history by chance. A stimulating freshman course on the English constitution at the University of Georgia led me to take other history courses until, without planning it, I had a major. But I found chemistry, literature, even math, equally interesting and dreamed impartially about becoming a medical doctor or the mother of six. In a vague way I thought I would have a career, but I had no notion what that involved, how it would affect marriage (which was also on my agenda), or what its substance would be. Indeed, I can think of no one of my female classmates who had the sophistication and sense of direction about future possibilities which are now commonplace among women students.

If my journal is to be believed, I went out into the world in 1940 in search of fame, fortune, and a husband, in no particular order. As to how that search was to be conducted, the journal is significantly silent. It was very much a matter of what might turn up.

Neither a job at IBM nor a brief turn in a graduate program for personnel managers seemed quite the thing (though my IBM boss promised the fortune would come in due course if I would only be patient). The first opportunity which struck me as leading in the right direction came in the form of an internship in Washington, where, along with thirty or so other recent college graduates, I was inducted into the mysteries of the federal government. After a California Congressman named Jerry Voorhis made a compelling talk to our group, I attached myself to him as an intern. Happily for me, he was a man who believed in encouraging the young. Senator Paul Douglas said, years later, that he had only known three saints in politics and Voorhis was one. Saint or not, he was a most unusual man, a Yale graduate of socialist inclination who had run a school for orphan boys before he came to Congress as one of the young radicals of the early New Deal. "When I came here," he said, "I planned to vote right on every issue; now after seven years I am only absolutely sure about one vote." Writing speeches for him and listening to his reflections made me so painfully aware of my ignorance that I went back to school.

An M.A. in political science made me a bit more employable; whether it made me any wiser is debatable. Still, it was 1944 and the war was opening new doors to women. The president of the National League of Women Voters, having watched much of her senior staff depart for higher wartime salaries in the government, took a chance on three very young women,

of whom I was one. The League, child of the National American Woman Suffrage Association, was still inhabited by, and to a degree run by, ancient suffragists: women of such force and power that I do not remember having for them any of the usual scorn of youth for age. While my work dealt with public affairs, economic issues, international problems, I was also learning—though I was not much conscious of it—a great deal about a certain kind of American woman and about the inner workings of a women's voluntary association.

I shared a house with three other women who had come to Washington as I had. The war gave a peculiar intensity to life— the men we had known in college came to visit on their way to countries we hardly knew existed and sent back letters from which all mention of place and time had been censored. In our various jobs, all of which dealt in some way with international relations, we believed ourselves to be helping shape the future of the country, even of the world.

Then came Hiroshima. In my mind's eye I can still see our household along with several friends, on that hot August night in 1945 gathered on an upstairs porch hearing the celebration in the streets but not feeling celebratory at all. We constituted ourselves a Ten Years To Live Club—it would take about that long, we said, for the atomic bomb to do us all in. The postwar world for which we had thought we were preparing would, clearly, be somewhat different from our hopes. Within three months two of us were married, and a third had enrolled in Columbia's Russian Institute. I was left to find new roommates and ponder the future—mine and the world's—while the League put me to work writing pamphlets about the control of atomic energy. That task made me again uneasily aware of how little I knew and how much there was to know, but if the world was doomed to self-destruction, did it matter?

Such musings were interrupted by an interesting and ebullient young man who invited me to marry him and go to Harvard—an offer I couldn't refuse.

Cambridge was an exhilarating place in 1947. For a while I almost took Harvard at its own assessment, which was not altogether a bad thing, since it made me work very hard. Being married to a strong-minded maverick who took nothing at face value and wanted to argue about most things—the more distinguished the faculty member, the more he wanted to argue—made this venture into higher learning different from earlier ones, and more productive.

Though the American Civilization program had requirements in history and literature, it was remarkably flexible and I continued to think of myself as a political scientist planning to write a dissertation in American political thought. Then, two days after the preliminary examination, my middle-aged mentor was made

a college president, and I turned to Oscar Handlin who, in addition to being scarcely older than I was, had been my most challenging teacher. Together we decided that I would tackle the Southern progressives, a term hitherto thought by most American historians to be a contradiction in terms. Thus for the second time, through a turn of chance, I found myself specializing in history—although still political history.

The dissertation was not destined to be written quickly. My husband, a notable workaholic, had taken his degree, and we headed back to Washington where he planned to gain some direct experience in international affairs.

All our planning was for his career; it did not occur to me to think this odd. Once we were settled, I took myself to the Library of Congress in search of those elusive Southern progressives. The Manuscript Division in those days was a small and friendly place in which I was made to feel entirely welcome and soon viewed as one of the regulars. Reading manuscripts fascinated me, though I was not entirely sure what I was looking for, or how it would all someday come together; at that stage I hardly knew the questions, much less the answers.

All this insecurity was temporarily laid aside in the summer of 1950 when our first child was born. Sudden immersion in parenthood is a traumatic experience: I could not imagine how one could combine scholarship with this voracious small being who never stopped demanding love, food, and care. With a very un-historical sense of time, I looked ahead and saw nothing but diapers and baby food for years to come. At the moment the president of the League of Women Voters came for lunch and offered me a job. I could work part-time, I could work at home, I could do whatever I wanted if only I would agree to become editor of *The National Voter*.

The baby, it turned out, managed quite well with a part-time nursemaid; and I found one could, after all, sustain attention and stretch one's mind on more substantial fare than Dr. Spock. In the 1960s when the need for part-time work for young mothers became a feminist issue I often thought of Percy Lee, that League president who, with no fanfare at all, recognized the problem and solved it and, in the process, kept me on track at one of those moments when it would have been easy to slip off completely.

The League was over its ears in debates about the cold war, the Point Four program, international trade, and a wide range of domestic issues. In preparation for the 1952 presidential election, we embarked upon a series of twelve articles on women's part in the political process for a mass circulation magazine. With so much going on in the present, it was hard to think about the past. By the time Rebecca was three, the idea that I might someday become a historian had receded into the distance.

But just then my husband decided he had finished his practical apprenticeship and was ready to join the academy. The snow-enclosed and male-dominated environment of Dartmouth College made it easier to write, and two chapters took shape before the next baby arrived. Then came another change of scene: we moved to Haverford College and had a third child. Once again my scholarly plans were in abeyance; once again a woman's voluntary association came to the rescue. Since the 1890s the American Association of University Women had been sustaining women scholars, generally by sending them to Europe to study. Mine may have been the first fellowship the AAUW knowingly provided to pay for a nursemaid. It made all the difference. At last—seven years and three children beyond the preliminary examination—the dissertation was finished.

The manuscript was safely in Cambridge; the degree was all but in hand. For the first time in years I could wonder, what next? without having a ready-made answer. Coming out of the library on a beautiful spring day, I met one of Haverford's two historians, who said that he was about to take a leave and wondered if I could suggest some young man who might like a one-year appointment in American history. I agreed to think about the question and started home. As I walked across the campus it suddenly came to me: here was a Job. I turned back and intercepted my friend: "Tom, why not me?" He looked surprised, but thoughtful: after all he was a committed Quaker and Quakers have long been given to treating men and women equally. He agreed to consult the acting president (who was, fortunately, a sailing companion of my husband's) and that is how I became a lecturer in history. My career as a historian had begun.

If I came to history by indirection, my decision to study the history of women was not, in retrospect, accidental.

Two images mark the earliest moments when I was conscious of women as part of history. Both are associated with a grandmother I barely remember, since she died when I was five. One is of her worn, leather-bound diary, with a rose pressed in its pages and a poem by Father Ryan copied inside the front cover. I saw this volume only once, in a disorderly storeroom supposed to be off-limits for children. The ink was faded, the handwriting difficult: I still remember my intense curiosity and frustration when I could not read the words. Years later, by then experienced in deciphering nineteenth-century handwriting, I searched in vain for that tantalizing volume.

The other memory is of a letter, found in the same store room (I was an inquisitive and disobedient child) in which my grandfather wrote to one of his sons in the year 1921 saying something like this: "Your mother is travelling around the state organizing for the League of Women Voters. They gave her a Ford car and her expenses, but of course I wish she were doing this for the church." That letter, too, disappeared, and it was

twenty years before I fully understood how much it told me.

My grandmother, according to family legend (which is about the only surviving record of her life) had longed to go to college, but found her very proper Virginia family adamant. She went instead to a teacher-training school in Nashville and married a friend of her Georgia roommate. She was beautiful, talented, and much constrained by a patriarchal father-in-law who forbade her, among other things, to sign the articles she wrote for the local paper. She seized every chance to carry on her education while raising five children. She was a mild supporter of suffrage, a leader in voluntary associations in her town and state, and died young. She was one of the few people her son-in-law, my father, admired without reservation. For that reason, and because of elements of the legend which, even as a small child, appealed to me, she has always been a presence in my life. One of my childhood fantasies was that she had not died but had lived to be my guide and friend.

My journal reveals other small foreshadowing events. In 1944, after I had seen Greer Garson's 'Madame Curie', I recorded a resolution to write a history of women, beginning with Eve. It was one of those passing thoughts, never referred to again. Yet when I left the League for the second time in 1953, my friends on the staff who knew me well chose as farewell presents Mary Beard's *Woman As Force In History* and Simone de Beauvoir's *Second Sex*. And in a file of old letters I find one to my father in June 1954 saying that I was sharing a room in the obstetrical ward with a woman who had just given birth to her fifth girl. "All her friends are commiserating with her," I wrote, "and since I am a moderately militant feminist this upsets me." This at a period characterized, we are told, by the domination of the feminine mystique.

As I searched the record for Southern progressives, I kept stumbling over women: well-dressed, well-spoken Southern ladies taking a strong hand in social and political issues. At first I was puzzled, since none of the people who had written on this subject had prepared me to find women there at all. But women were there, and they made a difference. So timid I was about this finding, arguably the only original part of the study, that it took up three or four pages at most.

But one thing led to another. Reading Congressional hearings I had been astounded to find members of Congress listening respectfully to a woman: Jane Addams. Who could this person be, I wondered, who could command the attention of old-fashioned Southern gentlemen not noted for their sympathy for women in political life? A passing comment by her friend Louise Young who called her "America's greatest woman" caught my interest. Someone told me that the Addams papers were not twenty miles away, and when summer came after my Haverford year I began spending four days a week in the Swarthmore Library trying to answer that question. The journal throws no light on my broader purpose (if there was one) unless it was to balance the responsibilities of child-raising with something less demanding, but before long I began to envision a biography of this woman whose papers steadily increased my interest in her and in the multiple currents through which she was navigating in the 1890s.

Just then my husband took a new job, this time in North Carolina. Jane Addams's papers were left 500 miles behind. With three young children and very little money, it seemed unlikely that I could travel about looking for the other widely scattered manuscripts that would be needed for a serious biography. With naïve optimism I sent off grant applications right and left, all of which yielded somewhat chilly form letters saying in a word, No. Only later did I discover that at that time grants were for established scholars, rarely for the ambitious beginner.

I did find a precarious part-time job in the history department of the University of North Carolina. A young colleague, perhaps intent upon astonishing his elders, asked me, the first and only woman in the department, to give a paper at a departmental seminar. I had four months to prepare: what to do? I remembered those women in the progressive movements and now, after a summer in the Addams papers, I knew they had not been a figment of my imagination. I took myself to the Southern Historical Collection, intent at first only on constructing a respectable paper for that all-male and highly traditional history faculty.

In the end the work thus begun would occupy much of the next decade.

Before I settled down in earnest to pursue my Southern women, two or three things happened which may have a bearing on this story. In 1960 Andrew was appointed Fulbright lecturer at the University of Bologna in Italy. A year abroad, with three children, in a city where English was rarely spoken; vacation camping trips to Greece and Spain and then to nearly all of western Europe and England; all this was worth ten years of ordinary life for stretching the mind and stirring up questions. While we were there, a letter from a member of the Duke history department for whom, in our youth, we had served as babysitters, asked if I would consider coming to teach for a year as a part-time instructor...a young man had left late in the year...they needed more time to find a suitable replacement. I replied by return mail, asking only (with considerable deference) whether a Ph.D. and three years teaching experience might qualify me to be a part-time assistant professor. That point settled, I went to Duke in the fall of 1961. Presumably the department never found a "suitable replacement" for the departed colleague, since I am there yet.

While we were in Italy, too, George Tindall had written asking whether I could be ready to give a paper on Southern women at the fall meeting of the Southern Historical Association. As with the job offer, I did not lose any time saying yes, so that by the time I met my first class at Duke I was hurrying to finish what would become "The 'New Woman' in the New South." The Southern met in Chattanooga; at the end of the session, and after a three-hour lunch with Oscar Handlin, I had committed myself to a monograph about Southern white women.

In retrospect the whole enterprise seems a little unlikely. I had always seen my work as something to be picked up and laid down as the family's needs and Andrew's career dictated. In 1961 he was busy at work on what would become The Revolution in Statecraft; faculty wives were then still expected to bear a hand with entertaining colleagues and students, with typing and proofreading; nor did I question the expectation. The Duke job, whatever the department thought, seemed to me to offer a possibility for a permanent attachment, especially if one were quick to publish. Yet here I was embarking upon a study for which there was almost no historiographical tradition and no network of established scholars. My temerity rested not on courage but on ignorance: if I had known what was involved I might never have begun.

I look back on my journal to recapture the flavor of that busy life. One sign of it are the long gaps in the record—occasionally months go by without a word. On October 30, 1961, I noted: "Time must be measured with different calipers here. It goes by all too fast. Thirty-nine days ago I began teaching and have hardly drawn a deep breath since. We are having a long beautiful fall...Andy is once again trying to grow a lawn...the children are doing well."

Nothing more for another twenty-seven days when I noted the trip to Chattanooga, a visit from my brother for Thanksgiving, and the need to get on with Christmas presents lest we "wake up Christmas morning with nothing done at all." By February the notations are staccato and telegraphic: "Up at 6:30, to Durham by 8:10 [first class]. Visit to Woman's College Library, sentimental journal through a picture book Europe. Picked up some intriguing items on women. Two other classes. Number of students dropping course etc., time a bit broken up. Worked on article on Southern progressives in Congress—why did I not do this last year? Atmosphere has much to do with what work gets done. Home. Walked around the circle with Mary Helen discussing School Board. Many children and dogs out enjoying the spring weather. Visit with Tan. Dinner. Chapel Hill *Weekly*. Phone calls. But a pleasant, interesting and demanding life. Rising to demands is the only satisfaction...Where has the Berlin crisis gone?"

And so the days went: teaching, neighboring, parenting; an occasional glance at public affairs—and trying to write a book.

Looking back I see that I was held to the course by several kinds of support. Andrew Scott was constantly encouraging, and

since he was a born parent (perhaps the best I have ever seen in action) the children never seemed to mind when I disappeared to the library on weekends. Then colleagues at the University of North Carolina and Duke and Oscar Handlin, off in Cambridge, kept offering encouragement, even enthusiasm. Then, there were the survivors: the Southern women in their eighties who had never doubted that they and their comrades were part of history, but who had long ago ceased expecting anybody to say so. How could I let them down? And there was Julia Spruill, who had meant, once, to write the book I was undertaking but, finding that the groundwork did not exist, had instead spent thirteen years creating her classic *Women's Life and Work in the Southern Colonies*. She was like a retired athlete urging a younger runner around the track. From Washington my friend Louise Young, like Spruill a pioneer scholar in the history of women, wrote embracing letters and offered a roof when I could get to the Library of Congress. It is hard to overestimate the importance of encouragement to anyone embarking uncertainly upon new terrain.

Though the history of Southern women became my principal work, Jane Addams did not disappear entirely. The news that three young men were embarking on biographies took care of my ambition to do that, but when first Edward James and then Bernard Bailyn gave me a chance to write about her, I did—and with enthusiasm—and I learned a great deal about what have become major themes of my work in women's history.

Then came another kind of learning experience. In 1963 Terry Sanford, the governor of North Carolina, like many young Democratic governors in that year, had taken John F. Kennedy for a model and decided to appoint a Commission on the Status of Women. How he hit upon me as a possible chairman I do not know. I had not the faintest idea about what such a commission could, or should, be, but some latent fantasy about being in political life led me to accept the job and thereafter to learn fast. I left my library study with its notes about nineteenth-century women activists and plunged into intense association with contemporary ones. It was a cold bath that cured me of many romantic images and taught me something of the complexity of human motivation—particularly the mixture of motives which lead anyone, male or female, into public life.

The commission functioned the way such things do in this bureaucratic age. Most of the work was done by committees or staff people, and the final report was a joint production. My task was to put it all together, wield a firm editorial pencil, and meet a deadline. The historian in public affairs is often, unconsciously, a participant-observer. While I worked hard on the problems we had set ourselves, part of my mind wondered, "How would anyone who has not been part of this process ever write an accurate account of this Commission's work?" I realized all over again how

partial even the best history must be. To be sure we left behind us a vast file of documents, safely deposited in the North Carolina Department of Archives, but the tough battles, the shaping arguments, took place face to face or over the phone and were never recorded. Nor were the complex motives of any of us, from the chair to the least active committee member, ever put into words.

The other great learning experience of the 1960s, for me as for so many people, was the Civil Rights Movement. As I watched my students, my children, myself caught up in different ways, I began at last to gain a faint glimmer of what it must have been like to have been part of the progressive excitement in the first two decades of the century or how it might have felt to be an ardent suffragist. I realized, too, that much of what I had thought I knew about Southern black women needed rethinking; that their history had not yet begun to be written.

With all this experience to ponder and its implications to incorporate in the manuscript I was struggling to write, I went back to the library. In 1970, in the midst of teaching, child-raising, and all the rest, there appeared at last a book—*The Southern Lady*—as well as two collections of readings in women's history, one for high school and one for college students.

The timing, through no forethought of mine, was excellent. Resurgent feminism was sweeping the country and bringing a demand for women's history; a considerable number of young scholars were enthusiastically creating a new field of study. I remembered Jane Addams, only six years after the founding of Hull House, writing her sister: "I am considered the grandmother of social settlements." (She was thirty-five at the time.) The handful of established historians of women who existed in 1970—most of us well beyond thirty-five—had much the same feeling. We were grandmothers, with a rapidly proliferating group of interesting grandchildren.[1]

Someday a student of the sociology of knowledge will write an illuminating article on the early development of the new women's history. Sparked about equally by feminism and the burgeoning interest in social history, a group of historians, mostly young, mostly women, began to appear on the scene in the mid-1960s. Dismissed as political or ignored completely by many colleagues, we responded by forming a community of scholars that cut across generations, ideologies, race, and class. Sharing ideas, sources, and material, instinctively seeking safety in numbers, we did the one thing that could develop a new field quickly. We learned from each other with an élan which is rarely seen in academic life. All in all 1970 was an exhilarating year; feminism rampant, women's history developing in all directions, and—in our family—the children growing up—Rebecca, indeed, was busy writing a college paper on "Women in Stuart England." But at the end of a nine-year endeavor, the actual publication of the book raised again the question, What next?

In the summer of 1971 I taught my first formal college course in the social history of American women, to an enthusiastic group of students at the University of Washington. It had been clear to me that history itself grew and developed when one brought women's experience to bear; now I began to see that pedagogy likewise benefited enormously from the introduction of this subject. I have taught many kinds of courses in twenty-five years, some good, but none has elicited the kind of hard work and commitment that this one did, and still does.

Developing the course and composing a number of public lectures complicated the question of what research to do next. There had been, briefly, some pressure from colleagues to do some "real history" (that is, with nothing to do with women) so that I might be viewed as a "real" historian. Happily this pressure diminished when two men with impeccable credentials wrote favorable reviews of *The Southern Lady*. The more serious problem was that so little had been done, the possibilities were so vast, and new ones turned up every time I prepared for a class or wrote a lecture. At first I wanted to do it all. There are an embarrassing number of false starts in the file.

The discipline I was having trouble imposing on myself came from outside in the form of an invitation to my husband and me to write an interpretive history of the suffrage movement. *One*

Half the People was our first joint enterprise to be labeled as such, though we had worked together for years, first on *Political Thought in America* (published under Andrew M. Scott's name) and then on *The Southern Lady*, of which I appeared to be sole author. Now we made our collaboration public. Our irreverent eldest child remarked that she could see, as she read the manuscript, where the historian left off and the political scientist began, but in fact the whole essay was the result of a constant exchange of ideas and drafts.

Somewhere along the line I had begun to define myself as a social historian. I found the intense discussions of social history in the 1970s giving me a way to define what I had been trying to do for a decade or more. In the spring of 1983 I was startled to hear a young professor, who had been in several of my undergraduate courses in the early 1960s, tell a group of his graduate students that I had introduced him to social history. Was it true? In the 1960s? As he and I talked, I realized that in the process of trying to reconstruct women's historical experience I had found my way to new kinds of sources and had looked to psychology, anthropology, and sociology for ideas to help me make sense of what I was finding. Without making a conscious shift from my earlier interest in political history I had begun, so he reminded me, assigning to students research projects which were similar to the work I was doing myself. For example, he had written an

undergraduate paper that was essentially a community study; the process of studying women had pushed me to ask questions about social structures and social change, and I in turn had pushed him. In *The Southern Lady* (then in its early stages) I was feeling my way.

Life, as well as other historians, has taught me a good deal. I have lived through a good part of the twentieth century and been a participant, as well as a recorder, of the history of American women. I have confronted many of the perennial issues: the interaction of personality and environment, of class and sex, of economic condition, race, education, war marriage, children, and dual careers. In retrospect, I realize that all kinds of seemingly irrelevant experience feeds into historical scholarship. "It is not in vain," Elizabeth Cady Stanton wrote to Susan B. Anthony in June 1856, "that I myself have experienced all the wearisome cares to which woman in her best estate is subject." She was thinking of their effort to bring about what she called a moral revolution, but a scholar seeking to understand the lives and experience of women long dead might say the same.

Probably few of us, looking backward, fail to find things that could have been done better had they been done differently. Reading the record, I am appalled at the amount of time I have put into university business with no visible consequence whatever. But perhaps even in those seemingly endless hours I was learning some things about human interaction that help me understand all the failed endeavors which are as much a part of the past as successes. In any case, in coming to terms with my own life I have been much helped by the women I have studied and have come to agree with Jane Mecom: "When I look round me on all my Aquaintance I do not see won I have reason to think happier than I am and would not change my neighbour with my Self where will you find one in a more comfortable State as I see Every won has ther Trobles and I sopose them to be much as fitts them best and shakeing them off might be only changing for the wors."

The world of the twenty-first century has many talented young historians, and occasionally one empathizes with John Updike's Rabbit: "The kids keep coming. They keep crowding you up." But most of the time the crowding is challenging and it keeps one alert. The history of women is now a flourishing field producing such a large quantity of good work that it will require considerable skill to make use of it in our teaching and our textbooks.

* A Historian's Odyssey, pp. i-xxvii from *Making the Invisible Woman Visible* (Urbana and Chicago: University Illinois Press, 1984)

1 To the best of my knowledge, when "The 'New Woman' in the New South" appeared in 1962, Eleanor Flexner, Alma Lutz, Janet Wilson James, Louise M. Young, Eugenie Leonard, and A. Elizabeth Taylor were actively engaged in scholarly work in women's history. Gerda Lerner was finishing a Senior Honors Thesis on the Grimke sisters at the New School for Social Research and teaching a course in women's history there. Julia Spruill, Elizabeth Anthony Dexter, and Mary Benson were no longer publishing. It is startling to realize that ten years later more than 1,000 people turned up for the first Berkshire Conference in Women's History held at Douglass College.

EPILOGUE

In the 1980s I composed this somewhat compressed autobiographical reflection as an introduction to my collected essays. It led to more correspondence with young historians than the essays themselves. Somehow they were much encouraged to find that one is not born a full professor with a long resume!

In the ensuing twenty years I have taught or lectured about women's history in many places, ranging from France and Germany to New Zealand and in many parts of the United States. What, when I began, was not yet even a sub-field in American history now flourishes almost everywhere, and very conservative male historians have labeled it the most exciting part of the social history now being written.

Why has this happened? It is a truism that academia, whether it knows it or not, reflects the broader world. In this case the link between the vast and on-going changes in women's roles, experience, expectations, behavior is clearly linked to the extraordinary efflorescence of the field in the last thirty years of the twentieth century. The lives of my granddaughters will be remarkably different from my own; one can only speculate how this change will play out both in life and in historical writing.

If, for the benefit of future historians, I tried to say what the most significant shaping events of my own life may have been, I think I would list these: being born in the poverty-stricken South and growing up in the Depression; the Second World War, which opened doors hitherto closed to women; the postwar prosperity which made travel and a widely varied experience possible...and a lot of luck in the form of being in the right place at the right time. A list of the people who have changed the ways I look at the world would be very long indeed; but the most important, I suspect, are members of my family: beginning with my parents, going on to my husband—who has steadily sustained my career— and now my children, whose high expectations of their parents have been a great and continuing force in our lives. Not least of their contributions have been the people they chose to marry and the children they have added to the family. Next in importance would be the responses of many of the more than 5,000 students whom I have met in classes across this country and in Europe.

As I look back over what is now a long life, I am struck by the fact that I have witnessed first-hand five generations of women in my family, women whose lives in some ways exemplify the changes in women's opportunities about which historians of women have written. My grandmother, born in 1873, longed to go to college,

but the most her family would permit was a teacher's college. Once married she continued to study, and when her daughters went to college (living out her dream) she went along and took courses in Boston.

My mother, born in 1896, went to college (not a common thing for a Southern girl to do in 1917) and married soon after graduation. She never worked for pay, but kept house, raised children, overcame the habits of her affluent upbringing to survive the Depression, was active in the League of Women Voters and never failed to vote. When my father ran for City Council, she actually campaigned a little and did a lot of the behind-the-scenes work. She tried to teach me to cook and sew, but I was inept and it was generally easier to do it herself, so I did not learn very much.

Encouraged by both my parents I (born in 1921) set myself to graduate from college at the head of the class, and, urged on especially by my father, went to graduate school intermittently until I finally had the Ph.D, and, ultimately, a somewhat late-blooming academic career.

My daughter, born in 1950, at the age when I published my first book and made it to full professor, has completed a term as department head and been designated as what is called "a chaired professor" in a highly regarded History Department. My older granddaughter at thirteen is already a champion swimmer (Title

Nine has helped make such things possible) and, in the family fantasy, on her way to being the first woman president.

The intriguing question is: what happens next?

"As I look back over what is now a long life, I am struck by the fact that I have witnessed first-hand five generations of women in my family, women whose lives in some way exemplify the changes in women's opportunities about which historians of women have written."

Anne Firor Scott

Anne Firor **Scott**

"*I had always seen my work as something to be picked up and laid down as the family's needs and Andrew's career dictated.*"

Anne Firor Scott

Anne Byrd Firor (Scott) was born in a small town in southwest Georgia and grew up in Athens, where her father was on the university faculty. Since Georgia public schools in those days had only eleven grades, and since she amused herself in summer by going to summer school (there being little else to do in the hot weather), she graduated from college at age nineteen and went out into the world to seek—she can no longer remember just what. The rest of her story is outlined in this essay.

Now in her eighth decade, she is writing, lecturing, teaching, and paying as much attention as possible to six grandchildren. She likes to say that she is a historical artifact: married to the same man for over half a century, and one of the dwindling number of Americans able to remember the world as it was before the Second World War.

Maya Angelou an interview

As a young girl, what were your dreams, and who were your role models?

I suppose my grandmother was my role model; she was beautiful to me, and so kind, and so strong.

Did you have dreams of being like her when you grew up? What did you think you'd become?

I thought when I grew up—not as a small girl, but when I grew up—I thought I would be a successful real estate broker, and have my own attaché case, and would wear matching leather pumps with a matching purse.

So how did your dreams change when you grew up?

Well, I started studying dance at about 13, and I continued studying; I found that that was what I *could do*. I had always written, since I was about eight or nine. Here at Wake Forest University, in the rare book room, there's a journal of my writing at nine years old. I'd always tried to do that. The dance came naturally, because I really loved it, but after a while my knees really—even as a young girl, my knees were very iffy. And so I started singing; I couldn't sing all that well, but I was a pretty good entertainer. People came

to see me...maybe not to hear me so much as to see me. And that's about it, I suppose.

In The Heart of a Woman, *you wrote that Billie Holiday told you that you were going to be famous. Did you believe her when she said that?*

Yes.

How did you know?

I didn't know. I just believed her. When she said, 'But not as a singer,' I knew that, too. (*Laughs.*)

You wrote that she said you sounded like her mother and stamped off to the bathroom.

Yes, in the nightclub—that was terrible.

What did you think that you might be famous doing, if not singing? Did you think it could be your writing?

Well, I didn't know about writing. I was always writing and writing music, too. I don't know...I suppose I was still thinking of the real estate world—buying and selling houses.

Did you have great insecurities when you were younger?

Oh, yes. Who didn't? Everybody...I mean, if you happen to be white in a white world, pretty according to whatever the fashion is in that world, rich in a world where money is adored, young in a world where youth is worshipped—you're still uncomfortable. It's almost impossible to grow up. Most people don't grow up, actually. What they do is they get older.

As you got older did you find that your insecurities changed?

Yes, but that point is worth listening to. Most people do get older; they don't grow up though. Growing up is an ongoing process which encourages one to take responsibility for the time he takes up and the space he occupies. The majority of people don't really want to do that, so they don't grow up. They get older, they have children, they find parking spaces, they honor their credit cards—and call that growing up. I don't know if one ever concludes that process, but I do know that insecurities change. They fade and new ones come up, new ones grow as some old ones fade away. I don't know if anybody's always secure. I mean, if you're living you can't be secure. People who are workers sometimes say that they are secure only as far as that next paycheck. Living things are only secure as that next breath.

What do you think in your life have been your greatest challenges, and also your greatest triumphs?

Oh, I don't know the triumphs. Every moment is a triumph that I'm alive and able to laugh. If I'm able to laugh as much as I

cry, I think I've achieved something. If I'm able to be kind when nobody's watching me, I think that's something. When I've failed, the failures I've encountered have, again, often to do with me. I forget that the brute or the batterer or the racist or the bigot...is a child of God just as I am. Whether he or she knows it or not, that's not my business. My business is for *me* to know it. When I've not known it and given short shrift, and been mean to somebody else, been angry, spoken harshly...that's when I've failed.

Is there one way that you've evolved as a person over the course of your life that makes you the proudest of yourself?

(*Laughs.*) I don't know about being proud.

Or the happiest?

Or the happiest, yes. When, as I say, when I'm kind in the dark...in private. That I'm grateful for. I thank God and I thank my grandmother.

Is there something in particular that gets you through difficult times?

I'm grateful to be a child of God. That comforts me all of the time.

Do you have dreams that are yet to be realized, either in your personal or your professional life?

Many, but none I can talk about.

Is there advice that you would give for young women either just starting out—or even older women thinking of a new career?

Absolutely. First, be honest. Be yourself. Be who you really are. If you're tremendously overweight, say so to yourself. If you have been lax in looking after yourself and your health, admit it to yourself—only to yourself. Then, decide what you want to do about it. If you want to do something about it then make a plan. It's your plan—it doesn't involve anybody else. Do something about it. If you really need that college degree—and you know if you need it better than anybody else—get it. It may take you two years, three years going at night, but get it. I think that all virtues and vices begin at home. I would like to encourage women to be kind to themselves—to yourself. You know what you need, you know what hurts you, you know what upholds you, what strengthens you. Be very quiet and look at yourself and admit—only to yourself—and then figure what you want and how you will go about getting it.

Is there a quality in yourself—other than your faith in God—that you think has enabled you to endure?

Yes, humor. I never trust anybody who doesn't laugh, who acts as if he or she is just serious and so has put airplane glue on the back of the hand and stuck it to his forehead. (*Laughs.*) I think, 'Oh no, you're not serious...you're boring as the dickens, but you're not serious.' If you're really serious, you came here to make a difference in your life and the lives of others.

Are there personal qualities in others that you admire the most—that you consider to be of the most value in someone that you meet?

I like kindness. I like courtesy.

What advice might you give for someone who found themselves a single mother as you did, and yet wanted to go forth and have a career?

Cherish the child, because that's going to be your greatest gift. Don't blame the child, cherish him or her. Because of the child you will educate yourself, because you'll want the child to be educated. You'll go to the library, you'll take books out, you'll follow a book club, you'll join a book club or you'll follow the book lists in the newspapers, and you'll read. You'll read to the child and that is the beginning of the most profound education. Always have something to laugh at with the child—not with any other human being—but something just funny about yourself. Let the child learn to laugh early.

Interviewed by Emily A. Colin

Maya **Angelou**

Maya Angelou was born Marguerite Johnson in 1928 in St. Louis, Missouri. She attended public school in Stamps, Arkansas and San Francisco, California. Angelou is fluent in English, French, Spanish, Italian, Arabic and West African Fanti.

She is the author of many autobiographies, including *I Know Why the Caged Bird Sings*, published in 1970, and *The Heart of a Woman*, published in 1981, both by Random House and Bantam Books. She has also written several children's books, including *Life Doesn't Frighten Me* (Stewart, Tabori & Chang, 1993). She has published numerous poems, including the Pulitzer Prize nominee, "Just Give Me a Cool Drink Of Water 'Fore I Diiie," "On the Pulse of the Morning," written for and recited on the occasion of President Clinton's Inauguration in January of 1993, and "A Brave and Startling Truth," recited at the celebration of the fiftieth anniversary of the United Nations.

An accomplished playwright and screenwriter, Angelou has written *Cabaret For Freedom*, a play produced off-Broadway in 1960 in collaboration with Godfrey, Cambridge, and *All Day Long*, a screenplay produced by the American Film Institute of Los Angeles.

Angelou's articles, short stories and poems have appeared in national publications such as *Black Scholar*, *Redbook*, *Ebony*, *Life* and the *Sunday New York Times*.

No stranger to stage or screen, she has made television appearances for such productions as "Maya Angelou: Rainbow in the Clouds," (WTVS-TV in Detroit), and "Afro-American in the Arts," both for PBS. She was featured in the *Tree of Life* episode of "Touched By An Angel." In 1977, she won an Emmy nomination for Best Actress for her portrayal of the grandmother in Alex Haley's *Roots*.

She is affiliated with numerous organizations, including the Harlem Writer's Guild, Unicef International, and the National Society for Prevention of Cruelty to Children in London, England.

Maya Angelou has received over forty honors and awards in her lifetime, including *Ladies' Home Journal* "Top 100 Most Influential Women" in 1983, the North Carolina Award in Literature (the highest honor the state grants) in 1987, the Distinguished Woman of North Carolina in 1992 and the Lifetime Achievement Award for Literature in 1999. In 1981, she was appointed the first Reynolds Professor of American Studies at Wake Forest University in Winston-Salem, North Carolina.

The Woman in the Red Wool Suit Ruth Moose

Most of my life I didn't need clothes to say who I was or stand for anything about myself. Dressing for success meant what I wore was well-made, appropriate for the occasion, fitted properly and looked attractive. The term "power suit" didn't meant a thing to me until the day I needed one. Desperately. Before then my clothes didn't make me, I made them.

I sewed like my mother and grandmother before me. My grandmother made dresses for her daughters, shirts, coats and trousers for her sons. She sewed all the pajamas and gowns needed by the whole family, and she made my first prom dress combining two patterns and using black velvet with mint green lace and net. The rest of the girls showed up in pastels, looked like Petit Fours. I felt I looked like Hollywood, or at least somewhere near the southern side.

I was often lulled to sleep as a child by the hum of my mother's Singer sewing machine. It sang under her fingers as she made most of my clothes, and hers.

In high school I took home economics I and II, thought I learned the "correct" way to sew, could teach my mother and grandmother new things. They listened and smiled and were kind enough not to say "I told you so," when I sat ripping out seams and sleeves, and mumbling mild expletives.

After I married I made curtains and drapes for our first apartment. They were easy. All straight seams. No yokes and sleeves. Then I made maternity dresses. By this time I could sew with some confidence and craftsmanship. A class in tailoring taught me all the things my mother and grandmother knew. I had long before developed a healthy respect for fabrics and the work that goes into a good garment. Here I made and fitted suits, did bound buttonholes, learned to pad and shape, wrestled with hair canvas and occasionally won. My suits, like Thoreau's proverbial firewood, warmed me twice...once while making them, again when I wore them.

⚬⚮

Then my life took a left turn and I landed in something my mother and grandmother called "public work," a profession with a desk and title that demanded working with assorted personalities in all sizes and personal agendas eight hours a day, five days a week. My job also required professional meetings. At my first "meeting" it didn't take me five minutes to discover that the males (and me) were the only ones in the audience wearing pants. Mine were a neat navy wool, nicely tailored, but the rest of the women wore suits...with skirts.

I began to build a wardrobe of suits. I bought suits in the usual grays and beige and blue. And a red one...a very red one because it seemed to say something to me and besides, it was on sale. Time to sew was out of the question. Even bits of mending were done at midnight. My life was that pressured.

The red suit hung in the closet through one winter and into the next. It was too bold for me to wear. I dressed in the expected, conventional grays, beige and blue. I blended into the fabric of my workplace quietly and well-behaved until the day I had to confront a misunderstanding. I had to slay a dragon-sized departmental power play. I had not only to defend myself, but take on two people who both outranked and outweighed me in position and influence. My job and a seven-year investment of my life were on the line.

I put on the red suit and as I did I felt I was girding my loins, dressing for battle. The red suit said I was mad as Hell. It said look out. It said don't tread on me. Don't touch me or you'll get burned. This was no Santa suit, this was one for Superwoman. My adversary slunk around the corner when he saw me coming. He couldn't miss me. I radiated power like a stun gun and I won. Nobody pinned a medal on my shoulder nor gave me a purple heart, but I won.

I didn't know I had the kind of courage it took to go into a situation like that, hold my cool and confidence, state my case and keep stating it and at the same time wearing a suit that said "I'm out for blood this round. Stop before you get hurt." Was this a 'power suit' that proved its worth? Did I truly dress for success and succeed? Could I have fought the same battle in navy blue or gray or tweed or twill? I don't think so. I think my red suit made a statement. I think it gave me confidence and courage. It did not say as blue or gray would have that I was 'conservative,' that I was playing 'corporate ball.' It said I will not go down without a fight.

A man in a red suit can sell used cars or play Santa. He can't go into a board room wearing one or he'd be thought more than a bit odd. Maybe the old Henry Higgins question needs a new twist, "Why can't a woman dress like a man?" And still make her point? Win a round without being considered shrill and pushy? The red suit said what I couldn't say in words—not the words of my professionalism, and certainly not the words of my Southern girlhood.

I learned courage comes from within, but if it takes a red wool suit of armor to protect you in battle...if the suit fits the occasion...then wear it.

Ruth Moose

Ruth Moose is on the creative writing faculty at the University of North Carolina at Chapel Hill. She is the author of two collections of short stories, *The Wreath Ribbon Quilt and Other Stories* and *Dreaming In Color*. She is also the author of three collections of poetry, *To Survive, Finding Things In the Dark*, and *Making the Bed*. In 1995, she received an award from the Robert Ruark Foundation for a short story in a competition judged by Anne Tyler. The story appeared in the *Crescent Review*.

Moose has received three PEN awards for short fiction, a North Carolina Literary Fellowship, and, in 1994, a MacDowell Fellowship. She wrote a monthly column for the *Charlotte Observer*, and for several years wrote thrice-weekly features and columns for the *Charlotte News*. Her poem "Blackberry Wine" is included in a Papier Mache Press Book, *I Am Becoming the Woman I Have Wanted*, which won the 1995 American Book Award.

Moose is a native of Stanly County, North Carolina. She is married to the artist Talmadge Moose and is the mother of two sons, Lyle and Barry.

Elle Puritz an interview

Why don't we start at the very, very beginning, your childhood and where you grew up, that sort of thing?

OK. I was born in Brooklyn, then taken right to Long Island, where I actually survived in a Jewish family, and my mother used to call me the world's most unhappy child. So they took me to a psychiatrist when I was in the third grade, and they put me on Valium. I was on Valium from the time I was in the third grade until I was twenty-three years old.

What did you feel about that?

Well, I added alcohol to it when I was sixteen, so at twenty-three I ended up in Alcoholics Anonymous, and I will have twenty-five years of sobriety this coming May 5th. So, that was my childhood. I don't really remember much of it.

Why do you think your parents made the decision to start you on Valium?

Well, my mother is a prescription drug fan to this day. She is probably the oldest living Percoset addict in North America. It was an easier way, to take a pill. That's the Jewish way, sometimes. Take a pill, you'll feel better. And so I was raised with a lot

of fears. They didn't want me to go to Manhattan because of the crime, you know. So, I led a very sheltered life.

Did your parents know when you started drinking?

My mother caught me one time going up the stairs with a bottle of cherry Kijafa in a paper bag, but she looked away. She had a lot of denial. She couldn't deal with a lot of it.

Were you an only child?

No, my brother is eight years younger, and he is a bum. He had many, many jobs, and he lives with my mother, and his wife and his two kids.

Did you make the decision yourself to go into treatment or was it something where you had no choice?

Well, I went to California after I graduated college. I bought a one-way ticket to L.A., and I really went out there because I wanted to die with the movie stars, where the movie stars were. I was a very big fan. I had read a lot of movie magazines, and my favorites were Sonny and Cher. You know, I just lived for these people. I remember when I was about ten or eleven years old, I went in to my mother and said, 'Mommy, I feel close to these people.' She said, 'What are you talking about? You are just a little kid on Long Island.' And the first job I got after I sobered up was the gofer on the Sonny and Cher show.

What did your mom say?

She's not very maternal; she's not very grand-maternal with my children, so she doesn't say much. But my father was really impressed.

Did they look strangely on your decision to go so far away, when they had been uncomfortable with the idea of your going into Manhattan?

Well, they didn't know, you see, I didn't tell them. I bought a one-way ticket and I left, and I would not come back.

Probably every Jewish mother's nightmare.
Uh huh.

It would be my Jewish mother's nightmare.

Oh, yeah. My mother called every hotel starting with A in Hollywood, because she just knew I would be going to Los Angeles. She just knew in her heart. And she found me at the Holiday Inn, which is now not there anymore in Beverly Hills, so I moved to the Sheraton, begins with S, figuring I would probably get a little more time out of it.

What happened after you got your job as gofer? What did you do next?

You know, I got a lot of jobs, because people were very kind to me. I was a gofer, and they were teaching me how to do payroll, and Union rules, and all that stuff, and then I went to work for a wonderful woman who called me and said, 'Come work for me.' And I said, 'Well, I don't know if I could do that job.' It was a production assistant. And she said, 'I will just be right down the hall. If you have any problems, you just scream.' She is an extraordinary person. She is very ill right now. So I did that, and then by age twenty-eight, I was the youngest associate producer in Hollywood doing musical variety shows.

Were you surprised?

Shocked. I was shocked. And I said, I remember I said to somebody, 'I don't understand why me? Why have I done this?' And somebody in AA said to me, 'The only reason that you are where you are is because obviously God thinks you could best carry the message from where you are. And that's why you are there.'

So, did you find that when you sobered up, you were happier?

Not in the beginning; I was very frightened to not have my friend alcohol and my friend drugs anymore to fill this hole, to be my companion and my shield to the world. So the people in AA literally took me in, and taught me everything about being a friend and being a worker and being a human being.

And then what happened?

Well, what happened in Los Angeles and in Hollywood was that there is always somebody younger and somebody smarter and the older you get, the production office for which you are working goes down for a while. It doesn't have a hit show, and then you have no work, because everybody else has their own people. And then I started going from producer to producer, job to job. In 1985 I decided I didn't want to do that anymore, so I opened a catering company. Actually, I bought a baking company from somebody in Los Angeles and turned it into a catering company and a wholesale bakery. I started with eight employees, and we started going out and catering to the people that I used to produce for.

Where did the idea come from? Have you always been into food?

No. It's just that I like baking, and it was at that time that the movie theaters were putting cafés in their theaters in California, and a friend of mine worked for AMC, which is a big movie chain out there. She said, 'They are going to open a café over there in Century City. You ought to bring your stuff.' And so I went into my kitchen and just whipped up my stuff. And they said, 'Do you have a bakery?' And I said, 'Oh, yeah.' And I thought: 'I have got to find a place to cook this stuff.' The first order he gave me was for twenty huge sheet pans of everything. So I went around to some of the caterers and asked if I could rent their kitchen at night. And after they would be finished, I would go in with a helper and we would be listening to Lite FM, you know, people calling in requests for love songs, and there we would be with the pastry bags, putting on seven to eight to ten dozen muffins. And then in the morning, I had this old Mercedes, and I would put everything in the trunk and deliver them before I went home, and then I went to bed.

Where did you learn to bake?

It was just a hobby. I liked it, because it is very chemical. You have to be exact. I like that. I'm into computers now, and building computers, and repairing computers. Because I like all that kind of scientific stuff.

So then how long did you run your catering business?

I sold the catering company to the woman who I first rented at night from. And she had ended up renting from me and then buying my company in 1991 as I lay in pre-term labor in Cedars Sinai intensive care. I went into labor at twenty-nine weeks with my son, Joel. So I laid there for five and a half weeks on a very aggressive intravenous drug to keep in him until he was cooked.

We could only keep him in to thirty-four weeks. And during that time I sold it, because I decided I was going to be a stay-at-home mom, and then that didn't work either, and so...

When in all of this did you meet your partner?

I met Joanna in AA in 1986. I had known her since she was sober. She just celebrated eighteen years. She was with somebody else, and I was with somebody else. And neither of us could understand why we were with these other people. But we were. So we were just friends. And, then I broke up with my relationship, and then she didn't; and then finally she broke up. And I decided that if I didn't scoop her up somebody else would because she is such a nice person. So, I did. And we went out on June 5th of 1987, and we have been together ever since.

Had you come out to your parents before you went out to California?

Oh, yeah. I came out to my parents when I was doing a show for the very first Kennedy Center Honors in 1978, and I had the woman I was seeing at the time with me. I was living in Los Angeles, and I was in Washington, and I said I am going to come see you after the show. And they said, don't bring your friend. And I said, 'Why?' And they said, 'Well, we want you all to ourselves.' So I called them back, from the telephone at the Kennedy Center, a pay phone, and I told them, and they acted so surprised.

I mean, you know, these people, parents of gays know, they know, but they don't want to know. So when you tell them they act really surprised. But they are not surprised.

Did they ever come around?

Oh yeah, totally. You know, my father, I think his death was the greatest loss of my life. The greatest unhappy event in my life. But he said to me, I don't care who you sleep with; I don't care what you do for a living; I love you. My mother calls Joanna her favorite daughter-in-law. She came out to the bris, you know, to California, and all that. She comes to visit once a year, which is enough.

She is like a drunk, you know. A very loud voice, everything is yelling. Even if she says 'I love you,' it is yelling. So, it's difficult for my kids who never hear yelling, because Joanna and I really get along really well. I mean, she is what I aspire to as a parent. She is much more patient than I am. She is the homework mom. She takes them to school. She stays and helps in the classroom, you know. She goes and does all the sports with them. And yet, they adore me. I am like the cuddly mom. My job is to get them up and ready in the morning, and put them to bed at night. And I hang with them, and I do computers with my son, Joel.

Was it hard for you to figure out the right way to parent?

Good question. I was very concerned about parenting and how it would be for me, and sometimes Joanna says, 'You sounded like Natalie just then.' And I cringe in my heart and say, 'I'll fix that.' I dreaded if I would have had a girl. Dreaded it. You know, I much rather wanted a boy, because I did not have a good mother/daughter relationship. When my brother was born, it was like Jesus Christ had made it back to the planet. It was—I mean, men in Jewish families—sons are it. I did not have the energy to learn to do a mother/daughter relationship. I love having sons. It's real easy.

How long had you and Joanna been together before you decided that you wanted to have a baby?

Well, let's see, we got together in 1987. I guess it was a couple of years after that, and she wanted to get pregnant first. She had just lost her mother and she had just lost her best friend to AIDS, and the grief just was keeping her from conceiving. So she looked at me. And, you know, I kind of identify a little more with the male side of me. It's the idea of doing this womanly thing, the most womanly thing I have every done. The most female thing I have ever done was get pregnant. I meant there were times I literally felt like an alien was in there. I thought, 'Wow! It's kind of like a guy getting pregnant, but I don't feel like a guy.' I mean,

I am more woman. I know that.

I am always like a cut-to-the-chase kind of person. I said, 'Look, we try twice. If I don't get pregnant, fertility drugs, because I don't have time to be doing this for years.' And I was thirty-nine.

We chose the donor. He was an anonymous donor. I had heard about another couple that went to this guy. His name was Paul Smith at Heredity Choice, and he had broken off from the Nobel Sperm Bank and taken nine guys with him, because he didn't like the restrictions they were putting on: nobody over thirty-five, you had to be married, not gay, and all that. So I called this guy, Paul Smith, and I said do you have any Jews with straight hair? I swear. He laughed and said, 'As a matter of fact I have one Ashkenazi Jew, which is Eastern European—Balkan. And I said, 'Send me the stuff.' And so he sent me the stuff, and he's 5'11" and 150 pounds, which means really thin, no fat cells. I thought, 'This is perfect, because I am always overweight.' And he has got straight black hair—I was born with very curly hair—an IQ of 160; in his early forties; has two kids of his own; a scientist at Cal-Tech.

Sounds good so far.

Hey, huh? His grandparents lived way past their seventies. And I thought, 'This is for me.' So I chose him. And this guy, Paul

Smith, he is very eccentric. They delivered a little tank of liquid nitrogen. The straws are very, very small because they spin out all the semen, and all that is left are little tiny, tiny drops of actual eighty million sperm. It is frozen, and they have a magnet on the end of these little straws, and they are buried in the liquid nitrogen, so they have to give you this magnet on a long stick, and you fish around in there and then you pull up this thing, let it thaw out and do it. And, he used to deliver it in a fire truck. He had this old 1939 yellow fire truck pull up in front of my door, and the neighbors are thinking, 'What the hell is going on in that house?' But, you know, he got me pregnant. Joel, today—that's his picture there on the right. And he is my greatest work.

Is his hair straight? I can't tell.

His hair is straight. See those other pictures over there?

Yes. Oh, what a face.

Yes, isn't that a face? He is gorgeous. All the girls swoon over him. It's really interesting to be two lesbians having two little penises running around. It must be engraved in them; it's in the testosterone; it's in the genes, that they know where they get their greatest source of comfort. Farting is funny, and belching is funny. It's a boy thing. You know, they don't hear us doing it, so obviously it is innate in them. And it is very funny. It is very interesting to watch.

Do you have little talks with them to explain, in case other kids in school ask them questions?

Yes, we talked to them. We said, 'You know, most of the time men fall in love with women and women fall in love with men. But every once in a while a man falls in love with a man, or a woman falls in love with a woman. That's what happened with us. And as you know, you need a man and a woman to make a baby, so we went and got some sperm from somebody who knew that we loved each other and wanted to have a baby.' So we don't call him 'the donor,' we call him the 'sperm guy.' We don't call him father or anything like that, and you can ask them does it bother them that they don't have a dad. And they say no. The kids in their class say, 'Boy, I wish I had two moms.' Joel is really happy he doesn't have a dad, because dads are rough and tough, and he says, 'Mom, I just want to meet a nice girl, get married, and have two kids.' He has already named his kids.

Oh, my goodness! How old is he?

He's eight. He said, 'But Mom, there is just one thing.' And I said, 'What?' 'Well, I am going to have to find a girl who would live here with us, because I am never leaving you.' I said, 'That's fine. I am going to write this down, and when you are twenty-two I am going to remind you that you said that.'

So your other son is adopted?

The other son is adopted. We decided we did not want Joel, who is very self-involved—The Prince, we call him—we didn't want him to be an only child, because the world already revolved around him. We wanted him to have a sibling. We are not young. We are not in our twenties or thirties, and we wanted him to have somebody to grow old with. So Joanna set about registering with an adoption agency in Los Angeles who did foreign adoptions, because first of all we wanted an infant. We didn't want anybody that came with a package of stuff that we had to deal with, because I feel we are too old. We wanted an infant, now that they have open adoption, I didn't want to be getting birthday cards from the birth mother and all that stuff, you know. So we wanted a child nobody else wanted.

So, lo and behold, two years after, because getting an infant is not easy, they called us and said, 'There is a little baby in a coal mining town three hours' drive from the Black Sea. We will send you a picture. The only thing is he has got a little club foot, a little problem with his foot. He was left in the hospital by his mother. There were twins. The twin died in childbirth.' The story went that the mother had an affair with a Polish soldier and the father was in jail, so she couldn't bring the kid home. She left the kid at the hospital. The kid was four months old.

Joanna says, 'We will take him.' So off she goes, February of 1995, to Russia. She takes Delta over to Moscow; Aeroflot from Moscow to Rostow; and a beat up car—a little tiny green car—three hours into the mountains to this coal mining town, and goes to this hospital. There is this baby boy all swaddled. They keep them swaddled there. They don't even diaper them. They change their swaddling three times a day. He was seven months old, he weighed ten pounds.

He had a broken femur, and he had the most deformed club feet that you have ever seen. I did not hear from Joanna for five days, because she was trying to decide whether to bring him home or not. And she decided to bring him home, and called me. He looks just like her—blonde hair and blue eyes. She brought him home, and he was so little that we had to give him these power bottles full of cereal and formula and stuff. We had to wait until he was a year old; on his first birthday, he had his feet fixed. The orthopedic surgeon at Cedars Sinai Medical Center said it was the worst case of club feet he had ever seen. They were actually facing up. He could look down and see the soles of his feet. So, now, they have been fixed. They are still kind of shaped and pointed inward, but they are on the floor.

Can he walk pretty well?

I mean, he doesn't walk, he runs. He is on the soccer team and it's hard for him to kick the ball. He kind of misses it. And sometimes it is more comfortable for him to wear his shoes on the other feet. Once in a while his feet hurt, you know. He has little marks where they tried to fix them, but couldn't. He has scars all around his feet. It was a very severe operation. But he is great. He's fabulous. They love each other. He's five and a half years.

Did he grow normally after a period of time?

No. They don't think he will reach his full genetic height. We kept him back, so he is in pre-K, and he has no hips. I mean, literally, his body goes like this; so he is still in like a 2T or 3T on the bottom, which is like the toddler size. And he only weighs thirty-two pounds. He's little, but he's fantastic!

Does he know the story?

Oh, yeah. He has a whole book on Russia, and he always says, 'Mama, tell me the Russian story again.' Mama is Joanna, and I am Mommy. Actually, he says Mommy with the black hair, and Mommy with the 'lellow' hair. She's the one with the 'lellow' hair, and she says she always tells him that Mama couldn't have the baby, so a lady in Russia had the baby for her, and she went and got him.

That's an incredible story; that's just amazing!

Yes, it is amazing.

So, then, when did you come to North Carolina?

So I gave birth to Joel. I decided to be a stay-at-home mom. That lasted six months. I was going out of my mind! So Linda Lavin—we became friends on a show I did back in 1975—I called her. I left her a message. I said: 'Do me a favor, if you know anybody that needs somebody to work for them. I don't want to go into production again and be away from Joel, and be in an editing room all night. But if somebody needs some help, blah, blah, blah.' So, she calls me back and she said, 'Oh, Ellesie, what can I do for you?' I said, 'Well I need some work.' And she said, 'Well, you are not going to believe this, but I was going to hire somebody that Warner Brothers wanted me to hire, because I was doing a show there. Tomorrow why don't you come in and see me?' So I went in. She said, 'It doesn't pay a lot.' I said, 'I don't care.' So it transcended from that day, which was in August of 1992, to when she fired her manager, she fired her accountants, and I became all of those things. And then she came here in 1995 to do a movie with Mary Tyler Moore, and she called me and said, 'You better get down here. I am going to buy a few houses.' And I thought, 'Just what I want to do is go to the sweaty South.'

Had you ever been in the South before?

I had been to Little Rock, which I hated, and Dallas, which was thunderstorms and humidity, and ugh, ugh! So I begrudgingly got on a plane and came here, and even as it landed, I couldn't believe it. This was like a fairy tale, paradise. She said, 'Could you live here?' And words came out of my mouth, I don't know from where, and I said: 'In a minute.' Joanna was thrilled because we were looking for places to move to. We didn't want to raise the boys in L.A.

How old were the boys then?

Joel was four, and David was one and a half. So they were babies. And Linda bought a house and rented it to us really cheap, which we eventually bought from her and added 1500 square feet to in Forest Hills. I was so depressed when I got here, because, you know, in L.A. I was somebody, and here I was nobody. Nobody knew who I was and blah, blah, blah. Anyway, that has since changed, and we have a great life here.

When I came here, I thought, 'Now this is really great. I am Jewish, I am gay, I am a woman, and I am moving to the South.' I just didn't even know what got into me. And I can't even tell you a bad experience we have had being a gay family. We are actually, to my knowledge, because I have researched this-we are the only family of our specific kind here. A lot of the gay women that have kids, had them when they were married to a guy. But nobody has done it 'our' way, you know, through our relationship had children.

One thing has led to another, and we have the best friends. You know, I say to Joanna, we are probably the most heterosexual homosexuals I know, because of the kids. We don't hang around with the other gay people in town, because we have nothing in common with them. I mean they don't want to be around kids. They like their singular life, and they like to party or whatever they do. 'Let's just go on a trip.' Well, I can't just go on a trip. I just went on a trip to Disney World. That's where my trip was.

We put the kids in Cape Fear Academy, because I figured in a private school we would have more control if there became a problem, and that they would grow up with the same kids year after year, and it would be no big deal. And that's exactly what has happened. And Joanna is in there with the mothers having those breakfasts and those coffees and all that stuff. We have been embraced by everyone.

What do you think was instrumental for you in terms of building a sense of community? Where did you start when you came here?

Joanna started. She went to the Temple, and she went to AA here. And she drug me out of the house. I became a recluse for about six months. I didn't want to leave the house, except to go to work.

So Joanna is Jewish, too?

She converted. She decided that the kids should have one last name and she changed her name to mine. And then she converted to Judaism in L.A. and waited until David came to put him in the Mikvah, which is the ceremonial bath. They went in the Mikvah together because we weren't sure if David was Jewish or not. And so we are all Jewish, and we are all one name, and that's how it started. From one person I met another person, and I have some very, very dear friends of Old Wilmington here. One of Joanna's best friends, a lady she plays golf with, is an eighty-year-old Baptist, who just loves us.

How did you find the Jewish community here? Was that something you wanted to get involved in?

Well, I figured that was something I would want to connect myself with, because it seemed like a safe place. And it was. We are very involved in the Temple. In fact, Joanna has taken it upon herself to do some fundraising for the Temple, and she is going to run a face-painting booth down at the Azalea Festival. So you see, this is what she does. This is how she endears herself to people. She's wonderful, wonderful, wonderful. I adore her. She is the finest woman I know.

And you're happy with the work that you are doing for Linda.

Yes. I love the work, and I love the fact that I travel and go to L.A. regularly. I just came back from New York not too long ago. Linda and I are very, very good friends, and she is a wonderful person. We mix the business and friendship part very well. It will be eight years, I believe, in August. And we are intensely together. You know, she gives me a lot of leeway to run her life and her real estate and her everything.

What have been the biggest challenges, do you think, for you along the way?

It's funny, I think the biggest challenge was losing my father. It was in 1983. He had a video they used to record all of the crawls at the end of all the shows I did, so that he would have all the crawls with my name on them. He was such a fan of mine. I just adored him. And, in 1983 my mother was giving a surprise sixtieth birthday party for him and I was in production. I flew in the Wednesday before Thanksgiving and I arrived at JFK at 4:00, and he had dropped dead of a heart attack in a restaurant at 3:00, on the eve of his sixtieth birthday. So, instead of going to a party, we went to a funeral. And it was the worst, I mean, I have a psychic scar, I can tell you. I haven't slept through the night since 1983. It has just devastated me. And, you know, it brought out a lot of fear of death in me. I have been working very hard on that.

That's been my biggest stumbling block.

I read a lot of books. I just finished reading this book called *Many Lives, Many Masters*, by a Jewish guy named Brian L. Weiss. He is a doctor. He is the head of psychiatry at the University of Miami at Mt. Sinai. I am thirsting for ways to find comfort within my soul.

I have always had a weight problem. That's been a big stumbling block for me. My sobriety has been easy. I have never really fought with the obsession to drink after I quit drinking. I go to meetings, of course, I still go to meetings, because every single person who went out drinking, whether twenty years sober or two years sober, said they stopped going to meetings. So, I don't. Every Sunday we go out to Wrightsville Beach. We get a babysitter, and we go out to lunch after the meeting. I can't say that I really have any big challenges.

When you stopped taking Valium, did it change your whole way of living?

Well, it did more than change my way. I had no way of looking at life. I just didn't look. So I really started opening my eyes. When I started using that Valium back in the third grade, my emotional life was arrested at that point, and I did no more maturing until I quit. So here I was, a third-grader being twenty-three years old. I got my feelings hurt and cried all the time. The old-timers used to tell me how I was when I was a newcomer—I just

couldn't sit still. So I really learned how to be a mensch, you know, how to get along with other people, how to compromise and be the kind of person I would like to pass on to my children.

What qualities in a person do you think are the most important?

Loyalty, love, somebody that has a good heart, and that cares about other people.

How are you trying to pass these qualities on to your sons? Are there concrete ways that you try in everyday life?

Yes. We do little things every once in a while. We go through the toys to give to the poor children. And I make them go with me to the place wherever we are going to do this, whether it is the Salvation Army or whatever. Actually, we were talking the other day about Joel, and about taking him to visit some retirement homes and play some chess or checkers with people.

And what qualities in yourself do you think really enabled you to get to where you are, and to overcome the challenges that were in your way?

Well, I am very tenacious. I am very stubborn. It is in my sign, the Taurus. I don't have patience for a lot of things. That's why I like computers so much. Computers—the answer is there. There is an answer to this problem, and Elle, you are smart enough, if you just read, or do whatever, try, you can do it. That's how I have lived my life. I am having a problem with the computer at home, so I am sitting here reading 'Fix Your Own PC.' And it is that way with relationships, too. You know, I believe in honesty with people except, I don't believe in brutality. So if I get some information about somebody, and I think to myself, 'Is this going to add to their life? Is it going to add to their life to tell them that their friends are talking about them? No.' So I am not going to tell them. That's how I base it. Not how am I going to look, but is this going to make them happy to hear that? And, if not, I don't say anything.

So, if a young woman came to you who was lost, or an older woman who was thinking of a change of career and didn't know what to do, is there advice that you would give them?

The first thing I would tell them is to never stop trying. If I stopped trying, I never would have made the life I had. If I had stopped trying to get pregnant, or if I had stopped trying to do this show or that show... We have a phrase in AA, 'contempt prior to investigation,' and before I say no, I need all the facts. What made me get on that plane to come to the South to have this incredible life when I did not want to go to the South? Just go, Elle. Just do it. Just investigate. Just put one foot in front of the other. It's like, action. And that's the other thing. Keep taking action. Because I can sit here and think all day. But until I start

getting out there, picking up the phone, doing something for somebody else, I am not going to feel better.

What do you think has made you the happiest, of all the decisions that you have made?

Having these babies, I think, has made me the happiest. Becoming a mother and not passing on the stuff that didn't work for me. To become a mother unlike the mother that I had. To be patient and listen and not yell right away, and have appreciation for these kids as human beings, that has brought me the most joy. Being a mother and being a friend. Just being the things I never thought I could be.

And have you been able to work on your relationship with your mom at all? Is it better?

I think it is much better than it was. We have an understanding. I love her. She loves me. We talk several times a week. We are who we are, she and I. We are very different people. We do the best we can for each other.

How did she react to your sobriety? Was she surprised?

In the beginning she was surprised. One year she came to a meeting in Los Angeles where I was speaking in front of about 200 people, and I thought well, she's here, so I had better tone down what I say about the drugs and all, and her with the drugs. So I am standing at this podium, and there was silence in the room. And all of a sudden my mother said, 'Go ahead, tell the truth. I can take it.'

So did you?

Yes. So she is very aware. You know, she will say things to me like, 'I love you. See, I said it first. Aren't I getting better?'

Yes. So did you at first blame your mom?

Oh, sure. Doesn't everybody blame their mom?

But for making that decision with the psychiatrist, saying 'Oh, yes. At age eight you can take some Valium.'

No, because you know why? Getting to AA was the best thing that ever happened to me. I use it as a program for living now. I use those steps every day, by admitting promptly when I am wrong, when I make a mistake, instead of holding on to it. You know, asking Him, God, to remove this thing, whatever it is—jealousy, or whatever. Help me with it. Now I have a place to turn. I have a way to raise my children.

Do you have dreams still that you want to fulfill, things you haven't done yet?

Everybody tells me I should write a book. So, I would like to do that someday. I just can't seem to sit down and have the patience to talk to myself about myself, you know? I would like to be thin once in my life, before I die. Now, am I willing to do what it takes to do that? In my mind I am. But other than that, I would love to see my children grow up and get married and have grandchildren. I am forty-eight now, so I would be a pretty old grandmother, but, you know, it is possible. That's it. I am happy. I don't ever want to leave Wilmington. I love it here. I love my friends, and I love my life here.

Interviewed by Emily A. Colin.

Elle *Puritz*

Born in New York in 1952 to two overweight, overprotective, overwrought, and overcome Jewish parents, Elle lived in her own private world. Her mother call her "the world's most unhappy child," so eventually Elle was put on tranquilizers in the third grade. She started smoking when she was 12 and drinking when she was 16. She graduated Hofstra University in 1974 and bought a one-way ticket to Los Angeles "to die with the movie stars."

Through a series of events and near death, Elle went into recovery and now has 25 years clean and sober. In 1975, she went to Beverly Hills High at night to learn typing and shorthand. She landed a secretarial job at an entertainment business management firm, but was forced to leave because one of their clients forced his intentions on her.

She was offered a job for less pay at CBS as a gofer on the Sonny and Cher Show. By age 28, Elle was the youngest associate producer in Hollywood for musical variety, her credits including shows for Bob Hope, Elvis, Cher, Bette Midler and the Kennedy Center.

In 1987, Elle met Joanna and their relationship continues today. In 1990, it was decided that Elle would try to get pregnant. They picked an anonymous donor and on November 13, 1991, Joel was born. Elle then went to work for actress Linda Lavin, managing her affairs. In 1994, Joanna went to Russia and adopted David, a 7-month-old orphan, weighing in at 10 pounds, with rickets, anemia, a broken leg and club feet. Elle and Joanna were the third same-sex couple in Los Angeles to co-adopt. Today, both boys thrive with their moms in North Carolina. David has just completed what is hoped to be his final surgery to straighten his feet at the Duke University Children's Hospital.

Penny Eisenberg   an interview

Where did you grow up?

On Long Island in New York. The town was called Roslyn. I went to Boston University and I was a music major. After that I went to North Bennet Street Industrial School and I studied piano tuning and technology.

What was your instrument?

Harp.

Tell me, as a child, what career dreams did you have?

None. (*Laughs.*)

That's the shortest answer I've had so far.

Isn't that amazing? I really didn't want to work. (*Laughing.*) I really wanted to get married and have babies, I guess. I don't know. What I really wanted to do was, I wanted to cook. But at that time if you wanted to cook, you had to do Home Ec. That meant you had to sew. I hated to sew. So, I gave up on that. In those days women didn't go to culinary school—at least women from where I grew up didn't. You had to go to college. Every-body went to college. Ninety-nine percent of the kids that I graduated with went to college. So it never occurred to me to do something like culinary school.

And where did the music come in? Did you take lessons as a child?

Yeah, I was always interested in music. Actually, music and art were really the two things that I loved—and cooking. But I wasn't very talented in art. Music—I played guitar, I played recorder—it was really just a hobby that gave me a lot of pleasure. When I went to college and didn't find an academic subject that gave me a lot of pleasure, I decided to go into music.

How did you decide to become a piano tuner?

Well, I wanted to make money with my music, to a degree. There's more to it than that. I was a teacher—I taught music in public school—and that was not very rewarding to me personally, because my success was out of my own control. For example, you could plan this wonderful lesson plan and you come into school and it's raining and the kids are off the wall. I found that very frustrating—the fact that I could work hard and still not have success. Piano tuning is very much in your own control. You work hard, you get an immediate result, and I found that very appealing.

Recount for me the path that you took from there to today.

Isn't that a logical progression? (*Laughs.*) I worked as a piano tuner and rebuilder after school. We were still living in New York at the time—New York City. Actually, before I went to North Bennet Street Industrial School I did an apprenticeship in piano tuning—that's when I was still in New York. I worked in a shop and then I decided to get further training and I went up to Boston and got the further training. Then we moved down to the South. I was pregnant. I worked as a piano tuner as long as I could until the baby was born. After the baby was born, I really didn't want to work as a piano tuner anymore. I didn't want to leave her with somebody else and go out. I didn't want people calling the house. So, what I did was I bought pianos and fixed them up in our home and then would sell them. The problem with that was that there was a lot of physical labor that I couldn't do because I have a bad back, and I like to work by myself. I really couldn't do that, so I decided not to.

Beth—that's my baby—she was a great sleeper. While she was sleeping I started to learn how to bake and how to cook. I have to say that I had very good basic skills, because my mother is a great cook and I always loved to cook. I was the only person in my dorm who cooked. So, we moved to Charlotte—this was twenty years ago. Charlotte had just gotten liquor by the drink, which meant that the restaurants were not very good up until then—because I guess restaurants need alcohol to supplement income. There were really no bakeries. There were no Jewish foods—when we moved here there wasn't a shop that had bagels—there was no rye bread, there were no pastries.

I had grown up in New York. I had also lived in Paris and I really loved good desserts and good food. There were no bakeries here except for, occasionally, the Southern-style bakery here and there. I figured if I want this food, I'm going to have to learn to make it. So I studied on my own while she was asleep and then when she got a little bit older and she was in Mother's Morning Out, I started to take a series of French cooking lessons, which I did with a Cordon Bleu chef who was in Charlotte. I did that for a couple of years. All along I was baking and stuff. I developed a reputation as a good baker, and so the Jewish Community Center asked me if I would teach classes. I started teaching classes and then I started teaching classes there, for non-profit organizations around town—you know, they would either raffle off a class or they would come to the house and I would do a class for a non-profit—things like that. I started doing some catering and it started to grow. Then, in 1994, I started not to feel very well. My health started to decline and I had to curtail a lot of my activity because it turned out I have fiber myalgia. The symptoms are very varied, but the major symptoms are muscle weakness, muscle pain, fatigue, mental fog...stuff like that. They think that it might have to do with neurotransmitters—that there might be a malfunction with the neurotransmitters that causes all these things.

Is that genetic?

There might be a genetic component. There might be a viral component. It might be injury-induced...they don't know. They really don't know and there's no cure at the moment. I wanted to do something that I could do at home, work when I was capable and not work when I was feeling sick. I thought I would write a cookbook, so...I did. (*Laughs.*) That's a whole procedure in itself which I could explain to you if you like.

Sure.

I don't know how extensive you want to get—you might want to pick and choose, but...what I did—the first thing that I did was I researched. I knew how to write a cookbook because that's what I do for my hobby. I have probably a hundred cookbooks—I read cookbooks all the time, I read recipes all the time and I had been doing that for fifteen years. So, I knew how to write a cookbook. I'm very organized and meticulous, so that was the easy part.

The best topic for me was Passover desserts, because for fifteen years I had been creating my own. Passover desserts are terrible generally. I knew that was a place that I could start to write. I did some research and found out there was not a Passover dessert cookbook on the market. So, I figured, 'OK, well that's a good thing for me to do.' I wrote the whole cookbook and they were all original, which meant every day I worked in the kitchen developing recipes and then I'd sit down and write them and do research on history and stuff like that—ingredients, supplies, equipment. All the recipes were my own and created in my own kitchen. Then I went to the library and read all about how to get an agent, how to get a publisher—I mean, what to do once you've got a cookbook.

I sent out fifty letters to agents and out of the fifty, I got back maybe ten or fifteen where they didn't feel they could represent me, but they thought that it was a wonderful cookbook and that I should pursue it. That gave me the encouragement to keep going. There are lots of reasons why agents don't want your book, like they've already got somebody that's in that field or they don't do Jewish cookery, or...stuff like that.

Eventually I had an agent from New York call me and say she loved the book and she wanted to represent me. Then she got me a publisher—within a couple of weeks she got me a publisher. Then I sent pictures—since I had made everything in my own kitchen, I had pictures of all the desserts.

The book was complete, which is very rare. Usually what you do is you write a proposal. I mean, that's the normal course of events. Well, I wrote the entire book, including the table of contents and the index, so when my editor got this he said he had never gotten a manuscript so complete. That was one of the reasons that he was able to accept it, because I'm not a famous chef and I didn't go to a famous school, but it was complete and they knew that they could get it out quickly and fairly inexpensively. He loved the concept because Passover desserts are usually terrible. These looked beautiful—they looked like French desserts.

Did they use your photos?

No. They didn't. There are actually no photos in the book—there are drawings but no photos. What he wanted me to do was to send him some desserts to make sure that they tasted good, which I did. I sent up twelve desserts packed in dry ice and I got a contract. Which was pretty amazing. Yeah, it was definitely amazing. From a major publisher—that one was Macmillan.

How did you feel when you found out that it had been accepted?

Oh, it was just thrilling. Absolutely thrilling. We were in Hawaii on a family vacation, and we had decided we would just go to inexpensive restaurants because we were with the kids. So we splurged and we went to this really expensive, famous restaurant in Hawaii to celebrate. It was really special.

And what has happened since?

That was published in '96 and I did a little of the publicity and a tour and it was great. I went on T.V. and learned how to do all of that. Then I thought in '97 I ought to start thinking about another one. At that time, my editor had left my publisher and that publisher was no longer doing cookbooks—so I had to start thinking about a new publisher. The second time around I didn't write the whole thing, I did a proposal.

The second one is light Jewish holiday desserts. It's the kind of thing I like to do. It's a real challenge and it's where I actually have to do the recipe development, which I like. But it was a challenge, and I did about fifteen just to make sure that I could get the results that I wanted. When I was secure that I could do that, then I sent out the proposal. It was bought by Morrow—which is another big name—and then I proceeded to write the book on a deadline, which was tough. With my fiber myalgia it was tough, because I had to work even when I didn't feel well. I did it, I think in nine months. I think I had a year, but I did it in nine months because I'm pretty compulsive and I was afraid it wouldn't get done. It was pretty intense. (*Laughs.*) So now I'm on the tail-end of that. That came out in September and we've done all of the publicity, pretty much. I'm still doing a little bit here and there, but I'm not actively working on anything else right now. You know, now I have to reevaluate again and see if I want to stay in this field, and if I do, which direction I want to go in.

Or whether I want to do something else. I like to change careers a lot. I did the piano tuning for maybe five years. I've done the cookbook writing for six years. I might stay with it and maybe take a different tack—maybe start doing some recipe development—which won't be as exciting. It's really exciting publishing a major cookbook. You know, you get to meet famous people and you get to have people tell you how wonderful you are and you get a lot of personal satisfaction. But unless you're a real big name, you don't get a lot of money out of it.

What has been one of the most gratifying episodes to come out of all of this for you?

Well, it's an incredible thrill to walk into a bookstore and see your book on a bookshelf. There were three things that happened that were, to me, just absolutely thrilling. Three really famous chefs or cookbook authors told me that they own my cookbook.

Wow. Who were they?

Well, I went into a restaurant in Florida called Chef Allen—his name is Allen Susser. I just happened to take my parents there for Mother's Day. It's an open kitchen and when we left I sort of gave a thumbs-up—you know it was a fabulous meal. He's a wonderful chef and he came out. Of course, I would never say any-thing but my parents said, 'Oh, and our daughter has a cookbook out.'

Parents are good for that.

I was so embarrassed. He said, 'Well, what is it?' and I said, '*Passover Desserts.*' He said, 'Oh, well, I own it and next year I'm going to modify something for use in the restaurant.' Which was thrilling! Then I had the opportunity to meet Jaques Pepin, who is one of the biggest names in the cooking world. He didn't have my cookbook, but he said, 'Ah, I've seen the little blue book and she's very nice.' Which was incredibly thrilling. The other one was Lora Brody, who's a very big name in bread baking and she has some products out that I use. I was on an elevator with her—this is at a culinary convention—I didn't know who she was. They were talking about bread and I made some comment and she turned around and I saw the label on her that it was Lora Brody. I was just thrilled to meet her. She asked me what I did and I said, 'Well, I have a cookbook out, *Passover Desserts,*' and she said she owned it. Stuff like that—you can't put a value on that. These are people that are just tops in their field that you admire. Stuff like that is just tremendously thrilling. When somebody comes up to you and says, 'Oh my gosh! It's Penny Eisenberg.' How can you put a value on that? It's so fabulous and so wonderful for your ego. And then, of course, my second book, I had other cookbook authors whose opinions I just treasure, to write wonderful things about my book and they put it on the back of the book.

As you've gone along this path that you've taken, what do you feel personally have been your greatest challenges along the way?

I think overcoming my feelings of inadequacy which I've always had. That's always the biggest obstacle—to believe in yourself. To say, 'OK, go for it. You want something? Go for it. And you can do it.'

What do you think has been most instrumental in your being able to do that?

My husband's constant love and respect.

Speaking of that, tell me about your family.

OK. I've been married for twenty-four years. My husband's a doctor—he's a radiologist. He's my best friend. We get along great. You know how some people say opposites attract? We're very much alike. There's just always been that respect right from day one. We have two kids. Beth is nineteen and she's at Vassar College. She wants to be a vet. She does cook a little. My son Eric is sixteen. He's a sophomore in high school and he has no idea what he wants to do. (*Laughs.*) Doesn't cook. My husband doesn't cook either but he's an incredible dishwasher.

That counts for a lot.

Absolutely. My kids are great. We have a wonderful relationship with both of the kids.

How have you been able to balance all your different careers and your family?

Pretty much whatever I've done has been around their schedules, and that was just something that I always wanted to do. I never just wanted to work nine to five. I really never wanted to quote-unquote work. I've always worked, but I never called it that. In between doing all this other stuff, I also spent about thirty to forty hours a week resettling Russian refugees, which I did for five years.

Wow. How did that come to pass?

It was through a Jewish organization and they needed help resettling them. I was just finishing my presidency of a Jewish organization. That was coming to an end and they needed somebody, and I just thought it was really important and I did it. It was practically full-time, but again, I worked it around the kids' schedule pretty much. When I couldn't, my husband and my in-laws would take over just for the couple times when I had to be out at night. But, even that—I never called that work.

What are some ways that you relax?

I cook to relax and I food shop. To me that's the most relaxing thing I can do. I do that almost every day. Pretty much I start my day by shopping and that, to me, is like a meditation. It's different when you're working on a recipe—it's pretty intense then. I read and I do computer stuff, which I find pretty relaxing.

What are some personal goals that you're currently pursuing or that you hope to pursue at some point?

I try not to make long-term goals. I sort of go along and I like short-term projects. Writing the cookbook, that's a one-to-two-year project and then if I want to go off and do something else, I can go off and do it. I try not to look too far ahead. I don't really make goals, like, 'OK, I want to do this or this...' Like right now we're thinking about moving into a new house, and that's what I'm going to do right now. That's it. I'm not doing anything else but that.

Looking for the house...

Getting this house in shape. Finding a new house and then doing what I need to do with that house. So that's what I'll do now.

Can you give me a laundry list of things that are your favorites, that are your likes—and this can be books, movies, food, music, T.V. shows...

I don't watch T.V. at all—ever. We love movies. We own probably a hundred DVDs. Of course, cooking is number one. That's right at the top. I would say movies are number two. I love to travel and I love to plan to travel, so that would be three. These are just personal things. This is not my family, my pets...that obviously comes before anything. The family and the pets—we have a lot of pets.

It seems like your vocation and your personal life are pretty integrated.
Oh yeah.

Is that important to you?
Yeah, it's really important to me. I think it goes back to the thing where I said I never wanted to work—but of course I work. I work really hard, but I don't ever consider it work, really. The only time I considered the cookbook work is when I knew that every day I had to be in the kitchen—where I had that deadline. That was not as much fun as just writing the cookbook, for example. But even teaching, I do a lot of teaching around town and I do a lot of baking for non-profits, and that's work, but I never consider it work. For me that's really important. I grew up in a household where my parents were self-employed and worked really hard, but they were home—they worked from the house.

My mother was always available—to take me places, pick me up, make parties—pretty much make her own time. I think that that is just sort of in me. When I say I never wanted to work, it was the idea of going one place and doing one thing for your whole life and from this hour to that hour you'd be there—never wanted to do that. All this other stuff, I think, revolves around that whole thing. What I love to do is what I do to make money—on my own time. That's real important.

What personal qualities do you consider to be of the most value in life?

I can only say in my life, I can't say this is for everybody's life. In terms of figuring out what you want to do for a profession, I think it's really important to know yourself. I think I would've gotten to this sort of professional life sooner—if I had realized that it was important to me to have control over my destiny, control over my success, I wouldn't have gone into teaching to begin with. But I didn't know that about myself until I did it. Piano tuning and what I've done with cooking are very close in certain ways. If I had known, for example, that I really like meticulous, detailed work—that's a connection between recipe development, not necessarily cooking, but recipe development and piano tuning—that you're doing things over and over and over again and getting better each time. You do that in both. To know your own qualities really helps you choose a profession.

So teaching was probably too general for you.

It was. Right. Too open-ended, too general. But I think that the thing that makes me good at what I do is that I care very much. I feel that what I do represents me and so whatever I do, I put my whole heart and soul into. It doesn't matter whether it's baking cookies for school or doing volunteer work—you know, being in an organization and taking on a job and doing that job—to the very best of my ability always. That, I think, is the most important thing. You can be smart but not a super-brain and go very far if you're willing to work hard and you're always willing to work to the best of your ability. A lot of people don't do that. They just don't. I think that is probably the most important thing in terms of work and in terms of self-esteem, which then spills over into how you feel about yourself and your personal life, and all of that.

What is the one way that you have evolved as a human being that makes you the proudest?

I think I've gotten much nicer than I was when I was young, and much less self-centered. That is a product of—of course, many things—but having children, having a husband who loves me and supports me no matter what, and also being involved in volunteer work.

What, if anything, would you do differently if you could turn back the clock?

Well, I probably would go to culinary school instead of going to college. I would probably do a combination culinary/college degree which you can do now. Of course, then I might not have met my husband, and so I wouldn't really do that unless I could be sure I would still meet him. What else? I think that's about it. I love my life. I have a wonderful life.

When you have disappointments, what are your sources of inspiration or renewal?

You know, when I found out I had fiber myalgia, I felt so crappy. I was really depressed—and I'm trying to think of how that got turned around...I don't know if I could pinpoint one specific thing that did it. Obviously when you have a lot of support at home it makes any disappointment easier to take. Some of it is just outlook, whether the glass is half-empty or half-full. That if this doesn't work out there's always something else. There will be another route, there will be something else that will be great. I think that I'm basically that kind of a person.

Of what professional accomplishment are you the most proud?

The first cookbook, because I was an unknown and to have that published by a major company is a truly amazing accom-plishment.

Of what personal accomplishment are you the most proud?

Well, I'm very proud of our family. We have a wonderful family unit—we all get along great. We didn't really have any of those teenage tantrum things and we're very close—all of us. I think it's an accomplishment.

As far as your part of it, what would you attribute that to?

I think that we've always treated our kids with a lot of respect. We've never put an artificial divide between us. The respect has always been there, but there's not that formality between the kids and us and never has been. From the time that they were little they were involved in decision-making with us, and we've always been very open with them about discussing things. I think that's really the key.

What career advice would you give to young women starting out, or older women considering a career change? You seem to be able to change pretty fluidly.

Well, the first thing is, you have to really know your person-ality constraints or what's going to make you happy. The more that you know about yourself, the better choice you're going to make. Then, of course you have to assess your skills and be real-istic about what your skills are and what you can do to increase your skills, or change your skills. I think those would be the three key things.

What dreams do you have that are yet to be realized, either professional or personal? In your case, as we talked about, it seems they're integrated.

I'd love to get my husband retired and my kids happily settled. Of course, that's not much in my control. What kind of dreams do I have that are in my control? I'd like to write another cookbook, but if that doesn't happen, that's fine. I'll just take a different tack, and who knows what the dream will be? I don't know. Again, I don't really think too much about the future. I'm so happy with my life. I don't really project out and say 'If only.'

How do you attribute your ability to live in the now that seems to be so difficult for so many people?

I don't know whether that's an innate thing, or whether it has to do with how happy you are in the present. I'm really, really happy in the present and so I don't expend much energy thinking about what could be.

Interviewed by Susan L. Comer.

"What I love to do is what I do to make money—on my own time."
Penny Eisenberg

Penny *Eisenberg*

Penny Eisenberg grew up on Long Island, New York and graduated from Boston University. She went on to graduate from North Bennet Street Industrial School where she studied piano tuning. She has lived in Madrid and Paris, but settled in Charlotte twenty years ago.

Having grown up with a mother who was a wonderful and innovative cook, Penny found Charlotte lacking in the excellent desserts and foods to which she was accustomed. She started to cook and bake, and began to pursue a culinary education. She studied with a Cordon-Bleu chef and then continued her education by reading as many cooking magazines as she could find.

Within five years, her desserts had gained a reputation and she began her career as a caterer and teacher. She currently has two books in publication: *Passover Desserts* and *Light Jewish Holiday Desserts.*

Penny is an active member of the Jewish community and is past president of the Charlotte Chapter of Jewish Women International, and currently serves on the board of the Jewish Federation of Charlotte. She is a member of ORT and Hadassah. She volunteers for Crisis Assistance Ministry, an agency to prevent homelessness, and for MedAssist, an agency that distributes medicine to needy senior citizens.

She currently lives in Charlotte with her husband and fifteen-year-old son, and has a daughter who recently left home to attend college. They have a dog and three cats.

Cathy Myerow an interview

Well, why don't we start at the beginning? Where you grew up, where you went to school, that type of thing.

OK. I grew up in a little town outside of Pittsburgh, Pennsylvania. It's called McKeesport. It was a small community that I lived in, a borough, actually, called White Oak. A very close-knit community. Went all through high school there. And left there and went on to Slippery Rock State University in Slippery Rock, Pennsylvania where I studied elementary education for four years. Left Slippery Rock in 1969 and moved to Connecticut, and taught there for twenty years. During that time I got my master's at the University of Bridgeport. And left Connecticut ten years ago and moved to Wilmington, North Carolina. Taught for five years here and decided that it was not the same type of career that I had experienced in the North and I just needed a change.

My husband died during that time period. He had been encouraging me to look for a career change because he knew I was dissatisfied with what was happening. And I, at that point, was thinking, 'Well, I'll just take some time for myself.' And I did resign the day that he was diagnosed with cancer. I resigned from my job and everyone said, 'Oh, you're just reacting.' But it was

then I think that I realized life is very short, and if you're not doing something that you want to be doing, then it's time to take the bull by the horns and make that change. So, I did.

He died four months after his diagnosis. So, during that time...it was a hard time...but I did a lot of soul-searching, thinking to myself, 'What am I going to do once he's gone?' We had no children. We'd only been married a short period of time. My husband, Jerry, had been on the board here (at the *Lower Cape Fear Historical Society*). And I can remember coming in this house and looking around and thinking, 'I would love to have a job like this,' because when we moved here I was really looking for a niche in tourism, where I would have something to do with tourism but it wouldn't be my total commitment. He and I had played around with opening different businesses, but we weren't ready to do that kind of thing. When I walked in here it felt *right*.

I had made the comment to someone at a cocktail party, 'I'd kill to be able to work in this house every day.' That was the last comment I ever made about it. After Jerry's death I went to Florida. I was visiting a friend there—just kind of regrouping my life— and I got a phone call saying that the director of the Historical Society was resigning and if I was interested in the job, to get on the next plane and get back to Wilmington. And I was. I was on the next plane and I came back.

Although I'd majored in elementary education, my minor had

been history and I really did love history. I interviewed for the job and the interesting part of the whole thing was—having no background in museums and having really very little background in historical society—I had listened to my husband talk about this organization of which he was a board member for three years and the places where he thought change needed to be accomplished. And with that in mind, when I came for my interview, I had listed all the things that I foresaw that I could do to bring about change and the change that I felt also needed to take place. That's what I was told by a board member got me the job. There was a panel of five that I interviewed with, and I think they had over eighty applicants for the position. But it was just having the foresight to have this list of changes that got me in the door. I'm happy to report I've been here four years next month. I took out that list the other day and I've accomplished all of it at this point. I feel really good about that.

What do you think enabled you to accomplish all of those things?

It was very easy. I think first of all, there was such a void in my life that this house and this career filled that void. With a historical home, if it isn't one thing it's another. Jerry had fallen in love with this house and he was in construction. So, when he walked around the house he did not see that the curtains needed to be replaced. He saw that the structure needed to be replaced.

I just started from there and I've worked my way through. And then I talked...talking to people I think is the biggest thing. Listening to what other people are telling you. Because they know where this business needs to go. And I think that's helped me achieve those goals...and set the goals in the right order.

What do you think has been the most enjoyable thing for you about working here?

I think the people I've worked with have been the most enjoyable. The board has been the most supportive group. We not only spend time together here working on this project, we also spend time socially and spend weekends together, travel together...so they have become a family to me. And that has been wonderful. The second thing that's wonderful—and again, it's in the people line—is the people you meet who walk through the door every day, the tourists. Sometimes I get so bogged down in paperwork that I don't get out there to do the tours. But the last few days I've been giving tours, too, and you just meet them from all over the United States. What a treat that is, to see people's interests: This person who walks through the door loves furniture. This person loves the history of Wilmington. This person loves the history of architecture and the architecture of the homes. So, you're never bored. Every person brings their own knowledge to the house, and you share your knowledge with them. It's basically taking that teaching background and applying it in a whole new area.

When you were a child, did you ever dream that you'd grow up to do something with history? Or did you always think you'd be a teacher?

I always dreamt of being a teacher. When other children were going home at night and playing Cowboys and Indians, I was setting up a classroom in our basement. My younger brothers and sisters were my students, and wherever I went I was always teaching. I love teaching. It was just time for a career change. I had taught for twenty-seven years by the time I left.

I ran into many of my students this weekend—Azalea Weekend—a lot of them were Belles. And it was so wonderful to get the embraces and the recognition of, 'This was my fifth-grade teacher and we had such a wonderful time.' You know that you've touched that child's life. In fact, one of our best docents is a former fifth grade student. One of the rooms in the attic was not restored, and he restored that room as his Eagle Scout project. I've also developed scouting programs where the children come in and they can do local scouting projects here in the house. So, I haven't left teaching yet.

What originally brought you to North Carolina?

The beauty of Wilmington.

Had you visited before?

I had visited in about 1985 with a friend. I was not married at the time and we had come down the coast. And I can remember sitting in a bar on Market Street and she looked at me and said, 'I'd kill to live in this town.' I said, 'It really is a pretty town.' Then we rode past the Bellamy Mansion and rode downtown. I thought it was real pretty, but I was going to have to teach in Connecticut the rest of my life.

Then Jerry was ready to retire at fifty, so we were looking for someplace and again, we came down the coast. We arrived in Wilmington, we walked around and he said, 'Cathy, this is it for me.' At that point I said, 'You know, I was in this town once before and just had forgotten it.' I said, 'I think this is it.' And we went home and sold the house and we were here within two months.

What qualities do you think are the most important in a human being? What do you respect the most?

I think the most important quality any human being can have is compassion and understanding of his fellow man. Being able to look at a person and see all their strengths and accept their weaknesses. That's very hard to do at times, but when you're working with so many people on a daily basis I think that is so necessary.

What qualities do you think have enabled you to excel at this job?

I hope that people will say it is a good listening ear that allows me to hear everyone's ideas and then use those ideas to implement new programs.

And what do you think some of your biggest challenges along the way have been?

I think the biggest challenge that is coming is looking at the Society and seeing what our mission is. Right now our mission is to collect and preserve records and materials and get that knowledge out about the Lower Cape Fear. However, this mission statement was written forty-four years ago. That was before the Local History Room became a part of this community. It was before the Bellamy Mansion was here. It was before the Cape Fear Museum was here, before the Foundation was here. Right now all of us are basically doing the same mission, though we have our own little twist to it. I think for the future what we need to do is to find our special niche and make sure that we are doing what we're setting out to do.

If there's one way that you've evolved as a human being that would make you the proudest, what do you think it would be?

Hmm...I think compassion is the one thing I've seen evolve the most over the years. Having gone through a lot of different crises in my own life, I hope it's made me grow as a person so that I can reach out to others who are going through crisis. I've become a Stephen minister in the last few years, and helping people through hard times is something I'm very proud of. It's very rewarding to me as a human being.

What enabled you to get through your hard times?

My faith. My faith in Christ has been...and I didn't realize how strong my faith was. It grew as each crisis came about. When I say crisis—it hasn't been a crisis-filled life. It's been a life of a lot of joy. But having gone through a divorce and having gone through the death of, actually the only person in the world who I had left, was very traumatic. I'll probably never get over it. And I just look at it and say, 'I have to live for both of us at this point.' And that's what I try to do each day when I get up.

Is it fulfilling for you in that way? That you're here doing this stuff that Jerry had been working on?

Yep. It sure is. I'll share a story with you. I hadn't been here but a day and Jerry had always talked about the roof. 'Everyone's worryin' about the drapes but the roof needs to be replaced.' It rained one day. It was the second day I was here, as a matter of fact. It didn't rain all that hard, but it rained hard enough that the room directly across the hall filled with water. We have two stories above us and I'm talking water this deep. I walked in and someone came and said, 'Cathy, you have to come and see this. There's this much water standing in here.' I went in and went, 'Oh my God.' And at that point someone from upstairs came down and said, 'Cathy, you have to come up because we have water going down the walls.'

So I went up there. I'm looking up there and trying to mop everything up and then I ran back downstairs. I thought no one was around and I just stopped for a minute. And I said, 'OK, Jerry. I got the message. The roof will be fixed.' I went around the corner and there was someone standing there laughing and they said, 'You know, we said that this is Jerry's way of getting what he wants!' My husband was very headstrong. It was his way or no way and they all knew it. And the roof has never leaked since. It was unbelievable. So, yeah. I feel very connected here. Because he loved the house, too. It was part of our time here in Wilmington.

Do you still have dreams that you want to fulfill? Goals that you've set for yourself?

I don't think so. What I'm looking for in my future is basically having time to enjoy life. And taking the time. I built myself a beach house and I have two dogs and we walk the beach. And I just want to be able to enjoy that beauty that I moved here to enjoy.

What do you do to relax, besides being on the beach and walking with your dogs? Do you have hobbies?

I love to play tennis. I don't have enough time to play right now, though. I love to spend time with my friends. At the beach house, we usually have about ten people every weekend. Most of them are from here. And we just sit and play games and talk and read and walk. So, that's...being with people. I really do enjoy that. With friends—true friends.

If a young girl came to you and needed some direction, or an older woman who, as you did, found herself on the cusp of change and needed advice, what would you say?

I'd say take each day and live it—to its fullest. And think how you can change this world and make it a better place. I really do stop and think about that frequently. In so many ways I feel like teaching was putting your hand on the future, and that made it very rewarding. And in this case, I'm putting my hand on the past, but it's only preserving it for the future. That's kind of an interesting concept for me to think about every once in a while.

Interviewed by Emily A. Colin.

Cathy *Myerow*

"Take each day and live it—to its fullest. And think how you can change this world and make it a better place."

Cathy Myerow

Cathy Myerow is presently the executive director of the Lower Cape Fear Historical Society where she oversees the works of the Society and the Latimer House Museum. This 1852 Italianate museum welcomes Wilmington visitors from all over the world and also houses the archives of the lower Cape Fear region.

Ruth Boettcher   an interview

Let's just start with a real easy question for a Sunday morning. Where did you grow up and where did you go to school?

I grew up in Chicago, Illinois. Actually, I was born in the city and then moved to the suburbs when I was four years old. I lived there until I was seventeen and went to school at Illinois State University. Did my undergraduate work there and got a degree in recreation and parks administration with an emphasis in resource management. Then I basically led a very irresponsible life from the time that I graduated until the time that I turned thirty.

I always remained in the field of recreation. I led bicycle trips for teenagers in the New England area. I actually worked for the American Youth Hostels for a summer. Umm...I picked apples. (*Laughs.*) I got a job up in northern Wisconsin as a Nordic ski patrol. Then I worked for the state, Wisconsin D.N.R., as a park ranger up in the Apostle Islands and on Madeline Island specifically. It's a really beautiful series of islands up there in Lake Superior.

What career dreams did you have as a child?

As a kid, I collected snakes and always had toads and snakes and turtles as pets. Reptiles and amphibians were the best thing ever—in the world. I hung out with the boys all the time and we'd go and collect critters. Where I lived outside of Chicago wasn't very conducive to all of that but we did it as much as we possibly could. I'll never forget the day when my father and I were going for a walk at a local arboretum a couple of towns over. I said to my dad, 'I'm going to find myself a spotted salamander.' He's like, 'Yeah, right.' So, I got my little plastic container and I looked under every single log that I came upon and didn't find anything. Then there was this railroad tie—I'll never forget this— there was this old railroad tie that was lying on the ground and it had a grasshopper on it. I stopped and looked at it—my family had gone on walking and were way, way ahead of me—and I turned it over and sure enough, there was a beautiful spotted salamander under there. I was like, 'Yes!!' I ran up to my dad and I said, 'Look!' and he said, 'All right. You were right, I was wrong.' So, yeah, I was a weird kid like that.

I was always interested in backpacking and doing long distance bike riding, and just doing those sorts of recreational pursuits. I would go and take trips by myself all over the country. I actually enrolled in a National Outdoor Leadership School course during my last year in college. I took an outdoor educator's course with them and hung out there for a while—you know, rock-climbed and did those sorts of things. Also, during the summers while I was at Illinois State, I worked at a kids' camp in Colorado and led a number of different backpacking trips and rafting trips and kayaking trips. So, I was into that mode of life.

When I moved to Wisconsin, I continued to cross-country there, of course, and then eventually met someone. In the mid-'80s, he persuaded me to move to South Carolina and that's when I actually discovered the field of biology. It was really weird, because when we moved, we moved down to Charleston—which was like this huge city versus the remote area where we were living up in northern Wisconsin. I moved to Charleston and I was like, 'Whoa!'—culture shock.

After about two weeks of living there I had to go take a drive. I was going crazy in the city, and I just wanted to go into the Francis Marion National Forest and kind of explore the area, and maybe do a little bit of bream fishing or something like that. I saw this sign for Cape Romain National Wildlife Refuge on Highway 17 heading north, and I was like, 'Well, maybe they have maps for the National Forest.' I had no clue where I was going. I walked into the Refuge office and I asked the secretary for some maps, and the Refuge manager got up out of his office and said to me, 'You don't want to go fishing, you want to go out with the sea turtle crew.'

I was like, 'What?' (*Laughs.*) I had no idea what he was talking about. He explained a little bit of what they did and what the whole project was about. It was an eight-mile boat ride from McClellanville out to Cape Island, which is this remote, uninhabited barrier island. They take all the sea turtle nests that were laid the previous night and move them into hatcheries. I was like, 'Sure. I'll go.' (*Laughs.*) And it changed my life.

We were only intending on staying down in Charleston for six months or so to help out with a family situation—and that sea turtle project, working with the turtles, kept us there. I became a volunteer and so did my friend Billy, and then the next year got hired on by Cape Romain National Wildlife Refuge to work the sea turtle project out there.

Then, the following year, we decided to work for the state. Tom Murphy, the coastal biologist down there, convinced me that I ought to go to graduate school. I was like, 'Well...all right.' So, I applied to various universities, and then Mark Dodge, a graduate student enrolled at Clemson, let me know of a new professor who had just come on board with the U.S. Fish and Wildlife Service Cooperative Research Unit. Her name was Susan Haig, and she was just this amazing fireball. She was very, very motivated, and she was looking for a graduate student. I went to the University and interviewed with her and she hired me on as a temporary technician to do some preliminary work. So, I did that for a summer and then enrolled in graduate school that fall. That changed my whole life. (*Laughs.*) I finally became responsible.

Anyway, so I was at Clemson through '94. I looked at the distribution of American avocets, which is actually a western species of shorebird. I got my thesis finished and published two papers out of that, and then, right after I graduated, I got a job with the Fish & Wildlife Service Cooperative Research Unit. I helped with an ongoing study looking at the impact of power lines on migrating birds. In 1995, I applied for and got this job. That's when I started here in North Carolina as the sea turtle project coordinator for the Wildlife Resources Commission.

Tell me about your job. What do you do every day?

(*Laughs.*) What I do is oversee the North Carolina Sea Turtle Protection Program. There are two primary objectives, or parts to it. One is, I oversee all the sea turtle nesting beach projects up and down the coast. I issue endangered species permits to those individuals who have been trained in the management and conservation of nests—hatchlings, nesting females, and all that other stuff. On a regular basis, I put on nesting workshops and make sure that everybody is doing the work in compliance with the Endangered Species Act—that includes handling nests, moving those nests out of areas where they may be in danger of frequent tidal inundation or just getting washed out.

There's just a myriad of responsibilities involved with that. Now, it's becoming even more difficult because we've had so many storms since '96, and a lot of the nesting beaches are heavily eroded. Beach bulldozing—what's called beach scraping—has just gotten completely out of hand. What people are doing is, they're actually scraping sand up and forming an artificial dune in front of their structures so that it serves as some sort of protection in a storm. Also, a lot of coastal communities are trying to see if they can enroll in some sort of beach re-nourishment program or maybe just a one-time re-nourishment project to widen and stabilize the beaches. We don't really know what impacts those kinds of activities have on nesting habitats. So, it's kind of a scary thing. The other part of the job is overseeing the sea turtle stranding and salvage network. What that involves is a huge network of volunteers and state and federal agencies that are on the beaches, or are able to monitor in-shore shorelines for sea turtles that wash ashore either dead or alive, but in some way debilitated. Right now, the data that is being collected by the stranding network—not only in North Carolina, but in other states as well—pretty much represents the only index of mortality that we have available to us. We don't have a real clear idea of the number of animals that do wash ashore, or what that represents in terms of total mortality. North Carolina, unfortunately, has a very high level of mortality. Last year we had over 600 strandings, which is just, I think, unacceptable. So, we're having to work with National Marine Fishery Service and also the State Division of Marine Fisheries, and now with fishermen as well in trying to figure out what is contributing to this high level of mortality.

What exactly is stranding?

It's when a sea turtle—and this is true for marine mammals and any critter—washes up dead, or still alive but either sick or injured. With sea turtles, they don't strand on purpose. Sometimes you'll hear about marine mammals who will become stranded in shallow waters for whatever reason. Turtles don't do that. Generally what happens with turtles—if they're still alive I'm saying—they're too weak to fight the current so they end up getting washed up. The dead turtles, of course, are being brought up on the shoreline from wave action and currents and so on and so forth. The stranding network then responds to these reports of animals on the beach and they collect a variety of data. They take measurements, they record any anomalies on the critters— any injuries or that sort of thing. Those that are still alive then get transported to the nearest rehab facility and get taken care of and hopefully, eventually get released.

What have been your greatest challenges along the path that you've taken?

I guess after I graduated from Illinois State my greatest goal was just to have fun. (*Laughs.*) I had just my own, selfish challenges. I really took pride in the fact that I could just travel any-

where and that I was self-sufficient and that type of thing. I actually learned a lot by doing that. I would go into areas and not know a soul, and I would take temporary jobs just to make enough money to get by. It was fun. You had to rely on and learn to trust strangers, basically.

Graduate school was probably the biggest challenge I ever faced in my life, because I didn't even know how to turn a computer on. (*Laughs.*) I was at a total deficit. My advisor, Sue Haig— bless her heart—she's the one who took me under her wing and had so much patience with me it wasn't even funny. She made us work really hard. It wasn't easy, but she was such an incredibly driven person. She also really cares about her graduate students. I look back at my graduate school experience and think I was just incredibly fortunate to have her as an advisor. I didn't know anything about experimental designs, or scientific writing, or anything like that. In fact, I had to make up undergraduate courses while I was in graduate school because I didn't take certain chemistry courses and that kind of thing. It was an interesting time. But, I made it through and nobody can ever take that away.

Working for the American Youth Hostels was a challenge, too. My first trip, I had a group of ten thirteen- and fourteen-year-olds. (*Laughs.*) I was the only leader and we went from the western part of Massachusetts to the coast. I had done a lot of work with kids' camps and stuff like that, but this group was not a good mix. Personalities clashed and it was—oh my god—it was a nightmare of a trip in a sense. After I finished that trip, I was convinced that all thirteen- and fourteen-year-olds should just be locked in a closet. (*Laughs.*) Their hormones are raging and it's like, 'Whoa!' Then I had another trip right afterwards, to Vermont. It was sixteen- through eighteen-year-olds and they would serve me breakfast in my tent. It was just a whole different ball game. So, my faith in kids came back, I guess.

When you get disappointed, or you have strife in your daily dealings, what are your sources of inspiration? How do you get renewed and rejuvenated?

Well, it's getting harder and harder. (*Laughs.*) I had a conversation not too long ago—the timing was perfect because I had just been through a series of very nasty meetings and I was feeling like, 'My god, this isn't going anywhere.' A friend of mine who works for the Fish and Wildlife Service called out of the blue. She's been in the business for twenty-five years and is, too, a workaholic and very inspiring person. She's a really neat lady. I met her when I was on Cape Island down in South Carolina—she helped us carry buckets of turtle eggs.

I just started to rant and rave, and she said to me—this was so weird—'You don't know how comforting it is for me to hear someone else say what I feel.' I'm thinking, 'But you've been in this business for twenty-five years. How can you take comfort in what I'm saying?' (*Laughs.*) Anyway, I asked her, 'How do you keep going?' and she said, 'You just have those days where things click. You actually feel like you've made some progress.'

For example, yesterday I had a good day. I gave a talk to a really neat group of people. They're actually a Cherokee Indian tribe, and they were so excited about the turtles and stuff. After that I had to zoom to Havelock to meet this guy who's a senior in high school and he's getting his Eagle Scout badge. He called me one afternoon and said, 'Well, I need a project,' and I just happened to be pricing plastic containers to carry live stranded sea turtles in. They were 300 bucks apiece and I was like, 'Man, how am I going to afford this?' I wanted to buy at least ten, and I had just found out that our stranding money from National Marine Fishery Service had been cut in half.

A light bulb went off in my brain when this kid was saying that he was in desperately in need of a project. I said, 'How would you like to make some wooden sea turtle carriers?' He's a herpetologist freak—he loves herps. I said, 'That would be perfect because we need them for the beaches.' He said, 'Sure!' So, it all worked out well, and yesterday I had to meet him in Havelock to pick up those boxes. I can't wait to distribute them. I guess little things like that—when you feel like you've really made some progress in trying to educate people and have them view the big picture versus just their own little part of the beach—I guess it's those kinds of things that keep you motivated.

You were telling me that, earlier on, you took a lot of temporary jobs to kind of keep yourself afloat. What is your favorite quirky temporary job experience?

God, I don't know, I've had so many. When I picked apples in Vermont, I guess I had the most wonderful experience because I didn't really expect it. It was kind of a short-term thing. It was crazy. (*Laughs.*) I had just finished working for the American Youth Hostels, leading a bike trip through Vermont, and it was really beautiful. I said to myself when I was in Vermont, 'Man, I'd love to grow old here.' I just really...had this feeling. You know how sometimes you go to a place and you feel really at home? So, I happened to talk to one of the guys who worked at the American Youth Hostels and he had mentioned something about going to pick apples in Putney, Vermont. A group of students from Evergreen State College go out every year to this particular apple orchard. He said, 'You can have a job if you want.'

I had no place to stay and it was going to start the following week. So, I was at my cousin's house in Connecticut, and I was fixing my bike out on her front lawn and this guy walked up—I'll never do this again, it was really stupid. He lived in Putney and he needed a housemate, so I moved into his house the next day.

(*Laughs.*) Turned out it wasn't the best move I ever made, but I had a wonderful time picking apples.

I ended up moving on to the orchard itself. A great group of people—played guitars every night and worked really hard during the day. I was able to climb huge, massive trees and look down this valley in the fall in Vermont, and the colors were just spectacular. It was fun.

Do you have a family now?

No. Well, I have no maternal instincts whatsoever. I have a friend—I guess my mate in life—and we have two doggies. (*Laughs.*)

What are some of the ways that you relax?

Umm...I don't really. Whenever I get a chance—which is less and less—I really still like to bike ride and stuff, but I haven't done a long distance trip in so long. We generally take the doggies to the beach and that kind of thing. My main thing is, when I consider my work day finished, then I just don't answer the phone or do anything like that because I really don't want to talk to anybody—which is kind of bad, but I just try to relax and then get ready for the next day.

What are some of your favorite things to do?

Probably first and foremost I like physical challenges—to do some really difficult physical things and to make it. I don't really want to get into hardcore rock-climbing or anything like that. I'm more into endurance things, being able to endure a lot of physical challenges. Also, not only physical, but I guess mental as well—things that are mentally challenging.

What personal qualities do you consider to be of the most value?

Strength in character, I suppose. Always considering the other person in situations. The biggest thing I have learned in this job is, realizing that there are always two sides to every story and that you need to consider both sides. Let's see...what else? Also the ability to make a decision to do something, then carry it through. Explore every possible way to achieve a goal. To always remember that there's a big picture to everything—and I'm guilty in this. You become so focused on a narrow perspective. It's so bad to do and it's so easy to do, and I think you always have to sit back and understand that there's a much bigger world out there—a much broader perspective that needs to be considered.

What is the one way that you personally have evolved as a person that makes you proudest?

Even though I have a hard time admitting it, I think the thing that I'm proudest of is the fact that I have done well in this job. I will always say that there is so much to be done, but I like to think that I've had at least some influence in making the sea turtle program in North Carolina grow. New policies that are initiated, new coastal management policies, fishery policies, that type of thing. I spent a lot of time trying to build up the stranding network, you know, get the folks trained on how to respond to these events. A lot of volunteers have been taking the ball and they themselves have educated the communities and given their phone numbers out as the folks to contact when somebody sees a turtle wash up. So, we have much better coverage on our ocean-facing beaches and also in some of our in-shore areas as well. I'm kind of proud of that, but we still have a lot more to do.

What qualities do you possess that make this a natural career choice for you?

I love the critters. I think it's a commendable pursuit to be able to do as much as you physically can for the benefit of the ecosystems that occur here. There's so much adversity that they face, especially along the coast. Our coastal environments are really sustaining a great deal of degradation because of development.

Sue, who taught me how to sink my teeth into something and shake my head as hard as I possibly can until I get it changed, is a truly amazing lady. What she has done in her career so far—she's made a heck of a difference in all sorts of disciplines. I always had admired that and I guess I kinda want to be like that as much as I possibly can.

What qualities of yours naturally create conflict or struggle that you have to work to overcome as pertains to your career choice?

That's a really good question. I have a very hard time doing what I had said earlier, about seeing both sides of the story. (*Laughs.*) Sometimes I have kind of a knee-jerk reaction. Although I try to hide it as much as possible, deep down inside I get really angry when I hear people say stuff that I don't necessarily think is correct, or I don't want to hear. I have a very hard time dealing with those kinds of things. I have to learn to let go and say, 'OK, there's got to be some sort of compromise or some sort of agreement that we can come to.'

Probably one of my biggest weaknesses in this position is the fact that I do work with a number of volunteers, and I really enjoy them, but I don't think I necessarily have that personality to do things for them, like plan activities and that sort of thing. The person that I hired this year has that kind of personality, where she pulls people together and organizes events. I've never been very good at that.

I guess I never feel like I get enough done. Just thinking that I should be doing more all of the time.

How do you explain the fact that your main goal early on was just to have fun, and you felt like you lived a pretty irresponsible life, but yet you turned into a person who is able to live every day with all this responsibility?

I don't know. I think once I went to graduate school, I got trained to do that, if that makes sense. I went into graduate school not really knowing what to expect. I have always been the type of person that, once I set my mind to do something, I was going to do it—whether it was to climb a particular mountain or go on a particular trip by myself. I carried that with me when I went to graduate school—I was going to graduate come hell or high water. That kind of set me up and made me far more disciplined in terms of, 'You have to sit down and you have to write this and you have to finish this.' My goals prior to that never involved any kind of desk work or actually writing up reports, per se. You know what I mean?

I don't want to sound like I was mentally inept prior to going to graduate school, but I was just always out for the adventure. I never took a position where I was responsible for drafting any kind of reports or coming up with management recommendations.

Graduate school taught me how to do that. I realized early on in graduate school that this particular discipline that I was going into was going to be a ton of work. At that point in time I said to myself, 'OK, you are going to dedicate your life to your career.' I made the decision at that point, and I want to continue to do that. I've never had the desire to have a family. So, I guess graduate school was sort of the transition to a life of responsibility. I will always give Tom Murphy a hard time over that. (*Laughs.*)

What, if anything, would you do differently if you could turn back the clock?

I can't really think of anything. I mean, life is hard now because I've put myself in that situation, but I had a lot of really good adventures. I don't think I would really change anything. Maybe one thing I would've tried to do is a lot more overseas traveling. I kind of short-changed myself when I was in my twenties and leading that irresponsible life. I always wanted to do the Peace Corps and I filled out a million and one applications, and for one reason or another I never pursued that. I maybe regret that. I think overall I've done pretty well. I'm pretty satisfied with what I've done.

If you could advise women who you would see as being very similar to you at those younger ages, what advice would you give them for starting out in their careers and in their lives in general?

To gain as much broad experience as possible. There are so many kids who go from undergraduate school directly into graduate school—and I'm just speaking from my own personal experience, that would have never worked for me—never. When I was that age, I didn't have a clue what I wanted to do. That was pretty obvious because it took me a decade to finally figure out. (*Laughs.*) Have as much adventure as possible. I think it's kind of sad nowadays—and it may be partially because of computers and stuff like that—that kids aren't really getting out as much and experiencing a broad range of things. You know, going out in the big world and just really seeing stuff. I know a lot of people are doing that, certainly, but I think more should. I think that's so important when you're first starting. I know there are some people who figure out right away what they want in life, but I can't fathom how anybody can do that. (*Laughs.*)

I still haven't figured it out.

I think young kids should just go out and live life. If they want to get married, wait until they're thirty or something like that, because you're still a kid in your twenties. You don't know what's going on. I mean, I did some really stupid things when I was in that phase of life, stuff that could have really put myself in a great deal of danger. I was pretty trusting. I think back to some of the things that I've done and it's like, 'I would never do that again.' But I was lucky I suppose, and I survived them. I had a great time. I learned a lot and got to see a lot of cool things. I think that's really important.

I think it's important also—and I keep telling myself this—

that because I'm turning forty soon, that's not a reason to stop doing that. That's part of the frustration that I'm feeling right now, is because I have stopped. For five years now, I've pretty much focused on one thing—and it's a good thing and I'm not regretting what I'm doing—but you gotta have that balance in life. Have some of that adventure as well, it keeps you mentally fit and physically fit.

What advice would you give someone who is approaching forty, and feels they want to make some type of career change?

Go for it. (*Laughs.*) I think age is irrelevant for the most part. If you feel good and feel healthy and you're up to the challenge, you should go for it. I don't think there's anything wrong with that. The only restraints you have are those you put on yourself. If a woman has decided to pursue a family life and have a family and suddenly has a change of heart, I guess there's always a way to work out a scenario where you can do both. I don't know. I'm now stepping on shaky ground because I don't know anything about raising a family. It's a big world out there and you've got a lot of opportunities.

I've never experienced one degree or iota of discrimination in my field. You know, where because I was a female, I didn't get hired, or anything like that. In fact, I will be the first to admit that it's helped me more than anything. Because I was fortunate in that I worked in situations where the people that I worked for were very open to having women work with them. My first supervisor that I had in my job, he said he would far rather hire women than men, because we're more responsible. (*Laughs.*) Part of the challenge is working out a scenario where you can make your goals happen.

What dreams do you have that are yet to be realized—both personal and professional?

I would like to get myself back in shape. That's a very important personal goal I have. I want to be able to have the time to get back into some serious reading, which I haven't done in so long. I want to embark on some new adventures. I want to be able to have time to travel before it gets too late. There's so much I want to see—different countries I want to visit—and I don't want to lose that.

Truly, a lot of it is to be able to feel physically fit again. I just am not there anymore and I don't like that. That's always been so important to me. I just feel like a slug now because I don't have time to go out. I used to be a bit of a maniac I guess, but it was never a big deal for me to just go out and ride 100 miles. I loved it because you would meet all these incredible people along the way, and they'd all think you're crazy. Or go on back-country ski trips and that sort of thing. I just miss it so much.

So, I guess those are some of my personal goals. I would like to do something creative again. I really enjoy crafty things—quilting and making baskets—and I just miss doing those things and being able to make gifts for people. I hate the fact that now I have to buy everything. I used to never do that. I kind of want to return to the way things used to be, but at the same time maintain a career in wildlife biology.

Professionally, my biggest dream—and it could actually be realized in this job if they were to hire on another person—my love in this job is actually overseeing the stranding network and dealing with in-water issues, and the whole mortality problem that we have here. The fact that North Carolina is so important for sea turtles—for young turtles, juvenile turtles. They use our waters as foraging areas and it just offers great developmental habitat, and yet so many of them are dying. I really want to pursue some really serious research in trying to ascertain what habitats these turtles use. How can we change fishery policies to reduce the possibility of turtles interacting with fishing gear that's in the water? I would love to sink my teeth in that whole part of this job and deal with nothing else. I would love to work one-on-one with the fishermen. I have far more respect for them than I do for politicians, because they'll tell me to my face that they hate turtles, and I would much rather deal with someone who tells me that honestly than someone who speaks out of both sides of their mouth. I just can't tolerate that.

There's so much that needs to be done in terms of changing fishery management policies here in order to protect threatened and endangered species in the water. I want to go out and just really conduct some really, really nice science—I think it's so critical for turtles that that be done. But until we get the money to do it, it's not going to happen.

Interviewed by Susan L. Comer.

About to release a small chicken turtle she rescued as a hatchling.

Ruth *Boettcher*

Since April 1995, Ruth Boettcher has been the sea turtle project coordinator for N.C. Wildlife Resources Commission Nongame and Endangered Wildlife Program. She oversees and coordinates a statewide sea turtle protection and management program involving numerous state, federal, and nongovernmental agencies as well as hundreds of volunteers. She has her bachelor's of science in recreation and parks administration from Illinois State University, and her master's of science in wildlife biology from Clemson University.

She currently lives in Gloucester with her best friend and lifetime companion who, through his keen insight and knowledge of the natural world, taught her to slow down and look at what was around her instead of simply blowing through the woods while skiing, backpacking or bicycling. Also living with them are their two dogs, Elke and Sadie, who give them reason to laugh every day.

Mary Upchurch Tobin an interview

Why don't we start with where you grew up and went to school?

I grew up here in Wilmington. I went to Hanover and UNC-W. And then, after college, I moved to Houston.

What did you dream of doing when you were a child? Did you know what you wanted to do?

I think I changed my mind a lot. I wanted to be a vet, and I wanted to be a pediatrician. I guess those were the two big things.

What did you study in college?

Therapeutic recreation.

Did you go on to pursue that as a career?

Yes. When I finished school I went to Houston and was a nanny for a year, or maybe a couple of years. Then I got a job in recreational therapy in Houston Hospital.

:

Will you describe for me what you do now?

Now my main job is a mother. I have a sign rental business, and I rent storks, and other signs that I am just now getting going.

I sell business startup kits to people around the country. Basically, my whole goal with that is just to help other stay-at-home mothers start up, or help them to leave their jobs and stay home with their kids.

How did you get from therapeutic recreation to being involved in the business you have now?

Well, the people I was a nanny for, their mother had died. That was probably the only kind of situation I could have gone into as a nanny. It would have been really hard, if not impossible for me to take care of kids whose mother just chose to go to work for twelve or thirteen hours a day. When I was working for that family, their stepmother was expecting twins, and I would try and find storks for them and couldn't. So I made my own, and then it just kind of started slowly from there. I started a business. I still worked for them, and then when I got the job in my field I just did it after work and on weekends. And it just kind of evolved. And I knew it would be a good business, that if I ever did have kids I would be able to still do.

So where did you meet your husband?

At the hospital, where I worked. He was a medical student rotating through. I met him and we had three kids really fast. I just kept doing the stork business, and it has really fit in with them. When I get calls, I can do it when they are napping.

How did you come to move back to Wilmington?

It just kind of evolved. I wanted to move here, and with small kids, I really needed the help. My family is here, and all my friends are here. So, my husband commutes to another town to work.

How old are your children?

They are a three-year old girl and almost-sixteen-month boy/girl twins. And so this fits in well with them.

How did you know that you wanted to be a stay-at-home mom?

Gosh! I just can't imagine leaving them. It's not a real popular opinion right now. There are so many people, I think, who have gotten to be where we think that day care is completely acceptable and okay. I mean, even now, at the age they are, I can't imagine leaving them with anybody else. I think that if you have kids, it doesn't have to be the mom who stays home. I know people who have stay-at-home dads, or the parents work opposite shifts and they never see each other. And that's fine, because

I think the kids need their parents. So it was just never even an option.

How do you handle being at home? I know you have your own business, but do you ever get lonely just being with the kids?

Yes. You have to have friends and meet people. We go to the park a lot. I have friends with kids the same ages, and they come over. You have to, or you would go nuts. You have to have somebody to talk to. We just came off three weeks of sickness, one thing after another. It was awful, because I was so isolated. Nobody could come over, or wanted to. And we couldn't really go anywhere. So, that's really important. I have even thought about doing a group, like for work-at-home mothers. I am a member of this group that is on the Internet. There are two other people, and one of them has contacted me also, just to make that connection.

How do you think you have been able to juggle having your own business and being an at-home mom?

I just don't sit still. I can't stand to. So, I just fill every minute. If they are happy playing, I run and do some little task. The good thing about what I am doing with the storks and the Internet is that it can all be done a little bit at a time. You can come back to it and leave it. It's not like I have people in or have to have business meetings or anything like that. I do a lot in the evenings, after they go to sleep.

What do you think of as some of your greatest challenges to get to this point?

Probably just getting the word out about it; and then the financial part. Now that my husband is getting his job established, it is not really an issue and that's good. That does make it easier. And now I have more money to work with as far as marketing, and things like that.

And how does your husband feel about your staying at home and having this business?

I think he wishes sometimes I did less with the business, because I definitely spend a lot of time on it.

Do you take any time for yourself to relax?

A little bit. For many years, doing the business stuff has been my getaway time. If I go out there and cut, or just work on that stuff without the kids right there, it really is relaxing. I have a hard time going out to a movie or things like that. It feels like wasted time.

How did you have the idea of starting your business? How did you get all

the pieces together?

Really slowly, over time. It has evolved just adding a little bit here and there. It isn't something you grow up with. Instead, everything is geared towards working for somebody else.

Do you find that having your own business adds a sense of isolation, because you are not in a job with other people?

No, probably the opposite. I still get the contact with the people who call. Everybody who calls me is thrilled. They are happy. They just had a baby. And so I get that adult contact, too. So that probably makes it less isolating than if I just worked at home and didn't have anything else. It is a concrete thing that is a tangible product. And that, I think, is one reason that people who are used to a career and then stay home don't like it, because it is the same thing every day. At the end of the day your kids are still there, and they are growing and all. And that's wonderful. But you don't really get the end results until so long down the road. And with this, you do it and it is great. I just made a sailboat this weekend for a beach birth announcement, and it came out so cute. And it is a tangible thing that you can look at and say: 'I just did this.'

Do you paint the signs yourself?

No. I am not really artistic at all. My brother is very artistic.

But the storks—I had a professional artist that did the design. And then, like the sailboat, it came out of a coloring book. I just went to the library and got an overhead projector, blew it up on the board, and then did it with chalk. And then my three-year old loves to help paint, so the first couple of coats that I put on, I let her do.

Do you find the other stay-at-home moms that you know find what you are doing inspirational?

I don't know. Most of them are really surprised. They don't know where I have the time, especially with twins also. But, yes. I guess so. I have a couple of friends who help me, like by going to town for me. The comment I get most is 'I don't know where you have the time.' But the people I get e-mails from are the best, because they are generally the people who are trying to find something. They really have to keep making money. I have just sold a kit to a lady in Arizona that I mailed today. She is a police detective on child abuse cases, and she doesn't want to do that anymore, because her kids are small and it's too close to home. So, she is just so excited about getting started and that keeps me excited about it. I'm glad that I don't really need to do it for an income anymore, so I can keep my price low, which will help other people get started.

Did you have a stay-at-home mom when you were growing up?

For the most part. When we started school, she would work during those hours. There was a period of—not even a year, I think—when we came home from school and went to a babysitter's house. I remember not liking it at all.

What qualities do you have personally that made this possible for you?

I guess just that I don't like to do nothing. I mean, I like to be very busy. My husband is very supportive. He will spend money. He will let me get whatever I need to do it, and he has gone early and made deliveries. And he is an emergency room doctor. He has taken storks for me that were going kind of far out, on his way to work.

So, he's in South Carolina?
Yes.

Goodness. How far does he have to drive?

Well, we have a place down there, too. And he works twelve- and thirteen-hour shifts. So, when he is working, he will go down there and stay for a few days and then come home. And if he is working night shifts, we will go down and stay there too.

Is that hard for you?

Yes. But also, part of it is we are both really strong-willed people and pretty independent. Kind of having that not-constant-together-time has probably helped us.

Is that something that you find a lot of people are kind of skeptical about? 'How do you do this? Does this work?'

Yes. And it wouldn't work for a lot of people, but we are both really strong-willed, and it just works for us. It is hard right now, because he is working so much just to get us all caught up. Once he is not working as much it will be easier, because he will be here more.

What accomplishment do you think you are proudest of?

Our kids. They are smart. They are a lot of fun. I just can't imagine not being with them.

Do you find that motherhood came really naturally for you?

: Very.

Did you think that it would?

Yes, I did. I started babysitting when I was ten. And I babysat all through college. I would go from one place to the next, and that was what I always loved to do. And, in fact, the kids that I used to babysit come and help me with mine, so that has been fun.

For you, was coming back to Wilmington a real good feeling?

Yes. And I never thought I would. I loved Houston, I really did, but once I had the kids I wanted to be back here.

What do you like about this environment, for children?

Well, I like the extended support. I like for them to have more family around, and friends. And I want them to be settled in one place and grow up. And then I am just familiar with this area. Their other grandparents live in the D.C. area, and that's only six hours away. It was really important to me, even if we didn't come all the way back to Wilmington, to be close enough that they would get to see all their grandparents. It wouldn't be just a once-a-year kind of thing. I wanted them to grow up being able to go up to their house, or for us to be able to go up there and visit frequently.

When all your kids are in school, do you think you'll want to be out of the house working, or to expand your business?

I would probably just expand this a lot more and spend a lot more time on it. I might, at that, work. I wouldn't mind working somewhere, having a retail store one day, that's baby- or kids-oriented.

Would you want to have your children at work with you?

Yes. Actually, there was a store here in town for sale, and I really considered buying it. The girl that bought it, she was pregnant and now has a new baby, and I see everything that she has had to do. There would have been no way I could have done it, when my kids are this age, especially with twins. And that would not really be fair to them. All three of them couldn't be in there. It is not like with just one baby. That is so much easier. But once they are in school, I definitely wouldn't mind having somewhere that they could come after school and do their homework. It would have to be big enough to where they could have their separate little room. Or maybe it would be something where I would just work during the day and then have somebody else there.

People tend to think: 'Oh, you have got to be there for the first three years and then they are fine.' But I talked to a lady who does storks in the New York area, and she has twins also, two of her five kids. And they are teenagers. She said, 'This time is probably more important, just because they have all that conflict and they don't want to admit they need you there, but they do.' And so, I definitely want to still be home, or be where they are, right on through.

Do you have dreams that you still want to fulfill and goals you are working towards, beyond what you are doing now?

I want those kits to—I would like to have 200 of them out there, people doing the same thing. That's where my goals really are, to help as many people get started as I can.

If you were talking to a young woman who was not quite sure where she might want to go, or an older woman who was thinking of changing careers, what advice would you give?

I tell everybody: 'Do whatever you really like to do.' It is such a cliché, but it is really true. And I have friends who think I am crazy. They can't imagine standing out in the garage and sawing and painting and doing all this. But I just love it. If you find whatever it is that you love to do, then it is not going to seem like work. And the money part will come after.

I would tell people also, don't have kids that you are not going to raise. I mean, there's nothing more important than that. No amount of money is ever going to get that time back in their lives. And if you can only afford one that you can take care of, then just have the one. So, that is the most important thing to me. I mean, I would have us all in a one-bedroom apartment and selling ice cream on the street before I would not be with them.

Interviewed by Emily A. Colin.

Mary Upchurch Tobin

Mary Upchurch Tobin is a native of Wilmington, North Carolina. She graduated from New Hanover High School and from UNC-Wilmington. Mary and her husband, Chris Tobin—an emergency room physician in South Carolina—have three kids: Caroline, three, and Michael and Meredith, seventeen months. They live in Wilmington and also spend time in South Carolina. She is a stay-at-home mom first, and The Stork Lady second. Her business offers sign rentals, gift baskets, and balloons to welcome new babies into the world. She also sells start-up packages for this business over the Internet, and currently has thirty locations—with more added each week.

"I have a hard time going out to a movie or things like that. It feels like wasted time."

Mary Upchurch Tobin

Shirley Pruitt an interview

Where did you grow up and attend school?

I grew up in Kalamazoo, Michigan, and went through my primary education and high school at Kalamazoo Christian schools. Then I was kind of unfocused and undirected and bounced around in community colleges in the local area until finally deciding to go to nursing school at Kellogg Community College. I got my associate degree in nursing in '84 and, from there, I started work as a neonatal intensive care nurse at Bronson Hospital in Kalamazoo and trained to be a transport nurse. But I only stayed at that hospital for a year before deciding to move down to Charleston, South Carolina, and was again in neonatal intensive care nursing. They were starting a transport team there and I got involved with that also. Meanwhile, I decided that, ultimately, I was going to be a lawyer, so I knew I had to get my bachelor's degree. I went to the Medical University of South Carolina right there in Charleston and probably carried about twelve credit hours a semester while working full-time. I graduated in 1989 and started law school that same year.

How did you reach the decision that you wanted to be a lawyer?

(*Laughs.*) Well, it was a long process. As I said, I bounced around in community colleges—I was in the physical therapy program, I was in medical office lab tech. So I was in the health field before I decided on nursing. And while I was in nursing school, I had kind of a euphemistic ten-year plan. I thought that when I graduated from nursing school, I would first do regular medical/surgical nursing, then work my way into neonatal intensive care, and then work my way into transport nursing. In my mind, I thought this would take quite a few years to accomplish. But when I was fortunate enough to get into the neonatal intensive care right away and start training for the transport team before the first year was up, I kind of then was getting a clue that my plan had gone much more quickly—and what was I gonna do for the rest of my life! (*Laughs.*)

I think, while, back then, I wasn't dissatisfied with nursing at all, somehow I knew that I wanted to keep growing and doing more. I mean, it's awful hard to look back now and remember what I was thinking, but I do remember the month before I moved down to Charleston, I had gone on a boating outing with some friends, and I remember sitting in a sand dune—and this is gonna sound very silly, but it's quite true. Other people were water-skiing and it was my turn to sit out, so I was just sitting in the sand dune in the sun and realizing that my life was about to change. I was going to a completely different state, doing completely different everything, and how was I going to change things?

One of the things I decided was that I would go back to school for a professional degree of some sort. And I leaned toward law because my sister-in-law had just finished law school about a year or two earlier so, even though she wasn't really practicing at that point, she was kind of encouraging me that law school might be a good place for me to go. So I started to think about it and, by the time I got to Charleston and got settled, somewhere in there I realized, 'OK, better make my plans. Law school's where I need to go and there's lots of stuff to do, so I better start now.' The first thing to do, of course, was to get a bachelor's degree. And I decided I should get my bachelor's degree in nursing since, if I was an absolute failure at the law, at least I could fall back on my nursing experience and degree. (*Laughs.*)

Tell me about the hybrid career you've created for yourself.

Since joining the firm after law school in 1992, I have concentrated exclusively in medical malpractice, and that's defense. We defend hospitals, doctors, and nurses who are sued for medical malpractice or wrongful death. When I started out, I did *everything*—I mean, broken legs, broken hips, operations that hadn't gone well, et cetera. Then I started to get involved with brain-damaged baby cases, because the senior partner in our firm had experience in that and we were one of the few firms in the area that did that kind of work. Within a couple of years, that's about all I did. I still would occasionally have what I call regular malpractice cases. But, primarily, I have focused in the area of obstetrical malpractice—either something has gone wrong with mother or something has gone wrong with baby. Brain-damaged baby cases, that's my specialty.

What attracted you to this particular specialty?

I think it was a natural segue because, doing neonatal intensive care, naturally I took care of sick babies. And in cases that involve allegations of brain damage in babies, one of the things you look at is what happens to the baby after it's born—how the baby reacts, whether it's having problems with the kidneys, the liver, the bone marrow, you know, signs of brain damage, et cetera, et cetera. So my experience working with sick babies made it very easy to read the medical records of sick babies. I mean, I understood what was being said in the records. I understood what the laboratory tests meant. I understood, to a certain extent, what the X-ray results meant. In talking with medical experts about the issues, I was able to very quickly understand what they were saying about whether this baby did or did not fit certain criteria—whether brain damage happened long ago during pregnancy, whether it was likely to have happened during labor and delivery, or whether maybe it happened *after* labor and delivery.

What career dreams did you have as a child?

(*Laughs.*) The one I remember the most is to be a truck driver. And I can't tell you how old I was, nor do I remember why that seemed so appealing. Maybe I was just fascinated by the big trucks.

Is there any childhood event or recollection you have that foreshadowed the career choice you ultimately made?

None whatsoever. I can tell you that, for me to have gone into nursing, to me, was a bit of a very funny coincidence because I had two brothers five years older than I, who had no use for a little sister. And they would always kind of tease me with, 'Girls grow up to be wives, teachers, or nurses.' I was just very much a tomboy growing up. My summer jobs and high school jobs were all manual-labor-type jobs. I worked in the celery fields. I worked in the flower business where we shoveled dirt and filled flats. And in *that* business, usually the women planted seeds and the guys hauled around the flats of flowers. I didn't plant seeds. I was with the guys, hauling around the flats of flowers—bound and determined not to be a 'girly-girl.' And I for *sure* was not gonna go to nursing school because that's what girls did! (*Laughs.*) So that's why it just took me quite a few years to get to nursing school, 'cause I graduated in '79 and I don't believe I started nursing school till '82. And I was in school all that time, just kind of, like I said, mucking around at different courses. Then it *finally* occurred to

me that, 'Well, I'm *interested* in the health field. I have touched on every aspect of the health field that *doesn't* interest me, so it must be that what I *am* interested in is nursing!' (*Laughs.*)

What have been the greatest challenges along your path?

Overcoming the fear. I was *terrified* of law school. It's awfully hard to articulate, but I was convinced that I would fail. And I have to say that I know one of the reasons I didn't go to nursing school right away, but kind of danced around the periphery, is not only because girls went there, but also because I thought nursing was terribly, terribly hard. And gosh, therefore, if I did *that*, I might fail! In fact, when I did start nursing school, I did very well and probably got As in almost everything. I don't recall getting anything less than a B+. Then that buoyed my confidence—you know, 'Well, yes, it *is hard*, but I'm certainly capable.' But I was absolutely convinced that law was out of my reach. So when I say I got my bachelor's degree in nursing as a fallback—in all honesty, I thought, you know, 'After a year—after I flunk out of law school, humiliated—at least I'll have a job.' (*Laughs.*) But I did very well in law school also. I'd have to say my biggest challenge has been believing in myself and being confident enough to do it. And there just came a point where I had to just go do it—and figuring the worst thing that happens is I don't make it and, 'Oh well, at least I *tried*.'

Were you a good student in grade school?

Yeah. I don't know why I didn't have real confidence, but I did quite well. I mean, I know I got As and Bs—and usually high Bs, like a B+. In fact, the first C I ever got in my entire life was in my last semester of my last year of law school on my last exam, Criminal Procedure. And, frankly, I deserved it because, to be real honest, that was a class I hated and I skipped it more often than not and figured—I knew I was going to do medical malpractice, so who needed Criminal Procedure? Still, I thought I'd done better on the exam than a C, and it really hurt my feelings to get a C on the last test I was ever gonna take! (*Laughs.*)

The way your life is going, maybe it's not the last test you'll ever take.

Well, you know, before my daughter—and now I'm expecting another baby—I had always teased that I might still go to medical school. But unless I have lots of energy and the kids are grown, I don't foresee school in the next little bit. I'm a little too busy. (*Laughs.*)

Speaking of which, tell me about your family.

I have a sixteen-month-old daughter, and we are expecting what may be a little brother—the doctors are not quite sure by the ultrasound—in four months. My husband is self-employed. And, as of the end of this month, I will be staying at home to take care of the kids. The theory is that I will do the paperwork for my husband and answer the phone calls as well as keep track of the kids and keep track of the household. And if we don't fall out in abject poverty, that's what will happen for the next couple of years.

So the plan is to lay out of your career for a time to focus on being a mom?

I think so. I'm not even quite sure, at my firm, whether we're calling it a resignation or a leave of absence. I mean, we talk about me being gone for 'awhile,' and I've not ever specified how long I'll be gone. In the last six months, I've had to travel extensively and it's come to a point where I just don't feel like I'm having enough time at home. And my husband can't grow his business because he's busy being at home taking care of things while I travel. Litigation is fairly time-intensive and your calendar is not always your own. And I just felt like I needed to step away and be a mom and see if we could financially afford for me to stay home and do the family thing for awhile. But I suspect that it won't be very long at all before I start doing hourly contract work for my firm, just because I know me and I usually can't keep my cotton-pickin' hands off of things and it's something that I'm very good at.

What sort of work does your husband do?

He is a home inspector and a general contractor. He does

about fifty percent home inspections and fifty percent of repair work in real estate deals.

What are some ways you relax from your really intense career?

Well, reading is my absolute favorite. And my preferences are the top-ten novels. Love magazines, books, whatever—I don't care to *learn* a whole lot when I'm reading. My husband likes to read history, biography. Give me a *story*! Get me immersed in a story. With a sixteen-month-old, there's just not a whole lot of time, and I have to admit to being very guilty at not taking time for myself. But I'm gonna work on that. (*Laughs.*) Just as soon as the new baby comes and I get everything straightened out.

Before Caroline, my biggest, biggest way to relax was to rollerblade. And it's still my absolute favorite way to have fun and get exercise because I never could run—I just was an awkward runner. But rollerblading would give me that sense of speed and yet not require the same intensity as running.

For the last four years, we've had boats. We started out with a pontoon boat and now we have a houseboat on the lake. And that's what we do on the weekends in the summertime. And of course, again, this is all pre-children when we used to be able to sit back and relax and read and swim and, you know, drink margaritas and just have a wonderful time. Now, that's not quite practical. (*Laughs.*) But, over time, we hope to get back to that.

What are some of your favorite things?

Books. Mexican food. Anything to do with water. Animals— we have two golden retrievers and two cats. In the summertime, when we're kid-free, it's my favorite thing to be with my husband on the bow of the boat with back-porch music playing on the radio and just sitting back and relaxing.

What are some personal goals or interests that you're pursuing or some you'd like to pursue in the near future?

This is not concrete. These are just musty ideas in my head about somehow finding the time to go and do something nice for people in nursing homes. Everytime I see people coming in with dogs and cats to nursing homes, or kids going caroling in nursing homes—you know, somehow I want to contribute. And the two ways I think of are with old folks in nursing homes or helping with animals, because that's another one of my passions. So many people treat animals so badly, or they get a pet and then tie it up in the backyard and leave it there. And I'm much more of a softy than that. Our two big stinky hundred-pound golden retrievers live *in* the house, shedding atrociously, but they're family just as much as my daughter is. So if my being home turns out to be financially feasible for us in the long haul, I hope to be able to have enough time to run the family and do something meaning- ful—and impart that to Caroline and the future baby. Just to do something good for other people instead of always *thinking* about doing something good. 'Cause I have the best of intentions, but, apart from giving financial support, I've never really *given* to the community. I very often have thought that I'll go work at the soup kitchen on Thanksgiving and serve up or help cook the food, but I've never done it. I always think, 'Next year I'm gonna fit that in.' But then we find we've traveled to visit the grandparents, or the grandparents are here, and you just allow yourself to get caught up in your own life.

What personal qualities do you consider to be of most value in life?

I guess I can only point to those things that I intend for myself and that I value in other people and that would have to be—the global term I would use would be 'integrity.' And, by that, I mean the smallest thing—doing what you say you're going to do—to honesty and fairness. One of the things I am most proud of myself for is that when something needs doing and when I have said it would be done, then I just do what it takes to get it done. Sometimes things are all just piling up, and if it means I stay at work until two in the morning and get back up at six because it just has to be for that particular moment, then that's what I do. So, while that might be a bit extreme, I certainly go crazy with people who say they're going to do something or constantly make promises and just don't follow up. (*Laughs.*)

Where do you find the personal strength and energy to go that extra mile?

I don't know. I think it's something I've always been able to do. I know that certainly when we were starting up the transport team in Charleston, the director and myself were the only nurses to run the team, twenty-four hours a day, seven days a week. And granted, because the team had just started, there weren't that many calls. But there would be times when—just when you've gotten home to go to bed, that's when your beeper goes off. So, you know, the old 'when duty calls...' You just pull it up from somewhere. And I think everybody has this capacity—it's just whether you choose to do it or not do it.

And when I got to law school, I needed to make some money, so I would work the night shift in the intensive care nursery while also going to school. I'd be in school all day and I'd nap a little bit in the evening. Then I'd put in my eight hours at work and take a nap for a couple of hours and go back to school. And I had done that while I was getting my bachelor's degree. I was working the night shift, seven p.m. to seven a.m. I would drive my car to a parking spot, set my little watch alarm, and nap for an hour and a half, then go to class.

When you decide it has to be done, I feel like you can do it. And sometimes it's just miserable. I don't think I'm uniquely capable of doing it, but I certainly seem to have done it a lot more than other people. Even now, I don't feel particularly well as a pregnant person, and about a week or so ago I had a time crunch to get something ready so, even though I normally am home and in bed by nine o'clock at night, I was staying at work until one to just get it done.

How do you take care of yourself physically, to be able to push yourself like that?

Well, you can only do it for so long and then you crash. Last week, for instance, I had been kind of pushing the envelope for several days in a row. Had a late night Wednesday night and a hard day Thursday. Then on Friday, didn't do much but lay horizontally—either in bed or on the couch—and took advantage of the fact that my daughter was still in daycare and just regrouped.

What is the one way that you have evolved as a human being that makes you proudest?

(*Long pause.*) I guess I am proudest of persevering and going for those things that I was afraid of. I was afraid of nursing school and I went for it. I was afraid of law school and I went for it. I was afraid of being a litigator and I went for it. And, you know, I guess that was my own personal demon—that even though I shouldn't have had such low confidence out of high school since my grades were fine, I did have low confidence. And because of my low confidence, I just didn't really have goals or direction and I kept

trying to find the easy way out. I kept trying to find some way to have a decent job that I didn't have to work too hard for. But I turned that around and didn't stop. I mean, I remember being in nursing school and saying, 'As soon as I get this degree, that's it! I'm never going to school again!' And clearly, that's not what I did.

It sounds as though an easy job would not be enough for you.

That's entirely true. And I remind myself of that everytime I complain about how hard my work is. I always tease that I wish I could go work at Wendy's and make hamburgers and be happy. Because, sometimes, I'm so stressed that I think, 'Goll, wouldn't it be great to just go in, do your time, and then leave and have your time be your own.' But I know that I would be terribly bored. I need to be challenged.

What qualities do you possess that make litigation a natural for you?

Probably that I'm competitive. (*Laughs.*) I think it's awfully hard to be a litigator and not be competitive. Between being competitive and a love of reading—because so much of the law involves reading—I'm either reading medical records or I'm reading medical literature or I'm reading transcripts. And in my particular line of work—and I think this is really true for most of the law—it's almost a *constant* learning experience. Even though I do brain-damaged baby cases and they're somewhat the same, there's always a distinction. There's always something new that's come up. So I think that's what's most exciting about it, is that it's not dull, it's not boring. Every time you're doing something, you're *learning* something. And then something happens that involves a new area of law that has to be researched. There's nothing stagnant about it, so I guess you have to be willing and open to learning.

On the other hand, what qualities of yours create conflict or struggle that you constantly work to overcome as pertains to your career?

Oh, that one's easy. I don't like conflict. (*Laughs.*)

A lawyer who doesn't like conflict?

It's terrible, isn't it? (*Laughs.*) That has probably been my biggest struggle because, for the most part, particularly in my field, it's kind of the same cast of characters. There are those defense lawyers that do baby cases and there are those plaintiff's lawyers—and I'm talking 'in our area of North Carolina'—that do baby cases, and we all kind of know the routine and we all know the drill and do almost everything by consent. I mean, those things that you really *have* to fight for, you do, but there aren't any *unnecessary* fights. There's not a lot of bickering. There's not a lot of posturing and puffing. We're all going for the bigger picture and we're not getting bogged down in point-by-point fights. But then, periodically, I do have to work with other lawyers who fight for *everything* and will argue with you about the location of a deposition or argue with you over things I'm accustomed to getting by agreement. And it's very hard for me to not internalize that—to step away, not take it personally. The worst, most horrible thing is when that's happening and you're engaged in this vicious fight with another lawyer and you feel yourself tearing up. It's awful. I mean, thank goodness, when that's happening, you're usually on the phone. (*Laughs.*) And I can count on one hand the number of times it's happened, but it's just horrible and you just have to remind yourself, 'This is not a fight about me. We're fighting for our positions.' But I cannot stand it. So that is my biggest conflict in doing litigation. Some people—and I know plenty of the very aggressive lawyers in our firm that live for that very thing—just go into battle with the other person. And that is my nightmare.

So what do you tell yourself to keep from taking it personally—because I can see how that would feel like a personal attack?

Oh, it does, it does. Fortunately, it is so rare in my particular area that I don't have to deal with it often. But when I do feel that coming on, I usually stop the discussion so I can get control. I'll say, 'We're just gonna have to agree to disagree right now and let me think about it—I'll get back to you.' And I have to admit there's been a couple of times my door's had to be closed while I've had to sniffle and snuffle and regroup, 'cause it's an embarrassing thing. (*Laughs.*) It's terrible to be crying when it doesn't have anything to do with you. And I have what I've always called my 'twenty-four-hour rule.' If something has upset me—if I pick up a letter or if I've had a phone conversation that just instantly makes my blood pressure go up and gives me that 'fight, fight, fight' sensation—I put that in the twenty-four-hour pile. I refuse to even talk to that other person or write a letter to the other person until I've had twenty-four hours to figure out, 'What am I reacting to?' And usually, within the twenty-four hours, I've gotten a grip. I've realized that, 'Yes, while on principle, I would love to fight and win, it's not worth it. I'm not gonna gain anything by doing that. So *what* if I'm right? We don't need to carry on like this.' So you move forward. But a 'time out' is the only thing that helps. (*Laughs.*)

What are your sources of renewal at those times?

Oh, probably talking to either a friend at work or my husband and just unloading it and having my little hissy in a safe environment. 'Can you believe this guy said this and that and the other thing?' Just having my little tirade someplace where it's quite safe to do so and feeling righteously indignant and getting it out of my system. That's when I usually figure out that this is not that big of a deal. (*Laughs.*) So venting. Venting in a safe place.

Do you see your two careers—a nurse, then a litigator—as related? Or do you feel you did a 180-degree turn from being a caregiver to being a warrior, so to speak, in the courtroom?

Not really, because it's just been a transfer of who I'm taking care of. I mean, I honestly did for awhile miss talking to parents of the children I would take care of. But now, my clientele is a doctor or several nurses who are *terrified* at the process. And, you know, contrary to what people may think, anytime doctors are sued, they take it very, very personally. I mean, their livelihood, their very *being* is being challenged. Certainly there are exceptions, but for the most part, these people are out there doing the very best they can and sometimes there's a bad result. And if there *is* a bad result, they're feeling horrible already. To then be accused of having caused a death or having caused somebody's child to be brain-damaged is a big deal. They need comforting and hand-holding. And I have found it to be extremely rewarding to be the person sitting there explaining to them what the process is all about, what to expect, explaining what has gone on, and having the capacity to understand where they're coming from because I used to be on that side of the fence. So I think they have gained some confidence in me because I can speak to them in their language. They can explain to me why they're right and I can absolutely go along with them—then explain, 'OK, now I have to take you to the *legal* side. This is why it's difficult. We may be right on the medicine, but now we have this law problem.' So, for me, it's always been the best of both worlds, because I had struggled with whether or not to go to medical school and ultimately decided I didn't want it badly enough to make the sacrifices that that was going to take. I have always felt like I've had both. I've never had to really step away from medicine—and then I get to add law to the pot.

What aspect of your career brings you the most joy?

(*Long pause.*) I think that has always been my very favorite part—dealing one-on-one with those people we're representing. And I guess the problem I'm having answering that right now is—I have been, for more than eight months, in a mental process of stepping away to do what I'm about to do, which is to be home with my family. So when you ask what about my job brings me the most joy, it's hard for me to even focus that way, because my joy right now is coming from my family—and my career has been something taking me away from my joy. Once I started making the decision that I probably needed to stay home with my family, it's almost like I've been mentally divorcing myself from the work that I do. It's very exciting, and you can get caught up in it. And

I *have* been caught up in it for seven years. I get to talk to—in person—some of the most renowned medical experts in the country, if not the world and, with some of them, I'm on a first-name basis. I can watch the news and they'll be quoting certain medical people and it's somebody that I know—personally. That's very, very exciting. And it's been a long process to wean myself away from that excitement and that sense of self-importance because, 'Gosh, look what I get to do!' (*Laughs.*) To kind of come back to where my heart *really* is, which is here at home.

Of what professional accomplishment are you most proud?

Oh, my law degree. That was just a pinnacle in my life, to have achieved what I was terrified of and to be in the top twenty percent of my class. I can recall with absolute distinction the hooding ceremony. That was just a tremendously moving moment for me.

And of what personal accomplishment are you most proud?

Being smart enough to hold still enough to realize the qualities of my husband and agree to marry him. (*Laughs.*) Because he was someone who, on sight, I had zero interest in; and *he*, on sight, was absolutely determined to get me to go out with him. He couldn't have been more opposite of what I thought I was looking for and, in fact, he's my soulmate. Certainly we have our arguments, but he's my very best friend. And just letting my life develop—letting myself personally grow so that I was a whole enough person—so that, when he and I met, we didn't have any of our own background mess to deal with and we could just go on together.

What, if anything, would you do differently if you could turn back the clock?

I have always regretted not going away to college for four years like everyone else does, you know, living in a dorm or living in a house with other people and having that particular experience. And to the extent my kids will pay any attention to me on that, that is probably something I would encourage. I don't think it's made any difference with my success in life, but I just think that that was an experience that I would've liked to have had. And it looks to me—and not having been there, of course, this may be a terribly romantic view of what it's like—but it just looks to me to be the perfect in-between time of being a kid and being an adult. If I could do anything differently, I would go to a four-year college instead of doing a community-college thing like I did.

What advice would you give young women just starting out in a career or older women considering a career change?

To *go* for it. I wasted a lot of time being afraid of something and certain I would fail. The worst thing that can happen is that you really *do* fail and then, so what? You just can pick up and do something else. But the likelihood is that you probably won't fail.

I think the other thing is just being open to opportunities. Don't box yourself in to one particular thing. And that's certainly something my husband and I have talked about 'cause he's had a very incredible career path, ending up as a self-employed contractor and inspector when his degree is in biology and chemistry and he used to be in pharmaceutical management. It doesn't seem to make sense. But it all just kind of builds on each other.

And I guess my biggest advice is—so *what* if you've gone to college and gotten a degree in accounting. That doesn't mean you need to be an accountant. You can look at other ways to use your degrees, look at other ways to use your experience. Go out and do what sounds good to you. And if you need to go back to school, go back, because it takes a lot less time than you think. I mean, I was twenty-eight, twenty-nine years old when I started law school, and I remember thinking, 'When I get out, I'm gonna have to establish myself with a firm and then I'm gonna have to be in a partnership track and I'm not gonna have any time for a personal life, and oh, boy, oh, boy, it's just never gonna work.' Worked out fine.

The person you are at twenty-five is not the person you'll be forever.

That's exactly right. I bear no resemblance to the person I was at twenty-five, and I think that's a *good* thing. I don't particularly think I was a great person at twenty-five. I wasn't a bad person either. But I hadn't grown, and the things I thought were important back then are not important at *all* now. And I'm sure in another ten years I may have a completely *different* set of priorities. Who knows? I just intend to stay open to the possibilities.

What dreams do you have that are yet to be realized, both personal and professional?

I don't know that I have any professional dreams right now, but that's probably because I just haven't given it any thought. My personal dreams, as I said earlier, are to be there for my family and to find some way to contribute. If I don't do it, that's one of those things I know I'm going to regret if I get to the end of my life and look back. Because good intentions are one thing, but actions are completely different. And so far I've only had good intentions. (*Laughs.*)

At heart, even though I've done this and that and the other thing, I'm an inherently lazy person and I do have this vision of getting to a point where my time is my own and I can rollerblade to my heart's content, I can read to my heart's content, and then I can do whatever those things are that I've decided I'm doing with my time. But I think that's gonna require being independently wealthy and I don't really see *that* coming. (*Laughs.*) When I hear people talking about, 'Oh, retirement is a terrible thing,' and 'I'm so bored,' I can't imagine how you can *possibly* be bored when you get to do whatever you want to do. To me, boy, I can't *wait* till I am completely justified in not working! But, knowing me, I'll probably be doing *something*.

Interviewed by Susan L. Comer.

Shirley *Pruitt*

Shirley Pruitt was born and raised in Kalamazoo, Michigan. She obtained an associate degree in nursing from Kellogg Community College in 1984 and began training as a neonatal intensive care nurse at Bronson Hospital in Kalamazoo. She moved to Charleston, South Carolina in 1985, and continued as a neonatal intensive care nurse at the Medical University of South Carolina, also serving as one of the charter members of the Neonatal Transport Team of MUSC (ambulance, helicopter and fixed wing aircraft transports).

Shirley obtained a bachelor of science in nursing from MUSC in 1989 and began law school at Wake Forest University in the fall of 1989. She graduated from law school in 1992 and began work with the law firm of Yates, McLamb and Weyher in Raleigh, N.C., specializing in medical malpractice defense with particular expertise in the defense of cases involving infants with brain damage. She went on a leave of absence on April 1, 2000 to care for her daughter Caroline (then eighteen months old) and assist her husband Charles in his home-based business. The couple is expecting their second child in late July.

Deborah Mastrangelo   an interview

Let's start with the beginning. Where did you grow up and go to school?

My dad was a military officer, and I lived all up and down the East Coast from Texas to Maryland. I spent four years in Europe, so I grew up everywhere. He retired when I was about thirteen or fourteen, and we lived in Virginia for a while.

I have been to seven different colleges. I finally ended up going to nursing school and graduated from nursing school in Virginia. Actually, I am an R.N.

Did you always know that nursing was what you wanted to do?
No. (*Laughs.*)

How did you come to that?

I was actually living in Iowa and was a pre-vet major working for a county hospital as a nurse's aide trying to go to school. I wanted to be a veterinarian. I realized that I couldn't see the light at the end of the tunnel. It was back in the 1970s, when a lot of women wanted to be veterinarians. It was still an all-male field, and in Ames, Iowa, there were probably eighty-nine openings and 900 applicants.

Wow!

If you had somebody whose father was politically or financially connected, who could give a donation, you would have a better chance of getting into school. It was very difficult. I was working in a hospital, had lots of friends who were nurses, and I became the hospital's first female EMT. Went through national and state certification, and ended up being a CPR instructor for the county and taught all the firemen and policemen CPR. I did that for a while and decided that I couldn't continue picking up people, hauling people out of ditches and out of their houses, and that the weight was just way too much, and decided to go to nursing school. And I moved back to Virginia and moved back home and went to nursing school.

And how long were you a nurse?

I did nursing for about seventeen years. I was a medical ICU nurse, ER nurse, and then I injured my back and was doing some clinical research for some of the drug companies and enjoyed that. Somewhere along in there I got married, and my husband is a physician and decided he wanted to go into private practice. We were both working for MCV, which is the Medical College of Virginia, in Richmond. He started looking at places and ended up, in 1985, in Wilmington. That's how we got down here.

After you got down here, what were you doing? Were you still in nursing at that time?

I did nursing; I worked at Pender Hospital. It was interesting, I went from a 1700-bed hospital to a forty-bed hospital. I went from having all the latest state-of-the-art equipment to Pender Hospital. It was quite a shock. In fact, one of the nights at Pender Hospital I went in, and we had a little monitor tech that was selling dead raccoons, and she had her styrofoam cooler sitting next to the monitor at the desk. I went in one night thinking, 'Oh, we must have somebody who has to get blood or something.' I was used to seeing the coolers with blood packed down, or with drinks if we were going to have a party. And it actually ended up that this little monitor tech said, 'I've got coons in here for sale. I'm selling them for $5.00.' Then she pulls one up, and it's a skinned raccoon! I said, 'Oh, God, what have I done! Why did I move here? Take me back to Virginia!' It was such a shock.

I can imagine.

It is very different going from a teaching institution to a private hospital, and also, this area is very different. The nurses are not paid the way they are up North. There is a lot of political stuff going on here with the nurses. I had done it for so long, and I just wanted to do something different. I got out of nursing for a while.

We moved two horses down here with us. We had them farmed out, boarded at a different place. So I started looking for land, and I spent one year looking. Ended up going door-to-door knocking, trying to find a piece of land where we could have a house and a barn and the horses. I wanted them in my own back yard. And I found thirty-two acres out on Sidbury Road, and a little man, whose wife was sick, and they decided to sell. We ended up buying the land, and twenty acres more next to it. So, we have fifty-two acres altogether.

So how long have you owned this?

We bought this place in 1987, I think, and the fields and the barns and everything were not here. This was nothing but rows and rows of cornfield. We lived in a little tiny house on the roadfront that needed a lot of work, and we sort of camped out for several years, trying to get the barn built, because the first thing I wanted to do was build the barn, get the horses moved home. My father-in-law, when he first came to see us—he lives in Stamford, Connecticut—he said, 'You drug my son off to the country!' He was just beside himself. Now he thinks the farm is really neat.

But we started with the first barn. We had Nickel Builders

come in from Fayetteville and build up the first structure. Then they put in two stalls, and I hired a guy during the wintertime. He and I built the inside of the barn, and we learned how to be chainsaw construction workers real quick. It was simple. You look at what was there and you just add, use your own creativity. And I built the rest of the barn.

The week before we were going to war with Kuwait, we bought our house for $3,000. It was an all-brick house, and we started taking it apart to move it. So we moved the house in six sections and we put it up here on the farm and rebuilt the house.

Oh, my goodness. Was that very stressful?

It was really a lot of fun. You have to sort of put things in perspective, on doing things like building some of the barns. We had some damage from one of the hurricanes one time, and I had this gentleman out who was helping me put the tin back on the barn. I told him, 'You know, this is really no different from sewing. You have a pattern. You have seams. Instead of using thread and a needle, you use a hammer and nails, and you just tack down.' And he got very upset with me. 'Lady, I don't sew!'

Probably would not want to think of himself as a seamstress.

Right. But it is really no different. It's not that difficult. It's just bigger pieces of material, and a little bit different type of ma-

terial, but it is the same principle, essentially. Instead of using needle and thread, you use a hammer and nails and tack it all together.

So, it has been a lot of fun. It's been really challenging. It's been very interesting, and I have met a lot of people and found out there are a lot of things you can do. And it has been interesting dealing with some of the local gentlemen. The first thing they want to do is deal with my husband, and I say, 'No, you have to deal with me.' And, so when you have them come to fertilize the fields and lime the fields, and you say, 'Don't go in that area,' they immediately drive out. They have eleven tons of lime on the back of their truck, and then they sink, and they get stuck, and then they come walking across and go, 'You need to get your tractor out and pull me out.' And I say, 'No, No. My little old tractor is only thirty-two horsepower. How do you think I am going to pull out an eleven-ton truck? No, it's not going to work.' So, it has been interesting dealing with some people like that.

And dealing with learning to be independent; learning that, if you have made a mistake, you have to back up and sort of go, OK, that didn't work. What will work? And being creative.

What's your husband's involvement with the stables?

He comes out and says it smells like a barn, and then he leaves. And he goes, 'When did you do that and where did this come from?' He doesn't know how many horses I have. He will ask me, and I'll go, 'I don't know. I don't count them. If I count them, then I have to tell you. And if I don't count them, I don't have to lie.'

Is he supportive of you?

He knows it is something that I really like, and this is what I have always wanted to do, as far as having the horses. We have done lots of horse shows out here. We've done clinics. We've had Debbie Connors from the United States Equestrian Team. We did an Anne Kursinski Clinic at Lake Waccamaw. She was the Silver Medal winner at the 1996 Olympics in Atlanta. She came and did a two-day clinic for us. So I have had lots of interesting people.

I think, for my husband, it is a little bit different. He grew up in the city, and he is just amazed with some of the things that we do and how things go. You know, if I said, 'Let's move to Landfall,' he would go 'Okay,' because he likes to play golf. He likes order, and things like that. And sometimes you don't always get order. When we get ready to go out to dinner, he says, 'You've got straw and hay all over you.' Or one of the horses will get sick. It's like having thirty kids with four legs, instead of having two kids.

Was he surprised when you went out and did all the construction and everything? Was he impressed?

He doesn't really tell me, but I know he tells people at work. I hear that. And he complains that I have too many calluses.

Oh, no!

I know that he is amazed at some of the stuff that I do. And I sort of have a can-do attitude, you know, 'I can do it.' When we moved this house, that was a big undertaking, getting it put back together. It was interesting. It was quite challenging, and I had some wonderful people help me with the house. I had a lot of fun. We tore up all the bricks and hauled all the bricks home. We cleaned bricks, and used the bricks, and are still using the bricks. You just have to go at it a step at a time and do a little bit each day. You always have to keep track of what your goal is and what you want to do, and it falls into place. It is just a lot of work.

So when you started out here, what was your idea for the stables? Were you just thinking of boarding, or were you thinking of having people come in and ride? What was your vision?

I wasn't really sure. I started out with the one barn with ten stalls, and really had no earthly idea, except that I was going to have my own horses, and maybe have a couple of boarding horses. And it just kept snowballing. It kept getting bigger. We kept adding more. We kept getting more barns. We are now in the process of building a covered ring. And we have got thirty-some horses out here.

We have tried having different trainers come out to do lessons. It is very difficult finding somebody to work in the horse industry as a trainer, as an instructor. It is a completely different world. It is very, very different from anything I have ever done in nursing. In nursing your only concern is the patient, and patient care.

There are lots of big egos in the horse business. A lot of it has to do with money, customers, clients, and can get very, very competitive. And it can get very, very cutthroat. I never realized it. I always thought I would take care of the horses, and everybody would like what I was doing.

What are some of the biggest challenges that you faced?

The biggest challenge, I think, is that, in the horse business it is more of who you are, what you know. You have a background, a reputation. It is very hard to establish a reputation in the horse business.

Most of the people that have been in the horse business have had family backgrounds: mother or father was a 'horse person' and the sons or the daughters grew up in it. I didn't. I just up and decided, this is what I want to do, not realizing what a big challenge it was, and that you really have to have a reputation to get into doing this—for your horses, your care. It is a really big pro-

cess. You have to have a lot of knowledge, and everyone is not always going to agree with you.

Horse people are very different. I have had a lot of boarders out here, and I think some of them think more of their horses than they do of their own children. If their horse has a cold, that's terrible. But if their child has a cold, oh, he'll get over it. It has been quite a learning experience. You cannot please everybody. It is like all businesses. There are certain horses that I really like and certain horses that I don't want in my barn. They are nasty. They are rude. It is a business where people can get hurt. And I have lots of rules. I am very safety-oriented, as far as people that are riding and having their horses here. It's just very, very different. Nothing like what I ever thought it would be. And I am still learning, and every day I learn something new and different.

In terms of running your own business, is that a really different mindset than being in nursing?

Yes. Running your own business and having a business. Any people who go into business for themselves are going to find out that if you are sick, it doesn't matter. If the employee is sick, you are going to be out there taking care of the horses. There have been days when I have had the flu, or something, and maybe the people I have working for me, they can call in and say, 'I am sick. I am not coming in.' But when you are the owner and you have got thirty horses standing out there, you have got to get your butt up out of bed, and you are going to have to go take care of them. And when it comes down to the last thing on the totem pole, you're it. You're the one who, if you want your business to succeed, you have got to get out there and do it. You've got to do everything from cleaning stalls to feeding, to watering, to haying, to unloading hay, unloading feed. All the scut work that goes with it as the owner of the business, you are going to be out there doing it. And you have got to be willing to do it to make it work. Unless you have got a bottomless bank account.

Was there ever a moment when you thought, 'Oh my goodness, what have I done? I am overwhelmed! This is a mistake?'

I don't think so, as much as I go through, 'That's it! I am cleaning house. I am closing up. I've had it. And I am going to just keep my own horses.'

I am not the most politically correct person. My mother always tells me that I am not very diplomatic at times, and I think that comes a lot from my nursing. In nursing and in taking care of critical patients, you don't have time to be diplomatically correct. I say what I think, and I think a lot of people don't know how to take that.

At times you get to a point where you think, 'Well, I just want to have my own horses. I just want to do my own thing. I want to

ride my own horses.' A lot of times, I don't have time to ride my own horses. I have to hire somebody to ride them. That's one big frustrating thing. When you are on the scale that I am, it is very difficult because the paperwork is just unbelievable, for keeping track of payroll, checking accounts, keeping all the equipment up and running, keeping the hay, the feed, the fencing repaired. It just never stops. A lot of times in the morning from when I get up in the morning until I lay down at night, I am constantly running. It is very, very busy all the time. Right now, because we are doing the therapeutic program, I have lessons every evening with the kids after school. So, it just doesn't stop. It is continuous.

Do you think it was your experience in nursing that led you to start Coastal Therapeutic Riding Program?

Yes. I always thought it would be fun to combine the nursing and the horses. And there is a lot to learn in that. I just went to a conference up in Virginia. I really met some very nice people up there. There is a whole new program with hippotherapy, which is using the horse as treatment, and as a therapeutic tool toward treatment. Basically, what I do right now is do riding lessons. I teach what I can to some of these children, and it may just be the basics of giddy-up and whoa, that they learn that they can say something and the horse does what they request the horse do. And it gives them a little knowledge and a little power and a little independence.

In hippotherapy, you use the horse to work as treatment in a problem that they are having. If they have somebody who is paralyzed, and they need to have that movement of walking, you put them on the horse's back, and it helps them increase their blood circulation, it helps increase blood circulation to the kidneys, it helps their muscles. It helps a tremendous number of things that go on in their body. A horse's walk is the closest thing to a human being's walk.

So, do you think the hippotherapy is something that you might want to do?
Yes. I eventually would like to get into doing some hippotherapy and get some training for it.

What's been the most satisfying for you with the therapeutic program?
The kids. They are a blast!

Will you talk a little bit about one kid, or how the kids in general respond?
You can bring out the inner child in you, because you get to play with them. And that's what's neat. And seeing the kids. Oh, they just light up, you know. They just have the greatest time ever with the horses, and my older horses, my senior citizen horses, that would normally be turned out to pasture and ignored, they get care. They get attention. They get something from the kids,

too. And they give back to the kids. It is just very nice to see the two of them working very well together. The horses stand there quiet, they are very patient with the kids, and so it is a neat interaction between the two of them.

How did you decide that this was something that you wanted to do?
I had read something about it and thought it would be sort of fun to try and see what happened. And then I sort of began and it snowballed. And I am having a blast with it. I really enjoy it. You see some of these moms out here with their children, and they are able to accomplish something, and the moms and the dads get so excited, because their kids actually can do more than they thought they could do.

I think everybody has a lot of potential, and sometimes people who have disabilities are told, 'No, you can't do that.' Why? Why not? You know, I just think everybody needs a chance to try, and a lot of these people find and adapt ways of doing things.

Some of these kids will not ever be Olympic riders, but they are the Olympic riders in their mom's or dad's eyes. It is just what you're satisfied with accomplishing. And you can accomplish as much as you want. These kids can accomplish a lot.

How do you juggle your personal and your professional life? Is there a clear distinction between the two?

Well, my husband being a physician, he is gone a lot. If I had kids, it would probably be really hard. I can't imagine how girls who take care of two children do it, but I have thirty four-legged children out there. So I think you just find ways.

I had a veterinarian friend of mine who had twins, and she had three children, all under the age of two. She used to do horse rounds. And I used to think it was absolutely amazing. She would bring all the kids. And if I had a horse that was sick, I would call Tina and say, 'I need you to come out.' She would say, 'Get sitters.' And I would have three people lined up. Everybody would take a baby. You just do things to find ways. And if you want it bad enough, you will find a way. It may not be the perfect way, or it may not be the ideal way, but you can find ways of doing things. And you just have got to be creative.

Because a man is given a hammer, it doesn't mean as a woman you can't pick up a hammer and nail too. God didn't make that hammer fit just a man's hand. Women can go out and be builders, you know. It is no different than being a seamstress. You just use different materials. You can be anything you want to be.

Have you had anybody give you funny looks or question your transition from nursing to doing this?

I don't know that I ever had anybody question. I think they are surprised that I will do what I have to. If it needs done, I am normally in the middle of everything helping to get it done. I have found there are things I don't like doing. I don't particularly like pouring concrete. That's heavy backbreaking work. The guys who do it, go for it, buddy! I don't like changing flat tires. I don't particularly like when we have had to have the barns wired; I am not interested in learning about wiring. I have had to learn how to fix plumbing, broken pipes, and things like that. Because water is one of the biggest important things for horses, keeping them up and going. And, so on a Sunday, if you have a broken water line, you learn how to fix it to get water to the horses.

You've got to like being outside. And I do like being outside, compared to being on the inside of the hospital. It's been a real challenge with Mother Nature and the hurricanes and things like that. The responsibility of having your own business is different than when you go to work, you go in and put in your eight hours and you go home. This is with you twenty-four hours a day, seven days a week, day in and day out. It doesn't matter if it's pouring down rain, or snowing, or freezing cold, you still have to get out there and do your job, and take care of the horses.

With the horses and the hurricanes, what do you do?

There's lots of things to prepare, to make sure that the generators are working and that you have fuel for the generators, you have got water for the horses. We have hay storage in two of the buildings, and we will split it up into a lot of different little areas, so if we should lose the roof of one barn, we'd have hay in another. The same thing with the feed. We braid identification tags into the horses' manes with our phone number on them. The last hurricane, we put identification tags in their manes and in their tails, so if they got out, and somebody caught them, we would have our identification there. So, hopefully, if they do get to running through the woods, if they lose one out of their mane, they will still have the one on their tail. We put halters on all of the horses in their stalls, in case we have to move them in the middle of the night, from one stall to another. All the stalls have a halter and lead line. The horses have their halters on, and there is a lead line in front of the door, so that you can go in and put your hands on them and get ahold of them and reassure them and move them to where it is drier. It is easier to do that, leave their halters on and have a lead line—especially at night, if you had to do it in the dark, no electricity, and flashlights—you can find everything right there. Being prepared, thinking ahead of time, having everything tied down, all the doors tied down, all the containers, everything put up and nailed down as much as possible.

What personal qualities do you think really enabled you to do this?

My personal qualities? I guess having my mom tell me I can. Moms are great.

This is something that your mom really supported you in?

Yes. Just having a mom that tells me that I can do anything that I want to do. She is just really neat. And having somebody that believes in me, I guess. There have been days when you get up and for every three steps you take forward, you get knocked back four, and you just sort of have to get up, dust yourself off, say Okay.

Do you think there are ways that you have changed through doing this whole thing?

Yes. I don't think things bother me as much as they used to. I don't take things as personally. If somebody doesn't like you for some reason, you just go, Oh, well. Whereas, in nursing, you just have a job. You are a nurse in uniform. Nursing is very regimented. You have a certain protocol for everything. Everybody does everything the exact same way. It is very structured. And as long as you do your job, there are no complaints. Here, if you don't do it the way somebody else thinks you should do it, everybody has an opinion.

I get a lot of people who will tell me how they think I should do things. And, it's like, I have done that already. I have tried that already. Everybody likes giving advice, and it is difficult sometimes to get people to realize that you have already tried some of this stuff. It just may or may not work.

It is difficult knowing how to be a boss and have employees, and how to handle that part—when they come in, if they don't show up, or if they don't call. It is difficult getting people here to work on a farm. Most people don't want to do manual labor. Most people don't want to clean out stalls. Cleaning out stalls to me is almost therapy, because you can get in there and clean out a stall and not have to think about anything else—turn on the radio and just do stalls. It is not a glorified job; it pays minimum wage.

You don't always have people out here that board with you who say 'Thank you.' They don't know what extremes you go to to keep their horses comfortable and safe. A lot of times my horses will go without the bedding in their stalls to provide other people's horses with bedding or better hay. Or I will go get in other people's horses first before I go get mine in. I will blanket other people's horses before mine get blanketed. You tend to do that, so your own end up getting neglected some times. And I don't think a lot of people realize that. They don't realize how hard you work, and how much you put into it. They don't realize that at ten o'clock at night I say, ' I think I will go and make sure everybody is OK.' There have been many times I walked out and I found something-one of the horses up against the wall for some reason. You just don't get a lot of thank yous. In nursing, when you have a lot of patients and families, and you are taking care of somebody that is sick, you know, you tend to get a 'You did a good job.' You don't

get that in this business. You get a lot of really nice boarders and nice people, but there are a lot that are not. They think that because they pay to board their horses with you that you work for them. And it can be a very thankless job. But I love the animals, and I love taking care of the animals, and I know with the therapeutic kids there is a purpose, and that's what I really want to do. I think they are going to be the fun part of this.

So what do you do when you're not working with the horses? Do you have any time to relax, and if so, what do you do?

Nothing. The last time my husband and I went on vacation, I said I wanted to go on a cruise with everybody seventy and older. I wanted to read. I hadn't read a book in so long. I like to read, and that's one thing I don't really get to do a lot of. I am too tired at night to sit down and read, you know. Just to be quiet and not have to be...It is very difficult sometimes, even coming to my house to sit down to have lunch, that I don't get a phone call from one of the boarders, or I get somebody knocking at the door, saying, 'Where do you go out on the trails? We want to go trail riding. Which way do you go?'

I'll be trying to sit here and inhale a sandwich, now. And it is sometimes very difficult to separate that from my house. People tend to just love the house, and it is very difficult to say, 'This is my house and that is the barn. That is the business.' Because everything is right here.

It's very difficult to have privacy. You know, everybody gets very intrigued by the horses. And they think that you should want to let them tell you all about their horses twenty-four hours a day, seven days a week. So when you say, 'I've had enough. I need to go run away for a couple of hours,' they say, 'Well, why?'

I like antiques, going to antique stores. And I might run away a couple of hours to do that, to go see something different other than a horse.

Does your husband get resentful that your horses take up so much of your time?

Oh, yes. It is very difficult for him. And he is very good and very patient about it. There have been times when we have planned to go out to dinner, and something has happened, and we haven't been able to. It's just very difficult trying to plan things and do things. Last time I went away, I left my aunt here housesitting, and some of the horses got out. She was calling me at midnight at the hotel in Virginia telling me, 'I've got three horses standing in the yard. What do I do?' And I go, 'Oh, God.' So, those things happen. You have to go, 'Okay.' Start calling this person and that person.

So, what do you think has been the greatest joy on the path that your life

has taken?

Finding out all the different things I can do. I have driven everything from a forklift to a bulldozer. We just got this building out, and I learned how to drive a sky truck, which is huge, a big forklift thing, to get the building unloaded. There is a great world out there. Young women need to know that there are unlimited possibilities. They can be anybody they want to be, if they have the ambition to try.

What advice would you give to someone who decided, as you did, to start over in mid-career?

Start a new career? Go for it, if it is something that they really want to do. There are lots of things I still want to accomplish.

Like what?

I want to try and get something patented to sell, and see that part of the horse business. I have some young horses. I would like to see them do well and maybe get them up and going. Eventually, one of the biggest things I would like to accomplish is being able to ride at some rated shows and work on my own personal riding skills, which I don't get a lot of time to do. I keep saying, OK, you are getting to that age. And you have to be realistic. I am not going to be a rider like a sixteen-year-old or a seventeen-year-old. I'll never be able to ride like they are, but I will be able to ride in my age group and be able to show. So, I think that would be fun, to get out and do some showing with my horses—the ones that I have raised here. Just get them out and see what happens.

Are there any decisions along your life that you regret, where you would have done things differently?

I don't know, because it has all been such a learning experience. I don't think there is anything I really regret; but it has been a real challenge moving to Wilmington, because Wilmington is not horse-oriented. So, I wonder if there is a purpose as to why we ended up moving down here. It was a big challenge. It was very frustrating. The first two years we were here, we didn't really have anyplace to live. It was very difficult moving. I had two very young horses. I didn't have any family down here. I was pretty much by myself. My husband was very busy with his practice. And so I ended up having to just sort of find myself. And it was difficult. I was very alone. But you make choices and you make decisions. And you have to say, 'Well, I am here, and what am I going to do about it?'

Was there anything that helped you get through that time period?

I don't know. Just work. People are so afraid of work today. To do this is not easy. To do any job is not easy. And you have got to be willing to do the work. You have got to be willing to get out there and get your hands dirty. A lot of people today want everything handed to them. It doesn't mean anything if it is handed to you. And you have got to do research and look at as much as possible. Don't be afraid to ask questions. That's the only way we can learn. And don't accept everything you hear as the truth. You can create your own. You don't have to go by what everybody tells you. But don't ever not make a decision. I think that is one of the worst things somebody can do, is to not make a decision, and just get stuck at a weird point and say, 'I am not going left, I'm not going right.' And just sit there. To learn and to grow, you have to make decisions.

And you learn from your mistakes. That's a big thing. Don't keep making the same mistakes. I think there is a bigger being out there that sometimes guides you along the way that you have to go. And you have to do with what you are dealt. And be glad that you have your health and to be able to do what you can do, to the best of your ability.

Young girls need to realize that it's okay to be different, to do different things. They don't have to be doctors, or lawyers—they can do anything they set their mind to. I think a lot of young girls don't realize that.

Interviewed by Emily A. Colin.

Deborah Mastrangelo

Deborah Mastrangelo is a self-proclaimed military brat. Though she was born in Ft. Bragg, North Carolina, she has lived everywhere. She attended seven colleges, eventually graduating from J. Sargeant Reynolds in Richmond, Virginia with an associate's in nursing. When she was twelve, she got her first pony—a landmark event, as it turned out.

In 1983, she married physician Michael R. Mastrangelo, whom she calls 'my non-horsey husband.' The couple lives in Castle Hayne, North Carolina, where Ms. Mastrangelo has owned and operated Castle Stables, Inc. since 1988. The corporation now owns thirty horses, and boards several more. Together with Linda Brett, a case manager for the Southeastern Center for Mental Health, as well as an active staff of volunteers, she organizes and operates Wilmington's Coastal Therapeutic Riding Program.

"Because a man is given a hammer, it doesn't mean as a woman you can't pick up a hammer and nail too. God didn't make that hammer fit just a man's hand."

Deborah Mastrangelo

A Stroke of Luck: The Story of How I Became a World Champion Kayaker Lydia McCormick Fonvielle

Rumor has it I could swim before I could walk. I don't know how true that rumor is, but I do have a picture that proves I had learned the crawl stroke by the age of two and a half. I swam competitively from the age of eight to eighteen, spent six summers of my youth lifeguarding at our local pool, and when asked to choose between a trip to the beach or a trip to the mountains, I always sided with the ocean because the volume of water was greater. Rivers invigorate me, waterfalls mesmerize me, rain captivates me, and a warm bath has the power to soothe my soul.

In the summer of 1991, after graduating from college, I got my first real job—field excavator on an archeological dig. You'd think that someone who loves water so much would take a job somewhere near it. I didn't. Like water I've always had a tendency to flow down the path of least resistance. I had a friend on a dig in New Mexico and she had the power to get me a job, so New Mexico it was. I loaded up my Honda and headed West.

New Mexico can be very hot or very cold, but it's almost always dry. Dry is not a good climate for a lover of water, but for an archaeology major, it's a great place to work. I assisted in the excavation of several Anasazi pithouses as well as a few Pueblo room blocks. I uncovered more than a few ancient pots and exactly one amazing stone pipe. I had the opportunity to view several native burials and had the pleasure of working with some of the most interesting people I've ever met in my life. Being a Southwestern excavator with an intense love for the water does have serious drawbacks, however. Showers are far and few between when you live in a tent on the reservation. Swimming holes can be found, but the drives are long. And time begins to pass slowly between trips to the lake. I eventually chose to return home.

Home is North Carolina. Hot and humid in the summer. Often humid in the winter too. It is a very green, very moist place with plenty of the water I craved so much during my two and a half years out West. Ahhh, contentment in the off hours, but what about a job? As for archaeology...well, my long-term prospects didn't look good. No major projects were scheduled in the East for some time to come. Hmmm, how about teaching? My mom was a teacher and I'd enjoyed those archeology talks to the students at her school. Fourth graders seemed nice. Why not? So back to school I went.

Wilmington, North Carolina seemed like a nice place to study up on my teaching skills. The university campus was only five miles from the Atlantic Ocean and the surrounding area was blessed by blackwater rivers galore. The only problem was, I'd shown up in January and the water was a little cold. My desire to get wet drove me to sign up for a kayak roll clinic in the university pool. My first exposure to kayaks was through the pages of a *National Geographic* article I read during my youth, and from that moment on I had the inclination that kayaking might be the sport for me. A craft that could allow you to enjoy the water regardless of temperature or state (whether it was calm or turbulent) had to be something I'd like.

Now rolling a kayak (flipping it over and then back up, all the while remaining in the boat) is no easy feat. I'd actually had an unsuccessful tangle trying to roll one during my freshman year in college. I like to blame that failure on my instructor rather than my own inability. He seemed more interested in my plans after the clinic than my plans to learn the kayak roll that evening. But one failed attempt wouldn't stop me from trying again. This session was being held at a different university with a far more

serious instructor and a far more mature and focused student. I managed to roll that kayak in two hours and was from that moment on forever hooked. In a short amount of time I found myself working for a kayak outfitter, putting my meager knowledge of elementary education to work teaching adults how to paddle, occasionally how to roll (the upside down thing isn't for everybody), and often leading tours.

Somehow I managed to weasel a demo whitewater boat from my boss for my personal use. Spare time in between classes and work were spent tossing about in the ocean waves. I'd seen others take kayaks into the surf, and although I had no clue what I was doing, I knew that I was having fun. If you're the type who finds the rush of adrenaline appealing, then imagine the following scenario. (If you're not a stimulus addict, bear with me a moment, keeping in mind that kayaking doesn't have to be a rush. It can calm and relaxing too. It depends on when and where you decide to paddle.) Okay adrenaline junkies, here goes ....

You're sitting approximately two to three feet above the water line, paddling out in eight- to ten-foot ocean surf. A wave has just crashed about fifteen feet in front of you and is now barreling your way. Your eyes widen and your lungs expand under the pressure of a deep breath. You lean back and put your paddle on top of the foam pile that is beginning to swallow you. Luck is with you today and you are jettisoned on top of the pile just in time to come face to face with a ten-foot monster curling up a few yards out. The paddle blades start digging under your command. You've got to get over this one. Getting crunched by the coming wave means you'll have to try that roll that you're not exactly hitting one hundred percent of the time. The strokes pay off and you launch over the crest and are blessed with a four-foot freefall off the backside of the wave. You land in the calm beyond the break and exhale as a big grin spreads across your face.

That's what it felt like when I first started surfing in the ocean with my kayak (riding waves like surfers do, but in a small kayak with a paddle). What a rush. I had no idea how to really surf in my boat, but it didn't matter because getting out past the breaking waves was fun in itself. Eventually a desire to learn what to do once I'd paddled out past the break got the best of me, and I started making friends with the other kayakers I saw on the beach. There weren't very many of them, but I hunted them down to ask their advice and learn from their techniques. I even started calling them at home, asking them if they were "free to come out and play." Most of these individuals were married men, and I think I may have made more than one wife suspicious, but eventually they came to see the reality of the matter. I wanted their husbands for one thing and one thing only—their ability to help me become a better kayaker.

I've made some wonderful friends kayaking over the years, but none will ever hold such a special place in my heart as the guys I came to know as The Big Water Associates of Wilmington. Ralph, the grand poobah of the group (AKA Papa Smurf) was always quick to offer a cold cola and a kind word after a session in the waves. Simon the Brit, the man with the quick wit, was always ready with a joke and a smile designed to make you laugh off any sketchy moment in the surf. And Stowe (AKA The Technician), known as such because he owned more gear than any one kayaker could ever use, was always there to make it clear how to do that new move or how to made that old move better. There were many other BWA kayakers who maybe weren't so easily nicknamed as the big three, but were just as instrumental in helping me grow as a paddler. We met on early mornings and late afternoons, weekends and weekdays, sometimes we even paddled under the light of a full moon. Not wanting to limit ourselves or our boats (they were originally designed for whitewater), we took river trips whenever we could. It was a magical first couple of years.

Eventually my education to become a teaching wizard was complete, and I found my second real job—fourth grade teacher extraordinaire. Teaching was supposed to be the perfect career for a kayaker because afternoons would be free for paddling....right? Well, I knew this wasn't true after pulling a semester of student teaching, but I had to give it a go. The kids were great, the hours were not. Between parent conferences, teacher meetings, creating lesson plans, and grading papers, I didn't find a whole lot of time for the water. Once again, I felt deprived of my greatest love. After a year of service in the teaching profession, I was done.

What now? I didn't want to teach (not school anyway) and returning to my life out West didn't seem like such a great idea either. All I knew is that I wanted to live at the beach and I wanted to paddle. I decided to spend the summer guiding kayak trips and instructing folks in the finer points of paddling. I'd make up my mind in the fall.

Fall came awfully fast, and at the end of the guiding season I was no closer to a career decision. A friend offered me a job helping him do a large upholstery project. I figured the time and physical labor would help me decide my future. He and I kayaked a lot in-between redoing chairs. As the end of the job approached, I had no answer to the career question. My friend then offered me a job painting his house. More physical labor and more time to think. Again, he and I did a lot of kayaking in-between brush strokes on the house, and by the time the painting was done I was no closer to choosing a new career. I was, however, kayaking great and very broke. Like water, I take the path of least resistance, but this time my stream was beginning to run dry.

Lucky for me, a friend who *doesn't* kayak offered me a job working on historic homes. The job was based in Raleigh, so I'd have to leave the beach, but it was time to sacrifice water time so I could get out of debt. Working on old houses very much satisfied the archeologist in me. Every house was an experience going back in time, and very nook and cranny taught a new lesson about the past. For the most part we worked exclusively on pre-civil war structures, which meant a lot of traveling, as there aren't a whole lot of really old houses left in North Carolina. The traveling was fun and my kayak went with me whenever possible, but after a year of living out of my car and in hotels, I was wearing down. It wasn't exactly the life I had in mind, but for a while longer I would have to keep plugging away.

Six months later I got an amazing call. A young man I'd known for several years called to announce that he'd just purchased the kayak outfitter in Wilmington that I'd done guide work for in the past and was wondering whether I'd like to come and work for him. Guide in the summer, manage the retail store in the winter, and as a perk, he'd foot the bill to have me attend a clinic in the mountains that would lead to my becoming a certified whitewater and calm water kayak instructor. In addition, part of my job description would include paddling when the waves were good and competing in all East Coast surf kayak competitions. How could I refuse? The money was reasonable and (more importantly) the benefits were excellent.

I started that job in September of 1998 at the age of twenty-nine. I had been kayaking for three years and had been competing in surf kayak competitions for two. I had some events and I lost some events, but every day I got better and every season I looked forward to competing again.

Three months prior to taking the job at my friend's store, word spread within the surf kayaking community that the Outer Banks would soon play host to the first-ever national competition held in the East. For ten years or more, the West had held a monopoly on the National Surf Kayaking Championships, as they had been the first to develop the sport in the United States. The nationals would be held at Rodanthe Pier near Hatteras, N.C. in late October. Better yet, team trials for an East Coast team would be held at the same location in May, and that team would compete for the United States in Brazil at the World Championships the following September. Timing on my job offer couldn't have come at a more fortuitous moment.

Of all the Big Water Associates (now known as the Kayakers Anonymous Club), I was the only one who had the time to attend the 1998 National Surf Kayak Championships, so I made the six-hour haul alone. Once I'd arrived, my solitude ended, as I became one of many East and West Coast paddlers hoping to surf well in the upcoming national event. My sights were not set on winning, however. I was there to learn. I'd heard that several high-ranking West Coast women would be competing, including a former World Champion. I hoped that at best I would do the East Coast proud and at worst I'd leave without embarrassing myself. To say the least, I was a little intimidated. What I hadn't considered, though, was the fact that surf conditions on the two major U.S. coasts differ drastically. While the West Coasters spent most of their time surfing on the type of big, peeling waves that allow a kayaker a clean face on which to play, I was used to the smaller, often tricky shore-breaking waves common on the East Coast. To my surprise, I had an advantage on my competitors. Shore-breaking surf can be scary if you don't know what to do to protect yourself when smashing into the beach. At the end of the weekend I hadn't lost a single heat, including the final round.

Winning a National Championship, especially one you didn't expect, can give you a lot to smile about, and my smile didn't wane for several days. Unfortunately, it also steals your anonymity and puts you in a position from which you can be removed. My training continued with an eye on making the East Coast National Team in May. Two months before competition commenced, I was informed that my points from winning the nationals had already qualified me for the team and competing would be unnecessary. At the team trials, three of my Wilmington friends also qualified for the team, and we soon began the task of raising money for our trip.

In September we loaded up on an airplane and headed for Rio de Janeiro, Brazil. Unlike the nationals held the previous year, I had high hopes for doing well due to the fact that two of the strongest teams competing in Brazil were U.S. East and U.S. West. And, as in the Carolinas, Brazil enjoys an East Coast surf break, although one touted to be far larger in size than what we generally experienced at home. What we found in the way of waves did not disappoint. They were practically identical in form to the those we surfed at home, and in size they were comparable to the large clean waves the Carolina coast often receives off the back side of a passing hurricane.

What we found in hospitality was a highly different matter. Customs decided to hold six of our kayaks hostage until we finally realized that $500 US would solve the "paperwork problem." I received the disappointing news that my name was absent from the official hotel guest list, so I wouldn't be able to stay in the room for which I'd pre-paid. I discreetly stayed in the room anyway, but none of us were too pleased to find out that the two-bedroom efficiency with a sleeper sofa that we were expecting was actually a one bedroom with an uncomfortable couch. There were six of us staying in the room.

Competition, however, did not disappoint. The Brazilians put on one heck of a show. Surf kayaking is a small sport worldwide, and participants are often asked to assist with the running of competitions. When not competing we often judge, tally scores, announce, and are always expected to help set up and tear down the site each day. Apparently the Brazilian government had taken an interest in the competition as a potential tourist attraction and revenue-generating event. They spent over $100,000 US on the 1999 World Surf Kayak Championships. We were blown away by a three-story stage, viewing area, and judging site that was divided into sections for the eight attending teams. Our judges and announcers were paid professionals, all our scores were computer-generated, and competitor scores were actually broadcasted loud enough during each heat that the competitors knew how they were placing while they were competing in the surf. We'd never seen anything like this before.

The following teams competed in the Brazilian Worlds: England, Jersey (a small island country off the coast of France), Scotland, Venezuela, Spain, U.S. East, U.S. West, and Brazil. As expected, U.S. West dominated both the team and individual events followed closely by England, U.S. East, and Scotland. To my dismay, I failed miserably in the competition class in which I'd expected to excel—the Women's High Performance Class (the event I won at nationals). But to my even greater surprise, I did well in the Ladies' International Class portion of the competition. In High Performance, each individual competitor may use any type of closed deck kayak they like. You'll see competitors using kayaks with fins and the boats can be any variations in boat length and hull design. In the International Class, competitors must all use the same type of boat—same length, same hull design, no fins. Before my first heat of Ladies' International Class, I'd practiced in a boat of this type all of thirty minutes. I didn't like the boat and wasn't looking forward to competing in one in Brazil. It was, however, a required part of the team event.

I won every one of my team heats in the Ladies' International Class and when I began advancing in the individual portion of the competition, no one was more surprised than me. I never felt comfortable in the boat, the waves only got bigger and more scary each day, and I really didn't know the finer points of handling that style of boat. I was used to shorter boats of maybe eight to nine feet. This was a twelve-foot-long monster. I was used to tough plastic boats. This one was made of fragile fiberglass. There were times when I feared I wouldn't get out past the breaking waves. I felt like a beginner again, only the pressure took away from the fun. Somehow though, I always made it out before the big one crunched me. Once out in the surf zone, I took the biggest waves I could find and went screaming down them praying that I wouldn't become surf munch. I saw more than one kayaker (male and female) swim out of their boats during the world championships due to a fierce pounding from the waves. At the end of the final heat I heard the announcer scream in Portuguese-accented English, "Black, you are the winner!" I looked down at my jersey color. I was wearing black.

Hearing those words at that moment, I think I felt more relief than happiness, although the joy did eventually hit. For me the competition was over. I'd succeeded in doing something that I'd never really expected to do, and I hadn't let down the approximately twenty friends and teammates who were screaming on the beach in expectation of my arrival back on dry land. More importantly to me, I'd be going home soon. That trip to Brazil, in spite of the victory, would never classify as one of my all-time favorite vacations. Many things had gone wrong—the hotel, the boat heist, not to mention a hurricane named Floyd that had smashed Wilmington while we were away.

Most of all, though, I'd had to spend two weeks away from my new best friend John. I'd been dating John for several months prior to leaving for Brazil, but I had no idea how much I'd miss him. I met him while teaching a kayak roll clinic, and although he is not the best student I've ever taught, he is by far the most determined. As I got to know John better (he took *several* roll classes from me) I learned that, like me, he had lived a life full of many twists and turns. Unlike me, he wasn't one to take the path of least resistance. This guy reminded more of a boulder rolling down a mountain. He was going to reach his destination (there was no doubt about that) and watching him get there was awe-inspiring. When I returned from Brazil it became very apparent that John was a good match for me. We complemented each other well. I had a feeling I might have a future with him, and in April of 2000 (just a month ago) we sealed that fate. John and I got married.

Once again, my life has taken a new and interesting turn. Kayaking still plays a huge part in my life. It is still my job to guide, instruct, and sell kayaks, but no longer is my kayak my significant other. John has filled that role. And while competing is still a great pleasure, it isn't my entire life focus anymore. Winning a world championship in surf kayaking pales in comparison to attempting to become a world-class wife.

Water still remains a strong passion, however—one which John thankfully appreciates—and I still seem to flow like water down the path of least resistance. John is of course leading the way down that path. Sometimes I wonder if I shouldn't become a more decisive individual—one who sets specific goals and goes after them—but I'm happy living life the way I do. When you don't know what to expect around the next corner, it means your life is an adventure, not a trip. Trips are planned. I prefer adventures to trips. Adventure is what makes life worth living.

When asked to compose a story about my world championship adventure in

Brazil, I must admit that I felt a terrible pressure to create something that would inspire others to do similar "great things." There is, however, no lesson here. While writing the piece I realized that my championship was no great feat, but simply a byproduct of how I choose to live my life. I don't make a lot of money, but I do have a lot of fun and if I could be an inspiration, I would inspire others to have fun in whatever they choose to do. I hope that I have.

The Ship's Store
7220 Wrightsville Avenue, Unit C
Wilmington, NC 28403
(910) 256-4445
shipsto@wilmington.net

Lydia McCormick *Fonvielle*

Lydia McCormick Fonvielle lives in Wilmington, North Carolina, instructing and managing for the outdoor specialty retailer, The Ship's Store. Born in 1969, she grew up in the small town of Lillington, located in central North Carolina. Lydia is a graduate of the University of North Carolina at Chapel Hill, has an elementary teaching certificate from UNC-Wilmington, and is an American Canoe Association certified kayak instructor. If you are interested in the sport of kayaking, call or e-mail Lydia at The Ship's Store or simply stop by for a visit.

"I don't make a lot of money, but I do have a lot of fun and if I could be an inspiration, I would inspire others to have fun in whatever they choose to do."

Lydia McCormick Fonvielle

Cathy Holt an interview

Why don't we start with where you grew up and where you went to school?

I grew up in south Florida, and I went to school at Santa Fe Community College in Gainesville, and then Evergreen State College in Washington State. A number of years later I went back to school at the University of South Florida in Tampa.

What did you study while you were there?

Well, I began in journalism and then switched to being a psychology major.

What was the lure of both fields for you and why did you change?

You know, I was young. Straight out of high school going to college, I really didn't have any idea what I wanted to do. As a young child I wanted to be a missionary to India.

How did that come about? That's kind of unusual.

I know. I had done a book report in fourth grade on India, and that became my desire as a young kid. That's what I knew I wanted to do. I was pretty active in the Baptist Church when I was a kid, and so that was my vision of what I needed to do. Then

I wanted to become an oceanographer. We always lived on the water when I was a kid. Then I kind of was just drawing straws and I came up with journalism, because I always liked writing and it was something I did well. I switched to psychology because I just became very interested in how we think and act—just how humankind operates. So, it's kind of interesting that I ended up doing something that had nothing to do with anything I ever studied with my life—except for psychology, of course; you use that every day of your life, in every relationship and so forth.

I was never too sorry. My parents were sorry that I wasn't pursuing anything I'd studied, but I feel like what college did for me was train me how to think. That could be applied to anything, any direction I took.

So, how did you go from there to becoming a goldsmith?

My husband—or boyfriend at the time—lived in Florida still and I was at school in Washington State. We decided that we wanted to get back together, so we both quit college and drove around the country for six months in a Volkswagen camper/van trying to find what we wanted to do and where we wanted to do it. Ended up he was in his last quarter of architecture school, so knew how to design and had done a lot of construction work, and we decided we were going to build furniture. So, we moved to Tampa and that's what we started doing together. For four years I built furniture with him.

After four years of living together and working together I decided that was really too much togetherness. But by then I was very attached to being self-employed and creating—being a *maker*. So, I went back to school at the University of South Florida and enrolled in the Fine Arts department to be a potter.

After studying there we then moved to outside of Athens, Georgia onto a piece of property. At that point, we were very much into the whole homesteading, alternative lifestyle. We wanted to be independent, to have some way to live off the land and have work that supported us—where neither of us would have to ever have jobs. But I didn't have any money left to be able to start a pottery business after we bought our little farmhouse and thirty-six acres there. I started looking through the paper for jobs, but if you live in a college town there's often all these highly skilled people and no jobs to go with them. That was the case in Athens. So I couldn't find any decent jobs at all in the paper. Then I saw an ad for 'experienced jeweler needed,' at this small jewelry store where the jewelry was all handmade. I went down and applied for the job—even though it said 'experienced jeweler'—but I was armed with my slides of the furniture I'd built and the clay objects I'd made. My rap was that I knew how to coordinate my hands and my eyes and my brain to work together, and that I had been hiring people myself in the furniture business for

several years. I knew what someone needed in an employee and that I would be able to switch gears easily and take what I'd learned. I was used to working with tools and I was used to creating and designing, and I felt like I could make the switch over to jewelry pretty easily. Actually, I must admit, I sort of professed to be much more interested in metalwork than I really was.

Isn't that always the way when you really need a job?

Well, I didn't know. I'd never really tried to have jobs before. I had just worked for myself. But I was willing to do anything at that point to find a decent job. Of course, they weren't interested in me. They were like, 'Well, that's nice, dear, but we need a jeweler,' and they sent me home. It shows me now how desperate I was, because I'm not usually a very aggressive person, but I showed up every day. When they would open the door, there I would be—pleading with them. 'Have you changed your mind? Will you let me give it a try? Just give me a shot.' They kept saying, 'I'm sorry, but we want someone with experience. We just don't want to have to train someone.'

But it was a small town and there weren't experienced jewelers applying, so I just showed up there every day. When they would open the doors, there I was again. They really just didn't know what to do with me. They'd send me home and then the next day they'd show up for work and there I would be again.

Finally, after doing this for five days in a row I said, 'OK, I've come up with an idea. How about if you let me work for you for free for two weeks? At the end of two weeks, if I'm not the quickest learner you've had—if you're not happy that you've let me join the troops here—I'll go home and I won't pester you anymore. You really have nothing to lose because I'm not even asking to be paid. Just give me two weeks to show you what I can do.'

I think they were as desperate to get rid of me being at their door as I was to get a job, so they just kind of looked at each other. It was two young women—not that much older than I was—two really bright women who had started this business. They finally decided, 'Well, OK. Let's just let her stay,' since they weren't going to have to pay me anything. So, at the end of two weeks they did hire me for a whopping $2.85 an hour, but it got me in. I eventually learned to love working in metal. It took me a while to be willing to change courses that way, but I eventually sold my kiln burners and my pottery wheel and all of my pottery equipment and switched over to metal.

Did you then go out and work on your own?

I worked for them for two years and then I borrowed $2000 from my father and built a body of work with it. I talked them into letting me work four ten-hour days instead of five days a week. So that gave me three days—Friday, Saturday, and Sunday—to create a body of work of my own with that $2000 that bought the gold and silver for me to do that. Then I entered my first craft show and had a really successful first show, and was able to give them my notice and go back to working for myself. That was always imperative for me—I was, I think, less attached to *what* I did than that I would be able to be in control of my life, the way you are when you're self-employed.

Could you describe for me the path that you took from there to get to where you are today?

Well, I went from what I just described as how I got started being a jeweler, and then I began going to Penland Craft School, which is here in North Carolina. I went there every summer for eight years.

I have a good friend who went to Penland for weaving.

Yeah, it's a place where magic happens. So, I would go there every summer for three weeks. I'd save up my pennies during the year, which was a huge investment at that point; I was making so little. But my husband taught at Penland—he was teaching furniture by then—so a mate could come for free. Some years when he would teach I would go that way, and other times I would just save my pennies and go.

I would take a quantum leap in skills and confidence every time I came back from Penland. Then I was asked to teach. My mentor, a fellow I had taken many workshops with, told a school in Connecticut—Brookfield Craft Center—about me. They were looking for some more people to teach workshops in the summer and they called and asked me to teach on his recommendation. Then I began teaching fairly frequently in different places—different craft schools, and different organizations. There're a lot of metalsmithing organizations. Most states have one, and they would invite me to come teach. From that, I learned how much I loved teaching.

Then I moved here to North Carolina. I knew I loved Chapel Hill, because I would always stop here any time I went on a marketing trip. Eight years ago my husband and I were divorced, and I decided if I was going to make that big of a change in my life, I was going to make a complete change. So I came here. After a year of being here I still didn't know one person, because I bought, again, a house in the woods in Chatham County. If you work alone in your home making jewelry and you don't have kids in school—I really had no way to meet anybody. You don't meet anyone on the way to the mailbox. (*Laughs.*) So a year later I still didn't know anyone.

Was that scary for you?

Yes. I was used to having very close friends, and I still do from living in Athens for so long. I had had really close friends and a husband since I was a youngster. To suddenly find myself with no close friends locally—no friends at all, I didn't even know anyone by name—was loneliness. I'd never been lonely in my life and I was very naïve, thinking you could just plop down in a new town. I'd always made good friends easily and I was like, 'Oh, I'll make good friends easily and I'll keep my own friends.' But it turned out that was a very difficult thing.

So, I took a job for two years as the executive director of the Chatham County Arts Council. It was a part-time job, so I was still able to keep up my goldsmithing. They needed somebody who had passion to really get the organization moving. Being my normally obsessive self, I got so into the job, I developed the Chatham County Studio Tour that's still in existence seven years later. There were all these exceptional artists here but no network involved for them to find each other or for the community to find them. If you wanted a stained glass window you went to Raleigh to a gallery, rather than knowing that, perhaps, your neighbor was making stained glass.

There're about fifty artists now on the tour in Chatham. People come from all over to take the tour, and artists from other areas of the country contact me about, 'How do you put together a tour like this?' It has turned into something I'm really proud of. I've probably done few things in my life that have affected so many people's lives positively.

I really got swept up in my whole commitment to the Arts Council for a couple of years. Then, once again, I came back to wanting that control over my own life that you can only have when you're self-employed—who I'm around and how my day goes. I did give it up and went back to full-time metalsmithing.

When you were working at the Arts Council, did you meet a lot of people who became your friends?

Almost every friend I have today I met in that capacity. But about two years ago, I developed metal toxicity. I'd absorbed too many metals over my twenty years of being a goldsmith. I started having all these problems with my arms at the same time, with repetitive stress injuries from having bad ergonomics and twenty years of working unwisely. The doctor wasn't sure if I was even going to be able to do jewelry anymore.

Two years ago I was at the acupuncturist trying to deal with this toxicity, and saw a notice on the wall about a yoga teacher training that was starting in Asheville. I hadn't been able to work in five months, and I was running out of savings. When you're self-employed and you live alone, you better think quickly as to an alternative of what you want to do. The thought of trying to get a job was almost out of the question at this point. I just knew

I had to come up with something. So I had been questioning myself about, 'What else do you like to do, Cathy?'

One thing I had done for a number of years was take a once-a-week yoga class and love it. When I saw this notice on the board at the acupuncturist, I called them up that afternoon and inquired and they told me that the training started in two days. I said, 'Well, but what about your next training?' and they said, 'The next one is in two years.' I said, 'Where else around here in North Carolina could I take a yoga teacher training to get certified?' My answer was, 'Nowhere.' I had to make an immediate decision. So, two days later I was on my way to Asheville for an eighteen-month program where you went for four-day weekends every week.

Wow. That's quite a drive.

Well, it was quite a commitment. I had no idea. Once again, I tend to be naive about what's involved. I just kind of jump into things assuming that everything will go all right. I had no idea the level of commitment it would take to get certified through this program. There was a just lot of studying, and homework, and learning. I knew yoga on such a superficial level, having just taken one class a week. The tradition goes very deeply and I had just skimmed the surface.

Once again, being true to my nature, I have now become

totally obsessed with this. I never would have thought that something else would grab my attention the way goldsmithing did. I didn't just do goldsmithing as a job; it was my life. I lived it. Now it's the same way with yoga. I teach four classes a week now. I love it. It is now the favorite part of my week.

What do you think have been your greatest challenges along this path?

First, just the discipline to work such long hours each week. It wasn't an easy path I chose. You make very little money as a craftsperson. I had to be willing to get up every day—whether I felt creative or in the mood or not—and go to the bench. That's hard to do. When you don't have a boss or any deadlines and so forth that motivate you, it has to be from your own inner motivation.

It was also difficult to keep up the level of craftsmanship that I was committed to having in my work. From the beginning I was committed to the fact that I would make the piece to the best of my ability—even when it was a simple design. My work is well done, and when you're broke and there's the constraint of finances where you know you would make more an hour if you could get the piece done more quickly...it sometimes is a challenge to keep that commitment.

Are there ways that you relax—beyond your craft and beyond yoga?

Besides the yoga, which is, of course, great for that, I love to garden. I love to take long walks and do so frequently. I love to play with my dog and just to be in the woods. I've always taken great care to make sure that I locate myself in a beautiful setting. The farmhouse that I moved to here in North Carolina was a disaster when I first bought it. It's now really quite lovely—eight years later. But the spot itself was wonderful. When I sit on my porch—I have a large screened porch where I hang out—that in itself is incredibly relaxing. I have many friends that come and use my porch and the setting where I live just for that reason.

Do you have personal interests or goals that you're currently pursuing, now that you've accomplished being a yoga instructor? What's next for you?

Really, mostly still the whole yoga quest. I'm new at this. I've only been teaching for a year, and I sincerely want to understand more. I want to learn—and I've been now around enough advanced practitioners to see that I will learn if I continue this level of commitment—how to focus the mind and how to be wholly present so that you really are in the moment. That's a skill that is hard to acquire and takes a lot of practice. The breath awareness, the meditation—really learning how to be more conscious. That's a pretty lofty goal, but it's one that this has all brought up for me.

What personal qualities do you consider to be of the most value in life—

either in yourself or in others?

Probably first and foremost is, I've always had the capability to devote myself wholeheartedly to a venture. I think it's hard to go far in a direction if you don't have that ability. I have a fire in my belly that makes me pursue excellence in whatever direction it is that I'm heading. I don't hold back. I'm able to whip myself up into enough of a frenzy that I can give a hundred percent when I pursue something. I think that one quality—I'd rather have that than I would talent. I've always felt like that was my biggest gift. I've known so many people who I actually thought were more talented than I was. I've had people work for me who I thought had more natural ability—more talent than I did. But they'd be working for me instead of me for them, because I knew how to apply all of what I do have towards something.

I think I have the courage to take risks and believe that improbable doesn't mean impossible. So often I've been told that something I wanted to do was impossible. I may not always have good sense—but I have courage. I think that's real important.

Is there one way that you've evolved or changed as a human being that's made you the proudest?

I think I've developed compassion to a degree I never had. For a long time in my life, everything just worked. When I went through divorce and my whole little world kind of turned upside down, I also during that same period was really ill for three years. In hindsight, that process of everything in my life falling apart at the same time did some marvelous things. One was really just developing a compassion for people when they are hurting and when they are having hardships. I feel more of a compassion now and an understanding about what's involved in that than I ever had—and much more of a realization now that our separateness is an illusion. I'm probably most proud of that part of my development than I am anything else.

Was it difficult for you to adjust to being single?

Extremely. I'd been with my husband since I was eighteen. It's still an adjustment. (*Laughs.*) It's been years. I really believe that in every problem comes a gift; and the gift for me was, I have learned to know me like I never could have if I had always been in a relationship. So much of my energy went into the man in my life and I'd never been alone—ever. So I never really had time to find out, who is Cathy when she's not being influenced strongly by anyone else? I still think a partnership is the most ideal situation. It's not like I'm bitter about marriage; I think marriage is great. But I see a lot of benefits that came from me having now learned to be alone and be comfortable with it.

Of what professional accomplishment are you most proud?

For a long time my goal was to someday reach the point where I would be respected enough as a metalsmith that Penland School would invite me to come, not as a student, but as a teacher. When they did that, that was a really large accomplishment in my little realm of goals. I guess another thing that has helped on the old resumé along the way is I had my work featured in *The New York Times*.

That definitely has got to help. Did you get a lot of feedback from that?

It's amazing to me how much. Not the people reading the article, but from that being in my portfolio, it opened more doors for me than the strength of my work. I have found that to be fascinating. When I would approach a gallery they always wanted to know, 'Who else thinks you're good?' It's almost like sometimes they don't trust their own taste; they want to know who else thinks you're good before they can determine if they're interested. Of course I Xeroxed™ it and put it in my portfolio, and when I would go on marketing trips and make appointments to go see galleries and had that as the second page you came to, that right away changed people's attitude and how they were talking to me. It was always amazing to me how that one little thing—I mean, *The New York Times* had no idea what they did for my career by doing that. You can't buy that.

On a personal level, is there one thing that you've accomplished that you're proudest of?

Yes, that I feel very well-loved in my life and that I have a big old heart.

Is there anything that you would do differently if you could turn back the clock?

Yes, I would not have waited until getting into my forties to start taking better care of myself. I think that some of my excessive habits were self-destructive and probably slowed down the progress I made on my path to trying to have a higher consciousness.

What specific qualities do you think were self-defeating in that way? What were you working against?

Being a party girl. I used to laugh and say it came from growing up in Miami. I was used to, and really for a long time, *needed* a lot of outside stimulation.

Do you find that's sort of an interesting paradox, given the fact that you choose to work alone?

Yes, and I think that there was guidance happening in that that I did choose to work alone. I think having the amount of time you have to think about your life when you're working alone was what offset the fact and made it possible for me to develop the way that I have, given that when I wasn't working, I was playing as hard as I was working. I think it's probably a really good thing that I spent so much time alone. I could have really gotten off-course otherwise.

Do you feel now that you've found a happy medium, or do you still seesaw back and forth between extremes?

No, I'm so different now. I'm more content than I've ever been in my life.

Was there a pivotal point for that—any one of those things you mentioned that really made the difference to you?

At the risk of sounding redundant, the yoga. That has made an incredible impact in my life. So many people think of yoga as just some physical activity, but the whole philosophy that goes along with the postures runs really deeply. I've spent so much time in the last two years reading the books and being around people that I'm really inspired by—centered, balanced people—it's affected me deeply. Even the breath work. There's a lot of breath work that goes on. There's people who believe that God is the breath within the breath. For people who haven't practiced this, I know it all sounds a little mysterious. But yes, I think that has affected me. For a long time after I moved here I still could

not make peace with being alone. I was used to having someone that I loved very much be around and somehow, being this active in yoga has quieted that neediness that I had felt for a long time.

Do you feel now that your sources of inspiration and renewal are different than they were when you were younger?

Somewhat. Some are the same. Some of them have been with me always. I go to the woods frequently. I live in the woods and there's a path behind my house that goes through hundreds of acres of Army Corps of Engineer land, so I have lots of woods right here at my disposal. Sitting quietly in nature changes my whole perspective. I can feel very disturbed about a situation and then go sit quietly in nature and somehow it brings about a much truer perspective of my life. It makes this little flip that happens where it's like, 'Oh yeah, that's right. I'm getting caught up in really insignificant things.'

I also travel a lot, and I've always used that as a source of renewal. There's something marvelous that that does for me and that's always been a priority—even when I had no money to be able to afford it, I did it anyway.

I have extremely close friends. They've been my lifeline a thousand times. And family—I've got family behind me a hundred percent. Those are gifts that are immeasurable as far as the value in your life and the solid base with which to reach out and throw yourself into life the way I have.

What advice do you think you might give young women just starting out in a career or older women considering a career change?

Well, being that I'm an older—as in mid-forties—woman who just made a career change, I can speak to that. I guess I would say find something that stirs your passion, then listen to guidance from your true Self—the one with a capital "S"—as to how to proceed. Then have the courage to do as you're prompted to do. You know, accepting the sacrifices that are involved because they're there, but then throwing yourself with wild abandon into the quest.

Where do you think people might look for that courage inside themselves, if it's not something that's part of their natural personality?

In the quiet moments. I have always been amazed how few people understand how necessary it is to have at least a half an hour a day alone with yourself. I did this even the whole time I was married; this wasn't a new realization for me. I have always told students there is no way I could have ever gotten where I've gone in life, without that half an hour a day. Now I'm trying to learn how to meditate, which is a separate thing. But I'm saying even for someone who just sits somewhere quietly where they can reflect on what it is they want to do, how to do it—you can't have courage if you don't have a plan. You can't make a plan if

you're in chaos all the time. A lot of people never have one moment during the day. They'll say they don't have time, but if you realize it's the most critical thing you can do the whole day—and that doesn't mean neglecting your children or your job or your whatever it is. All those things are going to benefit from the clarity you receive in spending that reflective time.

Interviewed by Emily A. Colin.

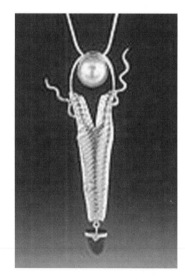

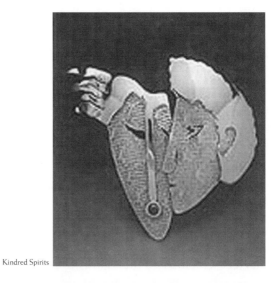

Kindred Spirits

Cathy *Holt*

Cathy became a professional goldsmith in 1980 and received numerous grants, fellowships and awards in the years that followed. She has studied with many leaders in the field and has led workshops for many years sharing the knowledge she has gathered. Her jewelry has been featured in the *New York Times* and in several jewelry books and magazines. Since 1998, Cathy has also been very involved in studying and teaching hatha yoga and has been certified twice.

Cathy has made her home in Pittsboro, a rural setting near Chapel Hill North Carolina.

Desirata

Billie Ruth Sudduth an interview

Where did you grow up and where did you go to school?

I was born in Suwanee, Tennessee, and moved to Birmingham, Alabama, when I was about two and a half. Graduated from Huntingdon College in Montgomery, Alabama, and then went to the University of Alabama for two years and received my master's degree. Got married the following year, moved to North Carolina, and been here for the last thirty years.

What were your school degrees in?

My undergraduate degrees were psychology and sociology, and my master's was in social work.

Since moving to North Carolina, have you always lived in the mountains?

We moved from Montgomery to Durham in 1970, and I actually worked as a medical social worker for the Department of Medicine at Duke. That was my first major job out of graduate school. Then we moved from Durham to New Bern. We were there thirteen years, and it was during that time that I started making baskets. We spent a brief sabbatical, so to speak, in the Mojave Desert—then came back to Wilmington, were there five years, and now we've been up here six years. Bakersville is a little bitty town in Mitchell County in the northern mountains. We're halfway between Asheville and Boone, and we don't actually live in Bakersville. We live right over the ridge from The Penland School of Crafts. It's not on the way to anywhere. I mean, when people come to my studio, it's because they actually want to come here. You don't just drive by it and stop.

That's probably good in and of itself.

Well, you wouldn't believe the number of people that find their way up here though. Penland School is the draw, and then, of course, the mountains themselves. But people from all over the planet visit us. It is unbelievable. Especially spring through fall. The winters are quiet. It's when most of us create new work, because it's wonderfully serene and quiet and there's no interruptions. And then we're all fussing along about the end of February that we haven't seen anybody in two months. It's a real mixed bag. Sheer isolation to unbelievable traffic.

Describe for me what you now do as a vocation.

Well, I am a full-time basketmaker. After I got married—what with nepotism, I could never work in a mental health program, which was what I was trained to do, because my husband was always the director of everything. (*Laughs.*) And I would either have to work two or three counties away, or change a little bit of my focus. So I went back and got certified in school psychology. I didn't actually get a second degree, but I have enough coursework that I probably could have a Ph.D in it by now. So I spent most of my career as a school psychologist. And one year, at the end of the school year, my boss told me that she felt like I'd really worked hard—the students were very demanding, and there were a lot of students with learning and emotional problems—and we'd survived the year. She said, 'Go do something for fun this summer.' And she knew I'd been collecting baskets all my adult life, so she said, 'You ought to go learn to make a basket.'

Well, Craven Community College in New Bern offered a four-session mini-course on 'How To Make an Appalachian Egg Basket.' So I signed up and went for four Monday nights, and I was there fifteen minutes and knew that that was it! You know, I wanted to do this thing. I stayed up half the night making other ones and playing with it. And when the sessions were over, there were no more ways to learn other techniques. There weren't many books on the subject, so I went to K-Mart and bought a lot of inexpensive imports and tore 'em up to see how they were made. That's really how I got started in it, and that was about eighteen years ago.

Well, it didn't take but about two or three years for me to leave my career and start doing baskets full-time. It was possible,

I think, because a lot of people responded to my work and encouraged me—mainly arts councils and things in the eastern part of the state. Then one thing just led to another and, before I knew it, I was doing major exhibits, and some museums were interested in my work. This is really an over-simplification, but I think just because I love making baskets, people have said they can see that in my work. And it was all the motivation and inspiration I needed to keep me going.

What career dreams did you have as a child?

(*Laughs.*) I don't know that I really thought that far past it. I always knew I'd go to college. My father, especially, very much stressed a college education. And I think the whole time I was in school and graduate school, I expected to be a social worker, and especially work with people with mental illness or emotional problems. Then when I went back and retrained in school psychology, I was very happy and very pleased with my career—working with students and seeing some change and growth and progress—although it was demanding. But it just sort of happened—it wasn't a grand design or plan. It just really evolved.

How do you think your two careers—psychology and basket-making—relate, if at all?

Oh, I think they definitely do. My work is based on Fibonacci's

Nature Sequence. Simply put, that's a thirteenth-century proportion theory that this Fibonacci figured out when he was studying patterns in nature. He realized that the same proportions are in the cap of an acorn or a pine cone or a flower petal. So that's why it got the name 'nature sequence,' because it's seen throughout nature. It's significant because the distance between the numbers in this sequence approximates the golden mean or the golden ratio. And that's been used to unify designs since ancient Greece—and influence DaVinci and Michelangelo in their art and Bartok in his music and Frank Lloyd Wright in his architecture and so on. And I use the same proportions that are found throughout nature in my baskets, so when people are responding to them, they're really responding to the same patterns and proportions that they see everyday.

I'm able to do it, I think, because of my background in statistics and measurements as a school psychologist—because my baskets are very mathematically based. I've even developed a curriculum called 'Math in a Basket' where I teach—and have taught teachers how to teach—math concepts through basket-making. So, when you look at my baskets, you'll see logarithms and Archimedes spirals and fractals. You might not know that's what you're seeing, but they're there, very purposefully. And I think if I hadn't learned how to calculate and measure, I never would've stumbled across this in my baskets. I probably would've loved the

process just as much, but my baskets would look very different than what they do look like because of the kind of training and background I've had.

Have you always been a mathematically-oriented person?

(*Laughs.*) No. In school, I struggled through math. And it's really amusing because I would always do extremely well on achievement tests. Then that would cause the teacher to write my parents and say, 'She has the ability. She's just not applying herself.' And it would get me in a heap of trouble, because whatever showed up on a standardized test, I certainly wasn't doing in the classroom. (*Laughs.*) I really probably stayed as far away from math as I could because I never really liked it. You know, it didn't appear necessary to me. And now, I truly regret not taking higher math, but it's more from an artistic standpoint because I think there's a lot more that I could do even now. I mean, I have college math professors and architects and engineers talking to me about my baskets. They give me ideas, and they've taught me a lot. And now I'm more into books on architecture and design in terms of learning what it is I'm really doing. You know, it's sorta like I started doing it, and then I went back and found out what it was called or what it is. But, no, I think it's all cumulative. I have no regrets about my, quote, formal education, and never had an art course in my life. It's amazing that, whatever I'm doing, it's just because of the passion I have for it. It's certainly not what I was trained to do.

As a self-professed former avoider of math, how did you even come upon the Nature Sequence and respond to it?

That's a good question. I was actually teaching 'Math in a Basket' in a middle school in Wilmington. The classroom teacher did a lesson plan on Fibonacci, and it dawned on me that what she was talking about is what I was doing in my baskets. Basically, she gave it a name.

So you were already doing this?

Yeah, but I didn't know what it was I was doing.

It was just instinctive to you?

Yeah.

What is it about basket-making that appeals to you so much?

Well, for one thing, the rhythm of the weave. Nature in itself is very rhythmic. But when you're weaving, I say that it's very much like playing a musical instrument. You can see the music I make although you can't *hear* it. But once you get going, it just flows. It's very soothing, very rhythmic. I also really like to see something evolve—you know, you start from just a pile of reeds

and an idea and you create this object that's called a basket.

And, I think, the fact that baskets are known in every culture and are probably the oldest of all the craft mediums. Potters used to make a basket and smear clay around it, then burn the basket away and have the pot, till it dawned on them they didn't have to weave the basket to get the pot—they could just fire the clay. Probably the oldest of all professions. But it's a very familiar object. And the ones I make, for the most part, I say that I make to hold your interest and not your objects. They're really not functional or utilitarian. They're more sculptural or decorative, but a very classical form. You know, it just feels good to me. That's why I do it. (*Laughs.*) I'm a happier person when I'm weaving.

Were you artistic as a child?

Nope. (*Laughs.*) I think I'm really one of these enigmas. As a young child growing up, my mother and grandmother and aunts crocheted and knitted and tatted and rug-hooked and all of these things that Southern women did. And I wasn't interested in any of it. I loved being outdoors and enjoyed sports and socializing, and didn't like sewing or hemming a dress or cooking or any of those things. I'm not sure what I *did* like, but I know I didn't like those. I was given a sampler when I was thirteen, and it took me, I think, until I was twenty-three to finish it. I just didn't like the needle and the thread. But I've always liked baskets. I've been married almost thirty-two years, and I got my first one on our honeymoon. You know, my family didn't have silver tea services. They had baskets they would put the rolls in. (*Laughs.*) So I've always been around them, but nothing like I am now. It's just something that I enjoy surrounding myself with. I enjoy making them. I love talking about them. I collect them, I make them, I write about them. Why—I don't know.

Did you think the first basket you made was any good?

Yeah. (*Laughs.*) My husband lovingly says that I found a way to make a living with my compulsiveness. I raised two sons and we had the whole menagerie of pets and all the things that little boys grow up with, so everything was always in disarray, just because it was a very lively, active family. And when I started making baskets, it was the one place where I could maintain order. And that is really what's become my signature, I guess, are these perfectly balanced, symmetrical, very tightly-woven pieces. I like doing them that way. And it does give me a sense of satisfaction that the baskets are as finely crafted as they are. Yet my house can still be a disaster, so I guess I've focused all my energies into these.

Do you still have that first basket?

I do. On my coffee table in the living room.

What do you think now when you look at it?

Well, that it really was a pretty good basket, especially with all I know about baskets now. But that it worked, and no wonder I like doing it because it was something that I was good at. You know, it was a success-right-off-the-bat kind of thing? (*Laughs.*) And then I had to obviously learn a great deal over a lot of years. But, in fact, other people that have seen it were sort of impressed that it turned out the way it did. (*Laughs.*)

Describe it for me.

It's an Appalachian egg basket. Not very big. It's real rustic-looking. But it's balanced, it's symmetrical, and it's very finely finished. A trademark of my baskets is that there's no loose ends sticking out. I mean, the detail work, I guess, is sort of a trademark. And that just sort of happened from the very beginning. But it's funny, that's the only early basket I have because, when we moved back from the West Coast, the movers lost nine cartons of my baskets and they never showed up. So I started collecting all over again. But, for some reason, I brought the first one in the car with me. Well, I've always had it around me. And it's light-years away from the techniques and the style of baskets I'm doing now, but the premise is still the same. The whole idea of basket-making is very simple. It's over and under. You gotta go over and under, and under and over elements to get 'em to be woven. So once you grasp that, then it doesn't matter what shape or form—contemporary, traditional, functional, non-functional. For it to be woven, it has to be these combinations of overs and unders. Once you learn that, there's nothing you can't do.

Do you think there was some serendipity in the fact that you carried that first basket with you in the car?

It must have been. You know, thank goodness! Although the head of the Renwick Gallery at the Smithsonian was here last summer, and I showed it to him, and I asked, 'Is it museum-worthy?' And basically he was saying, 'Just take care of it like you would an old quilt.' But the piece is not that special in terms of design. It's special because it's the first basket I ever made, but that's where the specialty ends. (*Laughs.*) He was basically saying that its intrinsic value is not that great—just 'cause it's the first one. It was special to me—or perhaps my family—but that's about as far as it goes in terms of it being special.

That alone is pretty special though.
Right, right.

What have been your greatest challenges toward reaching your level as a basket-maker?

One is knowing how to get the work out there, you know, the visibility. And I was really lucky because I was never afraid to ask for help. But when you're jurying for a show, you're so new at it, you know—'What makes a good presentation?' So I would ask art professors. I asked for a lot of help along the way—had a lot of mentors. But I think basically even knowing what to do or, what was a good way to approach being a visual artist. Do you sell to galleries? Do you do exhibits? Do you stand on the street corner and peddle your wares? (*Laughs.*) And I've done it all. I think you've just gotta sort of work to find where your niche is in all of that. But I don't think the schools train artists in the business end of things. They might teach 'em how to tap into that creativity, but then they may not have a clue about how to fill out their income taxes. And I think that's an obligation that arts schools, or any schools, need to perhaps address—that the common-sense end of things needs some attention, too.

Did you have challenges as far as the actual making of the basket?

Yeah. Oh, yeah. And I still do. You know, I can screw one up with the best of them. (*Laughs.*) But that's good, because I think you learn from those as well. I can get frustrated, the dyes will run—the depth of color is like cracking a pot in the kiln. I can carve through a handle putting it in and have to start all over, or have a piece finished and see a mistake and have to take it apart. And I think the longer I'm doing this, the more intricate the designs and patterns are becoming, or the shapes. And there's a bigger margin for error as you grow, but that's a part of it. Like 'Nothing ventured, nothing gained.'

When you get frustrated or disappointed, what are your sources of inspiration or renewal?

Weaving, always. I can have a particularly bad day or, you know, get bad news or somebody gets ill or sick, and I lose myself in the weaving. You stay focused. Coming from a clinical background, we were taught as students and then as clinicians that people have a much better chance of recovering from something if they're able to get their mind off of themselves where they're not just focusing on, say, pain or depression. And I think that's where baskets got a bad rap—you know, 'We'll go to the state hospital and make baskets,' or underwater basket-making. And that really evolved out of England. In, say, eighteenth-century England, a 'basket-case' was someone who was not able to walk, and you had to carry them. But now we equate it with somebody that's mentally ill. You know, 'Well, they're a real basket-case.' And *I* would consider it a compliment, because it means that you can focus and create. It's like with any art or music or writing— you get out of yourself and you're creating and your energies are on something other than just whatever it is that's troubling you. And I think that's probably a pretty healthy thing for *anybody* to

do, you know, whether it's write a book or play the piano or sing a song or act or whatever. The arts, I think, are a wonderful form of medicine.

Tell me about your family.

Well, I have a husband and two sons. One is twenty-nine and he's married and has two sons, age three and almost one, and they live in Wilmington, which is seven hours away. So when I'm a grandmother, I have to do it on long weekends, but it's still special. I have another son who's twenty-five, and he moved to London four weeks ago through his own hard work. He's with Bank of America. Let's see, my husband dabbles in photography—is quite good at it if he had more time to do it—and is very musically inclined. He's done everything from singing opera to singing in a barbershop quartet. And both of my sons are very creative, but neither one of them weave.

My whole family's very musical but me. Until this weekend, I used to say I had no musical talent. We met a musician who plays for the Atlanta Symphony, and he said that there's two areas of music that you look for talent. One is rhythm, and one is melody—I think that's how he said it. And he said, no doubt, I had the rhythm—maybe I was short on the melody.

How have you balanced family and career?

I think pretty well. Our kids were lucky that they're fairly well-adjusted, bright children, and I think the proudest day of my life was when both of them finished college. The same expectation my father had of me, I had of them. There were a lot of years that we didn't do a whole lot except raise children, you know, the soccer games, the Cub Scouts, the little theater—we were always there, always involved. But as I got into baskets, you might see me weaving at a soccer game on the sidelines. I would just take it with me. It was a high-energy family, and just tons of interests and everybody going in seventeen different directions. And, fortunately, a two-parent family and two kids—one parent can go one way with one of them and the other parent, the other way, and then you meet in the middle and swap back and forth. I was a Cub Scout mother and Sunday School teacher. My husband coached soccer. And we were very involved in raising them and missed them terribly as they grew up and left home, but, at the same time, feel like we did a really good job because they were *able* to grow up and leave home—all the way to London. I told my husband two weeks ago, I wished I hadn't made my children feel so independent that they would go to another country!

Were your children involved in your career, for instance, when you went to a show or to teach?

They were probably old enough that we either left them home or with friends. They've been involved in terms of how much responsibility they had to assume once I started really getting into the basket-making. And there were a few years that I had *both* careers, as a school psychologist by day and a basket-maker by night. So they learned earlier, I suppose, than other children how to do laundry. I didn't teach them to cook as well as to call Domino's or open a can of soup—you know, 'This is important to me and I'll make sure you get fed, but I might not be the one cooking it.' There's been a time or two—which is really terrible and it made me feel very guilty at the time—that they actually had Thanksgiving dinner out of a Styrofoam box because I had an exhibit in another city, so they got carry-out. But they were teenagers, so I think they survived it OK. And now they're very proud of what I do. There was a time that I think the younger one was sort of embarassed to let his friends know that I was a basket-maker, and now he's quite proud of what his mother's doing.

What ways other than weaving do you relax?

Uh, weaving. *(Laughs.)* I'm serious. The weaving is the payoff for all the other things that you have to do as a craft artist, like fill out show applications and do interviews—no offense, please *(laughs)*—or answer the mail, answer the e-mail. The bookkeeping end of it is horrendous. It is like, 'Be careful what you wish for, 'cause it may become yours.' You know, I think I'd always hoped that people would respond to my work, and it was that way almost from the beginning. But as it has evolved and, I guess, become more recognized, the demands for my time are getting where it is hard to relax or to have a life or to do things that aren't just baskets, baskets, baskets. And it was last summer, I think, that I realized that if I'm gonna be around another fifty years to make baskets, then I need to start taking better care of *myself*. So I've started an exercise routine and more gardening and getting outside—and getting away from it a little bit every day. But I would say there was at least a fifteen-year period that that's just about all I did. I love it so much that I don't think I would've done it any other way, and now it's really difficult for me not to be weaving, because that's what I really, really *like* to do and want to be doing. For me to take time out to, say, go exercise or go cook or clean or do laundry—you know, I'd just as soon not do that. I'd rather just sit here and weave.

What are some of your favorite things?

Well, my favorite movie's 'Forrest Gump,' and I think that's because I love that generation and it just sort of, I think, detailed all the kinds of things that us folks that came of age in the sixties were involved in. And the fact that they portrayed him as being in Alabama, and my being an Alabaman—the legendary Bear Bryant and some of the expressions and the simplicity of it. My husband proposed to me in Mobile Bay out from Bayou La Batre where the shrimp boats were in 'Forrest Gump.' And I think the other thing—having worked in schools with kids that maybe weren't as bright as other students, but had such talent in other ways that you really have to realize that not everybody is created equal, but everybody *does* have something that they're good at.

And I love shrimp. Foodwise, shrimp—and chocolate, but shrimp. I love the old comedies on T.V., 'I Love Lucy.' I like listening to music from the sixties, 'Peter, Paul, and Mary' and some of those. (*Laughs.*) I think probably I rebelled at a much later age than most other people in the sixties in terms of leaving my career and sitting up on the top of a mountain making baskets. And the older I get, the more I value friendship and people and relationships and nurturing them. And I love to see the stars up here in the mountains at night. It's brilliant. I used to like the four seasons, but we've had so much snow that I've decided I don't like winter too much anymore. (*Laughs.*) Springtime!

Uh, what other kinds of things? My dogs! Oh! I have two springer spaniels. And I've had springers and dogs my whole life. I love dogs! I *want* a cow. I don't have one, but I *want* a cow. Mmmm, favorite things. I don't read as much as I should. Leon Uris used to be my favorite author. He wrote *Exodus*, and this is dating me, too. A lot of us up here listen to 'books on tape' while we work, and I always read before I go to bed at night, but it might take me a month to get through a book because I'm usually so tired after being in the studio for twelve hours! (*Laughs.*) Oh, and Birkenstocks! I could not live my life without them. I think they're representative of the freedom that I now have.

What personal qualities do you consider to be of most value in life?

Honesty. Dependability. Well, I love happy people, you know, good personalities, somebody that can make you laugh. Really, I think, probably playing it straight with people. I'm very outspoken, but at least people know where I stand. Just being yourself, not putting on airs.

What is the one way that you have evolved as a human being that makes you proudest?

Persistence. (*Laughs.*) That's another quality I like in other people, too, although it can drive you nuts. Well, I think, the fact that I just followed my passion, and I know that's a real simple kind of answer, but it wouldn't have mattered to me, I don't think, if anybody ever bought the first basket. I just like doing this so much. I guess it was the first thing in my life that I'd ever done just *for me*. I guess when you're true to yourself, then these other things happen. And maybe that's what it has been about the baskets because, growing up, I was the good daughter, and I *am* the good wife and the good mother, and there's nothing wrong with

that, but I think there are expectations of 'This is what a *child* is supposed to be like, this is what a *wife* is supposed to be like, and this is how *parents* are supposed to be.' I even knew what a social worker or a school psychologist was supposed to be like, 'cause they trained me to do that. But when I started doing baskets, there were no expectations. You know, it just happened. One thing just sort of followed another and it grew and it developed and I think it was more—what's the word I'm looking for?—*spontaneous*. That's something else I like in people, too, is spontaneity.

What qualities do you have that make basket-making a natural for you?

I work hard. I'm motivated. Compulsive, absolutely—but I don't want to come across as being obsessive-compulsive. (*Laughs.*) I think the passion for what I do, and I think perhaps even the ability to articulate what it is about what I do that matters.

On the other hand, what qualities of yours create conflict or struggle that you constantly work to overcome as pertains to basket-making?

Well, I don't take rejection well, although I'm getting better at it, because the more you do it, obviously, the more rejections you get. (*Laughs.*) So maybe practice makes perfect on that. I think the worst quality I have with my basket business is that after all these many, many, many years, I still don't know how to pace myself in terms of what I should be doing versus what can be done another day. I start out each day trying to get it all done, and then something obviously *doesn't* get done. Just setting priorities maybe. And because I started making baskets when I had a career, I usually couldn't weave until after work, after dinner, after the kids were in bed. So my mentality still is that my best work comes later in the evening. But the truism is I have all morning, all afternoon, all night. You know, I could do it starting in the morning, but I just still tend to do all these other things, then after dinner's when I create the best work. *(Laughs.)* And then I don't have enough time to do it all, so I stay up late. But I think you're asking very poignant questions because I probably don't self-evaluate enough. I doubt any of us do. I guess I've evaluated *other* people just about my whole life, as a career, so when I went into basket-making, I just put that on the back-burner and said, 'Hey, you know, enough is enough.' *(Laughs.)*

Of what professional accomplishment are you most proud?

Well, there are really three. I guess one that is really significant to me was being named a 'North Carolina Living Treasure.' Number two, having a basket on the cover of—and I'm not talking about a major magazine—*Mathematics Teaching in the Middle Schools.* That was sort of an indication to me that the baskets were making a difference in terms of how people were not only looking at baskets, but how they were looking at art and education

integrating, where it's not separate, but you can incorporate arts into the curriculum and teach and yet still have arts. That was a very proud thing for me, because there's more substance to what I do than just making a pretty object. And I guess the third thing was when the Smithsonian acquired a piece for their permanent collection.

And of what personal accomplishment are you most proud?

My children, my marriage. You have to really work at those things. Very proud of my children, my husband and I raising them together, and our relationship now. My immediate family, no doubt about it—and then my grandchildren!

What, if anything, would you do differently if you could turn back the clock?

Well, two or three things. One, I would never gain weight—*(laughs)*—I'm gonna have to work so hard to get it off now. Two, definitely taking much harder math classes in high school so I could learn more about what I'm doing. And, three, probably traveling more when I was single, before the kids came.

What advice would you give older women considering a career change?

Do it! *(Laughs.)* I would say, 'If you've got the passion, go for it!' When I quit my paying job—my career—my son just started college. So we go from a two-income professional family to almost *no* income from me, because I'm making baskets and probably not selling that many. But you've just gotta do it—you've gotta take a chance. And, you know, without being stupid about it, you can live on less *things*, less *fluff*, and have a much better life because you're happy with what you're doing. I would say the material things are probably the farthest down the list of *anything* with me because of the quality of my life and my relationships. But I would say, 'Follow your passions.' And don't put it off until you're too old to do it. I know there are a lot of people that would trade places with me in a heartbeat. You know, they wish they could quit their jobs to throw pots or to write that great novel or to paint a picture, but they dare not do it. And you've just gotta do it!

What about young women starting their careers?

I think probably for young women, there's nothing like a good liberal arts education. That way, you're not so tied down in any one area, but you've got a lot of basics, a lot of tastes of things. View college as a time to grow and learn. And you may still not know what it is you want to be when you grow up, and that's OK, too.

What dreams do you have that are yet to be realized, both personal and professional?

Well, personal is to spend time in Europe with my son since he's living there—to travel, to see places I haven't seen. Last year, the craft council from South Africa visited me, and they've been wanting me to come over and work with some Zulu basket-makers. But to really see more cultures—and *baskets* in those cultures—and more places.

Professionally, I think just doing what I'm doing. I never really had these lofty career goals with my baskets, and maybe that's a good thing. But, you know, to make the best baskets I can make and to find the time to try more ideas. I'm very happy doing what I'm doing, so I'm not sure that I've set goals for where I want to be ten years from now. I hope to be healthy enough and not have carpal tunnel or arthritis, so that I can still be *doing* this ten years from now. 'Cause there's really not anything else that I can think of that I'd rather be doing.

Interviewed by Susan L. Comer.

Billie Ruth *Sudduth*

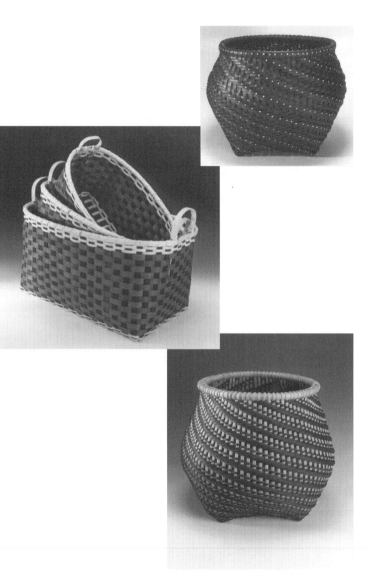

Billie Ruth Sudduth was born in Tennessee and grew up in Birmingham, Alabama. She holds a M.S.W. from the University of Alabama. As a basket-maker, she is primarily self-taught. Her baskets can be seen in exhibitions and collections around the country and around the world. Some of Billie's most impressive exhibitions include "The Renwick at 25–The Reinstallation of the Permanent Collection" at the Smithsonian Institution, National Museum of American Art in Washington, D.C., and in museums in Germany and Denmark. Billie and her work have been featured in numerous publications, including *American Style* and *The Chicago Tribune*. She lives in Bakersville, North Carolina.

My Crazy Quilt Life Carol Auclair Daly

In the spring of my fifty-third year, I find myself looking back upon my life as if it were a familiar crazy quilt—a quilt with which I have become quite comfortable. To review one's life—the beginning, the roads taken, the goals and destinations reached, the things we were unable to accomplish despite best efforts—is to realize that we are all very much "the sum of our parts"—the whole being formed by bits and pieces of bright, colorful moments joined by the everyday fabric of life. And as I look ahead to the future, and all the new and wonderful moments and experiences ahead, I realize that all the significant bits of my past will also have roles to play in the challenges ahead.

I know now that we are not born the people we become. It is those bright little moments, the crazy little pieces of fate that don't quite seem to fit at the time, and the seemingly random choices that we make over the years that ultimately form the complete person. Life is a classroom, and our experiences are our teachers. Not until we have lived several decades do we fully realize that no day is without a lesson. No relationship is accidental. Nothing we do for someone else is ever wasted time. No prayer goes unanswered, whether or not the answer we get is the one we want to hear.

I know too that some things in life, especially as they apply to relationships, are undeniable: A kind, caring husband, secure within himself and supportive of his family and their dreams, is a gift to be treasured for a lifetime. Every child is a special child with a unique gift to be recognized and nurtured. Every mother works. "Family" is more than a word. Love endures and faith sustains.

None of these are earth-shattering revelations. Similar thoughts can be read in a multitude of places from old ancient readings to new Internet web sites. But, like generations before me, and those that will follow, my complete acceptance came with the journey, not in hearing the words from someone else. The proof is in living. My life—that crazy quilt of bits and pieces—has been an evolution—all the many "parts" of me coming together in harmony to become a complete person.

My Parts: I

Beginning life as the oldest of four children in a rather conservative New England family, I grew up with very distinct definitions of "right" and "wrong." But my evolution has taught me that not everyone shares those definitions, and that there are indeed gray areas where compromise of values, without loss of my personal character, is possible—they call this "tolerance."

I have learned that not judging others' views does not mean I must compromise my own values. I must be my own person, and have every right to expect others to respect that. No apologies for my beliefs are necessary; nor should I expect anyone to apologize to me for theirs.

My lesson: Respect is a two-way street.

My Parts: II

Life is fraught with ups and downs, and mine has been no different. No success was without a preceding failure; but no failure has been without a lesson. No goal was attained without obstacles to overcome; but no obstacle was greater than my ability to find a solution, as long as I was willing to try.

When I was sixteen, my family moved from Massachusetts to Florida and I became an angry teenager, certain that I had been cheated by fate. But almost twenty years later when my husband's employment caused us to make the first of several moves to several cities, that painful experience and the memory of my own youthful devastation enabled me to help my children through the same pain and feelings of loss.

One of our moves came a year and half into my return to college to fulfill a long-standing dream of becoming a nurse. College is different when you go back as an adult. I was focused...serious...dedicated...a Dean's List student with her eye on the prize. And then came the news of the transfer that would prevent me from finishing. We were sent to an area where the commute to a new college would have placed an undue hardship on the family. As mothers often do, I accepted the disappointment even while questioning "Why?" Years later, I knew why. A nursing degree for me wasn't God's plan. But having a good basic understanding of medical terminology, physiology, anatomy and nutrition were. I would need those things to help me understand and cope with a serious medical situation that would affect our family. That training would also enable me to get me a job after the move that brought us finally to North Carolina. The job market was tight then, and I didn't think I'd find work; but amazingly, an attorney I met at a Boy Scout function needed someone who could understand medical terminology well enough to converse with insurance company representatives, and understand medical record notations. I could do that; and so found work in an unlikely place and time.

My lesson: Things happen as they are supposed to. If life doesn't make sense—wait—it will.

My Parts: III

I am a woman, a daughter, a sister, a wife, a mother of four, a baby-boomer, an employee many times over, a volunteer, a businesswoman in her own right, a survivor by nature, and like all of us, a complex human being. And despite all legislation and the cries for equality that have surrounded me and obsessed the women of my generation for most of my lifetime, one thing remains clear— you cannot have it all. Our actions always have reactions. While a woman certainly does have the right and the capability to become whatever and whomever she chooses to be—still, there is no free lunch. There are prices to be paid.

As a stay-at-home mom in my children's early years, I found great pleasure in reading to them, taking them to the park, teaching them their ABCs, witnessing the awe of life that is only visible through the eyes of a child.

When I went to work part-time in the evenings, I gave up the right to enjoy some of those things; but instead watched my children develop a wonderful and enduring bond with their father that resulted from increased sharing of parental responsibilities and nurturing.

As "Mom, the full-time college student and part-time employee," I gave up sleep, any semblance of a social life, and many of the "fun" moments of family life. But I studied with my children, doing our homework together at the dining room table— and we all learned more than our lessons.

When all the children were in school, and I returned to work full-time, I found "me," but gave up a little piece of them. But the pain was mine—not theirs. They had received all the love and attention and encouragement they needed to become well-adjusted, happy people. The "space" they received as a result of my going to work allowed them to develop independence and self-confidence; but all the time knowing that I was quite literally "only a phone call away."

My lesson: There is something to be learned and enjoyed in every situation. No woman needs to feel guilty about what she can or cannot offer her child on a given day. Witnessing "grace under pressure" may be the best gift of all.

My Parts: IV

I've learned that "The Empty Nest" does not signal "the end" for a woman, although I'm sure that it does have that effect on those who would allow it to happen; for it "sneaks up on you" when you least expect it. Just about the time you feel you have the "parenting thing" down pat, it's over. Early in my parenting career, our parish priest gave a sermon about parenting that had a tremendous impact on me. I can see him still...standing there and saying so gently, "God has given you a great privilege—the privilege of caring for, nurturing and raising His little ones. They aren't YOUR children. He has only loaned you these children—HIS children—to raise as your own. And to do your job right, you must raise them to leave you."

My lesson: Plan for the inevitable. Parenting is a temporary position by the very nature of the job description. There needs to be a life plan for the time that follows. For me, it has been a time of re-awakening—a time to use the many skills and lessons learned throughout my life—to explore the reaches of my own talents and interests—and to share those things with others.

The Sum of My Parts

Here in the year 2000, at the beginning of a new millennium, I find myself the owner of a small business on the Internet—working via microchips and telephone wires alongside small business owners whom I've never met, from all over the world – many of them half my age and much more computer savvy than I. But no

matter; because you see, I also find that in this new cyber-marketplace, all things and people are equal. We don't deal in politics, religion, age, education, nationality, personalities, or race—we care only about helping each other to grow and prosper. We respect each other's differences, share our talents and our skills, and rejoice in individual successes.

Perhaps man has finally succeeded in finding a small corner of peace on earth—a bit of Heaven—in the unlikely world of cyberspace. And I so look forward to exploring it further as I continue to add pieces to my crazy quilt life!

Carol Auclair Daly

Carol Daly has resided in Jacksonville, N.C. since 1987 and lived for three years previously in Statesville, N.C. She worked for several years with Onslow County Government, being one of ten winners statewide of the first Ralph Ketner Employee Productivity Awards for government employees who implement innovative and cost-saving programs.

In 1996, she left her job as the county's public information officer to organize and administer a Disaster Relief Program at Onslow Community Ministries, Inc., to aid victims of Hurricanes Bertha and Fran, and initiated a Group WorkCamp project for teenagers to help repair homes of the elderly and poor in Onslow County. As a volunteer, she worked with Boy Scout Troop 357 in Jacksonville for eight years; is past secretary of the Onslow County United Way Executive Committee; and member of both the Public Relations and Steering Committees of Onslow's CHIP (Community Health Improvement Process).

She is currently the owner of Creative Enterprises, which is both a small business community site and an online publicity and promotion service. Visit Creative Enterprises on the World Wide Web at *http://www.creativethought.com.*

Pass It On: Testimony of a Quilt Artist   Valarie Jean Bailey

There's a church song that says, "When I look back over my life, I have a testimony!" It's a spirited song; it makes you want to stand up, raise your hands and say "Awomen!" I was brought up in the Black Church and I know that Testimony is serious business. It is telling your story to God before the congregation. Testimonies demand correctness; no pretense, no lies, no "showing off," just righteous truth from the heart about life's experiences.

When I look back over my life, I can bear witness to the fact that there is Love in this world. On any given day, at any given time or place I can stand up and testify that I have been loved in this life. Some people like to believe that love does not exist here, or that there is not enough to go around. It's the most common excuse for a lack of humanity and the resistance to love and be loved. I believe that in order to thrive in this life—not just survive, but triumph—one must be loved. You have to feel it bone marrow deep. It must surround you, wrap around you like a quilt, warm and protective. The existence of Love, like air and water, is necessary to sustain life. I did not always know this. I did not always feel loved. Now, however, at the mid-century point in my life, I know the value of Love—its preciousness and its joys.

I've learned from the lessons of life the importance of self-love, the acknowledgement of love received, to extract the love I need from the places I least expect it, and to keep on moving.

My testimony is an affirmation that quilts are love. It gives evidence to the fact that where there are quilts, there is Love. I've been a Quilt Artist since the early '80s, but looking back, I realize that I've been a quilter-in-progress all of my life. The story of how I arrived at quilting takes a little while. First I have to tell a little about my life and the people I've known and loved on the path that has led me to the quilt.

I was born an Artist and the artist spirit living inside me has kept me sane, and has been the guiding force for my hopes and dreams. The Goddesses have bestowed upon me the gift of prophecy through needle & thread. As an artist, I believe that I must know the basic human needs of this world and translate them into art that can be understood and appreciated. True, I'm more Ain't than Saint, so my prophecy is limited. God is love and through God's love the beauty and Peace of life is ours. It is incumbent upon each of us to grab hold of the love that comes our way, and pass it on. Love demands reciprocity; we get it and must return it in kind. I suppose I'm really talking about a generic kind of love, the simple, unconditional kind. Because love can get complicated and spin spirals of emotions through your brain, not to mention what it does to your heart.

Being birthed in rural North Carolina in the middle of the twentieth century meant that I was born on the front lines, thrust smack dab in the center of an old struggle that in my generation would renew and intensify. Many times I've had to take disadvantage in this world because the advantages were not available to me. I came into this world black and female in the segregated facilities of a small hospital, near my hometown of Lillington in Harnett County.

Carrie Haymer Bailey was a tender, nurturing mother and, as best she could, provided a wonderful home for myself and my siblings in our early years. I've seen pictures of this plump, smiling woman standing outside of our weathered clapboard house facing the sun without a squint in her eyes. I have memories of her soft breasts and her laughter. Her nickname was Jolly, and the daylily tattooed on my right wrist represents the strongest recollection I have of her. She planted them all over the place. Remembrances of the daylilies, their spontaneous bursts of color along the landscape, appear often in my work. My mother was the first artist that I knew. Her canvas was the earth around her and the many flowers she planted, her palette. She passed away when I was four years old. She has been missed every day since.

After my mother's passing, my greatest blessing was that my Aunt Mae stepped up and raised us. Lillie Mae Hamer was the "knee baby" in the family, (the next child up from the youngest) who had gone North in her late teens, and after working for some time as a live-in maid in Connecticut, settled in Elizabeth, N.J. Aunt Mae reigned as the Supreme Matriarch of the family, and her goal was to keep her sister's children together.

In my fourth year of life, I found myself relocated up north to live with Aunt Mae. I exchanged my dirt road drawing board for coloring books and crayons. There were no trees in the projects like my Carolina pines, and yes, people did sit outside at night, but did not put the children to sleep on blankets underneath the trees while they fried fish or roasted pigs and watched the sunrise. For many years I thought black folks forgot how to raise children once they went North. Later, I learned it was just the stress of the day-to-day in the factories and never making ends meet that left them angry and unable to love with consistency. And that bears some forgiveness.

Before I started kindergarten, I was informally adopted by Mildred and Livingston Taylor. They "kept" me until the end of my third-grade year. During those years away, I experienced a great deal of emotional and physical abuse which resulted in my having horrific nightmares. One night was especially bad. I was being chased through a foggy and dense cemetery in the middle of the night by a pack of wild dogs. I awoke trembling and crying. Then miraculously, a soft light appeared near the foot of the bed. When I looked up I saw my mother sitting there, her hands gently stroking the covers. She was smiling and telling me things to comfort me. Then, I fell into a deep sleep and when I awoke again, she was gone. The sunlight of a new day lit the bed where she had sat.

When I decided to tell Aunt Mae what had happened, she was skeptical at first, but soon realized I was telling the truth when I described the clothes my mother wore. She turned to me with the most sympathetic look on her face and said, "That's what we buried your mother in." Aunt Mae always understood me, no matter how crazy I got or how tired she was. The joy of having my aunt's love was that she never tried to replace our mother's love, but worked in concert with it.

I managed to survive childhood because as folks say, "God had a plan" for me. Looking back, I realize it was revealed to me in the fourth grade when I was living at Aunt Mae's with my brothers and sisters again. I was in a new school and that was frightening. It was difficult to readjust to being with my siblings full-time after being an only child and being "spoilt" by "Sugar" (Livingston Taylor's nickname). He was more "father" to me than my biological one. In the few short years I lived with them, he did all the things for me that little girls dream of. The one time he had to whup my behind, he cried afterwards. When I told you that I had to give up my dirt road drawing board for coloring books and crayons, he was the one who gave them to me. He saw the artist long before I understood what I was, and he sought to bring it out. We'd spend hours at the kitchen table drawing this one figure of a woman until I got it right. Later there were expensive paint sets, the paint by number kind; and he was first to tell me that I really didn't have to paint by the numbers given, I could use my own imagination. We were bonded for life, although in later years I didn't see much of him because we lived in different cities and it was just too painful. There's a special room in my heart for him—it holds the treasures of having had the best father a girl could have. He was a precious gift in a transient and painful childhood.

⇥

Aunt Mae used to make skirts and things for us to wear. She began to teach me to sew on her sewing machine and do basic hand sewing. My aunt introduced me to fabric. We would go to the local merchants, shopping for everything from cotton for blouses, wool for winter skirts, to fabrics for upholstery, curtains and the like. Little did I know those trips were basic training for the countless hours I spend as a quilter in fabric shops, browsing catalogs and exchanging pieces with fellow quilters to find the right fabrics for my work.

Aunt Mae was an avid gardener and had a "green arm" for growing everything she touched. We lived on the second floor of a three-story building and Aunt Mae got permission from the landlord to use the back lot for her garden. Every summer she transformed that ugly, wine-bottle-strewn space into an urban paradise. Not only was it beautiful, but it provided us with food for the winter. She would recruit my sisters and I to assist in the cleanup first, then the planting and tending of her garden. Later in the summer we would help her can vegetables and fruits. Aunt Mae worked as a meatpacker at a factory in Newark and she always brought home the best cuts of meat. We never knew a hungry day in her house. She taught us how to cook in the country tradition of our ancestors and that meant countless hours of shelling peas, shucking corn and cleaning greens until they met her approval. She took the most mundane domestic chores and turned them into an art. She never returned to North Carolina to live, but North Carolina always lived in her.

Looking back to this time in my childhood, I sense that it was the point where I embraced the artist in me and began developing the curiosity and skills that go into my quilts. Also, I believe the transition where I began to know who cared about me and who didn't—and how to respond to the love I was receiving—

started at this point in my life. Because I loved my aunt so much, I tried to do the things she taught me to demonstrate my love. As a result, I developed a love for learning, an appreciation for art, a respect for nature and a sense of family that I carry to this day.

⤝

I'm supposed to be telling the story of how I arrived at quilting, but it's an impossible tale to tell unless I explain the situations in my life. Artists create from their life experiences. It's what we know best.

During the early '60s I lived with my Aunt Mae on a consistent basis. Elizabeth, N.J. was a city of neighborhoods and diverse ethnicities. We lived in the "Port," a working-class neighborhood where there were forty-eight identified ethnic groups (I found this out from a human interest story I clipped from the newspaper for class once). So I went to school with just about everybody and learned to deal with just about anybody. By the time I was in junior high school I was on a roll. I had friends of all nations and my art career was flourishing. In ninth grade I was put into Mr. Tagliaferro's class. We called him "Mr. Tag" and he had, by far, the greatest impact on my art career. I had a course that year called Elective Art. It was a small class and those of us fortunate enough to be there were on our own in terms of how we executed our assignments. I learned words like chiaroscuro and practiced by drawing eggs in a basket over and over again. He took us to see Michelangelo's Pietá at the World's Fair in New York. I wanted to be a beatnik and go to Paris when I got out of high school. In fact, it was my desire to just get out of school and go anywhere I could take care of myself and not rely on anyone in my family.

Aunt Mae's daughter had the responsibility of taking care of us during the week. She'd had this responsibility ever since we came North. Looking back, I realize it was quite a heavy responsibility for a young woman who'd been recently divorced and had lost her only child to SIDS shortly after my mother's death. Her anger and frustration at life was taken out on us. The emotional and physical abuse we were encountering during the week intensified as we grew older. We didn't want to tell Aunt Mae all that was going on because she was working very hard, and we didn't blame her for her daughter's disposition. There were some good days in between the rough ones and we learned to cope. There was no Child Abuse Hotline back then and most abnormal behavior in families was kept secret. By ninth grade, the years of abuse had taken a toll on me and my sisters.

Mr. Tag was privy to all that wasn't going good in my life and on days when I was just not interested in attending the other classes, he would leave the door to the supply room open and I would paint or draw or sculpt or work on whatever project I was involved with at the time. I survived that year because of the love I received from this man. At the graduation ceremony I received the Art Award. You couldn't tell me then that I wasn't going to be a famous artist when I grew up. I had applied to Edison Technical & Vocational HS and had been accepted to study Fashion Design. At the end of a very tumultuous and rebellious summer of 1964, Aunt Mae told me that she was sending me down South to live with my father and his wife because I wasn't getting along with her daughter and it was creating discord in the house. Somewhere along the way, abused children learn to fight back, to resist, and rebel.

Along with the problems I was facing in the house, the world outside was going crazy, too. My favorite president had been assassinated in November of 1963. Black people were being brutalized and denied rights all over America, and the civil rights struggle was intensifying, especially in the South. Watching this on television created a conflict within me that is not easy to explain. I knew that I didn't hate all white people—I had good friends that were white—but I did hate the Bull Connors and George Wallaces of the world. At the same time, I was torn because I knew all too well that black people were hurting each other too. I was damaged by my relatives long before I entered the greater society, and to put all that behind me to blame the white man for the suffering of my people seemed wrong in some way. So I tore my drawers a little; I was a teenager with a bruised heart and needed some relief—but nothing more than sneaking out to be with my friends, and being rowdy on occasion.

When summer came to an end, it was time to pack and leave for North Carolina. I didn't want to go. I wasn't ready for yet another transition in my life and most importantly, I didn't want to leave my little sister Carrie. She not only loved and adored me, but depended on me a great deal as she was younger and had been the recipient of most of the abuse. Carrie was devastated by my leaving and clung to me, crying, when I was getting in the car to go to the bus station. It was a very sad time for us. I went down on the Greyhound bus, determined that no one would ever hurt me like this again.

I entered an entirely different world than that to which I had been accustomed. Lillington was still segregated, and older relatives seemed to accept that way of life. I tried to cope with life as it was. Food became my refuge and every day after school I'd hide in my room and devour all the sweets I could. By the time Christmas rolled around I weighed 164 lbs and couldn't fit into any of my clothes.

--⇒

I went to the white school in Lillington my junior year for the "movement." They were desegregating the schools there and I felt obligated in some way to go. I had known some terrific white folks in New Jersey and I felt that the experience of living among them had prepared me for this venture. I was so wrong. I didn't know enough about Southern white folks, and while I wasn't afraid of them, I was not prepared for some of the cruelty they dished out on a daily basis. I couldn't turn the other cheek as Martin Luther King, Jr. said. When they came at me, I gave it back big time. I competed both in and out of the classroom and except for being sent home once in awhile for fighting, I fared pretty well. My sister Jackie got sent down South that year too, so I had some backup.

Our rebelliousness came to a head the summer of '66 when our father, sparked by my stepmother and cousin (both schoolteachers), called the sheriff on us because we refused to stop going to the house of one of our friends, whom they deemed unacceptable. When our father came to the house to get us, he said that there was someone at home who wanted to see us. My sister Jackie and I left thinking it was a relative or someone and we were anxious to see who it was. When we got near the yard and saw the sheriff's car, there was blood in our eyes. We were so angry we couldn't think straight. I told the sheriff that he had no right to tell me who I could and couldn't hang around, since he never stopped traffic for me once when I attended the white school that year. He was a racist and would stand there and get a real kick out of making me wait to cross the street to go into school each morning. He would act as if he didn't see me or my sister and then wave us across like he was doing us a favor. Calling him to intervene in this family problem was a despicable act on my father's part and I have never forgiven him for that.

In the fall of 1966 I began my senior year at John W. Ligon High School. I found a job through the school and a room with Miss Dixie Montaque, and kept on moving. I was finally "on my own"—or at least I thought I was. I was sixteen years old and all I wanted to do was get my high school diploma and go to art school. I loved being in Raleigh back then.

I can never forget the day the most important influence of my senior year came into my life. It was the first week of school and I was changing classes. As I approached the door, it opened suddenly and the finest young man I'd ever seen stepped through and held it open for me. My heart stopped as I looked into the biggest brown eyes I'd ever seen. It was like being struck by lightning. I must've nodded or smiled a "thank you" and kept on going, but my heart was racing and I was curious as to who this young man was. It didn't take long to find out.

A day or two later I went to art class. The rural schools I'd attended didn't have nor care about art, but Ligon was advanced and I had the opportunity to take art again. I couldn't wait to get to class. By the time I got there, the front tables were filled with students, so I made my way to the back. To my surprise, there he sat—the young man with the magnificent brown eyes. His smile was translucent; he lit up the entire room. I tried not to look excited, but I couldn't help myself. We introduced ourselves and the rest is history. Reuben Thomas Peppers became my high school sweetheart and the love of my life. We were the best of friends. We shared our hopes and dreams for the future. It wasn't about sex in those days, because he was intent upon keeping me a virgin until our wedding night. It was about watching over one another and making sure we got through the day-to-day.

I worked at Colonial Food Store in Cameron Village after school and weekends. They had just started hiring "Negroes" in front positions. Since I was in the Distributive Education Program at school—where we were supposed to learn about the world of work through active participation in the job force—I got a job there as cashier. I did an excellent job and had customers lined up to have me wait on them. Both the manager and his assistant relied on me and gave me thirty-nine hours a week, the maximum for part-time workers, because they knew I was on my own trying to finish school. I learned a great deal about people working there. I worked hard, and having my own source of income enhanced this feeling of being on my own.

At the end of my senior year I graduated with honors! I was so proud of myself. A list of high school valedictorians and honor students was printed in *The News & Observer*, and many of my customers from the Colonial Food Mart came in and congratulated me. My Aunt Mae came down on the Silver Meter in grand style for the graduation ceremony. I wore a white pique dress under my cap & gown that came from one of the finest shops in Cameron Village. One of my regular customers owned the shop and gave me a huge discount because she thought I needed to look my best. I felt wonderful at graduation, as if I'd leapt the biggest hurdle in my life and reached the sky. I had applied to and been accepted at Shaw University and planned to study art.

In the summer of 1967 Reuben signed up for the Marine Corps and was in Basic Training when I entered Shaw in the fall. For the first time in many years, I felt alone. These feelings would intensify as I began to realize that I didn't have the resources I needed to complete my education. By Christmas I was disillusioned with school. Shaw did not have the facilities I needed to pursue an art career, and I had used all my savings. When Reuben came home on leave he told me that he was going to Vietnam. It was not a good time.

I left Shaw in the spring of '68 and lived with my sister and brother-in-law for a short time. My sister was pregnant with my nephew Junior at the time and her marriage was just getting started. Martin Luther King, Jr. was assassinated a few weeks before my nephew was born. I had starting seeing Andrew Fowler, a student at Shaw from Washington, D.C., by that time. I learned that Reuben had been with someone else while he was on leave and I felt betrayed. I lay on my sister's couch for three days and cried. Then I wrote him a letter and said that we were finished. I convinced myself that I liked Andrew because I didn't want to think about my heartbreak over Reuben.

I stayed with my sister for about a month and then I left North Carolina for Newark, N.J. to stay with my roommate from Shaw for a while. Once I was gainfully employed, I got an apartment in Newark and my sister Carrie and her son, Gregory came to live with me. I maintained a correspondence with Reuben because I still loved him. In all good conscience, I couldn't leave him in that war alone.

After several temporary jobs that summer, a friend I'd met at Shaw got me a job in New York City. On September 16, 1968, I started work as a receptionist at the New York City Community Development Agency, the community action agency for the city.

After the riots of the late '60s, the government was pumping much money into the inner cities for all kinds of programs. CDA, as it was called, was teeming with the best minds in the country and was the largest community action agency among anti-poverty programs in the country. I was in awe of most of the staff and my co-workers became my new family. I was thrilled to be working there.

Shortly after I began work, I got a call from Reuben. He told me that he'd just gotten home from the war. I hopped a plane that Saturday morning and held my breath until I saw him. Seeing him again was joyous and it felt like nothing had ever gone wrong. The war had matured him and changed him in some ways, but he was still the same person I loved inside. He wanted me to come back to North Carolina and marry him, but I was studying at the School of Visual Arts at night and I had a great job in New York. I wasn't ready to come back just yet. He got stationed in Hawaii and I continued to work in New York.

⇥⊙

By the time Reuben came home on leave again, I was pregnant by Andrew. I was too ashamed to accept his offer to marry me and take care of my child. He said it didn't matter to him and that everyone would think it was his child anyway. Deep inside I couldn't commit to him. A part of me cared for Andrew and I wanted him to accept me and our child. Until that happened, I couldn't give myself over to anyone else; not even the one I truly loved.

During the Christmas break Andrew came to Newark to see me. I was showing by then and that frightened him. He told me that he didn't want any part of this experience and that I was on my own. His words cut like a knife, but I was no stranger to rejection and found the strength I needed to carry on—although I was in a kind of pain too torturous to even talk about. I had my job and that was sufficient to mask the pain. My commute from Newark to New York on the "Tubes" (a commuter train that runs from Penn Station, Newark to the World Trade Center) kept me viable and active during my pregnancy. I was huge, but that didn't stop me.

I had planned to spend a few days with Sherry, a dear friend from Shaw who lived in Rockville, Maryland. I wanted to rest before I gave birth. Sherry had also left Shaw and was staying with her mother. I had a clinic appointment at two o'clock, and then I planned to take the train down to D.C. where Sherry would pick me up. While I was being examined, the doctor told me that I was "four fingers dilated" and I asked her what she meant. When she told me that I would be giving birth shortly, I cried. Not only was it a total surprise to me because I wasn't having the kind of pain I'd heard about, but I wasn't sure that I was ready for mother-hood.

Regardless of whether or not I was ready, Jason was. He came into the world on Monday, March 23, 1970 at 5:24 p.m. I had one labor pain and cried out for my mother. Although I didn't see her that time, I felt her presence. I gave birth alone at Beth Israel Hospital in Newark. No one except me and the doctors knew Jason was in the world until the next day, when I could get to a phone and call my sister Carrie. She had walked me to the hospital, but I didn't think I was in labor, so she caught the bus to Elizabeth. She figured I was in the hospital because I hadn't come home that night, but it wasn't confirmed until I called the next day. She brought the suitcase I'd packed for my trip to the hospital and we had a good laugh.

I loved my son the moment I laid eyes on him. He just popped right out of me without pain or fanfare. He was plump and had a head full of hair. One of the nurses told me that she'd never seen a child who looked so much like his mother. I had wanted a different kind of life for my son, one with two parents, but this was the hand I'd been dealt and I was determined to play it.

Jason got sick with viral meningitis when he was six months old and I almost lost him. When he got out of the hospital he weighed only eleven pounds and wasn't the happy, bouncy baby he'd been. But he was alive and I was determined to get him back

on track. I'd taken some time off from work while he'd been in the hospital. This time we did go down to Maryland to see Sherry at her Mom's house to rest and recoup. While there, Miss Bunny convinced me that I should call Andrew and invite him over to see his son. He jumped at the chance. So, when Jason was six months old and weak from surviving meningitis, his father saw him for the first time.

⊷⪤

In November 1970, I moved to Park Slope, Brooklyn. By this time I was working in the Resources Library at CDA with Carol Capizzi, who became Jason's and my Jewish mother and friend for life. Carol was also an artist and had been a teacher and librarian before coming to CDA. After watching me in a demonstration, protesting a police brutality incident that had occurred during a meeting at the Council Against Poverty, she decided that I was smart and witty enough to work with her. She was instrumental in helping me move to the city and in caring for my son. At the same time I met Carole Stern and Jocelyn Cooper, who would become my extended family for life. Carol and Carole were feminists and gave me an education I couldn't have gotten in any college or university.

The Resources Library became the CDA Underground and

much political activity was launched there. We were on the front lines of the movement in New York City. I found a home there like I hadn't had in my life. I was able to use my talents and skills in many ways. I had plenty of assistance with the care and nurturing of my son.

I spent the next two decades working, going to Visual Arts at night trying to get a Fine Arts degree, parenting and generally, just involved in the business of living the day-to-day.

When I left Visual Arts in the summer of 1981 I planned to return and complete my studio courses and get the degree. But I didn't. Painting and drawing were the things I loved best. When I walked into my studio at the end of a day's work, sometimes after making dinner and doing laundry, it was only to get to my bed which was located in a little room next to it. I love oils and could never master acrylics; oils simply mix colors better for me and I absolutely love to explore color. So when my palettes would dry up and I'd look at the pieces I was working on and couldn't remember where I'd left them, let alone the point of departure, I stopped painting. During my one summer camp experience, a middle-aged woman who always seemed to be stressed out by something or other was responsible for our cabin. She was quick to dispense advice at every minor incident that occurred. One day she gave this long rap about "second choices." It was her belief that most people have to settle for the second choice in life, that usually we don't get our first choice. I never forgot her spiel and I never forgot how determined I was after listening to her to do all I could to guarantee that I get the first choices in life. When I put my paintbrushes down I thought of that counselor's advice. If I could not paint, I was going to find something creative to replace it that would bring me as much satisfaction.

In the mid '70s someone asked me to make them a set of Raggedy Ann & Andy dolls, but they wanted them to be Black. I used a pattern to make them. I was doing crafts then to supplement my income and made several of these dolls to sell. Then someone suggested I make my own doll instead of copying someone else's. So I designed "Chocklat Chips," a doll that looked just like me. I got a few commissions, but soon gave it up because they took so much time and it wasn't all that profitable.

After I saw the play "For Colored Girls Who Have Considered Suicide When The Rainbow Is Enough," I made a doll for Ntozake Shange. It was left at the theater for her and a long time passed before I got any feedback on it. Then, one day—by fate or destiny—I met her in Brooklyn. I said, "I made a doll for you and left it at the theater…" Before I could finish the sentence, she screamed in delight and told me how much she enjoyed the doll.

Later on, at Ntozake's request, I was called by *Essence Magazine* to design dolls to be included in a collage they had commissioned artist Joan Hall, to create for the excerpt of Ntozake's *Cypress, Sassafras & Indigo*. After the book was published, she called me one day to tell me that she was scheduled to do a reading from the book at the Public Theater, and asked me to create a quilt for the stage. I had dabbled a little in quilts by making them for some of the dolls I'd made, but these were small pieces and very non-traditional. So I began to design this quilt without any real knowledge of materials or basic quilt construction. I was still in Visual Arts then, so I asked one of my fellow students to help me with parts of it. The top of the quilt was a panel that we painted with fabric paint and acrylic, then the middle had some sort of triangle design in it. And the bottom was black fabric that I stamped gold stars on for background on which to hang the dolls I had to make for this piece.

I remember that there wasn't a whole lot of time to complete this project. I made this quilt as big as the floor in my studio and moved everything out of the way to work on it. It was humongous in my studio, but "Indigo Dances Around Her Dolls" looked like a postage stamp on the stage. I wasn't too happy about that, but everyone else seemed pleased with it. The reading was a one-time performance, so they took the quilt down and gave it back to me to take home. That ended my experience of working with Ntozake, but started my journey into the quilt.

It soon occurred to me that the difference in designing quilts and painting was that I could put my work away in a shoebox somewhere and come back to it months later without losing the train of thought. The fabrics didn't dry up or lose color. This was a very good thing, because the artist was put on hold while I went about the business of living. Jason and I lived on the third floor of a brownstone apartment building that was being "co-opted," and not being able to afford to buy it, I had to move. I held out as long as I could. It broke my heart, but I left Park Slope and moved to Harlem.

I began working there part-time as a curator at Aunt Len's Doll & Toy Museum. Aunt Len had a fabulous doll collection and had received a grant from the N.Y. State Council on the Arts to begin cataloging it. I moved my work and my son to Harlem to be near the museum.

It was not easy living in Harlem, but learning a new place is never easy at first. Yet, living in the borough of Manhattan was exciting. I started taking classes at the Quilt Center down on Houston Street & Broadway to learn basic quilting techniques. The center was a unique place. The first workshop I attended was about using color in quilts and the instructor used an exercise that I'd done in art school many times. I knew then that I just had to apply the same theories of color to my quilts that I'd applied in my painting. Eventually Linda Cross, from the Eldercraftsmen Training Studio, called and said they had been funded to locate and document anonymous textile artists in New York City and would like to interview me.

—⊶⊫⊙—

This testimony is an affirmation that quilts are love, like I've already said, and believe me, it gives evidence that where there are quilts, there is love. Linda Cross and Pamela Richardson of the Eldercraftsmen, Inc. became the threads that bound me to quilting forever. They featured my work in the Textile Project first, a tireless effort that included so much more than photographing my work and documenting my history. They are both visual artists and we'd spend hours talking about our work and the creative process. They helped restore my confidence as an artist and believe in the work I was doing. At the same time, they taught me all that I didn't know about grantsmanship and solicited my participation in projects they were planning. I taught my first workshop at the Eldercraftsmen's Training Studio. Then I was hired as an Outreach Worker for the next phase of the Textile Project and was introduced to numerous textile artists.

In 1991, Linda and Pamela received funds from NYSCA to sponsor an apprentice program with Master Quilter Fannie Roberts Chaney. They developed this project to document the Southern tradition of African-American quilt making through Mrs. Chaney's work and train two apprentices. The project got started in 1992, and during weekly sessions at Mrs. Chaney's quilting frame, Quassia Tukufu and I learned how our ancestors made quilts. Mrs. Chaney made the best greens I've ever tasted, too, so going there was more than a classroom, it was like going home. After a year of the apprenticeship program, we produced many quilts and quilt tops that were shown in an exhibit called "Mississippi Patchwork In New York." Quassia is a gifted artist as well as a quilter. She curated the exhibit and secured the Countee Cullen Regional Branch Library in Harlem as the venue for presentation. It was held during Women's History Month in March of 1993.

—⊶⊫⊙—

Where there are quilts, people, there is love. Whenever the pressures of work and home got the best of me, there was always someone there to encourage me and renew my spirit.

Jason was always there. He was growing up, finding his way in the world without a father and trying to be supportive of his mother all at the same time. Jason enlisted in the Army after graduation and I decided it was time to move back to Brooklyn—

it was my home and I missed it.

Eventually I joined the Empire Quilters' Guild and right away I knew I should have come on board years earlier. The guild was a diverse group of women and men who were totally absorbed in the art of quilt making. As time passed I met a lot of African-American women at the meetings and learned that there had been a chapter of the Women of Color Quilters Network in New York. Eventually the chapter was reactivated and I served as Chairperson for almost three years. Our biggest project was creating a quilt for the Dance Theater of Harlem. When it was completed it measured 10' wide x 14' long and it was hung from the third tier of the New York State Theater at Lincoln Center for the company's premiere engagement there.

Once I was settled back in Brooklyn, I got a call from Sandra McGill and Viviane Arzoumanian, who were starting a quilter's guild in Brooklyn and wanted it to be a diverse group. "Can you get African-American women involved?" was the question, and of course I did, but I also brought a lot of other women to the group. Fifty-three women were at the first meeting which was held at Sew Brooklyn, a quilt shop in Park Slope, and the Quilters' Guild of Brooklyn was launched. Soon my Saturdays were taken up with quilt guild meetings. I was putting out a monthly newsletter

for the Women of Color and trying to produce my own work, too. When I look back now, I'm amazed at the amount of activity I was involved in and the number of women I was working with. Joan Fielstra came into my life around this time and became my aide de camp. She was a member of Empire Quilters and several guilds on Long Island, where she lived, but wanted to join the Women of Color. She asked me one day, "Do I have to be a color to join this group?" I got so tickled, I said, "Yes." "Well, I'm pink, can I join?" And join she did. Joan would drive in from Long Island and pick me up for all the meetings we attended. She would even clean out her Subaru so we could fit all our stuff in. At times she would pick up two other quilters and all their stuff. I don't know how we did it, because we were all women of ample proportions. It was hilarious and glorious to boot. The Quilters' Guild of Brooklyn became yet another extended family for me and its members were my sisters.

At the beginning of 1996, I had been employed at the Community Development Agency for over twenty-eight years. I was a tenured civil servant and enjoyed the work that I did. I was always outspoken and questioned authority, but I never had any fears about my work life until the Guiliani Administration. After he took office the atmosphere in the agency changed. There was a physical move as well as departmental changes. I'll cut to the chase and tell you that on March 23, 1996 my employment with CDA was abruptly terminated. I knew it was coming and had prepared myself somewhat, but one is never really prepared for that kind of sudden change in one's life. Part of me was relieved that it was over, I'd been subjected to the cruelest kind of treatment by the administration and co-workers I'd known for many years, for six months prior to the termination, and I was tired. Yet, part of me was sad, too, because CDA had been more than a workplace, it had been a home for me for all those years. I had served on the front lines of the anti-poverty struggle for all that time and I had the respect of the community I had served, and that was my downfall. The administration had made some very bad funding decisions and when it hit the papers they blamed myself and a few other co-workers for leaking information. They used my time and attendance as the basis for my termination. It was all planned and they had connections, so I left that Friday and have not been inside its doors since.

I struggled on unemployment for a while, but I was also being evicted from my apartment because it had been bought by an unscrupulous landlord and he wanted more money. We went to court and they gave me six months to relocate, which ended in November. Over that last summer in Brooklyn I can't tell you all the people who came to my emotional and financial rescue. If the administration at CDA thought they had broken me or my spirit, they were wrong.

Looking at my uncertain future without a means of support or a place to live, I decided to take my sister's advice and come home to Carolina.

⚬──⚬

I decided to go to Lillington first. My stepmother Rachel Bailey was still living and she was elderly and needed someone in the house with her. I made the decision to go there because I had put all the bad memories behind me. I wasn't going to stay forever, but I needed a base to start out. I had numerous offers from folks in Brooklyn to move in until I got myself together, but I wanted out of New York. It was no longer home to me, but a place of horror and fear. We packed most of my work and supplies in a van and left the rest of my things in the apartment as I shut the door and headed for North Carolina.

It was a few days after my forty-eighth birthday when I arrived in North Carolina. As the sun came up, we found ourselves outside of Zebulon on I-95. I called my sister Jackie and told her where I was and she said she'd meet us in Lillington. She and Carrie arrived shortly after I did. We found a storage space for my work and later that day, the four of us moved my things from the van to the storage unit—it has remained there to this very day. I had been a collector in New York. Wherever I lived, I collected things. People were always bringing me fabric. And while I never painted, I never threw away my art supplies—that is, until I moved back to North Carolina. This experience taught me the lesson of not putting too much value on material things. You've heard the saying that you can't take it with you when you die; well, I'm here to tell you that sometimes you can't take it with you when you're living either. When I closed the door of that apartment and left, there was so much stuff left behind, it looked like someone still lived there. I can imagine the look on the landlord's face when he walked in. Later on, when I collected myself and began to take a mental inventory of what I had and where it was, I remembered that there were some boxes I'd never unpacked from my move back to Brooklyn from Harlem. In those boxes were my collection of dolls, posters, books, Christmas ornaments, bric-a-brac and whatnots; I didn't have time to look through every single box. If the landlord took the time to look in the boxes before he threw them out, he would have found many treasures. I hope he didn't.

I lived the first six months in Lillington in a kind of haze. I went through the motions of getting through a day, but my mind and heart were closed for repairs. I had come to a point where I had to live outside of myself in order to survive. I had come to a second-by-second existence. I wasn't emotionally ready to look for a job and I didn't have to. Before I left New York, Gurusurya held a sort of birthday/going away soirée for me at her house. I was surprised to see so many of my friends there and it was all I could do not to break down. Usually quilters give baskets with fat quarters of fabric donations in them for special occasions. So when the lights went out and I saw them coming towards me with a basket, I thought it was full of fabric and I got excited. But it was full of little origami figures, birds and frogs and the like, with bills folded in their beaks or legs. They were sitting on a pile of money. That basket supported me for a very long time. *Now* can I get a witness? Quilts and Love go hand in hand!

I spent almost three years in Lillington and made one quilt the whole time. Actually I finished a small quilt I'd started in Brooklyn, "Mudd Biscuits," and sent it to New York for the Empire Guild Show at the Puck Building in March of '97. Shortly after I got to Lillington I attended a pine needle basket workshop with Dee Glover at the Harnett County Public Library. Dee said I was a quick study and soon I was going with her and assisting in workshops. I made a few small baskets and sent them along with the quilt to the Empire Show and everything was sold. I could make baskets on the porch or just sitting outside in the yard, I didn't have to deal with surface design or color or block arrangements and that was sufficient for awhile.

My sister Jackie kept telling me that things were going to work out for me and to keep motivated. She encouraged me to apply for the 1998-2000 N.C. Arts Council Touring & Residency

Artists Directory and my application was accepted. I went to Wilmington for the 1998 Arts Market and met enough North Carolina artists to know that I had come home to a good place where art lives. Although it was on a respirator in Lillington, and about to flat-line.

By March, 1998 my case against the City of New York was settled and I was officially retired. I got my driver's license on the third of March and bought a '96 Honda Civic with the small settlement I received on March the thirteenth. Two weeks later I drove myself to RDU Airport and took a plane to New York. I was going to attend the Quilters' Guild of Brooklyn's Quilt Show and then go to Lancaster for the Heritage Quilt Festival. Before I left for New York I received my QGB Newsletter. Although my friends were careful not to let it leak that they were making a quilt for me, they neglected to omit it from the "Show & Tell" column that month. Under Gurusurya's name was "Valarie Jean's Quilt." It has thirty-six blocks on the front and four on the back, meaning that forty of my friends participated in the effort. It is beautiful; each block is different and reflects the work of the individual quilters.

There was some debate between my friends and I over what should be done with it. Some of them felt that I should take it home and sleep under it and be blessed by the good spirits and love that went into it. I felt that it was truly a fine piece and should be shown at whatever shows we could get it into. I especially wanted it to go to Lancaster. The quilt won some ribbons at the N.Y. Quilt Festival that year. I was sure that I didn't want to bring it to Lillington—the vibes were not good for it. I took it to Elizabeth with me and when I went to visit Aunt Mae she loved it.

⇥⊖

"We Miss You, Valarie Jean" is a testimony about me. It was an exhibit of African-American quilts at Medger Evers College in Brooklyn during Black History Month this year (2000) and Carl Blumenthal wrote a review of the show in his column <u>Art Out Loud</u> in the *Brooklyn Journal*. Speaking about the quilt, he said, "...this patchwork quilt was assembled from squares created by the friends and students of Valarie Jean Bailey, one of the founding members of Quilters of Color Network of New York, who moved back home to North Carolina. Not only is it amazing how elaborate each square is, but the thirty-six pieces complement each other beautifully. There are variations on stars, squares, diamonds, and rectangles. It seems as if each square shows how each quilter was inspired by Valarie Jean. In other words, the quilt is a very dense but lively message of love with many layers but none hidden." Somebody say, "Awomen!"

Being able to drive gave me a new sense of freedom and I

started looking for a job. It wasn't easy and I was determined that this time I was going to have a job in the arts. I sent resumés everywhere to no avail, even drove as far as Durham for job interviews. By September, I had one car payment left in the bank and there were no more days left on my job search calendar. So I went to Plan B. I took a job at the Pantry. I dubbed my sales associate job my "red pepper job" (from a favorite saying of my friend Jocelyn), and went on about the business of living. It was hard work for me at the beginning, but then as I got to know my customers and their routines, there were days I actually looked forward going to work. Secretly, when I had two days off in a row, I'd go to New Bern, check into the Hampton Inn, pull out my sewing machine and sew. Jackie would bring me food, and there was a respite for a little while.

The new year started out being the most grievous time of my life with the passing of my beloved Aunt Mae on February 2, 1999. When she passed away I felt like I was letting go of two hands instead of one. I was so young when my mother left, I never knew the full impact of witnessing her passing.

As I stood over Aunt Mae in her hospital bed the evening prior to her passing and asked her if she was ready to go, the full burden of loving someone hit me so hard I felt like I'd been hit by a train and thrown into the middle of the earth. "Are you at peace?" I asked. "Yes," she answered softly, shaking her head. When I looked at her, I saw the most beautiful smile I had ever seen on her face and all I could say was, "Then I'll have to let you go!" Love teaches us to put the needs of those we care so deeply for before our own. When I learned Aunt Mae was in intensive care, I felt that I could pull her through. When I boarded the plane, all I could think of was that she would pull through this, I needed her and that was that. But when I walked into the room with monitors and tubes and beepers everywhere, I knew it was time to let her go. The need to end her suffering superseded any selfish needs I had to keep her here. After her passing, my grief was compounded by the fact that the connections to my mother through my aunt were gone, too. I found comfort, though, in the knowledge that I had been there with her and helped to send her joyously to the other side. While other family members were at the hospital in the final hours, I sat on her bed and lit a candle to light her way, thinking, too, that she'd find my mother much more quickly in the light.

When I returned to Lillington after her burial, I had to confront my heartbreak somehow and find the strength to move on. I had a workshop scheduled for February 20th at ArtQuest in Greensboro and a meeting at SECCA in Winston-Salem on February 16th to begin planning a story quilt project to be conducted in the fall in the Forsyth County public school system. I prayed to the Goddesses for deliverance, and both ventures were successful.

My good friends Joan Fielstra and Nancy Russell-Cooley came down on March 10th and we got a suite at the Jameson Inn in Dunn. We quickly turned it into a quilt factory. For three days and nights the sewing machines hummed and the quilts started coming together on the walls. Joan had taken me to the hospital to visit my aunt the day before she passed away and knew how grieved I was. Nancy had worked with me at CDA and I brought her into Empire and the Brooklyn guilds. We have reciprocated our love for one another over the years, and I know that they love me; why else would they drive so far?

When the heat of summer hit me—coupled with the loneliness I was feeling missing Aunt Mae and my friends, and with my work still on hold—I really sank into a pool of despair. I believe that on this plane, there are a number of Goddesses to meet our needs. And I prayed to just about all of them on a daily basis. I wanted desperately to leave Lillington and thought I'd look for a job in Winston-Salem when I went there in the fall for the quilt residency. However, my prayers were answered one day at the end of July as I stood behind the counter waiting on customers and a pair of familiar brown eyes smiled up at me. The rest, as they say, is history!

I called my friend Sherry that night and asked her, "Guess who came into the Pantry today?" "Reuben Peppers" was her answer, before I even got the whole question out. "How did you know?" "I could feel it in your voice," she said, "you've been waiting for him ever since you got back to North Carolina!" I had left my number in his mother's mailbox one day when I was in Raleigh and tried to visit with her. She called me right away and told me that she didn't see him that often, but when she did see him again, she'd give him my number. Several months passed before he called and when he did, we had a very pleasant conversation. Nearly a year passed, and with all the other things going on in my life, I stopped thinking that I'd hear from him. I always felt way down in my soul that we would get back together again. And we did.

Reuben is a hard-working man. He's not consumed by my work, but he is consumed by his. He is passionate about providing a way for me to get the quilts done, rather than being passionate about the quilts. He would rather cook dinner for me when I have a quilt to finish, than critique a quilt. I'm learning to accept his ways again. His smile still excites me in much the same way it did thirty-some years ago. I have to tell you that in the wee hours, on a full-moon night, I watch him sleep peacefully; then I know I've finally come home. In our house there are quilts and Love.